Determining the Economic Value of Water

Determining the Economic Value of Water

Concepts and Methods

Robert A. Young

RESOURCES FOR THE FUTURE
WASHINGTON, DC, USA

An RFF Press book
Published by Resources for the Future
1616 P Street, NW
Washington, DC 20036–1400
USA
www.rffpress.org

Library of Congress Cataloging-in-Publication Data

Young, Robert A. (Robert Alton), 1931–
    Determining the economic value of water : concepts and methods / Robert A. Young.
        p.   cm.
    Includes bibliographical references.
    ISBN 1-891853-97-X (hardcover: alk. paper) — ISBN 1-891853-98-8 (pbk. : alk. paper)
    1. Water-supply—Economic aspects. 2. Water resources development—Economic aspects. I. Title.
    HD1691.Y675   2004
    333.91—dc22   2004021904

The paper in this book meets the guidelines for permanence and durability of the Committee on Production Guidelines for Book Longevity of the Council on Library Resources. This book was copyedited by Steven Jent and typeset by Betsy Kulamer. The cover was designed by Maggie Powell. Cover art: "Pure Water Flowing from Faucet" © Matthias Kulka/CORBIS.

ISBN 1–891853–97–X (hardcover)   ISBN 1–891853–98–8 (paper)

About Resources for the Future *and* RFF Press

Resources for the Future (RFF) improves environmental and natural resource policymaking worldwide through independent social science research of the highest caliber. Founded in 1952, RFF pioneered the application of economics as a tool for developing more effective policy about the use and conservation of natural resources. Its scholars continue to employ social science methods to analyze critical issues concerning pollution control, energy policy, land and water use, hazardous waste, climate change, biodiversity, and the environmental challenges of developing countries.

RFF Press supports the mission of RFF by publishing book-length works that present a broad range of approaches to the study of natural resources and the environment. Its authors and editors include RFF staff, researchers from the larger academic and policy communities, and journalists. Audiences for publications by RFF Press include all of the participants in the policymaking process—scholars, the media, advocacy groups, nongovernmental organizations, professionals in business and government, and the general public.

To my wife, Lynn

Contents

PART II
Applications of Valuation Methods

Preface

Water economists are called upon to answer some difficult questions:

- What types of goods and services are produced by water? Why are prices for water seldom observed on normal commodity markets?
- What do economists mean by "value" or "benefits" in relation to water resources? Is the economic benefit of an increment of water the same at all times and places and for all purposes? Why are estimates of water-related policy benefits important?
- What nonmarket valuation methods can be used to estimate economic benefits of water-related policies? Which methods are most appropriate for producer goods and which for consumer goods uses of water?
- How are the various methods applied in practice? What are their advantages, limitations, and appropriate roles?

Water management, historically always important, is an increasingly timely subject. In its varied forms, the water resource supplies important benefits to humankind, ranging from commodity-type benefits in agriculture, industry, and households to environmental values, including biodiversity and recreation. However, significant water management problems can be found throughout the world, and in many areas they are rapidly becoming worse. Growing populations and incomes increase demands for water for agricultural, industrial, and residential uses from limited surface and ground water supplies. These same forces of economic and population growth add to the pollution discharged to the world's waterways, and to the encroachment of human activities upon lowlands vulnerable to flooding or upon important natural ecosystems. Increased prosperity carries with it amplified demands for improved water quality, for more access to recreational and amenity uses, and for preservation of biodiversity and natural ecosystems.

The price signals which reflect scarcities of goods and services and which are successfully used to guide investments and resource allocation in the private sector are usually absent or distorted for water, complicating public sector decisionmaking related to the resource. A premise of this work is that, although market prices will play an increasing role in water allocation, the market's function will continue to be limited; consequently, applied economic valuation procedures can play an important role in guiding public policies related to water. To address the many public policy issues arising when markets are absent or imperfect, economic researchers and practitioners have adapted the neoclassical economic model to public policy decisions, developing the evaluative procedure termed cost–benefit analysis. A major portion of that effort has been devoted to formulating, perfecting, and applying nonmarket methods for measuring benefits, forgone benefits, and costs of proposed public policies and programs relating to the natural environment. These efforts have often been directed to evaluation of changes in water resource supplies and quality. Tools have been developed and refined which are conceptually consistent with market prices and which permit increasing confidence in bringing economic efficiency considerations to bear on public decisions relating to water (and other environmental resources).

This book is broadly about putting a monetary value on goods and services provided by water. More formally, it is intended to introduce the reader to the application of welfare economics principles to the measurement of economic benefits in the context of assessing water-related policies (intersectoral water allocation and reallocation, investments or policies to augment water supplies or qualities, pricing, or other water planning decisions). A major aim is to provide professional economists (both field practitioners and advanced students) with a consistent conceptual foundation for comparing the economic values of water across alternative uses and with costs of investments. It will show readers the concepts and techniques for applying alternative empirical approaches to measuring the economic benefits of water-related policies or investments, illustrate how to understand the strengths and weaknesses of these alternative approaches, and provide guidance to the more technical literature.

For several reasons, the emphasis here inclines toward offstream and private good issues, valuing water in agricultural crop irrigation, industrial, and municipal uses. First, my professional research has mainly focused on such issues. Second, although there is considerable diverse literature on valuation of water in offstream private goods cases, there is no single volume that attempts to integrate this literature with the much more fully developed literature on valuation of environmental goods and services. Moreover, nonmarket methods for valuing water in the production sectors have not received the comprehensive attention devoted in recent decades to environmental issues. Agriculture accounts for the largest consumptive use of water in the United States and worldwide, and industries are also important water users. Accordingly, this volume gives special emphasis to valuing water as a producers' good; it critiques a number of methods frequently employed, and proposes improved approaches. Thus, it attempts to fill the gap in the existing literature regarding application of nonmarket valuation techniques to commodity uses of water in agriculture, industry, and municipalities in a framework consistent with that already well-developed for public environmental goods and services.

The book is organized as follows: Part I sets the stage. Chapter 1 identifies the physical, economic, and social attributes of water and describes a number of standard water policy issues for which economic analysis is frequently needed. Chapter 2 briefly reviews the basic conceptual and analytic issues underlying the neoclassical approach to the economic valuation of water. Chapter 3 introduces applied methods of nonmarket valuation, reviews the procedures appropriate to measuring water values in producer uses of water, and describes their advantages and limitations. Chapter 4 covers issues of applied benefit measurement for consumer uses of water, primarily public good benefits (such as obtain from water-based recreation, preservation values, and water quality enhancement).

Part II describes and evaluates applications of the various methods to specific water use categories. Chapters 5, 6, and 7 discuss the applications of these methods to offstream or withdrawal uses in agriculture, industry (including hydropower), and municipalities, respectively. Methods and applications of measuring the value of water as public environmental goods are addressed in Chapter 8, which reviews methods for addressing such issues as instream flow valuation, environmental preservation, and flood risk alleviation.

The scope is mainly limited to the estimation of direct benefits (and benefits forgone) of water-related policies. A number of broader treatments of the principles of cost–benefit analysis—including the validity of secondary benefits, the rate of discount, the planning horizon, decision criteria, and the general issues of setting up and performing a cost–benefit analysis—are available (e.g. Boardman et al. 2001; Fuguitt and Wilcox 1999, etc.).

The analysis should be, for the most part, accessible to those with training in microeconomic theory, mathematics, and statistics at the upper-division, undergraduate level. The text should also be helpful to water engineers, environmentalists, planners, policymakers, and other noneconomists who make use of water valuations or who interact with economists on water policy and planning activities. It should be a useful adjunct to more general textbooks in academic courses in natural resource and environmental economics and in water planning and management.

To the reader and potential user of the materials presented here: *caveat emptor.* First, no single magic number represents the economic benefits of water used for any given sector. Just as the market prices for goods and services are typically specific as to *place, form,* and *time,* nonmarket valuations (often called accounting prices) for water also vary according to these dimensions. They further vary with the situation, the underlying factors, and the policy proposal being evaluated. Given the relative lack of transportability of both the public and private attributes of water, values for water can be expected to vary even more widely than do prices for more conventional goods and services.

Second, noneconomists and those economists who are new to the field should be aware that accurate economic valuation of the impacts of water-related polices is seldom quick, easy, or simple. Developing appropriate and reliable estimates of the value of water requires substantial skills, time, and research resources. To adequately perform the assignment calls for command of many if not most of the technical skills of the applied economist. Rigorous estimation of economic benefits of water policies and projects must begin with a close understanding of microeconomic theory. Successful shadow pricing of water in any particular use will further demand proficiency in one or more forms of quantitative economic modeling. Competence with advanced statistical and econometric techniques is a necessity for developing sound contingent valuation, travel cost, and hedonic price estimates. Probably the quantitatively least demanding of the commonly used methods of valuing water and other nonmarket environmental goods are simple benefit transfer techniques, but advanced approaches here too call for considerable statistical skills. For valuing water as a producers' good, an essential foundation is familiarity with production theory, business accounting, and spreadsheets. Moreover, mathematical optimization and computable general equilibrium modeling are increasingly used for addressing this type of problem. Finally, careful collection of accurate and representative primary data or selection of adequate secondary data is an often underemphasized requirement. Only a handful of economists have the training, native abilities, resources, and time to become proficient in more than a few of the many types of issues that arise in shadow-pricing. Specialization, as elsewhere in the economy, is here a necessity.

This volume arose from numerous assignments and collaborations during my work on water economics over the past four decades. I became interested in water valuation as applied to arid-area water policies in the mid-1960s working with William Martin and the late Maurice Kelso at the University of Arizona. Subsequently, as a visiting scholar at Resources for the Future, I was fortunate to collaborate with Charles Howe in several research efforts, an association that has continued intermittently since we moved to different state universities in Colorado. Applied economic valuation of water became a major research focus of mine at Colorado State University where, with Lee Gray and others, a two-year effort for the National Water Commission developed a conceptually consistent framework for estimating the economic value of water in alternative uses and applied it to various regions across the United States (Young and Gray, 1972). Research and consulting assignments with the U.S. Agency for International Development, the World Bank, and the Asian Development Bank provided an international dimension to the research agenda. Particular thanks are extended to Lee Gray for his valuable contributions to the conceptualizations and implementations of specific valuation techniques and, more recently, for his administrative support. For over two decades I taught a graduate course in water resource economics at Colorado State University which emphasized water valuation techniques, and supervised graduate students' research in water economics. Numerous students, both in the classroom and in applied research, posed valuable questions and challenges to the concepts and methods discussed here. Several years ago, in a consulting capacity, I prepared a technical report on water valuation for the World Bank (Young 1996). More recently, the Government of Switzerland provided a grant to the World Bank that enabled me to update and expand that work toward completion of this monograph. Particular acknowledgments are due to Ariel Dinar of the World Bank for encouragement and support of this effort and for discussions and advice on the subject and content of the work. Several anonymous reviewers provided useful and insightful suggestions for improvements on earlier drafts. Susanne Scheierling deserves special mention; while on leave from the Asian Development Bank, she read and commented on the entire draft manuscript and was very helpful in improving both the content and the presentation. I am grateful to all of those mentioned above for help in refining and clarifying the ideas presented here.

ROBERT A. YOUNG

Part I

The Economic Value of Water: Concepts and Theory

Water, Economics, and the Nature of Water Policy Issues

Economists are interested in the subjective values associated with the sources of individual satisfaction because of their concern with the economy's ability to allocate resources and coordinate production and distribution so as to create the greatest benefit to society. For many needs and desires, competitive markets are a relatively good means for determining and responding to individual preferences. There are limits to this solution, however, because not all sources of satisfaction go through markets, and markets may fail in other ways as well. National product and income estimates as measured by market transactions are therefore incomplete, and inadequate measures of overall welfare. Correcting for this by estimating values uncounted by the market can help, although this is often difficult, and at times virtually impossible.

Tibor Scitovsky, 1993

Public policies relating to water supply and quality can have significant economic consequences for households, communities, farms, and business firms. In many parts of the world, under past and current policies, water is allocated to less valued uses, water quality continues to decline, groundwater basins are overexploited, public amenity values receive inadequate attention, and floods and droughts take an unnecessarily severe toll of life and property.

Descriptive statistics illuminate broad water use and consumption patterns and place water allocation issues in context. In the United States, crop irrigation continues to be the major user of water, accounting for 42% of withdrawals and 84% of consumption in 1995. (*Withdrawal* refers to an amount of water diverted from a surface source or removed from a groundwater source for human use, while *consumption* is understood as that part of water withdrawal that is transpired through plants, evaporated, incorporated into products, consumed by livestock or humans, or otherwise removed from the immediate water environment.) The domestic-commercial category represented 11% of withdrawals and 7% of consumption, while industry took 8% and 5% and thermoelectric power accounted for 39% and 4% of the same categories. Elsewhere, water withdrawal and consumption patterns reflect climate, degree of economic development, and other factors. However, as in the United States, crop irrigation represents the major consumptive use of water in the world. (See Solley et al. 1998 or Rogers 1993, for national and regional data on water withdrawals and consumption by sector for the United States, and Gleick 1998, for both a global overview and detailed data on water use.)

This chapter begins with a review of some of the physical, economic, social, and political characteristics of water important for designing water polices. Then it describes the significant issues that confront analysts and policymakers. Finally, it addresses the broad approach to economic appraisal of public policies.

1.1 Why Is Nonmarket Valuation Needed?

Water is distinguished from most other resources and commodities by a number of special characteristics that pose significant challenges for the design and selection of water allocation and management institutions (see Young 1986). Water's unique characteristics are described below under four headings: hydrological and physical attributes, water demand, social attitudes, and legal-political considerations. These considerations explain why water is for the most part a good not traded on regular markets, why nonpriced side effects frequently accompany water use, and why synthetic estimates or shadow prices are important for water allocation and investment decisions.

1.1.1 Hydrologic and Physical Attributes of Water

Water Is Mobile. Typically found in liquid form, water tends to flow, evaporate, and seep as it moves through the hydrologic cycle. Mobility presents problems in identifying and measuring specific units of the resource. Primarily because of this attribute, water is what economists call a "high-exclusion cost" resource, implying that the exclusive property rights which are the basis of a market or exchange economy are relatively difficult and expensive to establish and enforce.

Supplies Tend To Be Highly Variable. As a generally renewable natural resource, basic raw water supplies are mostly outside human control; they are typically variable and unpredictable in time, space, and quality. Local water availability usually changes systematically throughout the seasons of the year (with climatic variations) and over longer cyclical swings. Significant global climate changes—from both natural and human causes—are forecast, raising concerns about longer-term supply trends. The extremes of the probability distributions of supply—floods and droughts—bring problems for humankind. Abnormally large rainfall or snowmelt and consequent flooding can impose significant costs, and most governments have undertaken programs for mitigating the risks of floods. At the opposite extreme, droughts can devastate economies, particularly those heavily relying on agriculture.

Water Is a Nearly Universal Solvent. Water—when in plentiful supply—provides (from the private perspective) an inexpensive capacity for absorbing wastes and pollutants, and further for diluting them and transporting them to less adverse locations. Managing the assimilative capacity of the hydrologic system should, then, be understood as the management of a scarce collective asset. In many situations, water quality considerations are as economically important as are direct use and other public benefits.

Interdependency Among Users Is Pervasive. Water is rarely completely lost to evaporation in the course of consumption or production activities. So-called "water uses" generally result in return flows to surface streams or aquifers. In crop irrigation, for example, it is not unusual to find that 50% or more of the water withdrawn from watercourses is returned, in the form of surface runoff or subsurface drainage, to the hydrologic system. An even larger proportion is typically returned from municipal and industrial withdrawals. Downstream users or those depending on the same lake or reservoir are affected (usually, but not always, for ill) by the quantity, quality, and timing of releases or return flows by upstream users. These interdependencies lead to effects called *externalities* (or "spillover" or "third-party" effects), which are uncompensated side effects of individual economic activities. The presence of externalities implies that the full costs of economic activity are not recognized in individual producer or consumer decisions, and outcomes for the society will be less than optimal.

Water Problems Are Often Site-Specific. Because of variations in water supply and local demand, problems with water resources are typically localized, and policy often needs to be adapted to local conditions. The relative supplies of surface and ground waters at any site depend, of course, on climatic variations (precipitation in the form of rain or snowfall), as well as on the available aquifer storage. Water demand and quality issues are likewise specific to the population size and level of economic development.

Supply Facilities Exhibit Economies of Large Size. The capture, storage, and delivery of water (especially surface water) typically exhibit economies of large size (i.e. falling unit costs). When costs decline over the range of existing demands, a single supplying entity can be the most economically efficient organizational arrangement. For example, the least-cost approach to capture, storage, treatment, and delivery of residential water supplies in an urbanized area is usually by a single public utility: a classical "natural monopoly." Accordingly, public ownership or public rate regulation of water supply industries is often invoked to avoid monopolistic pricing.

Goundwater Supplies Have Distinctive Attributes. Groundwater deposits, or aquifers, supply much of the world's water. Unlike surface water, groundwater flows slowly, and it is difficult to assess the potential yield and quality of an aquifer. Most size economies are achieved at relatively small outputs. Moreover, these may be partially or completely counterbalanced by increased pumping costs and rising third-party spillover costs due to water table drawdown.

1.1.2 Water Demand: Characteristics from Users' Perspectives

Because the different benefits obtained from water usually call for specialized management approaches, it will be useful to group the types of values into five classes. These are (a) commodity benefits, (b) waste assimilation benefits, (c) public and private aesthetic, recreational, and fish and wildlife habitat values, (d) biodiversity and ecosystem preservation, and (e) social and cultural values. The first three are treated here as economic considerations, because they are characterized by increasing scarcity and the associated problems of allocation among competing uses to maximize economic value. The final pair, preservation and socio-cultural issues, are discussed separately as noneconomic values.

It may be most useful to begin by recognizing that the economic characteristics of water demand vary across the continuum from *rival* to *nonrival* goods or services. A good or service is said to be rival in consumption if one person's use in some sense preclude or prevent use by other individuals or businesses. Goods that are rival in consumption are the types that are amenable to supply and allocation by market or quasi-market processes, and are often called *private* goods. When goods are nonrival in consumption, one person's use does not preclude enjoyment by others; these are often called *public* or *collective* goods. Nonpayers cannot be easily excluded, so private firms cannot profitably supply nonrival goods. Water for agricultural or industrial uses tends toward the rival end, while the aesthetic value of a beautiful stream is largely nonrival.

The significance of nonrivalry can be better understood by noting its association with high exclusion costs. *Exclusion cost* refers to the resources required to keep those not legally entitled from using the good or service. Water is frequently a high-exclusion-cost good because of its physical nature: it is difficult and expensive to limit the use of the good to those who have helped pay for its costs of production. The refusal of some beneficiaries to pay their share of the provision of a public good, from the benefits of which they cannot be excluded, is called the "free rider" problem.

To circumvent the problem, public goods must normally be financed by general taxes rather than by specific charges.

The first type of benefit mentioned above is the commodity benefits: those derived from personal drinking, cooking, and sanitation, and those contributing to productive activities on farms and in commercial businesses and industries. What are here called commodity values are distinguished by the fact of being rival in use, meaning that one person's use of a unit of water necessarily precludes use by others of that unit. Hence, commodity uses tend to be private goods.

Some additional distinctions will be helpful regarding commodity-type uses. Those types of human uses of water that normally take place away from the natural hydrologic system may also be called *offstream* uses. Since they typically involve at least partial consumption (evaporation or transpiration), they may be further distinguished as *consumptive* uses. Other types of economic commodity values associated with water may not require it to leave the natural hydrologic system. This group may be labeled *instream* water uses, hydroelectric power generation and waterways transportation being important examples. Since instream uses often involve little or no physical loss, they are also frequently called *nonconsumptive* uses. Although instream uses do not "consume" much water, in the sense of evaporating it to the atmosphere, they do on occasion require a change in the time or place of availability. This is, for example, the case with reservoir releases for hydropower or navigational purposes. So these uses exhibit some aspects of the rivalness of a private good.

The value of waste disposal is a second type of economic benefit of water use. Bodies of water are significant assets because of their assimilative capacity, meaning that they can carry away wastes, dilute them, and, for some substances, aid in processing wastes into less undesirable form. The assimilative capacity of water is closer to being a public than a private value, because of the difficulty in excluding dischargers from utilizing these services.

The values for aesthetics, recreation, and fish and wildlife habitat represent a third type of economic benefits from water. Once regarded as luxury goods inappropriate for governmental consideration, these types of benefits are increasingly recognized as important matters of public concern. The populace of developed countries, as income and leisure time grow, more and more often choose rivers and streams distant from their homes for recreational activities. In developing countries, water-based recreation is often an inexpensive form of leisure activity and a basis for tourism. Significant instream values may be found in the recreational aspects of habitat for wildlife and fish. Like waste assimilation, recreational and aesthetic values are also nearer the public good end of the spectrum. Enjoyment of an attractive water body does not necessarily deny similar enjoyment to others. However, congestion at sites such as waterfalls may lessen total enjoyment of the resource.

Nonuse (often called *passive use*) values constitute another potential economic value of water. In addition to valuation of goods and services which are actually used or experienced, people are willing to pay for environmental services they will neither use nor experience. Nonuse values are benefits received from knowing that a good exists, even though the individual may not ever directly experience the good. The benefits reflected by voluntary contributions toward preserving an endangered fish species are an illustrative example. Although still a controversial concept, most resource economists now agree that nonuse values should be included with use values so as to more accurately measure total environmental values (Carson et al. 1999; Freeman 2003, Chapter 5).

Some advocates for the environment object to policies that acknowledge the commodity aspects of water, because they fear this will lead to the sacrifice of important public benefits. It is likely more fruitful to recognize both the commodity and environmental characteristics of water demand, and to design policies with this duality in mind.

Water Is a Low-valued Commodity. Although there are exceptions (bottled drinking water, for example), the economic value per unit weight or volume of water tends to be relatively low, placing water among commodities which economists call "bulky." Capital and energy costs for transportation, lifting, and storage tend to be high relative to economic value at the point of use. For example, in irrigated agriculture, much of the raw water used on crops may yield direct economic values—roughly speaking, the return net of production costs available to cover the costs of supply—of less than US$0.04 per ton. Even water intended for urban residential uses—after being captured, filtered, treated, stored, and delivered by municipal water supply systems—typically costs the user less than US$0.50 per ton. Extensive water-conserving technologies (closed conduits, recycling, metering) as well as incentives for conservation (marketable property rights, increasing block pricing) are presently found only where water is recognized as scarce and valuable. Although water is generally a low-valued commodity, it nevertheless may still be underpriced relative to the cost of supply or opportunity costs.

Demand Varies. Variability affects demand as much as it does supply. The needs of agriculture oscillate in response to temperature and rainfall patterns over the seasons of a year and over longer cycles. Residential and industrial water demands also vary depending on daily, weekly, and seasonal considerations. Both storage and conveyance systems and management institutions must be prepared to satisfy peak loads in high-demand periods.

1.1.3 Social Attitudes Toward Water

More than for most commodities, social and cultural values relating to water are often are in conflict with economic values. Because water is essential to life, and because clean water and sanitation are essential to health, many argue that market allocation mechanisms should be rejected in favor of regulatory approaches. The Dublin Conference on Water and Environment in 1992 asserted as one of its guiding principles for action that "…it is vital to recognize first the basic right of all human beings to have access to clean water and sanitation at an affordable price" (UN 1992). The significance of water for life is even greater in arid regions, where crop irrigation is essential to production of that other staff of life, food.

For many, water has special cultural, religious, and social values, and these people prefer not to have water treated as an economic commodity. Goals other than economic efficiency play an unusually large role in selecting water management institutions. Boulding (1980) has observed that "the sacredness of water as a symbol of ritual purity exempts it somewhat from the dirty rationality of the market." Many people intuitively reject pricing of a resource that is necessary for life, and some cultures or religions proscribe water allocation by market forces.

However, an exclusive focus on the necessity of water for life as the basis for designing allocative institutions tends to obscure the fact that in most societies only a tiny fraction of water consumption is actually used directly for drinking and for preserving human life. Most direct water use is for convenience, comfort, and aesthetic pleasure. In the arid western United States, for example, average residential water withdrawal frequently reaches 500 liters per capita per day. Only a fraction of a percent of this use is for drinking; nearly half may be applied to irrigate lawns and gardens, and most of the remainder is for bathing, flushing toilets, and washing cars (Gleick 1998).

1.1.4 Legal and Political Considerations

A number of considerations for water policy design fall on the border between economics and political science, or what is sometimes called political economy.

Transactions Costs Versus the Relative Scarcity of Water. The term *transactions costs* refers to the resources required to establish, operate, and enforce a resource allocation, management, or regulatory system. Transactions costs may be also termed "ICE" costs, because they comprise the costs of obtaining information (such as knowledge about the needs and attitudes of other participants), contracting costs (resources required to reach agreements) and enforcement costs (the expense of enforcing contracts and public laws and regulations). Given the supply and demand characteristics of water noted earlier, transactions costs for water management and allocation tend to be high relative to its value. Where water is plentiful relative to demand, water laws tend to be simple and only casually enforced. Where water is scarce, more elaborate management systems have evolved. In many regions, water supplies are only now becoming scarce enough to require formal management systems. Increased resource scarcity and technological advances which reduce the transactions cost of monitoring and enforcing regulations both act to encourage innovations in allocative institutions, so as to economize on the scarce resource.

Cumulative Impact of Many Small Decisions. Water policymakers must often confront the problem aptly termed the "tyranny of small decisions" (Kahn 1966). This issue arises when markets or other mechanisms to ration resources are absent. Even though each individual act of water use, taken alone, might have a negligible impact, the sum total of many individual decisions can be of major importance. Numerous small decisions become important for policy in groundwater extraction by numerous individual small wells, nonpoint pollution from chemicals carried by runoff from farmers' fields, and sediments arising from forest harvest. Effective public regulation of many small, scattered decisionmakers is exceedingly difficult and expensive, but increasingly necessary.

Water as a "Common Pool" Resource. Common pool natural resources (often inaccurately called "common property" resources) are defined by two characteristics (Ostrom et al. 1994). The first is rivalry (or subtractability), meaning that a unit of resource withdrawn by one individual is not fully available to other potential users. The second is that the exclusion costs (the costs to a government or a cooperative private entity of preventing potential unentitled users from exploiting the resource) are relatively high. In addition to water, other fugitive or mobile resources, such as petroleum, wildlife, or migratory wildfowl can be common pool resources. Common pool *dilemmas* arise when resource use decisions that are rational from the individual's perspective bring about a result that is not optimal from the perspective of the exploiters as a group, or of society. When no one owns the resource, users have no incentive to conserve for the future or to consider the forgone benefits to others, and the self-interest of individual users lead them to over-rapid or excessive exploitation. The characteristics of the economic institutions governing their use is the fundamental issue in managing common pool resources.

In sum, we see that the unique characteristics of water make it a truly unusual resource; for numerous physical, economic, social, and political reasons, it presents special challenges to measuring benefits and costs and establishing appropriate institutional arrangements.

1.2 The Role of Economic Valuation in Water Management

The Dublin Statement does not, as some have believed, urge that markets be generally adopted for allocation of water. Indeed, as described earlier in

> **Water has an economic value in all its competing uses and should be recognized as an economic good.**
>
> …Past failure to recognize the economic value of water has led to wasteful and environmentally damaging uses of the resource. Managing water as an economic good is an important way of achieving efficient and equitable use, and of encouraging conservation and protection of water resources.
>
> *Source: Principle No. 4, The Dublin Statement on Water and Sustainable Development* (International Conference on Water and the Environment, Organized by the United Nations; Dublin, Ireland, January 1992.)

this chapter, market failures relating to the services of water (including externalities, public goods, and decreasing costs of production) are common enough that markets will be applicable in a limited number of situations. However, the Dublin Statement can be interpreted as recommending that water allocation policies be analyzed with economic evaluation techniques (cost–benefit analysis), thus justifying the framework and procedures presented in this book.

Estimates of the value of water provide signals of relative scarcity that are not available due to the absence of markets. River basin management calls for measures of benefits or value of changes in water availability. A standard example is investment in capturing, storing, delivering, and treating new water supplies. Another would be a proposal for reallocating water among competing water-using sectors. Further examples where marginal values of water might be useful include optimal groundwater basin policy, improved water quality, flood risk mitigation, and pricing and cost recovery for investment in water supply systems. These cases are discussed below in more detail.

1.2.1 Investment in Water Supply, Storage, and Conveyance Facilities

Consider a proposed investment in a multi-purpose water project which is being assessed for its economic feasibility. The economic feasibility criterion can be written:

$$PVNB = \Sigma_t \left[\frac{\Sigma_i (B_{it})}{(1+r)^t} \right] - \Sigma_t \left[\frac{C_{it}}{(1+r)^t} \right] - \Sigma_t \left[\frac{D_{jt}}{(1+r)^t} \right] \tag{1-1}$$

where:

    PVNB= present value of net benefits;

        B_{it} = incremental benefit (willingness to pay) for incremental water use or availability in sector *i* in year *t*;

        C_{it}= capital and operating costs in sector *i* in year *t*;

        D_{it}= incremental project-induced disbenefit (forgone benefits or external costs) to sector *i* in year *t*; and

        r= the discount (interest) rate.

The economic feasibility hypothesis to be tested is:

Is *PVNB* > 0 ?

Of course, the test can be also expressed in the alternative, but largely equivalent forms of the benefit–cost ratio or the internal rates of return. See any standard text on benefit–cost analysis, e.g. Boardman et al. 2001 or Fuguitt and Willcox 1999, for further discussion.

In implementing this test, economic valuation (shadow pricing) will normally be required for the terms B_{it} and D_{jt} and possibly for elements of C_{it}.

1.2.2 Intersectoral Competition for Water

Changing demands for water, particularly in the more arid regions, bring about a need to consider reallocation of water from lower- to higher-valued uses. Irrigation of agricultural crops is the largest user of water worldwide, particularly in arid regions, although its value at the margin is relatively low. One source of increasing demands for water is growing needs for off-stream uses: residential, industrial, and commercial uses. Demands for instream uses, such as power generation, waste load dilution, recreation, biodiversity, and fish and wildlife habitat, are also increasing. Proposals for major water storage and conveyance projects to meet these demands often confront the reality that the low cost sites are already utilized. Moreover, increased costs for energy and capital and a rising public recognition of the potential forgone environmental benefits arising from water developments represent additional scarcity considerations. These factors combine to encourage a search for water supplies from existing uses the marginal economic value of which is less than the cost of developing new supplies.

When a likely economic welfare improvement opportunity from reallocating water among use sectors arises, the question facing the analyst is: can a reallocation from sector *i* to sector *j* yield incremental gains to sector *j* in excess of the forgone benefits in sector *i*? In applied cases, the hypothesis of suboptimal allocation is tested for specific proposals for reallocation.

Consider a proposal to reallocate water from agriculture to municipal uses. Indirect impacts are expected on the hydropower sector. The economic feasibility test can be expressed by developing measurements for two conditions (Howe and Easter 1971; Young 1986). The first condition is that the benefits (both direct and indirect) to the municipal (purchasing) sector exceed the sum of forgone direct benefits to the selling sector plus forgone indirect benefits to the selling sector plus forgone indirect benefits to the hydropower sector. This can be written (assuming all benefit and cost expressions are in present value terms, employing a consistent planning period and price level):

$$DB_i + IB_k > FDB_j + FIB_k + TPC + CC \qquad (1\text{-}2)$$

where:

DB_i = direct economic benefit (value) to receiving sector;

IB_k = economic benefit to indirectly affected sector(s), if any;

FDB_j = forgone direct benefit (value forgone) in source sector;

FIB_k = forgone benefit in indirectly affected sector(s);

TPC = transactions and planning costs (for information, contracting and enforcement of transfer agreement plus project design costs);

CC = physical conveyance and storage costs.

A second condition is that the forgone direct benefits in the source sector should be the *least-cost* source of water for the purchasing sector:

$$FDB_j + FIB_k + TPC + CC < AC \qquad (1\text{-}3)$$

This second condition thus asserts that the proposal's costs (the sum of direct and indirect forgone economic benefits and the transactions and conveyance costs) should be less than AC (the cost of the next best alternative water source).

Economic analysis of both issues—as well as the other resource allocation and cost recovery problems mentioned previously—require the estimation of marginal or incremental benefits and benefits forgone of changes in water supply or use. The overall task of our study is to critically examine methods for estimating the various manifestations of marginal benefits.

1.2.3 Management of Groundwater Deposits

Although groundwater deposits are usually renewed to some degree from rainfall, runoff, and seepage from streams or linked surface water bodies, typically the rate of renewal is much slower than surface water. In the extreme case, aquifers are nearly nonrenewing (similar to ore and petroleum deposits), so the optimal rate of using up the fixed supply over time becomes an issue for economic analysis.

The economics of managing groundwater as a nonrenewing resource is addressed in a fairly extensive literature. This line of investigation focuses on two issues: the optimal rate of use over a long planning period, and the appropriate institutional structure to encourage individual pumpers to achieve this optimum. Groundwater has often been unregulated—left as an open access resource—and over-rapid exploitation and external costs (land subsidence, intrusion of poor quality water) are two of the major inefficiencies which occur in the absence of adequate collective management. In the most advanced analyses, the optimal allocation is derived by dynamic optimization procedures that balance diminishing returns to present period use against the effects of increased pumping costs and the discounted benefits of future uses. Decision rules specifying the optimal rate of pumping for each year of a long-term plan are derived. See Provencher and Burt 1994 for discussion of optimal groundwater management and a review of alternative institutional arrangements for groundwater allocation.

1.2.4 The Benefits of Improved Water Quality

In addition to quantity available, the quality of water also influences its economic value. Water in natural environments is never perfectly pure, and natural processes of erosion and transport of plant and animal materials add to the load carried by water. Humankind uses water bodies as sinks for disposal of numerous wastes from production and consumption activities. The extent to which micro-organisms and dissolved or suspended constituents are present varies greatly; in sufficiently high concentrations it can affect health and reduce aesthetic values and productivity. Therefore, the content of pollutants, or conversely the degree to which the water is treated for various uses, is important in determining its economic value.

Estimating benefits of improved water quality raises some complex and challenging policy issues. For the important cases of degradable effluents—those which are transformed after discharge into receiving waters—the detrimental effects depend on the nature of downstream water uses, the distance downstream, the temperature, rates of flow and the quality of receiving waters. Willingness to pay for a given project or regulative policy aimed at water quality improvement is usually assumed to reflect the damages avoided by subsequent users. See Spulber and Sabbaghi 1998, Chapter 2 for a rigorous exposition of this type of model.

A related example is the need to measure economic damages from releases of hazardous materials into public water bodies. This issue has increasingly come into prominence in the United States, exemplified by enactment of the Comprehensive Environmental Response, Compensation and Liability Act (CERCLA) of 1980 (see Kopp et al. 1997).

1.2.5 Policies for Alleviating Flood Hazards

Throughout the world, floods damage property, disrupt economic activity, and cause injuries and deaths every year. By some measures, floods cause more damage and deaths to humankind than any other natural hazard (Rodda 1995). Most governments have programs to change flood flow regimes and influence land use behavior by citizens in order to reduce loss of life and property and optimize the use of valuable floodplain lands. The benefit of public floodplain management programs is alleviation of the risk of flooding.

Benefits of flood alleviation projects typically are measured as the difference between *expected* flood losses with versus without the intervention. The evaluation is, of course, site-specific, depending on both hydrologic conditions and the nature and density of present and prospective future human activity on the floodplain. The principal technique for estimating urban flood risk reduction benefits has been the property damage avoided (PDA) approach, which reflects the present value of real (inflation-free) expected property damages avoided by the project or policy. (See Chapter 8 for a more detailed exposition of the economic model of flood risk reduction.)

1.2.6 The Role of Economic Valuation in Water Management: Summing up

To summarize to this point, the reader will find a common theme running through the above survey of water management and allocation issues. All of these are water management problems that involve choices as to how water should be combined with other resources so as to obtain the greatest public return from scarce resources. Included are the classic microeconomic resource allocation issues: how much of each input to use in production; how to proportion inputs in a production process; which products and how much of each to produce with scarce inputs; and how to allocate use of resources and consumption of goods and services between present and future uses (Varian 1997). Therefore, these issues can be usefully cast as resource allocation problems and can be best understood within an economic framework. Where markets are absent or ineffective, economic evaluation of resource allocation decisions requires that some means of estimating resource value be found.

It is a truism of applied policy analysis that "decisions imply valuation." Rational decisionmaking presupposes the forecasting of consequences and the assignment of values to these consequences. Because of the limited role played by market forces in the allocation of water, market prices upon which to base water-related resource allocation decisions are seldom available. In the jargon of the economist, *accounting* or *shadow prices* reflecting the value of water must be developed in their place.

Economists have in recent decades developed a number of techniques for measuring the economic values or benefits associated with nonmarket allocation relating to the environment and natural resources. These techniques call for a wedding of economic theory and applied economic practice. The theoretical foundations of nonmarket economic valuation of environmental resources are well developed (e.g. Freeman 2003). Progress with methods for estimating economic benefits in actual cases is also well advanced.

Although much of the applied resource valuation literature has dealt with water resources in one or another of its many ramifications, there is no single publication that brings all these disparate methods together under one cover. Moreover, although many of the resource valuation methods, particularly on the topic of environmental quality, have been subject to critical scrutiny and testing, some areas of water valuation have received less attention. Especially for the intermediate or producers' goods derived from water—such as crop irrigation, hydroelectric power and industrial water use—procedures for empirical applications of valuation methods appear to be less developed and have received less application and critical testing.

Conceptually sound and empirically accurate estimation of the economic benefits of water applicable to a specific policy proposal is most often a task demanding more time, resources, and technical skills than is generally recognized by nonspecialists. It requires familiarity with positive and normative microeconomic theory and the tools of applied quantitative economics. Water valuation rests on the normative framework of neoclassical welfare economics, as it is a particular application of cost–benefit analysis (Just et al. 1982; Johansson 1993). Positive microeconomics provides the conceptual framework for the analysis of behavior of producers and consumers (e.g. Varian 1997). Additionally, any of the numerous techniques from the quantitative toolkit of applied microeconomics may be used, ranging from survey research to econometrics to optimization modeling.

The discussion now turns to a brief presentation of how economists evaluate public policies.

1.3 The Nature of Economics and the Evaluation of Public Policies

Economists study the way in which individuals and societies respond to the scarcity of means available for achieving a multiplicity of wants. Economic analysis is designed first to understand the functioning of the economy and second to anticipate and assess the impacts of alternative policies over the longer term and on all affected parties, not only on those immediately affected. Water and the resources required to both exploit and protect it are increasingly scarce; hence, it is in the interest of the public that economic criteria be applied to water management decisions.

The Economic Approach

It is a *method* of analysis, not an assumption about particular motivations. ...The analysis assumes that individuals maximize welfare *as they conceive it,* whether they be selfish, altruistic, loyal, spiteful or masochistic. Their behavior is forward-looking, and is assumed to be consistent over time. In particular, they try as best as they can to anticipate the uncertain consequences of their actions. ...While this approach to behavior builds on an expanded theory of individual choice, it is not mainly concerned with individuals. It uses theory at the micro level as a powerful tool to derive implications at the group or macro level.

Source: Becker 1993 [emphasis in the original].

1.3.1 Positive versus Normative Economics

The activities of mainstream or neoclassical economists can be divided into two types. (The differing perspectives of some of the principal alternative schools of thought among economists are discussed later in this chapter.) *Positive* economics is concerned with observable facts and recurring relationships; it seeks to describe, explain, and predict economic phenomena. For example, what are the effects of changing prices, incomes, policies, or technologies on water consumption patterns? What role does water play in regional economic growth? The second type, *normative* economics, is concerned primarily with criteria for policy and questions of optimal policy (but rests in important ways on positive economics). Normative economics employs the empirical studies and predictions of positive economics, and combines them with value judgments reflecting notions about the ideal society in order to derive policy recommendations. For instance, are government administrative agencies or markets preferable in accommodating changing patterns of demand for water? How much pollution should be permitted and with what type of policies? Should a particular water supply project be undertaken?

Formal policy analysis is, by definition, normative. Questions of *ought* or *should* reveal dissatisfaction with the current state of affairs, and identify a policy problem. Moreover, normative criteria are a necessary basis for identifying an "improved" policy. Policy analysis presupposes ethical principles that provide a standard of evaluation for existing and proposed policies. The normative branch of economics is called welfare economics. It combines value judgments regarding the nature of the desirable organization of society with positive studies of empirical economic regularities to develop policy recommendations.

Normative analysis relies on the selection of appropriate normative criteria. Normative economics of the mainstream variety is based on a variant of Utilitarian ethics, which can roughly be characterized as holding that policies should be decided on the criterion of the "greatest good for the greatest number." Applied normative economics of the mainstream variety is based on criteria proposed by Vilfredo Pareto, an Italian economist who wrote in the early twentieth century.

Cost–benefit analysis (CBA) is the term used to label the practical application of the welfare economics test for potential Pareto improvement. Empirical economic methods are employed to predict whether a proposed policy initiative would produce beneficial effects in excess of adverse effects, both expressed in commensurate monetary terms. Beneficial effects are those which produce positive utility or remove anything that causes disutility, while costs are reductions in desired things or increases in undesired impacts. The normative framework for applied CBA is developed more fully in Chapter 2. (More generally, see any of the numerous texts on applied cost–benefit analysis, e.g. Boardman et al. 2001 or Fuguitt and Wilcox 1999.)

Normative economic analysis also must be based on some positive economic studies. Most economic policies can be described as incentives (which positively or negatively change the payoffs or incomes to members of the economy) or constraints (which impose limitations on the range of permissible economic activities). Examples of incentives are taxes and subsidies, such as a tax on pollution emissions or a subsidy to encourage pollution-reducing activities. A constraint might be a limited right to use water in a stream or canal, specified by, say, rate of flow. Any economic evaluation of a proposed policy will rest—in addition to normative criteria—on empirically based (positive) predictions of the response of water-using consumers or producers to policy initiatives.

1.3.2 The Economist's Approach: Basic Concepts

A number of fundamental concepts identify the economist's view on the way an economy functions and how policies should be designed. (Rhoads 1985 provides a sympathetic review and critique.)

Opportunity cost refers to the benefits forgone when a scarce resource is used for one purpose instead of in its next best alternative use. Spending and regulatory decisions that use scarce resources impose costs in the form of forgone alternatives (that is, opportunities that can no longer be undertaken).

Marginalism, in the context of resource allocation decisions, emphasizes the importance of considering incremental gains relative to incremental costs. Rather than setting spending decisions or ranking problems by judgments of their seriousness, spending should be prioritized on the basis of the marginal potential gains relative to incremental costs.

The Water-Diamond Paradox

The case of water was involved in one of the most famous intellectual conundrums in the early history of economic thought: the *water-diamond paradox*. Why, it was asked, are diamonds valued more highly than water? Although its price is low, water has enormous value *in use* to humans because it is necessary to existence. Diamonds, in contrast, are not at all essential, but have high value *in exchange* (on the market). This puzzle was subsequently resolved in two ways. One was by what came to be known as the distinction between *value in use* and *value in exchange*, and with the additional distinction between total and marginal values. The total utility of water clearly exceeds that of diamonds. However, the marginal utility of diamonds is greater than the marginal utility of water. The second explanation points to the cost of production of the two commodities. The cost of mining diamonds is much larger than the cost of obtaining water, and prices must reflect these relative costs. Thus, combining the two explanations, because diamonds are scarce (the marginal costs of acquiring more are high) and the marginal utility for diamonds is high, diamonds are priced higher than is water.

The notions of *diminishing marginal returns* and *resource substitutability* are closely linked with marginalism. Diminishing marginal returns refers to the fact that increases in the use of a given input (when all other inputs are assumed to be held constant) lead to decreasing increments to production. Similarly, additional consumption yields decreasing increments of utility or satisfaction for the consumer. Resource substitutability means that consumers and producers are not limited to fixed proportions in resource use in their consumption or production activities. Changing relative prices or scarcities may make it attractive to substitute plentiful resources for scarce ones. Farmers will take more care and expend more labor in crop irrigation under scarce water conditions than in relative plenty; householders may replace inefficient plumbing fixtures as water prices rise.

Another important idea is that *incentives matter*. Based on the belief that individuals act to maximize their own welfare as they see it, economists expect the individual producer or consumer to adjust behavior when incentives change. Since the time of Adam Smith over two centuries ago, an emphasis on designing institutions to make private interests more consistent with public goals has been a main attribute of the economist's approach. Recognition of private interests in designing government programs will frequently permit important goals to be achieved more cheaply.

Economists also emphasize the study of *unintended consequences* of human action in that part of the social system encompassing production, exchange, and consumption of goods and services (O'Driscoll 1977). Economics goes beyond direct observation. The nonspecialist can recognize the immediate effect of policy decisions: a policy of holding water prices below costs makes the resource less expensive and improves the economic well-being of some consumers. In this case, however, an additional consideration is that other consumers (or taxpayers) must pay part of the costs. Another example: provision of a reliable, high-quality water supply may provide increased employment and income to the regional economy. However, economists attempt to also address the hidden impacts of these policies and illuminate considerations not readily recognized. Low-cost water will lead to overuse and waste of the resource, while the financing of an investment in water supply implies forgone employment and income elsewhere in the economy.

Valuation of *nonmarketed* goods and services pervades environmental and resource economics. Economists recognize that people value things—including many important services of the earth's water supply—that they do not purchase through a market or that they may value for reasons independent of their own purchase and use. Further, not everything that reduces utility—such as pollution—is costed in markets. Although practitioners of the "dismal science" are sometimes equated with Oscar Wilde's cynic who "knows the price of everything and the value of nothing," environmental and resource economists in fact spend much of their professional efforts attempting to estimate the public's value (often called a shadow price) for nonmarketed goods and services. The modern economic paradigm assumes that values of goods and services rest on the underlying demand and supply relationships that are usually, but not always, reflected in market prices. Economics is not just the study of markets, but more generally, the study of preferences as an aspect of human behavior (Hanemann 1994).

The principal strengths of the economic approach to rational policy making are its focus on assessing the consequences (both beneficial and adverse) of policy actions and its attempts to be sensitive to the particulars of a decision. By expressing consequences in terms of a common denominator of money value, it provides a method of considering and resolving tradeoffs among competing and valued ends, including taking account of the economic costs (forgone benefits) of achieving those ends.

1.3.3 Alternative Viewpoints among Economists

Noneconomists should be aware that economists who study resource and environmental problems do not all speak with the same voice on how economics should be applied to research and policy issues. As in the discipline as a whole, and indeed in common with other social and policy sciences, resource economists exhibit a spectrum of methodological perspectives on studying the economy as well as diverse ideological views on the appropriate role for private and government entities in managing natural and environmental resources. They differ widely on the uses and limits of economics as a policy tool.

This book takes what can be called a mainstream or *neoclassical* viewpoint. Neoclassical microeconomists mainly focus on explaining the behavior of prices and the allocation of resources in a market economy. Economic efficiency is presumed to be a primary goal of society. Where conditions exist such that markets do not function properly, neoclassical economists apply their tools and concepts to understanding such conditions and prescribing remedies that enhance economic efficiency. As exemplified by this book and others, environmental and resource economists have adapted these concepts to nonmarket valuation for purposes of policy analysis.

But other schools of economic thought also deal with environmental and natural resource issues. In contrast to the perceived mainstream focus on markets and prices, *institutionalists* have emphasized the importance of studying the effects of economic institutions on the creation and distribution of incomes, usually with descriptive rather than quantitative tools. Economists in the institutionalist tradition further tend to question the mainstream's emphasis on economic efficiency as a criterion for policy analysis and, from a policy stance skeptical of the results of an unfettered market mechanism, emphasize the importance of other values such as fairness and equity of income distribution (e.g. Bromley 1991).

At the other end of the spectrum are the *Individualists* or *Austrians*, who emphasize the role of individual liberties as much as the importance of economic efficiency, and urge decentralization, definite and enforced property rights, and market institutions for resolving water and environmental problems (e.g. Anderson and Leal 1990).

The *ecological economists* represent a growing and increasingly influential departure from the techniques and policy prescriptions of mainstream economics. This school of thought arose in tandem with the worldwide awakening to environmental problems in the late 1960s. Perhaps the key premise of the ecological economics movement is that growth of the world's economy will, in the not-too-distant future, be limited by the biophysical capacity of the earth's environmental system. Accordingly, they challenge the complacency of the mainstream view that the world economy could continue indefinitely along the high-growth path of the past, a path that has been powered by technological change and has enabled increasing consumption levels for more and more of the earth's population. (For an introduction, see, for example, Edwards-Jones et al. 2000.) Ecological economists are strongly skeptical of the potential of market allocation systems and technological innovation for dealing with potential long-term environmental problems. Rather than highlighting maximum economic growth as a primary social goal, they emphasize a policy of sustainability or "development which meets the needs of the present without compromising the ability of future generations to meet their own needs." (World Commission on Environment and Development 1987).

By raising difficult questions and challenging mainstream tenets, these various competing viewpoints force a continual rethinking of economic theory, adding to the contribution of economics in understanding and steering the economy. However, none of the competing paradigms offers viable alternative models of nonmarket environmental valuation. For this reason, I have no hesitation in adopting the mainstream neoclassical framework.

1.3.4 Concluding Thoughts

Earlier in this chapter appeared a well-known quote from the Dublin Statement on Water and Sustainable Development to the effect that water should be recognized as an economic good: managing water is an important way to achieve efficient and equitable use, and to encourage conservation and protection of water resources. This premise implies that economic criteria should be among the tools employed in evaluating water management policies. It does not imply that policymakers should always choose the market system as the means of allocating water resources. Although water is increasingly allocated by market mechanisms, its unique attributes make it a classic example of the market's potential failure to achieve an economically efficient allocation. Externalities, public goods, decreasing costs in supply, and high transactions costs are among the reasons why unfettered markets will not always best serve society in allocating water resources. Thus one is led to the need for nonmarket valuation techniques to provide measures of value and scarcity for economic policymaking related to water. The next chapter describes the conceptual framework for economic valuation of nonmarket goods and services as applied to water resources. The remainder of the book describes the standard methods, assesses the strengths and limitations of each, and illustrates the various approaches with case examples.

Conceptual Framework and Special Problems in Valuing Water

To lay the basis for the subsequent analyses, this chapter summarizes the broad conceptual framework for economic valuation of nonmarket goods and services as applied to water resources. I begin by reviewing some of the basic concepts and definitions used in measuring economic value or benefits of public water projects or policies. The main focus is on valuing changes in water supply for reallocation and investment choices, but changes in water quality and reliability are also addressed. Next comes a discussion of some issues in valuation unique to the water resource. The chapter concludes with a classification system of types of benefits, broad types of measurement techniques, and methods by which water is valued in applied contexts.

2.1 Economic Value Versus Other Concepts of Value

To paraphrase David Pearce (1993, *13*), there is no activity that can be properly called "valuing water." Resource and environmental economists performing nonmarket valuations actually try to assign *monetary measures of individuals' preferences for outcomes of policy proposals or events*. In the present context, the outcomes of interest are often improved water supply, quality, or reliability. Similarly, economists seek monetary measures of the loss in well-being because of inadequate or excessive water supply or degraded water. Using the measuring rod of money for valuing inputs and outputs facilitates comparisons with money costs of investments and with values in alternative uses, such as with environmental public goods.

2.1.1 A Preliminary Sketch of the Economic Valuation Process

The fundamental concepts used as measures of value are *willingness to pay* (WTP) or *willingness to accept* compensation (WTA). Resources have economic value or yield benefits whenever users would willingly pay a price for them rather than do without, or be compensated to do without the good or service (of which, more later). Effective market operation results in a set of market values (prices) which serve to allocate resources and commodities in a manner consistent with the objectives of producers and consumers. In many parts of the world, water has been plentiful enough to be regarded as a free good and, until recently, institutional arrangements for managing water scarcity have not been of serious concern.

When markets are absent or ineffective, economic valuation of resource allocation decisions requires some synthetic means of estimating resource value. Resource value is measured in the context of specific objectives. The value of the resource reflects its contribution to the objectives. In water resources, governments have identified several major objectives, any of which may be relevant: enhancing national economic development (equivalent to enhancing what economists term economic efficiency from a national perspective), enhancing regional economic development, enhancing environmental quality, and enhancing social well-being (U.S. Water Resources Council 1983; Organization for Economic Cooperation and Development 1985).

2.1.2 Alternative Approaches to Resource Valuation

Other approaches to assigning values to natural and environmental resources are available in addition to that developed in economics. Philosophers divide values, broadly speaking, into either *extrinsic* or *intrinsic*, both of which are relevant for water and environmental policy. The distinction rests on whether the basis for valuation derives from consequences for human welfare. Extrinsic (sometimes called *instrumental*) values are those that arise because things or acts are instruments for humankind for attaining other things of intrinsic value. As an example, water resources may be valued extrinsically for their contribution to human health, welfare, or satisfactions. Intrinsic values, in contrast, are assigned to things, actions, or outcomes for their own sake, independent of means of providing or attaining other items or situations of value for humans (Anderson 1993, *204–206*). People often value environmental resources for other than their own use or consumption; for instance, they wish to preserve endangered species or protect delicate ecosystems, without consideration of whether these offer immediate human utility. (See Randall 2002 for a thoughtful treatment of the role of cost–benefit analysis in public policy formation where economic efficiency is not the sole criterion.)

Both approaches to valuation are legitimately applied to environmental and resource policy. However, the prevailing—though not unanimous—view among philosophers is that neither extrinsic nor intrinsic values are necessarily absolute. When values conflict, as they often do, a dilemma arises. The solution is to reconcile the competing goals (McLean 1993). Morgan and Henrion (1990, 27) describe a widely-used approach—called the *approved process* approach—which, roughly speaking, requires all relevant parties to observe a specified set of procedures or apply a concept of due process to estimate a proposed policy's impacts on relevant measures of value. Any decision reached after an appropriate authority balances the competing values under the specified procedures is deemed acceptable. Standard water planning manuals—including the United States Water Resources Council's *Principles and Guidelines* (1983) and the Organization for Economic Cooperation and Development's *Management of Water Projects* (1985), although neither acknowledges the underlying philosophical premises—appear to reflect an approved process approach. Both manuals call for a determination of environmental impacts (intrinsic values) to be balanced against human (both economic and social) welfare considerations (extrinsic values). Moreover, both manuals emphasize that the task of technical analysts is not to come to a decision, but to display impacts in the appropriate metrics. The ultimate resolution or balancing of conflicting values is assumed to be made at the political (legislative or upper executive branch) rather than the technocratic level.

The economic values discussed here are extrinsic, in that they reflect people's assessment of contributions or decrements to human welfare. These economic benefits will be appropriate in either a stand-alone economic analysis or a more general multi-objective or approved process approach.

2.2 Economic Criteria for Resource Allocation and Valuation

Although improving the distribution of income, enhancing environmental quality, and attaining other nonmarket goals are important, our analysis pertains exclusively to the objective of economic efficiency in the development, allocation, and management of water resource supply and quality. There are two major reasons for this. First, under conditions of increasing scarcity and growing competition among water users, economic efficiency becomes an increasingly important social objective, and efficiency values have viable meaning in resolving conflicts. Second, within a broader multiple-objective framework, efficiency values provide a constructive means of assessing the opportunity costs (forgone benefits) of pursuing alternative objectives.

2.2.1 Evolution of Cost–Benefit Analysis Applied to Water Resource Planning

Systematic comparison of the estimated benefits with the estimated costs of federal water projects has been required for many years in the United States, provisions in the Water Reclamation Act of 1902 being an early example. However, methods of evaluation were exceedingly crude by present-day standards, often consisting only of comparisons of expected gross revenues received by beneficiaries with expected total project costs. Little or no attention was paid to the often considerable associated costs that must be expended to enable beneficiaries to use project outputs. (Such costs might include those for building and operating conveyance systems to move water from a point of capture to the point of use.) Also uncounted were the benefits from what we would now call nonmarketed environmental goods and services. Further, the forgone benefits from precluded alternative uses of water were disregarded (a situation that has continued to this day). In the early part of the twentieth century, economists began to formulate the methods of normative economic analysis that came to be known as welfare economics. The well-known requirement in the United States Flood Control Act of 1936—"if the benefits to whomsoever they may accrue are in excess of the estimated costs"—has been said to be the basis for establishing welfare economics as the conceptual foundation for feasibility tests on federal water projects and set the stage for later development and refinement of cost–benefit evaluation techniques. (See Hanemann 1992 for a more detailed discussion of the evolution of environmental valuation techniques in the United States.)

By the late 1940s, a few academic scholars, mainly working in the "land economics" tradition in colleges of agriculture, had studied issues relating to water allocation and had begun to work out nonmarket methods of estimating economic benefits and costs, mainly in the context of agriculture. About the same time, several reports on evaluation methodology were issued from within the federal government, most notably the *Proposed Practices for Economic Analysis of River Basin Projects* (Federal Inter-Agency River Basin Committee 1950), known informally as the "Green Book." However, it was not until after mid-century that some resource economists began to adapt rigorous microeconomic and welfare economics concepts to public investment and allocation issues relating to water. These economists brought several relatively simple concepts—such as opportunity costs, demand as willingness to pay, marginal analysis, nonmarketed costs and benefits, and distinctions between private and social benefits and costs—to the economic evaluation of water allocation issues. But major changes in analysis and policy were implied.

The new era of serious development and application of the welfare economics conceptual framework began in the late 1950s. Eckstein (1958) and McKean (1958) provided expositions of the appropriate concepts combined with rigorous critiques of the then-current practices in federal evaluation procedures. Also at the same time, Krutilla and Eckstein (1958) emphasized the physical interdependence of water projects within a basin framework. They argued that because water had an opportunity cost value in alternative uses in the typical case of an already developed river basin, these costs should be routinely taken into account in federal project appraisals (wisdom that routinely continues to be ignored). Several other works on water economics appearing about that time were extremely influential in the emerging field of applied natural resource economics. Contributions by Marglin and by Dorfman in the Harvard Water Program's summary report (Maass et al. 1962) provided, respectively, the most rigorous statement up to that date of the welfare theory applied to water resources and an exposition of the economic theory of production as related to water resource development.

Several other major themes emerged. One central idea—still controversial—was that water in private goods uses could be fruitfully thought of as an economic commodity, and that suitably adapted exchange institutions warranted consideration as mechanisms for water allocation. Economists also realized that underpriced water resources created an artificial demand for water in urban and industrial as well as agricultural uses, implying that what were widely perceived as important water "needs" were better understood as merely wants for cheap water. Full-cost pricing, perhaps implemented with an increasing block rate structure, was proposed as an appropriate solution to many artificially created "water shortage" problems.

This work in the late 1950s and early 1960s provided the conceptual underpinnings for the outpouring of applied studies of water economics and policy that were soon to follow. The next section sketches the received conceptual doctrine on the goal of economic efficiency and implementation via the Pareto Principle.

2.2.2 The Pareto Principle and Economic Efficiency

Economic efficiency may be defined as an organization of production and consumption such that all unambiguous possibilities for increasing economic well-being have been exhausted. Stated somewhat differently, economic efficiency is an allocation of resources such that no further reallocation is possible which would provide gains in production or consumer satisfaction to some firms or individuals without simultaneously imposing losses on others. This definition of economic efficiency—termed Pareto optimality—is satisfied in a perfectly functioning competitive economy. Abstracting from the mathematical elegance found in textbook expositions (e.g. Just et al. 1982) and abstracting further from the time consideration in outputs and inputs of economic activities, Pareto optimality can be expressed quite straightforwardly in terms of the attainment of (a) economic efficiency in production of goods and services, (b) economic efficiency in distribution of goods and services, and (c) resource allocation in a manner consistent with consumer preferences. Put another way, Pareto efficiency is achieved when the marginal benefits of using a good or service are equal to the marginal cost of supplying the good.

Pareto optimality rests on several central value judgments (Mäler 1985). The first of these is the judgment that individual preferences count; the economic welfare of society is based on the economic welfare in aggregate of its individual citizens. Second, the individual is the best judge of his/her own well being. The third, more restrictive, value judgment is that a change which makes everybody better off with no one becoming worse off constitutes a positive change in total welfare.

2.2.3   From Welfare Theory to Cost–Benefit Practice

Translating from the welfare economics theory to applied cost–benefit practice requires further steps. Because, in a complex modern society, few policy changes which improve welfare for many would avoid lowering welfare of some individuals, few proposed changes would meet the strict Paretian standard of making no one worse off. However, welfare theorists circumvented this problem with the *compensation test*: if gainers could compensate losers and still be better off, the change would be judged an improvement. In practice, compensation is often impracticable; identifying and compensating all adversely affected parties is expensive and time-consuming. Hence, the compensation test becomes a test for a *potential* Pareto improvement. If gainers could *in principle* compensate losers and still be better off, the change is deemed acceptable, whether or not the compensation actually takes place.

Also, rather than evaluating all possible allocations in a continuous function framework, cost–benefit analysis (CBA) typically examines fairly large discrete increments of change to assess whether the move is in the direction of Pareto efficiency. An action which generates incremental benefits in excess of incremental costs is termed Pareto-*superior*, because it leads to a condition superior to the *status quo ante*.

Beneficial and adverse effects are often abstract and ambiguous concepts. As noted earlier in this chapter, mainstream economists treat values as extrinsic and propose to measure impacts in terms of satisfaction of human preferences. To transform the concept of welfare into a single metric, the suggested measuring rod is that of money. The change in a person's welfare from some proposed improvement is measured as the maximum amount of money a person would be willing to forgo to obtain the improvement. Conversely, for a change which reduces welfare, the measure is the amount of compensation required to accept the change.

The economic evaluation of projects or proposals is based on systematically balancing the predicted beneficial and adverse effects generated by the proposal. *Benefits* are the "good" or "desired" effects contributed by the proposal, while *costs* are the "bad" or "undesired" impacts. (For detailed treatments of the overall approach to CBA—some of which is applied to environmental and natural resource problems—the reader may consult the extensive literature in that field, e.g. Boardman et al. 2001; Fuguitt and Wilcox 1999; Brent 1998; Johansson 1993).

The valuation of policy outcomes should be based on the concept of willingness to pay: *Benefits are the sums of the maximum amounts that people would be willing to pay to gain outcomes they view as desirable; costs are the sums of the maximum amounts that people would be willing to pay to avoid outcomes that they view as undesirable.*

Boardman et al. 2001, *70* [Emphasis in the original].

Willingness to accept (WTA) compensation is an important welfare measure in some contexts. WTA is the payment that would make an individual indifferent between having an improvement and forgoing the improvement while receiving the extra money. Alternatively, it is the minimum sum that an individual would require to forgo a change that otherwise would be experienced. (Analysts initially expected that empirical estimates of WTP and WTA for the same good would be quite similar and that the Marshallian consumer surplus would lie between them. However, empirical studies— mainly in applications of the contingent valuation method—have shown fairly large divergences between WTP and WTA. This subject is addressed below in Chapter 4.)

Figure 2-1, patterned after concepts demonstrated by Smith (1985), illustrates the comparison of Pareto efficiency and cost–benefit criteria. The curve denoted $B(W)$ is a representation of aggregate benefits (i.e. consumer or producer surplus) of alternative levels of water services (W), while $C(W)$ represents the associated aggregate costs. These curves measure social welfare (or aggregate utility) and cost. Their general forms reflect the conventional assumption that benefits increase at a decreasing rate with increased output and costs increase at an increasing rate. The Pareto-efficient solution is at W^*—the maximum vertical distance between $B(W)$ and $C(W)$. At W^* the marginal benefits equal the marginal costs.

However, as noted earlier, rather than seeking a full optimum solution, cost–benefit analysis in practice typically considers whether a change from given conditions would represent a desirable shift. In Figure 2-1, such a change would be represented by moving from W_1 to W_2. The conventional CBA test compares the aggregate increment in benefits (GH) with aggregate incremental costs (EF). If incremental benefits exceed incremental costs, as they are drawn to do in Figure 2-1, then the change is a Pareto

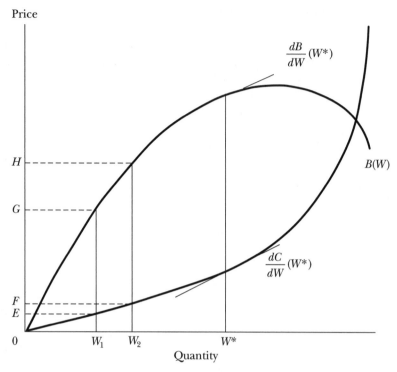

Figure 2-1. Pareto Efficiency and Cost–Benefit Criteria Compared

Improvement. Any act or policy judged a Pareto Improvement could be recommended as preferable to the existing situation.

2.3 Economic Valuation in the Absence of Market Prices

Alternative water management policies can effect significant variations in the quantity of water available, its quality, and the timing and location of supplies for both in- and off-stream uses. In general, these impacts have an economic dimension, either positive or negative, which should be taken into account in policy formulation. Specifically, the public decision process (and resolution of conflicts) is improved by identifying and comparing the benefits and costs of proposed water resource developments and allocations among alternative and competing uses.

2.3.1 The Need for Accounting Prices

Paraphrasing Howe (1971a), policy impacts can be classified into four categories:

1. Impacts for which markets exist and market prices reflect scarcity values;
2. Impacts for which market prices may be observed, but such prices fail to accurately reflect true social values, although they can be adjusted to more accurately do so;
3. Impacts for which market prices do not exist, although it is possible to identify surrogate market prices; and
4. Impacts for which market prices or surrogate prices are not meaningful.

Cases 2 and 3 are most typical in CBA for water resource planning. In these instances the prices employed are called *accounting prices* (or sometimes *shadow prices*).

Benefits and costs must be expressed in monetary terms by applying the appropriate prices to each physical unit of input and product. Three general types of estimates are employed. A primary source of the prices used for CBA is observation of market activity; in CBA applied to water resources planning, this approach is more often applied to the cost side than to the benefit side of the analysis. Second, it may be necessary to make adjustments to observed market prices—for example, when agricultural commodity prices are controlled by government regulation or when minimum wage rates are set above market clearing prices. Finally, it is often necessary to estimate prices which do not exist at all in any market, such as the value of water used for power generation or in outdoor recreation. The second and third types would be accounting prices.

2.3.2 Defining Accounting Prices: The Willingness to Pay Principle

The presumption that the prices used in CBA are interpreted as expressions of willingness to pay or willingness to accept compensation for a particular good or service is obvious for market prices, because the equilibrium market price represents the willingness to pay at the margin of potential buyers of the good or service. For nonmarketed goods, WTP is the theoretical basis on which shadow prices are calculated. The assertion that willingness to pay should be the measure of value or cost follows from the principle that public policy should be based on the aggregation of individual preferences. Willingness to pay represents the total value of an increment of project output, i.e. the demand for that output. (Some authors, unfortunately, in addition to this broad meaning, use the term "willingness to pay" to refer to a particular type of nonmarket valuation study which directly questions people on their valuations for environmental changes. To avoid ambiguity, these specific techniques would best be identified by the name of the relevant elicitation process, e.g. "contingent valuation.")

Therefore, *benefits* are defined as any positive effect, material or otherwise, for which identifiable affected parties are willing to pay. *Costs* are the

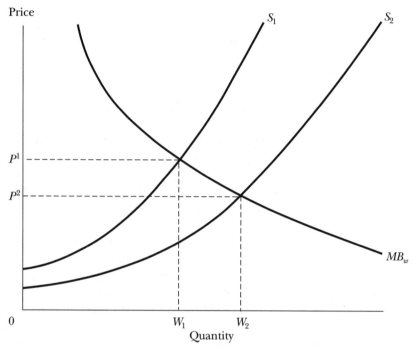

Figure 2-2. Price and Quantity Effects and Change in Economic Surplus from Nonmarginal Shift in Supply of Marketed Commodity

value of the opportunities forgone because of the commitment of resources to a project, or the willingness to pay to avoid detrimental effects.

2.3.3 Economic Surplus and Measures of Benefit

Economists further base the concept of economic value on a decision framework within which rational individuals make the best use of resources and opportunities. The framework assumes that the individual members of the economy react systematically to perceived changes in their situation. Such changes can include—in addition to the quantity and quality of the water resource of primary interest here—prices, costs, institutional constraints and incentives, income, and wealth.

Figure 2-2 illustrates the concepts of economic (producers' or consumers') surplus under marketed commodity conditions. The curve denoted MB_w in Figure 2-2 is a familiar demand curve, reflecting the maximum amount of the commodity (here denoted W) that consumers would be willing to take as dependent on price. The demand curve slopes downward to the right, reflecting the desire for consumers to take more of the commodity W only as the price declines.

The inverse demand function, which reflects the converse relationship (the value assigned by consumers as a function of quantity) can also be interpreted as the marginal willingness to pay for alternative quantities, so it is conventionally labeled in CBA, as in Figure 2-2, a *marginal benefit* (MB) function. The inverse demand function is more frequently applicable in water economics, because the issue is finding the benefit or shadow price where quantity (of water) rather than price is the decision variable. (See e.g. Randall and Stoll 1980.)

Consumers' (and producers') surplus is defined as the area above the price: it represents the difference between the maximum that users would be willing to pay and what they would actually have to pay under a constant price per unit. The supply curves S_1 and S_2 represent a nonmarginal shift in supply, such as from a project that increases the supply of some productive factor (e.g. water for crop irrigation).

The trained economist will note that the measures shown are for the ordinary *Marshallian* concept of demand and consumer surplus. More precise welfare measures, called Hicksian measures, are provided in the price theory and welfare economics literatures (Just et al. 1982). The Hicksian *compensating* version refers to the amount of compensation (received or paid) which would return the individual to his/her initial welfare position. The *equivalent* version refers to the amount of money that must be paid to the consumer to make them as well off as they could have been after the change. Marshallian demand functions are sometimes easier to estimate. Moreover, when purchase of the good or service in question accounts for only a small part of the household budget, it has been shown that the Marshallian measure is often a quite close approximation to the Hicksian measure. (See Freeman 2003 for a more complete analysis.) In evaluating water resource policies, since water is a small fraction of most consumers' budgets, the differences among the measures are frequently smaller than the errors in estimating the functions econometrically. Thus, the Marshallian approximation will usually be acceptable in most practical applications.

Figure 2-3 portrays a common case in nonmarket valuation of water resources (Randall 1987, Chapter 13). It represents an increase in the availability of a commodity such as water for a nonpriced use from W_1 to W_2. Perfectly inelastic supply curves S_1 and S_2 shift from W_1 to W_2. The curve MB_w, as before, shows the downward sloping marginal benefit function. The area under MB_w between W_1 ("without change") and W_2 ("with change") represents the economic surplus attributable to the changed water supply. It is this area, bounded by the points W_1ABW_2 that the economic analyst is attempting to measure in nonmarket valuation of changes in water supply and environmental amenities.

Note that the curve MB_w can represent consumer demand *or* producers' willingness to pay. In the latter interpretation, MB_w is the producers' Value Marginal Product (VMP) function, the marginal net return to an increas-

Marginal Benefits

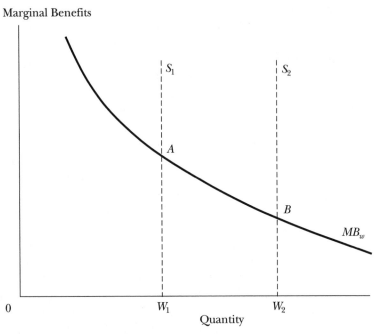

Figure 2-3. Change in Economic Surplus from Nonmarginal Shift in Supply
of Nonmarketed Commodity (e.g. Water)

ing level of input. (See Chapter 3 below for a formal derivation of these
properties of producers' valuation of inputs.) This interpretation is, in fact,
frequently more applicable to valuing increments in water supply than the
producers' surplus depicted in Figure 2-2 (i.e. the area above the supply
curve *S* and below the price line). Also, in parallel with the Hicksian adjustment for income effects to consumers' surplus measures, a corresponding
adjustment for cost-minimizing allocation of other inputs or technology is
appropriate for producers' surplus measures (Johansson 1993).

To recapitulate, the economic value of an environmental resource is
measured by the sum of many users' willingness to pay for the good or service in question. Willingness to pay is a monetary measure of the intensity
of individual preferences. Therefore, we can say that *economic valuation is
the process of expressing preferences for beneficial effects against preferences contrary
to adverse effects of policy initiatives in a money metric.*

Increasingly of interest are measures of opportunity costs of water
resources. Opportunity costs are the benefits forgone when a scarce
resource is used for one purpose instead of the next best alternative. When
evaluating tradeoffs of proposed reallocations, one needs a measure of the
benefits of the proposed new use as well as the reduction of benefits associated with reduced water use in the sector currently benefitting. Hence,
opportunity costs are the reverse of incremental benefits. Returning to Fig-

ure 2-3, a measure of opportunity costs would be the area under MB_w from, this time, W_2 to W_1. This is the same area bounded by the points W_1ABW_2 described before.

2.3.4 Other Considerations: The With–Without Principle and Standing

In applied economic evaluation in water resource management, three useful policy-driven concepts are: the *with–without principle, standing,* and the *accounting stance.*

The With–Without Principle. The with–without principle holds that policy appraisal should compare the "state of the world" as it would be *with* the policy to the "state of the world" as it would be *without* the policy. The implication is that policy evaluation is not adequate if it simply compares conditions *before* implementation of the policy to conditions *after* its implementation. Many changes in the world from "before" to "after" would have occurred without the contemplated policy or project, so only the effects due to the intervention should be credited or charged to it. The intent is to identify only the impacts that are clearly associated with the project or program, not changes in the economy which would have occurred even without the policy or program. Otherwise, policy evaluation is likely to overstate policy impacts.

Which Population Has Standing? The term *standing* refers to the question of *whose* benefits and costs are to be counted. (Whittington and MacRae 1986). For purposes here, the term refers to the population in a specified geographical area or political entity or subdivision thereof (such as a region, a province, a state, or a country), the benefits and costs to whom are counted in a specific economic evaluation.

One basic principle for deciding on who has standing is to base the decision on the widest conception of who will enjoy the benefits and bear the costs of the policy intervention under study. A project's benefits and costs may be confined to a local region, or they may extend to the whole country or even internationally. However, practicality may dictate a less ambitious effort. Even though benefits and costs of a proposal may be expected to be widely dispersed, the ever-present constraints of time and resources for data collecting and modeling of impacts in performing a CBA may limit the geographic scope of project planning. Modeling of small impacts in distant locales may be beyond the state of the art.

The most frequently used basis for standing in CBA is the population of a country. However, where impacts extend across national boundaries—as often happens in international river basins—a supranational area may be the appropriate unit of standing. Valuations may be, and in water resource planning often are, performed for subnational entities (e.g. political subdivisions such as states or provinces, or geographic regions). However, because impacts often extend beyond such regional boundaries, this approach should be used with caution. For example, an irrigation project may generate direct benefits in a local area, but some of the direct costs may be paid by the national government, so that a national accounting stance is appropriate. Another example is the indirect or external costs, such as forgone electric power generation or lower water quality imposed on downstream water users, that may accrue well beyond the borders of the area benefited. Indirect benefits outside the project region can also occur. For example, interception of waters by irrigation or power reservoirs may yield indirect flood reduction benefits far downstream.

Ideally, all real beneficial and adverse economic effects, both direct and indirect, are accounted for in a full economic evaluation. Thus, the population granted standing in CBA should be as encompassing as possible; impacts should be accounted for no matter how far away or in what political jurisdiction they may occur, and whether they are direct or indirect. However, in practice, the choice of the population with standing must be made on practical grounds, balancing the gains in accuracy against the increased costs of planning associated with spreading a wider net. Most national planning agencies suggest a national perspective wherever possible. Whittington and MacRae (1986) further consider whether the impacts of illegal activities should count—probably not—and whether impacts that extend to future generations should be counted—probably so.

Accounting Stance. In this context, *accounting stance* refers to *how* benefits, costs, or other impacts are counted in a CBA. The primary distinction is between *private* and *social* accounting perspectives. The private accounting stance measures impacts in terms of the prices faced by the economic actors being studied. In contrast, for the social accounting stance, social prices are those adjusted for taxes, subsidies, and other public interventions. To simplify a complex subject, social prices are those prices anticipated to occur at a free market equilibrium. The most common element of CBA adjusted for accounting stance is the interest rate, an issue so significant that most CBA texts devote an entire chapter to it (e.g. Boardman et al. 2001, Chapter 10). The distinction between private and social accounting stances also often arises in agricultural water use, since many governments intervene in both commodity and input markets relating to agriculture.

Although *financial analysis* and *economic analysis* are used for this same distinction in some CBA manuals, particularly those from the World Bank (e.g. Gittinger 1982), that terminology is avoided here. This is because these terms are quite ambiguous and confusing to nonspecialists—economists and noneconomists alike. So-called "financial" and "economic" analyses both employ the same basic economic methods. The main distinction is that they use different prices.

2.4 What Types of Water Values Can Be Identified?

A number of particular economic, political, and physical characteristics of water policy decisions create distinctive problems for the task of water valuation. It must be recognized that there is no single economic value of water. Of course, there is no single price for any marketed good and service. But values of water differ more widely than do prices for most goods and services traded on markets.

When a value of water is being estimated, what is being measured is the welfare change associated with some policy-induced change in the attributes of the commodity. Because the appropriate measure differs according to the specific attributes of the situation and decision in question, it is important to keep clear what these attributes are. A number of these issues are discussed below.

2.4.1 Long-Run versus Short-Run Values

Policy decisions relating to water can range from major long-lived capital investments to one-off allocations in the face of immediate events such as droughts or delivery system failures. So we must distinguish carefully between long-run and short-run values. This distinction relates to the degree of fixity of certain inputs, particularly where water is a producers' good, as in crop irrigation, industry, and hydropower.

To give more realism to the static model of early neoclassical microeconomics, more than a century ago Alfred Marshall formulated a somewhat complex, but still workable, market price theory that reflected some additional realities of a dynamic economy (Blaug 1997, Chapter 10). Marshall's distinctions, with little substantive change, are still in use today for many applied economic analyses, including most of those discussed here.

The aspect of Marshall's theory of price determination of immediate interest here is its differentiations among various "periods" usually referred to as *lengths of run*. In the *market period* (which seldom arises in water policy analyses), supplies of goods are completely fixed in quantity. In the *short run*, plant capacity for production is fixed but production can be increased or decreased somewhat through changes in use of variable inputs. For purposes of water planning, a short-run formulation is appropriate for modeling temporary variations in water supplies, such as during a drought. In the *long run*, plant capacity becomes variable. Costs of such capacity are then included in the analysis. Finally, some more recent authors propose a *very long run*, which allows for change in the technology of production.

The use of the terms "market period," "short run," and "long run" can be perplexing, sometimes even to experienced economic analysts. The terms misleadingly suggest the notion of calendar time. However, Marshallian periods are better understood as a concept of "operational time." Short-run and long-run situations are distinguished not according to any actual time in days, weeks, or months, but corresponding to the degree that economic actors can adapt to changing conditions (Blaug 1997, Chapter 10).

Anticipating the model to be developed in more detail in Chapter 3, consider a rational producer's net returns to water. In the short run, where some inputs are fixed, the estimate of the increment in net income can regard the cost of fixed inputs as sunk and ignore them. In the long run, where input costs must all be covered, these costs cannot be ignored. Therefore, we would expect that, for the same site and production processes, values estimated for short-run contexts will usually be larger than values for the long run. Similarly, domestic water users exhibit different responses in the short versus the long run. Price elasticity of demand is less (in absolute value) in the short run when decisions are constrained by factors such as the technologies embodied in water-using appliances, than in the longer run when adjustments to shortages are possible. Accordingly, willingness to pay in the short-run planning situation is once again typically higher than in the long run.

The long run is the appropriate model for most of the important investment or intersectoral allocation problems in the water resources field, and is therefore essential for our purposes. Failure to observe this distinction has caused many nonspecialists to ignore fixed costs and thus to erroneously attribute too high a value to producers' water uses. Sometimes, however, as in drought planning, short-run values are appropriate.

2.4.2 At-Site versus At-Source Values: Commensurability of Place, Form, and Time

Marketed economic commodities are priced according to spatial, quality, and temporal attributes, and shadow pricing of water should follow similar principles. For example, petroleum is always priced in terms of grade, as well as location and time of delivery. A look at a daily newspaper's business pages reveals that prices for crude oil at the point of production or delivered to a refinery are much less than the cost per unit volume of refined gasoline in bulk at some specified distribution point, which is in turn much lower than the price of gasoline at the local retail station. These considerations apply to water, and oblige analysts engaged in comparative water valuation exercises to ensure that the chosen measure of water value is *commensurable* in terms of a common denominator of place, form, and time.

Consider first the aspect of place. Because of the low value of water at the margin, the capital and energy costs for its transportation, lifting, and storage often tend to be high relative to economic value at the point of use.

Therefore, the economic value of water of similar quality at the point of use may differ widely from the value at the source. Second, the form or quality is important. Water in its raw (untreated) form in a river—or even in a reservoir or canal—is a distinctly different commodity than treated water delivered by a public utility under pressure to a business or residence. Third, because of seasonal variations in demand, the value may change with time. In many places, water has little value for irrigation in winter, but it may be quite useful at that time for power generation or industry. When comparing values among uses (for intersectoral water allocation choices), one must recognize that aspect of the problem. Comparing values among uses is best performed in terms of raw water supplies at some specified point of diversion.

These considerations all point to an important distinction in offstream water uses, particularly for comparing marginal values between and among sectors. For any offstream use, in addition to the demand or value at the site of use, we can think of a derived demand for water at the source. The water at the source must be captured, transported to the site of use, and perhaps stored and treated to convert the raw water to the commodity with the place, time, and form attributes desired by the user. Each of these processes incurs some resource costs. Irrigation water is seldom treated, so it may be only stored and transported, but domestic and industrial water supplies are typically filtered and treated to remove or reduce sediments, microorganisms, and chemical contaminants. Hence, willingness to pay at the site of use is greater than that at the source of the water, the difference reflecting the costs incurred to convert raw water in stream or aquifer to the time, place, and form most useful to the water user.

Although the distinction between the values of water to the user and the derived demand for raw water at the water source have long been recognized, its significance is not always acknowledged. Even some experienced resource economists have incorrectly inferred a misallocation of water resources solely on the evidence that charges to urban water users were found to exceed charges in agricultural uses.

In order to clarify the distinction, I will call these concepts, respectively, *at-site* and *at-source* values. At-site values will exceed the at-source values by whatever costs are incurred in capturing, storing, transporting, and treating the water. This distinction will be invoked at several points in the subsequent analysis.

2.4.3 Per Period Versus Capitalized Values

Some values can be expressed for a single period (*per period*), while others represent the value of a capital asset. Water values are usually expressed or computed as of a single period, usually a year, but sometimes less; a year may be subdivided into smaller seasons, such as six-month winter and summer periods. The alternative is to estimate the capitalized present value of a stream of periodic or per period values. The distinction is the same as that between the annual rental charge and the price of purchasing full ownership in a capital asset such as a house. Hence the capitalized value may be sometimes called a *capital asset* value. The capitalized value will of course be much larger than the per period value, by a factor depending on the interest rate, the number of future periods over which the annual value is capitalized, and whether the annual values are assumed to be constant or are assumed to vary. In the most frequently used model for relating annual values to a corresponding capitalized values—which assumes a constant interest rate, a constant annual value, and a long time period—the capitalized value will typically be 10 to 20 times larger than the annual value. (This relationship between per period and capitalized values will be discussed in more detail in Chapter 3.)

2.4.4 Use, Nonuse, and Total Economic Values

In addition to the familiar notion of *use values*, the notions of *nonuse value* and *total economic value* (TEV) have become key to environmental economics in recent years. Total economic value is the sum of direct use values plus a remainder, called nonuse values (also called *passive-use values*). (The origins of these notions are usually attributed to Krutilla 1967.) Use values are the conventional preferences measured by WTP for actual recreational or aesthetic enjoyment of an environmental resource. Nonuse values apply when individuals who do not use or intend to use a given environmental asset would nevertheless feel a deprivation if the asset were to vanish or be withdrawn. Such individuals may wish to see certain environmental objects or entities conserved for their own sake, or to ensure their availability for others ("existence value"), or out of altruism toward future generations ("bequest value"). Nonuse values are public goods in the usual sense of the term, meaning that they are nonrivalrous and nonexcludable. Since its origin, the concept of nonuse value has been controversial, although the idea itself now seems firmly entrenched in environmental economic theory and practice (Kopp 1992). (See Bishop et al. 1997; and Carson et al. 1999; and Freeman 2003 for more detailed discussions of theory and measurement of nonuse values). (This issue will be discussed further in Chapter 4.)

2.4.5 Appropriate Measure of Water Quantity

To assign an economic value to a unit of water in evaluating intersectoral allocation options, one must express it as a monetary value per unit water volume or quantity used. Several concepts of water quantity are in common use (Solley et al. 1998), and the choice of measure can be quite significant in its effect on the estimated unit value of water.

For offstream uses, the quantity variable can be expressed as any of three possible measures. One concept, *withdrawal*, refers to the amount of water removed from a surface or groundwater source.

A second measure, *delivery*, expresses the amount of water delivered to the place of use (farm, home, or factory). The quantity of water delivered differs from the amount withdrawn by the amount of delivery (or conveyance) losses, i.e. the amount lost in transit (usually from leakages) from the point of withdrawal to the point of use. The amount withdrawn and that delivered may be quite similar. This can occur when the use takes place essentially at the point of withdrawal (such as with industrial use of ground or surface water pumped at the manufacturing site). However, conveyance losses are often significant. Throughout the world, irrigation water is often transported in unlined earthen canals that frequently lose 20% or more to seepage between the point of withdrawal and the point of use. Even piped urban water systems lose significant amounts. Some developing country megacities lose a third or more of the water from leaky pipes and connections between the point of withdrawal and the places of eventual use (Nickum and Easter 1994).

The final customary water quantity measure is the *consumptive use*, sometimes called the *depletion*. It is the part of the water withdrawn which is transpired or evaporated into the atmosphere, incorporated into crops or products, or otherwise removed from the water environment.

The magnitude of these distinctions is clear from the data on the crop irrigation sector in the United States in 1995 (Solley et al. 1998). The amount of water delivered was about 80% of the amount shown as withdrawn. Further, the amount consumed was reported as about 60% of that delivered, so the net amount consumed is less than half of that originally withdrawn. These figures, of course, have an important implication for water management policy, since water losses have significant environmental and economic ramifications. For purposes of economic valuation the concern is that estimated values of water will differ greatly, depending upon which measure is chosen. In reporting and interpreting an economic value per unit of water, it is essential to understand what water quantity is being measured.

Moreover, the choice of withdrawal, delivery, or depletion as the appropriate measure will depend on the purpose at hand. For the economist interested in predicting user response to changing prices or entitlements, the delivery measure is often most appropriate, because that is the measure upon which individual water users base their allocation decisions. However, regional or river basin planning models often express water quantities in terms of withdrawals or depletions. For economic modeling and analysis purposes, it appears preferable to begin with delivery as the primary measure of water use and, where necessary, make subsequent *ex-model* adjustments to express benefits per unit depleted or withdrawn.

In nonconsumptive or instream uses, none of the above variables are precisely relevant. One must treat any change in place, form, or time as a measure of use. In evaluating instream versus offstream uses, a hydrologic model which can adjust for all these interdependent factors in geographic terms becomes a vital aid (e.g. Booker and Young 1994; Booker 1995).

2.4.6 Uncertainty and Sensitivity Analysis

Estimating benefits for long-run water investment or allocation decisions requires forecasting the behavior of a number of economic, technological, and social variables for a period of years. Because of the unpredictable nature of these factors, no analyst can expect to be perfectly accurate. Some recognition of uncertainty should be incorporated into CBA. Basing a plan simply on best-guess projections may lead to excess confidence in the results.

A number of formal treatments of uncertainty are applicable to evaluation of water investment and allocation decisions (e.g. Morgan and Henrion 1990). However, implementation of the advanced techniques recommended in these sources—usually based on estimating objective or subjective probabilities of occurrence of key variables—will usually require too much statistical expertise, study resources, and time to be practical under actual planning conditions.

A more practical alternative for acknowledging uncertainty is to use "sensitivity analysis." The effect of (sensitivity to) important variables on the estimated value of water is determined by varying one model element at a time to determine the sensitivity to erroneous forecasts (Gittinger 1982). For example, a study of the economic benefits of a proposed investment in crop irrigation should test for sensitivity to assumptions about crop yields and crop prices, and perhaps for assumptions on the opportunity cost of capital. Performing a sensitivity analysis does not change the potential future facts, nor does it reduce the actual risk of a plan. Sensitivity analysis shows the impacts of incorrect assumptions regarding key parameters and helps avoid the impression of certainty in a world in which little is in fact certain.

A variation on sensitivity analysis is the "switching value" test (Gittinger 1982), which investigates how far a key element in the analysis would need to change in an unfavorable direction before net benefits would fall to zero.

2.5 Looking Ahead: An Overview and Taxonomy of Water Valuation Methods

The numerous methods of nonmarket valuation of water have their strengths and limitations; each may be more appropriate to specific types of water uses. No one classificatory terminology has yet found general acceptance. Hence I propose two ways to broadly classify methods of measuring the economic values of water uses. The first distinguishes between private and public water-based goods and services, the second between inductive and deductive quantitative methods.

2.5.1 Broad Classification of Methods According to Types of Water-Based Goods and Services

One basis for distinguishing water valuation methods is the type of good or service being studied. It is useful to classify goods and services yielded by water as either public and private. Although these notions were introduced in Chapter 1, they deserve further elaboration. Those goods and services for which one person's consumption or use reduces the amount available to other consumers are called "rival in consumption" or rivalrous. Institutional arrangements, such as property rights, may be established so that potential users of a resource are excluded unless they pay for use. *Private goods*, then, are those which are both rivalrous and exclusive. For such goods, users can be excluded if they don't pay, users can be required to pay for any benefits received, and any use by one person lowers the amount available to others. Most offstream uses of water—agriculture, industries, and households—approximate the characteristics of private goods closely enough to be so labeled here.

Private goods can be usefully further classified into producers' goods and consumers' goods. A product or service used to make other goods or services is called a *producers'* (or sometimes an *intermediate*) good, in contrast with *consumers' goods*, which are used directly by consumers. For example, irrigation water is used to produce crops, which, after adding inputs for processing, transportation, packaging, and marketing, eventually become consumers' goods (i.e. food on the table). Water used for irrigation (and by industries) is thus a producers' good. Water used in households—for drinking, cooking and sanitation—is, in contrast, best treated as a form of final consumers' good.

In contrast to private goods and services, the other main type of benefit of water use is often called a *public good* benefit. For some goods and services yielded by water, consumption by one individual does not diminish the amount available to others; it has zero opportunity cost of consumption. Another characteristic of public goods is that exclusion of nonpayers is not feasible. Such resources are not readily amenable to management under a pure property rights regime. Establishing and enforcing exclusive property rights might incur costs in excess of any benefits yielded by such a process. Thus, public goods are both nonrivalrous and nonexclusive.

Some uses of water are examples of public goods. Streams and lakes valued for aesthetic or recreational pleasure furnish one instance; one person's enjoyment of a beautiful waterfall doesn't reduce the enjoyment of others (although, because of congestion, the public good attributes of many bodies of water are becoming economically scarce enough that one or another type of property regime is being established). Nonuse values (such as biodiversity preservation), water quality improvements, and flood risk reductions are largely public goods.

Although there is some minor overlap, the valuation methods most appropriate to private goods differ from those appropriate to public goods valuation. Next, we consider the different quantitative methods that can be brought to bear on valuation of water.

2.5.2 Broad Classification According to Techniques for Quantification: Deductive and Inductive Techniques

Approaches to water valuation can be classed according to the quantitative techniques employed. Most methods of water valuation fit into two broad categories that differ in the basic mathematical procedures and types of data employed in the valuation process. One class, termed *inductive* techniques, employs inductive logic, usually as formal statistical or econometric procedures, to infer generalizations from individual observations. The other broad type of technique, the *deductive* method, involves logical processes to reason from general premises to particular conclusions. Deductive techniques employ constructed models comprising a set of behavioral postulates (i.e. profit or utility maximization) and empirical assumptions appropriate to the case at hand.

The terms "inductive" and "deductive" are chosen here in preference to the *positive/normative* distinctions often used to differentiate types of applied economic analysis, because the positive/normative distinctions don't seem to be precisely descriptive of the approaches found in nonmarket valuation studies related to water. First, what are often called normative models in applied economics are not, strictly speaking, normative in the sense of being derived from basic moral or ethical premises (e.g. from Pareto optimality). Rather, they are characterized merely by the incorporation of an hypothesis of self-interested optimization in resource allocation. Thus I choose to group these among the broad class of deductive techniques. Second, the term "positive technique," which likely derives from the now largely outdated philosophy of science school called "positivism," has little present-day descriptive content or meaning for either students or noneconomists. I here choose to include studies which are sometimes called "positive" or "positivistic" models within the more general grouping of inductive techniques.

Inductive techniques, which are the techniques most often applied to valuation of public environmental goods, involve a process of reasoning *from the particular to the general*, i.e. from observations to general relationships. Observations made subject to inductive or statistical analysis may come from observed transactions, from responses to questionnaires, or from secondary data from government reports. The accuracy of inductive techniques depends on several factors, including the representativeness and validity of the observational data used in the inference, the appropriateness of the assumed statistical distribution, and the functional form used in fitting the data. When based on appropriate observations of real-world behavior or responses to surveys, inductive methods have an advantage of reflecting actual economic behavior. (Exceptions are found in those types of nonmarket valuation approaches, notably the expressed preference methods, that analyze survey respondents' replies to hypothetical scenarios with inductive techniques.) Most inductive techniques, as represented by formal statistical analysis, can also provide measures of variance and goodness of fit, which furnish valuable indications of the reliability of inferences made from the observations. A corresponding limitation is that this observed behavior is historical; future behavior and valuation may need to be forecast by assuming out-of-sample parameters. It may be difficult or inappropriate to infer future demands and values from past conditions. For example, for producers' goods, the estimated value or accounting price depends greatly on assumptions about product prices, prices of other inputs, and technological parameters. In addition, inductive methods tend to demand statistical and computational skills on the part of the analyst. Collection of suitable data, whether from original respondents, actual experiments, or secondary sources, may be time-consuming and expensive.

Deductive techniques, on the other hand, are the most used for valuing water in its producers' good manifestations. This general approach involves reasoning *from the general to the particular.* Deductive techniques require construction of empirical and behavioral models, from which specific parameters or shadow prices are deduced. The deductive techniques described in this book commence with abstract models of human behavior that are fleshed out with appropriate data. In addition to the behavioral postulates (e.g. profit or utility maximization), the data to fit a deductive model will typically include assumptions about technology of production or consumption and the relevant price or prices. The data for constructed models may be provided by empirical studies of production or consumption processes, published government reports, and expert opinion. The accuracy of the results of deductive reasoning depends on the validity of the premises and the appropriateness of the model specification. Examples of deductive techniques applied to valuing water as producers' goods range from simple budgeting via spreadsheet to dynamic optimization models. Deductive techniques offer the advantage of flexibility, as they can be constructed to reflect any desired future economic and technological conditions. Assumptions can be varied and sensitivities of the results to varying assumptions can be determined. Certain deductive models of water value, including some applied to valuing an irrigation water development, are quite simple in concept and demand relatively little in the way of data and computational skills. More realistic and complex situations call for extensive data collection and significant model-building proficiency. A note of caution about the application of deductive techniques: it is important to begin with a sound conceptual basis for a deductive model, supported by an accurate and adequate data base. The hurried and inexpensive application of an apparently simple process may lead to conceptually incorrect or inaccurate—and therefore misleading—results.

It would perhaps be more accurate to describe these classes of methods as "*mostly* inductive" and "*mostly* deductive." Deductive methods typically require some inductive steps to arrive at the initial empirical premises, and inductive methods usually involve some deductive reasoning to proceed from the results of the statistical analysis to the desired willingness to pay measure.

2.5.3 A Taxonomy of Methods for Nonmarket Valuation of Water

Table 2-1 provides a taxonomy of methods of nonmarket valuation of water investments and policies, broadly classified according to whether they are based on an inductive or a deductive technique. The methods mentioned in the table are described in more detail in the following chapters. The reader unfamiliar with any of the methods can first consult the Glossary, where each method is defined and briefly described.

Table 2-1. Main Types of Nonmarket Water Valuation Methods, Their Characteristics, and Uses

Valuation Method	Description of Method and Data Sources	Useful for Valuing Water as:
Inductive Methods		
1. Observations of Water Market Transactions	Observed prices from transactions for short-term leases or permanent sales of rights to water.	Actual at-source or at-site WTP manifested by transactions within or between agricultural, industrial, municipal, and environmental uses.
2. Econometric Estimation of Production and Cost Functions	Primary or secondary data on industrial and agricultural inputs and outputs analyzed with statistical (usually regression) techniques.	Producers' (agricultural or industrial) at-site valuations.
3. Econometric Estimation of Municipal Water Demand Functions	Primary or secondary municipal data analyzed with statistical methods.	At-site demands for municipal sector (including residential, commercial, and government) deliveries.
4. Travel Cost Method (TCM)	Revealed preference approach using econometric analysis to infer the value of recreational site attributes from the varying expenditures incurred by consumers to travel to the site.	Valuation of recreational services and derived at-source valuations for changes in water supply.
5. Hedonic Property Value Method (HPM)	Revealed preference approach using econometric analysis of data on real property transactions with varying availability of water supply or quality.	At-source demands for changes in water quantity or quality revealed by transactors in residential or farm properties.
6. Defensive Behavior Method	Revealed preference method using reductions in the costs of actions taken to mitigate or avoid incurring an external cost as a partial measure of the benefits of policies from reducing the externality.	Valuation of reduced water pollution from biological or chemical contaminants.

continued on next page

Table 2-1. Main Types of Nonmarket Water Valuation Methods, Their Characteristics, and Uses *(continued)*

Valuation Method	Description of Method and Data Sources	Useful for Valuing Water as:
7. Damage Cost Methods	Maximum willingness to pay given as monetary value of damages avoided.	Valuation of reduced water pollution or flood damages.
8. Contingent Valuation Method (CVM)	Expressed preference method using statistical techniques for analyzing responses to survey questions asking for monetary valuation of proposed changes in environmental goods or services.	At-source valuations of environmental (e.g. instream) water supplies. Also at-site valuations of changes in residential water supplies.
9. Choice Modeling (CM)	Expressed preference method using statistical techniques to infer WTP for goods or services from survey questions asking a sample of respondents to make choices among alternative proposed policies.	At-source valuations of environmental (e.g. instream) water supplies. Also at-site valuations of changes in residential water supplies.
10. Benefit Transfer	Benefits estimated for one or more sites or policy proposals employed to assign benefits or value to other sites or policy proposals.	Adaptable in principle for any case: producers' or consumers' goods; and collective environmental goods including nonuse values.
11. Benefit Function Transfer/ Meta-Analysis	Statistical synthesis of the results of previously reported studies of the same phenomenon or relationship to distill generalizations.	A potential basis for benefit transfer in all producers' and consumers' valuation contexts. Also valuable for assessing role of methodological assumptions in research results.
Deductive Methods		
12. Basic Residual Method	Constructed models for deriving point estimate of net producers' income or rents attributable to water via budget or spreadsheet analysis.	At-site or at-source estimates for offstream intermediate goods (agriculture, industry) for single-product case.

continued on next page

Table 2-1. Main Types of Nonmarket Water Valuation Methods, Their Characteristics, and Uses *(continued)*

Valuation Method	Description of Method and Data Sources	Useful for Valuing Water as:
13. Change in Net Rents	Constructed residual models for deriving interval estimate of net producers' income or rents attributable to increment of water via budget or spreadsheet analysis.	At-site or at-source estimates for offstream intermediate goods (agriculture, industry) for multiple-product, multiple-technology cases.
14. Mathematical Programming	Constructed residual models for deriving net producers' rents or marginal costs attributable to water via (usually) fixed-price optimization models.	At-site or at-source valuation of offstream intermediate goods (agriculture, industry) for multiple-product, multiple-technology cases.
15. Value-added	Constructed models of net producers' income or rents attributable to water via value-added measure from input-output models.	Seriously biased (overestimate) method that has been used mainly in offstream intermediate goods (agriculture and industry).
16. Computable General Equilibrium (CGE) Models	Constructed models for deriving net producers' income or rents attributable to water via price-endogenous optimization models.	Recently adapted method used mainly for offstream intermediate goods (agriculture and industry).
17. Alternative Cost	Value attributable to cost savings from next best alternative source of service (e.g. electricity, transportation).	At-site or at-source valuation of intermediate goods offstream (agriculture, industry) and instream (hydropower, transportation). Also for water as private and collective consumption good by households.

Methods for Valuing Producers' Uses of Water

As mentioned in Chapter 1, the largest consumptive users of water in the world are, by a significant margin, the producers' good types. Irrigation of agricultural crops accounts for a major portion of the world's water withdrawals, and represents the largest single consumptive use class. Industrial (including manufacturing and commercial) uses account for another important part of withdrawals, but, because less evapotranspiration is involved, for a smaller but still significant amount of consumptive uses. While most industrial firms withdraw and consume at least some water, the major uses in this category are electrical power generation and the manufacture of chemical, paper, foods, and beverages.

Measures of producers' welfare have received less consideration from welfare theorists and from applied environmental and resource economists than have measures of consumers' welfare. The standard authorities of welfare theory do give some attention to producers, but stress welfare effects of output and input price changes rather than the considerations of primary interest here—input quantity or quality changes. Exceptions are found in Freeman (2003, Chapter 9) and Johansson (1993, Chapter 5), who extend the basic analysis to incorporate welfare measures of changes in quantity or quality of resource inputs into production processes.

This chapter has two purposes. One is to introduce and extend the general conceptual framework for valuing inputs in producers' goods contexts, particularly in offstream production uses, such as agriculture and industry. It provides a set of models that reflect the special conditions of water-based production while staying consistent with approaches used in nonmarket valuation of public environmental goods. A second goal is to describe the various methods that have been developed for applied valuation of producers' uses of water, both in agricultural and in industrial uses, and to assess these methods for consistency with the conceptual framework and the empirical setting of water-using production activities. Section 3.2 describes the conceptual apparatus developed for measuring welfare changes in the context of water-using producers. The remainder describes and evaluates the various nonmarket methods that have been developed to measure producers' values of water.

3.1 Some Preliminaries

Recall from Chapter 2 the four characteristic issues that must be addressed in evaluating producers' uses of water:

- whether a long-run or a short-run planning context applies;
- whether water is a variable or a specialized fixed input in production;
- whether an at-site or an at-source value is needed; and
- whether the prices used in the analysis should be private or social prices.

The problems encountered in valuing producers' goods are as challenging as those that have received much more attention in the arena of public environmental goods.

Long-run or Short-run Models? Conventional welfare analysis for producers tends to emphasize the short run rather than the long run. Problems of short-run water allocation are frequently encountered in water policy analysis, such as for assessing potential economic damages from drought damages, but in applied assessments of major water management policies (such as proposals for investment in water supplies or for permanent reallocations of water rights to potentially higher valued uses), long-run models often are the most appropriate. Thus, translation of received theory to practical application calls for adaptation. Further, in the field of water resource management, we need to assess the welfare impact of changes in water supply more often than the effects of potential changes in output prices. Finally, the textbook treatments typically focus on theoretical derivations, assuming that prices and production functions are known. The practical problems encountered in performing *ex ante* predictions of welfare change from proposed policy changes are not addressed in the primarily theoretical literature. In general, *ex ante* analysis of water policy proposals requires formulas and procedures for approximating the theoretical concepts over the long run. Also needed are practical procedures for forecasting unknown price, cost, and technological parameters over the long run.

Water as a Variable or a Fixed Input? One issue in valuing water in production is whether to treat water as a standard fully divisible and variable input, or as a specialized fixed input. If water in production is viewed as fully variable, then the conventional theory of producers' demand is applicable. However, although this point has received little attention in the literature, if water is a specialized fixed input in production, the theory of economic rents is the more appropriate model.

Casual observation of the agricultural sector would point to water as being a fixed input. Rather than being available for purchase at will, irrigation water supply is usually allocated by a system of limited annual rights to use a prescribed amount of water, often linked to ownership of arable lands. Moreover, the fixed allotment of water is typically less than the producer would prefer. Moore and Dinar (1995) and Moore (1999) used data sets from irrigated agriculture regions in California to statistically test whether water is more appropriately treated as a fixed or a variable input. Both studies found that the fixed input approach better fits the data.

Conversely, informal consideration of how nonagricultural industries obtain their supplies, whether self-supplied or purchased from a water utility, suggests that in most industrial uses the firm is free to choose the optimal level of water use. Thus, the assumption that water is a variable input would seem to fit the industrial case. Dupont and Renzetti (2001), employing a statistical technique similar to that used by Moore and Dinar (1995), tested the hypothesis on data from three annual surveys of manufacturing water use in Canada over the period 1981–1991; they concluded that intake water is appropriately modeled as a variable input. Accordingly, alternative applied frameworks for valuing water both as a variable input and as a fixed input will be developed in this chapter.

At-Site or At-Source Measures? The distinction between at-site and at-source values arises because "water" can actually be many different products, depending on attributes of place, form, and time. The filtered and purified water delivered under pressure to a domestic consumer is a much different commodity than the water taken from a river as the raw material for the delivered product. Quality criteria differ across industries, so treatment costs may cause differing values between at-site and at-source locations. Conveyance costs and losses may be significant, so the at-site value will typically exceed the at-source value.

As used here, the at-site value of water is calculated at the place of use (such as in the farm, home, or factory for offstream uses, or at the relevant location on the river, lake, or reservoir for nonwithdrawal uses). By convention (but not by necessity) the at-site measure is the value used in investment evaluations, to be compared with costs of supplying water to the same site. In contrast, at-source values are calculated at the location where the water is obtained (such as from a stream, reservoir, or aquifer). For withdrawal uses, at-source values are derived demands lower than at-site values by any costs of capture, transport, and treatment to be put to use by users. For theoretical reasons, evaluating certain policies, such as comparing intersectoral allocations, calls for at-source values. Obviously one needs to make clear whether one is discussing an at-site or an at-source value, since they can differ markedly in otherwise similar conditions.

Private or Social Prices? Another important decision is whether private or social prices are relevant. The question arises where input and output prices are subsidized or taxed or otherwise influenced by government policy, such as in the agricultural or energy sector. To begin, note that for studies that employ deductive models for *ex ante* evaluation, the choice is open. For evaluation of investments in water supply largely financed by a national government, social prices are appropriate (Gittinger 1982). For analyses based on observed prior behavior, as in hedonic property value analyses or other land value-based investigations, the data will be of necessity based on a private accounting stance. Conversion of estimates based on observed behavior from private to social measures would be difficult to accomplish, and I am unaware of any examples.

3.2 Basic Welfare Concepts for Valuing Water in Producers' Good Uses

Production of any good or service requires a combination of resources or inputs, including expendable materials, equipment, labor, management, capital, and land. Each of these inputs contributes to the total value of production. *Estimating the economic benefits or values of a single (often) unpriced producers' good such as water entails isolating that portion contributed by water to the total value of the output from the contributions of all other inputs that go into the production process.* For producers' goods, such as water used in agriculture or industrial production, the neoclassical economic theory of production and the theory of the firm provide the major theoretical basis for valuing the economic welfare implications of changes in input supplies. The theory of economic rent is also relevant in a more general and realistic formulation.

As Just et al. (1982) put it, measurement of producer welfare helps answer the question: Is the producer better off from some change in price or quantity of inputs or outputs, and by how much? A basic point of departure is the static deterministic theory of the firm from neoclassical microeconomics. (The reader not familiar with this literature may wish to consult textbooks such as Varian 1997.)

3.2.1 A Sketch of the Theory of the Firm as Used in Economic Welfare Analysis

In mainstream microeconomic theory, the firm is the basic production-side decisionmaking unit in the theory of supply. It is understood to be a legal entity (such as a proprietorship, partnership, or corporation) that owns some inputs (also called factors of production) and purchases others, transforming these inputs into outputs of goods or services. A central assumption of the standard model is that a *production function* serves as the technical description of the firm. (A production function is a relationship that shows the maximum production which can be obtained from all possible combinations of given inputs at the given state of technical knowledge. It may be expressed in graphical, tabular, or mathematical form.) The behavior of the firm may be characterized a number of ways, but here the focus will be on profit-maximization or cost-minimization. The firm is viewed as combining inputs according to one or the other of these criteria so as to produce intermediate or final outputs, or both. This model of the firm explains how changes in resource availability and relative prices influence the quantities produced and the distribution of factor incomes.

Consider now the derivation of the appropriate measure of the firm's welfare change from changes in an input. (The presentation follows Johansson 1993, Section 5.1. See also Freeman 2003, Chapter 9.) Begin with a profit-maximizing firm using a number of priced variable inputs, plus a fixed input, to produce a single output. It is assumed here that the quantity (or quality) of water (denoted W) used in the production process influences the output from given amounts of the other factors of production. The output is denoted Y and its price P_y. The vector of variable inputs is X, and P_x represents the prices of those inputs. A fixed factor K also contributes to the production process. The firm is assumed to face perfectly elastic supplies for factor inputs and perfectly elastic demand for its output, so that prices are known and constant. The firm's production function is:

$$Y = Y(X, W, K).$$

The welfare (or profit) function $\Pi(\cdot)$ of this firm can be written:

$$\Pi(P_y, P_x, W, K) = P_y Y(X, W, K) - P_x X(P_y, P_x, W) - K \qquad (3\text{-}1)$$

where $Y = Y(X, W, K)$ is output and $P_y Y(X, W, K)$ is Total Value of Product (TVP). The production function $Y = Y(X, W, K)$ is assumed to be twice-differentiable in all its arguments. Fixed costs are, by definition, those that cannot be avoided even if the firm ceases operation. Equation 3-1 therefore asserts that profits equal the revenues minus both variable and fixed costs.

The conditions for solution of the maximum problem are:

$$\frac{\partial \Pi(\cdot)}{\partial X_j} = \frac{P_y \partial Y(X, W, K)}{\partial X_j} = P_{x_j} \quad \text{for all inputs } j \qquad (3\text{-}2)$$

The expression $\partial Y(X, W, K)/\partial X_j$ is the marginal physical product and the entire expression $[P_y \partial Y(X, W, K)/\partial X_j]$, incorporating the price of the output, is termed the Value Marginal Product (VMP) of the input. Equation 3-2 asserts that at the profit-maximizing optimum, VMP for each input must equal its price.

Welfare analysis of producer decisions in response to public policy interventions is usually grounded on a model in which one or more inputs are assumed to be fixed, and is based primarily on the concept of *producer's surplus*. Producers' surplus is defined as the difference between revenues and the variable costs of production, and thus is the return to fixed inputs. Producers' surplus then is: $P_y Y - P_x X$. (Producers' surplus may also be called quasi-rent. See the discussion in Section 3.5.)

Producer welfare is measured by the change in producer surplus associated with a change in an element of the welfare function. These elements, which may be changed by public policy intervention, could be prices of product or inputs, or quantities or qualities of an input, or technology. Here we are mainly interested in measuring welfare effects of changes in quantities or qualities of an input.

(The welfare economic theory adopted here employs the highly abstract model of the firm as optimizing subject to a known production function and known input and output prices. Emerging alternatives to the primary paradigm—see Ricketts 2002—rely on a more realistic description of the human actors in the firm and the role of organization theory in understanding the behavior of the firm. In one strand of this literature, the firm is understood as a response to the problem of adapting production activities to meet continually changing but imperfectly foreseen conditions. This model emphasizes the role of transactions costs entailed in such adjustments and the enforcement of agreements with contractors for services to the firm. Another strand, representing what are called behavioral or managerial theories of the firm, hypothesizes that the firm's managers are motivated by criteria in addition to strict profit maximization, such as gross sales, assets, or personal utility. Since these alternative theories have not been adapted into a welfare economics framework emphasizing input demand, they are not further discussed here.)

3.2.2 The Basic Measure of Producer Welfare

The immediate concern here to derive a welfare measure from changing the quantity or quality of water as an unpriced input. The welfare measure of a change in quantity of an input can be obtained by taking the partial derivative of equation 3-1 with respect to the chosen input. This gives:

$$\frac{\partial \Pi(\cdot)}{\partial W} = \frac{P_y \partial Y(X, W, K)}{\partial W}$$ = P_w (3-3)

As indicated above, the expression $\partial Y(X, W, K) / \partial W$ is called the marginal physical product and the entire right hand side of equation 3-3, incorporating the price of the output, is the VMP of water. VMP tells the effect on the welfare function of a unit change in the input. Where the input is fully variable, *VMP is an appropriate measure of the producers' benefit or willingness to pay for changes in the quantity of the input.* (See Johansson 1993, Chapter 5; and Freeman 2003, Chapter 9 for further discussion.)

In Figure 3-1, for any specified amount of water, say W^0, the marginal value can be read off the VMP_W curve at P_{W^0}. Also of interest is the value of a discrete increment of input, say between W^0 and W^1 (where $W^1 > W^0$). The shaded area under the curve between W^0 and W^1 represents the value (change in producer surplus) of the discrete increment $W^1 - W^0$. Technically, because the VMP_W curve reflects an assumption that the producer cannot adjust levels of other inputs, it represents a lower bound on the change in producer surplus. The full input demand function as given in equation 3-3 does permit adjustment of other inputs so as to increase profit, and therefore it reflects the correct welfare measure.

Concluding, the value of water as a variable input in production can be measured by the concept of the VMP of the input. Much of the remainder of this chapter will address what empirical methods yield valid measures of this notion and related concepts in applied evaluation contexts.

VMP Versus Rents as Measures of Welfare. The above analysis assumes that the input being valued (water) is continuously variable, the selected amount is chosen according to the profit criterion, and the VMP function represents the welfare measure. As remarked earlier, these assumptions fit the case of industrial use of water.

An alternative situation obtains in much (although not all) water use in agricultural irrigation: the farm typically has an institutionally fixed annual allotment of water that it cannot exceed. A welfare model recognizing an input whose supply is inelastic and based on the theory of economic rent is the more appropriate welfare measure (see Section 3.5).

As indicated in Section 2.5, the various applied nonmarket valuation techniques can be classified as inductive or deductive. The remainder of this chapter first discusses the deductive techniques, mainly the residual method and its extensions as well as the alternative cost method (Sections 3.3 to 3.11). An overview of several inductive techniques follows, including analyses based on production function and derived demand, observations on water markets, and the hedonic property value and related methods (Section 3.12). The valuation of producers' uses of water is summarized in Section 3.13.

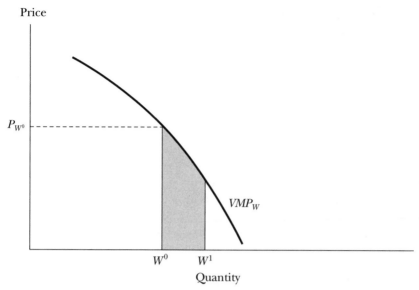

Figure 3-1. Measuring Change in Producer Surplus When Quantity Is Changed

3.3 Applied Valuation of Producers' Water Uses with Deductive Techniques

Deductive techniques derive an accounting price from postulated empirical models of individual economic decisions made by firms and households. They can also be described as *constructed* models, because they typically fit real-world data into the appropriate conceptual framework. Since empirical parameters can be changed at will, deductive techniques are particularly useful for *ex ante* evaluation of hypothetical policy options, a key activity in applied water policy evaluation. They can also be adapted for *ex post* evaluation of conditions and policies, but they are less well suited for this purpose than the inductive techniques.

Four methods apply deductive techniques to derive suitable measures of benefits of water as a producers' good. The residual method is the basic deductive technique (Sections 3.4 to 3.7). It has two closely related extensions: the Change in Net Rents and the mathematical programming models (Section 3.8). Critiques of two additional methods that are judged inappropriate—the value-added method and the average value product method—are provided in Section 3.9. A summary evaluation of the residual method is in Section 3.10, and a fourth method, alternative cost, is discussed in Section 3.11.

3.4 The Basic Residual Method 1: The Product Exhaustion Theorem

The conceptual framework reviewed in Section 3.2 implies that the VMP function provides a key measure of producer welfare. For practical non-market valuation of producers' goods, the so-called *residual* (or *residual imputation*) method has been the most frequently used approach to approximating VMP, in particular for evaluating policies on the irrigation of agricultural crops. It is a deductive technique, deriving the benefit or value estimate from a constructed model of individual producer decisions, the model being made operational with data representing the specific application. The residual method finds the value of water as the remainder or net income after all other relevant costs are accounted for. In the agricultural sector, the residual imputation method has long been used as a framework for applied estimation of values of fixed assets, primarily for land and real property, e.g. Heady 1952, *402–414.*

The basic residual method can be derived from the neoclassical theory of the firm in either of two conceptual approaches. The first, more conventional approach involves the approximation of the VMP via the *product exhaustion theorem.* However, the assumptions of the product exhaustion theorem approach fail to reflect the most typical situation in agricultural water use. Hence, in Section 3.5, an approach that employs the theory of economic rents and quasi-rents is derived to approximate the residual value of water in agricultural production. Both approaches, it turns out, lead to the same residual formula, but the rent model explains phenomena that are left unaccounted for in the approach via the product exhaustion theorem.

3.4.1 Wicksteed's Product Exhaustion Theorem

The product exhaustion theorem can be adapted to estimate VMP via the model of input demand sketched in Section 3.2.1. Philip Wicksteed is credited with formalizing the product exhaustion theorem near the end of the nineteenth century. (Interested readers can find detailed discussions and references to the original writings of Wicksteed and others in Blaug 1997.) The theorem (also often called the adding-up theorem) can be expressed: if firms operating under competitive market conditions optimize by selecting input quantities such that the VMP of each input is equated with its corresponding marginal factor cost (as in equation 3-2), the sum of the value marginal products, each weighted by the amount of the corresponding input, will, in long-run equilibrium, exactly equal the total value of product. Expositions of the product exhaustion theorem can be found in almost any intermediate or advanced price or production economics theory textbook. Blaug's presentation (1997, *419–435*) is among the most complete and accessible.

Specifically, Wicksteed showed the conditions under which the total value of product will be exactly exhausted by the distributive shares of the various inputs. However, this proposition holds only in the event that the total value function is, in mathematical terms, homogeneous in the first degree. In economic terms, a production function homogeneous of the first degree exhibits constant returns to scale. Later writers showed the precise conditions under which Wicksteed's product exhaustion theorem would hold, drawing on the mathematical proposition called Euler's Theorem and making explicit the further assumption that factor inputs are perfectly substitutable. Other commentators on Wicksteed (particularly Wicksell) pointed out that these results hold under less restrictive conditions than first degree homogeneity, showing that the product exhaustion proposition does not entirely depend on the shape of the production function. Specifically, if the cost curves are U-shaped, competition drives all firms to produce at a scale where their average costs are at a minimum. In long-run competitive equilibrium, where product price equals minimum average cost, production choices by firms will approximate choices made under constant returns to scale. In the neighborhood of firms' minimum average costs, constant returns to scale are approximated, and profit-maximizing actions make a factor's price equal to the value of its marginal product. (See Blaug 1997, *435–436.*) Readers interested in a more advanced theoretical treatment may consult Makowski and Ostroy 2001. Their approach to distribution theory and the product exhaustion theorem, although at least as realistic as the standard model, is based on a less demanding set of postulates.

The product exhaustion theorem opens a way for applied economics to find a point on the unknown VMP function (or benefit measure) of any one unpriced input, such as water used in production. In general terms, if the production function and the quantities of all other inputs are known, and accurate prices can be assigned—by observation of market activities—to all inputs but one, invoking the product exhaustion theorem allows the imputation of the remainder of total value of product to that input (the *residual claimant*).

3.4.2 Algebraic Derivation of the Return to the Residual Claimant

It will be useful to set out a more formal statement of the product exhaustion theorem. The derivation requires two principal postulates. First, under conditions of competitive equilibrium (or equivalently, in the event that the total value of product function is homogeneous in the first degree) the fundamental product exhaustion proposition stipulates that the total value of product can be divided into shares, so that each resource is paid according to its value marginal productivity and the total value of product will be exactly exhausted by the distributive shares. Second, profit-maximizing producers are assumed to add increments of each input up until the point where value marginal products are equal to price or opportunity costs of the inputs. The competitive equilibrium assumption implies that for all inputs, producers equate returns at the margin with the prices of those inputs. Observed or expected prices can then be substituted for unobserved value marginal products, yielding a formula for the residual claimant.

To illustrate the use of the product exhaustion theorem for residual valuation, consider a simple production process in which it is desired to impute a value for the nonmarketed input: water. Assume a single product denoted Y which is produced by several factors of production: purchased materials and equipment (M); human input, e.g. labor (H); equity capital (K); other natural resources, such as land (L); and the residual claimant: water (W). The production function is written:

$$Y = f(X_M, X_H, X_K, X_L, X_W) \tag{3-4}$$

Inputs and outputs are assumed to be continuously variable, and the level of technology is given and unchangeable. Production is modeled via a static, deterministic model of the profit-maximizing firm, as outlined in Section 3.2.1.

By the first postulate, if all inputs are paid according to their value marginal products, the total value of product is exactly exhausted:

$$(Y \cdot P_Y) = (VMP_M \cdot X_M) + (VMP_H \cdot X_H) + (VMP_K \cdot X_K)$$
$$+ (VMP_L \cdot X_L) + (VMP_W \cdot X_W) \tag{3-5}$$

where $Y \cdot P_Y$ represents total value of product Y; VMP_i represents the value marginal product of resource i; and X_i is the quantity of the ith resource. Equation 3-5 asserts the fundamental product exhaustion theorem: the amount of inputs weighted by their value marginal products sum to total value of product (or total returns).

Given competitive markets for the purchased inputs and perfect knowledge and foresight, prices for these inputs may be treated as known constants. The second postulate (which asserts that for each input i, the producer chooses the level of input such that $VMP_i = P_i$) permits substituting P_i for each of the VMP_i into (3-5) and rearranging:

$$(Y \cdot P_Y) - [(P_M \cdot X_M) + (P_H \cdot X_H) + (P_K \cdot X_K) + (P_L \cdot X_L)] = (P_W \cdot X_W) \tag{3-6}$$

If we know or can empirically estimate the appropriate values for all price and quantity variables on the left hand side of (3-6), the right hand side can be derived to find the (unknown) contribution of water to the total value of product: $(P_W \cdot X_W)$.

The analyst will normally wish to go one step beyond finding the full contribution of water and find a unit value of water (in, for example, dollars per acre-foot or money per gigaliter). A unit value of water is helpful in converting the value estimates into a common denominator of value per unit volume, particularly as needed for evaluating intersectoral water allocation choices. Since it is assumed that X_W is known, the expression can be solved to find (impute) the desired unit value or shadow price of the residual claimant, denoted P_W^*:

$$P_W^* = \frac{(Y \cdot P_Y) - [(P_M \cdot X_M) + (P_H \cdot X_H) + (P_K \cdot X_K) + (P_L \cdot X_L)]}{X_w} \tag{3-7}$$

The solution to equation 3-7 is usually termed the "value of water" (in production) or, in practical settings, the "net return to water." For simple production processes, the empirical application of equation 3-7 is reasonably straightforward. Particularly in the determination of expected benefits from added irrigation water supply, it has seen extensive use throughout the world. With the appropriate data (including input requirements, corresponding product yields, and expected prices), the calculations can be readily performed with spreadsheet software on a desktop computer.

Short-run Values via the Residual Approach. A further remark on the formulas represented in equations 3-6 and 3-7 is warranted. Since these equations treat all nonwater inputs as variable factors of production, they can be termed as long-run models, and the values derived from them are long-run values. Although long-run values are those that economic analysts are most often called upon to estimate, values derived from short-run models are appropriate for many water policy decisions. An example would be for valuing water for a short-term drought situation. In such cases, some or all of the costs of fixed or owned inputs (equity capital, land) may be treated as having zero opportunity costs and omitted from the calculations.

$$(Y \cdot P_Y) - [(P_M \cdot X_M) + (P_H \cdot X_H)] = (P_W^S \cdot X_W) \tag{3-8}$$

Not shown here is that some labor inputs not yet introduced may also be properly regarded as fixed costs. Other things equal, the solution to this short-run equation would, of course, yield a substantially larger residual estimate of the economic value of water than the long-run case.

3.5 The Basic Residual Method 2: The Theory of Economic Rents

Although deriving the residual method via the product exhaustion theorem is adequate in theoretical terms for continuously variable inputs, an alternative derivation employing the classical concepts of *economic rents* together with further notions from Alfred Marshall can provide a complementary foundation for valuing water as a producers' good. These ideas are useful when water at a particular site of use is a limited input, as often occurs in agriculture or in hydroelectric power production. The theory of economic rents will help to further explain some anomalies which arise in the valuation of producers' uses of water, especially in agriculture.

Once again, our concern is to measure the value of changes in the availability of water—as an unpriced resource—to a producing firm. The subsequent analysis draws on the formulation by Just et al. (1982, Chapter 4), whose discussion of the applied theory of welfare changes from producers' allocation of inputs is perhaps the most detailed available. In this case, changes in rents and quasi-rents are taken as the measures of welfare changes from changes in supply of producers' goods. However, it will first be useful to introduce the different concepts of rents and quasi-rents as they are used by economists in production and price theory.

3.5.1 Concepts of Economic Rent

In technical economic terms, economic rent refers to a type of surplus: the earnings of a resource over and above the minimum amount required to induce that resource to be supplied. ("Rent" takes on a somewhat different meaning in economic theory than in everyday English, where it refers to a related but distinct concept, the periodic payment for use of a capital asset, most often for leasing land, dwellings, or other forms of property such as vehicles.) Alternatively put, economic rents are payments in excess of the price required to bring a resource or input into production or the returns which a factor would earn in another industry. In the final analysis, rents are determined by supply elasticities and appear whenever the supply schedule of a factor is not perfectly elastic with respect to price. There are several different types of economic rents, some of which are applicable to the discussion here.

The initial rent concept formalized in the economic literature is now called *Ricardian* or *differential rent*. Proposed almost two centuries ago by David Ricardo and other English thinkers, it arose from the wish to explain the empirical phenomenon that an important part of the national income was paid for land ownership, and particularly the observation that prices for use of farm lands (both annual rentals and outright sales prices) varied according to the quality or productivity of the land for producing crops. Ricardo proposed that land rent is the "payment for the original and indestructible powers of the soil." Lands of higher productivity earn a differential income over and above the other costs of producing agricultural crops, but this extra income is not due to any special input or effort of the landowner. Land is assumed to be in fixed supply but of differing quality or productivity. The differences in agricultural productivity among parcels of land may be due to soil characteristics, such as texture, fertility, slope, or microclimatic factors (rainfall and temperature). Other things equal, the most productive lands are always the first to be used, and less productive tracts are brought into production at a later stage. Therefore, as economic growth causes demand for outputs of land (and prices of these outputs) to grow, more inputs are applied, lands of lower productivity are brought into production, and higher rents are earned on the more productive lands. Land that does not return enough to break even or return a rent stays idle. Ricardo called the boundary of lands where no rent is earned the *extensive margin*.

Rent theory implies that potential buyers of land will bid more for the more productive lands (those with the potentially higher stream of future incomes), so both the annual rents and the market price of land vary with its productivity. Land market prices also depend on the interest rate at which market participants convert the expected future stream of land rents into sales prices. (The interest rate reflects the returns available from alternative investment opportunities.) This process is referred to as *capitalizing* the annual differential rents into land prices. Consequently, the rents to land become a part of fixed costs.

A further concept termed *locational rent* was introduced later in the nineteenth century by the German scholar Johann H. von Thünen, who addressed the effect of the costs of transporting products to market on the rent earned by land. For example, an advantage of favorable transportation costs accrues to those land parcels lying closer to central (usually urban) markets. These cost advantages of productivity and location are reflected in lower net costs of production and marketing, and hence in higher land rents. As with differential rents, locational rents are in turn capitalized into higher land values. The locational aspect highlighted by von Thünen tends to be more important in urban land valuation, while the productivity considerations emphasized by the Ricardian tradition are usually more important in agriculture. See Keiper et al. 1961, Bronfenbrenner 1971, or Blaug 1997 for extended discussions of theories of land rent, and Eatwell et al. 1987 for a good brief summary.

In the late nineteenth century, Alfred Marshall introduced the idea of *quasi-rents* (see Marshall 1920, the last edition of his treatise). Recognizing that resources other than land could be temporarily limited in supply and hence yield a return over their opportunity costs, Marshall added further concepts to the theory of economic rents that became important in welfare economics theory. Since Marshall reserved the term *rent* strictly for the Ricardian concept—those payments arising from differential productivities of land—he termed these temporary returns to other resources quasi-rents. When the supply of a resource is unresponsive to price changes in the short run, it can lead to an excess return to the fixed resource that is similar (for that short-run period) to a differential rent. For example, buildings, machinery, and equipment may earn quasi-rents in the short run because the supply of these items of durable equipment cannot be expanded quickly or adapted to other uses. However, in the long run, existing equipment and machinery can be put to new uses or sold, and new machines can be obtained, so in a competitive economy, quasi-rents are typically being competed away. Over a longer planning period, quasi-rents will induce further supply of nonspecialized resources, and the quasi-rents will disappear.

Marshall provided little elaboration to his quasi-rent concept, and the notion has been somewhat difficult to pin down. The meaning has evolved and is now generally understood to refer to "returns to investments regarded as fixed in the short run, ...conventionally defined as total payments to fixed factors plus excess profits" (Blaug 1997, *359*). It is in this sense that the term will be used herein. Examples of fixed factors whose returns are included in a firm's quasi-rents are equity capital, special technological knowledge, natural resources (such as land), and perhaps labor and management services contributed by owners of the firm.

Armen Alchian (Eatwell et al. 1987, *141–143*) renewed attention to a second, little-known Marshallian rent concept called the *composite quasi-rent*. Marshall uses this term when a combination of resources yields a return exceeding the opportunity costs of the inputs required to generate the output. The resources are worth more together than separately, made so by a unique investment to make the resources specific to each other, so that the value of each resource is dependent on the other. It is interesting to note that Marshall used water resources in energy production to illustrate the concept. His example was a grinding mill (for converting grain into flour) together with a water-power site (comprising a diversion structure and a water wheel) to energize the mill. The combined investment could be worth more than the sum of the opportunity costs of inputs required to construct the facility, leading to an excess return (as composite quasi-rent). Although the economic literature tends to pay little attention to the concept of composite quasi-rents, I believe that they play a significant role in valuing producers' uses of water. In the example of irrigation of agricultural crops, combining water, nonirrigated land, and an irrigation water supply system likely yields composite quasi-rents. Further, the return over maintaining the capital invested in the water supply system ordinarily accrues to the owner of the land. Hence, a portion of the composite quasi-rents from initiating irrigation will appear in the periodic payments for the use of land. These rents will further be capitalized into the price of irrigated land, just as will differential and, if any, locational rents. Hydroelectric power sites represent another important case where water and capital may earn a Marshallian composite quasi-rent. As the costs of alternative energy sources increase with scarcity of fuels, rents to hydropower sites have risen over time, a trend that can be expected to continue.

This concept raises a question that challenges any residual approach to valuing water. Applied water valuation studies where water is a limited resource can be interpreted as attempts to analytically measure if and to what extent potential composite quasi-rents will be forthcoming from an investment in water supply or from a proposal to reallocate water to alternative higher-valued uses. The difficult question is what proportion of the composite quasi-rents are appropriately attributed to water and what portions to the other fixed resources contributing to the output. Any such investment will require inputs of risk capital and entrepreneurial creativity in addition to water, hence the returns are to a composite of resources. For accounting purposes of a private firm, there may be no need for any further breakdown into the individual contributions of the various contributing resources. But if the economic analyst wants, as we do, to break down any composite quasi-rents into their component parts, the problem is to isolate the individual contributions.

Marshall's notion of composite quasi-rent is a positive economic concept that explains a significant phenomenon of producing firms in market economies. Only those rents that can be specifically associated with the water input can be a measure of the benefits of producers' uses of water. Since the concept was introduced prior to the development of welfare economics as we now understand it, one is not surprised that the early discussion did not go into the normative question of how composite quasi-rents are to be allocated among the combination of resources that yield those rents. (This question will be taken up in Section 3.7.)

One should not expect to find consequential water-related composite quasi-rents in cases where water is not a significant production input, or where water is not limited in supply, as is the case for most manufacturing industries. Even though it is a helpful concept in arid-area agriculture and in hydroelectric power generation, the relatively limited role of water in most industrial production activities, the fact that water is seldom fixed or specialized to industrial firms, and the presence of capital and technological substitutes for water will limit the relevance of composite quasi-rents to a few cases.

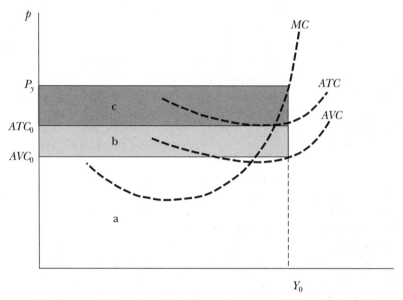

Figure 3-2. Distinguishing Standard Quasi-Rents and Water-Related Rents

3.5.2 Derivation of the Residual Method via the Theory of Economic Rents

It is next shown how the residual method can be derived from an alternative conceptual framework that emphasizes the concepts of costs and rents, rather than the production function approach of Section 3.4. Figure 3-2 illustrates aspects of the theory of the firm important for this derivation. As before, this simplified version of the neoclassical model assumes that the supply curve for variable inputs is perfectly elastic: the firm is able to buy all the variable inputs required at a constant price. Similarly, the producer is a price-taker in the output market, so product price (P_y) may be assumed constant for the period of the analysis. Total Revenue (TR) is output (Y) times the product price:

$$TR = Y \cdot P_y$$

In this context, a significant cost concept is marginal cost (shown as MC in Figure 3-2), which refers to the incremental cost of producing another unit of output. The profit-maximizing producer selects an output level that equates product price with marginal cost:

$$P_y = MC$$

In Figure 3-2, the optimal level of output (where $P_y = MC$) is shown as Y_0.

It is often useful to distinguish inputs as fixed or variable. Fixed factors are those that cannot be evaded, even if the firm ceases operation. Fixed costs are initially assumed to be priced at market price or opportunity costs, as relevant. (The problems of implementing this assumption are considered in Section 3.6.) Variable costs are those that can be evaded if the firm produces no output. Total variable cost is represented by the area denoted a in Figure 3-2. Average variable costs (AVC) and average total costs (ATC) are defined, respectively, as total variable cost and total costs divided by Y. In this derivation, the residual claimant—water—is assumed to be in limited and fixed supply.

The concepts of rents and quasi-rents are fundamental to this approach to producer welfare measurement. Broadly speaking, in welfare economic theory applied to producers, *the welfare effects of changes in prices or quantities (of either inputs or outputs) can be measured by corresponding changes in rents and quasi-rents.* Following conventional definitions (i.e. Just et al. 1982), the sum of rents plus quasi-rents is defined here as the difference between total revenue and total variable costs. As described earlier, economic rents are any payments made to an input over and above the amount needed to attract any of that input into its present employment. Quasi-rents are in present-day usage understood to be total payments to fixed factors. The sum of rents plus quasi-rents composes that portion of total revenues in excess of total variable costs. That is, total revenue is made up of total variable costs plus normal quasi-rents, composite quasi-rents and economic rents. As noted earlier, economic rents arise only if one or more resources are in limited supply. If all resources can be purchased on competitive markets at constant prices, no economic rents will be forthcoming.

For present purposes, we can further distinguish two types of economic rents. One type, *water-related rents,* comprises all those rents that derive from the use of water in production. For this type, found primarily in agricultural crop irrigation, water is assumed to be fixed in supply; hence it can earn economic rents. Denote these water-related rents as R^w. Further denote nonwater-related rents as R^{nw}. These are mainly composite quasi-rents as discussed in Section 3.5.1. However, in certain cases, particularly in specialized agricultural activities like as fresh fruit and vegetable production, water-related rents may include significant differential rents and perhaps even locational rents as well, which may arise when productivity or locational considerations relating to water create special returns to certain types of water-using production activities. The water-related rents are depicted as the area c in Figure 3-2. The remaining rents (area b in Figure 3-2) consist of normal quasi-rents (QR) plus (if any) all other rents, i.e. the returns to the other nonwater fixed factors of production (generally, the returns to equity capital, but also in some cases to entrepreneurial, managerial, land and other nonwater natural resources inputs).

The above definitions, as remarked by Just et al. (1982, 57), point to an algebraic representation of the measures of producers' welfare. Total revenue equals the sum of total variable costs, normal quasi-rents, water-related rents and nonwater-related rents. Symbolically, we can write:

$$TR = TVC + QR + R^w + R^{nw} \tag{3-9}$$

Equation 3-9 can be rearranged to solve for R^w:

$$R^w = TR - TVC - QR - R^{nw} \tag{3-10}$$

If both total variable costs and all quasi-rents and nonwater rents can be isolated and measured, we can then derive water-related rents (R^w) as a measure of long-run water-related producer welfare.

Note that equation 3-10, in which a residual measure of the value of an input is derived via the concepts of rents and quasi-rents, is essentially the same as equation 3-7 which is derived by finding the VMP via the product exhaustion theorem. In applied contexts, both R^w and P_W^* are calculated by subtracting all estimated nonwater costs of production (including nonwater rents as payments to owners of scarce resources) from estimated total revenues. Water-related rents (R^w) and net return to water (P_W^*) are both measures of the incremental contribution of a unit of water to the economy. Hence, the residual method of estimating the value of water or, more generally, the welfare changes from varying the water input, can be approached through either conceptual framework.

As remarked earlier, the framework based on rents best reflects the situation in agricultural irrigation, where water is mainly a fixed or limited input. In contrast, the VMP approach via the product exhaustion theorem is most appropriate in industry, where water can usually be regarded as a variable input. The subsequent section on practical issues in applying the residual formula is expressed in terms of the rent concepts, although the discussion would change little if the focus were on VMP.

3.6 Practical Issues in Implementing a Residual Analysis

Those few environmental economics textbooks that mention valuation from the producers' good perspective tend to dismiss the issues of empirical implementation as too straightforward to need discussion. In fact, a competent, conscientious implementation of the residual method can be quite a challenging task. It requires not only a correct theoretical model, but judgments and decisions on several empirical issues specific to the policy problem being studied. Once the theoretical concepts are satisfactorily addressed, the empirical issues of implementing the residual method center on the availability of adequate data. As with any other deductive analysis, the conclusions derived from a residual analysis are only as trustworthy as the data inputs. Two additional empirical features are important, particularly in the usual case where the benefit measure is to be forecast not just for the current or immediate future time period, but over a long (e.g. 30–50 or more years) planning period, as is frequently required for evaluating water supply investment and reallocation proposals. One consideration is calculating the outputs associated with various levels of inputs for each year in the planning period, i.e. determining the relevant physical production function(s). Another empirical element is estimating the prices of outputs and inputs (including valuing owned inputs as well as purchased inputs) particularly over any long planning period. This process involves characterizing the market and policy environment relating to the scenario(s) being evaluated.

3.6.1 The Aggregation Problem and Data Needs

All deductive techniques aggregate from the model of a single firm to that of the collection of producers in an industry or region. This is called the aggregation problem. Actual individual firms within a broadly defined industry may differ widely in their resource endowments, the specific products they produce, and the technologies they employ. Clearly, an analyst operating on a limited budget and schedule cannot model every firm in a given industry or region. The usual response is to employ the concept of the "representative firm," another Marshallian invention. A representative firm is intended to reflect the average or some other measure of central tendency regarding size, technology, and product line of the individual firms in the population under study.

However, data are often not readily available to define this construct. Data collected by public agencies, such as for census or tax collection purposes, may not precisely reflect the data needed or, more likely, they may not be available to researchers because of disclosure or privacy regulations. Some public data may not be collected with proper random sampling techniques and may not yield unbiased estimates of the desired parameters. A special interview survey is the preferred approach, but may be expensive in time, skills, and budgetary resources to implement. Classic and still valuable discussions of the problems of assembling and using data in applied economic analysis are found in Morgenstern (1963) and Kamarck (1983).

3.6.2 Specifying the Physical Production Function

Accurate specification of the relevant physical production function is a major issue in applying the residual method. The production function can be thought of as a "recipe," describing the amount and mix of inputs needed for producing any particular quantity of output. Determining a production function within a reasonable degree of accuracy can be a daunting task. Of course, the effect of a changing water input level on output will vary with the level of other inputs, so for any residual analysis the investigator needs to make clear the appropriate levels of the other inputs and how they affect output. Production processes, particularly biological processes applicable to agricultural production, are very sensitive to the timing as well as to the quantity of water inputs and to a number of environmental attributes, such as climate. The yield response of an increment of water applied to crops may vary greatly depending on when in the growing season it is applied. Quantifying the effect of degraded water quality on output—needed for the evaluation of policies for improving water quality—is also a difficult assignment. More important, over a long planning period, one must address the question of whether to assume that production technology remains constant.

Specialists from the appropriate biological or physical disciplines should be relied upon in deriving an empirical production function. Agricultural production functions may be obtained via field experiments or interview surveys, or based on opinions of experts from the relevant disciplines. Industrial production functions are more often developed by engineering specialists, although survey or census data are sometimes available from which a production function can be approximated with statistical methods.

In applying the residual method, two important issues relating to production functions may be identified. One issue is accurately forecasting the actual future levels of output associated with given factor inputs. Over- (or under-) estimates of the level of production possible from a given bundle of inputs will bring about a corresponding over- (or under-) estimate of the residual. Because of the arithmetic of the process and because the contribution of water typically represents only a portion of the total value of product, any degree of error in forecast output and associated revenue will be magnified several times in the residual.

The principal issue, however, is listing and quantifying the predicted amounts used of all relevant inputs (including that of the residual claimant). It is essential to avoid what might be called the *omitted variables* problem. Since the process is to calculate a net return to water, if the costs of one or more important factor inputs are omitted from the specification of the production function, the productivity of any omitted input is erroneously attributed to the residual claimant. The calculated net return to water would be correspondingly overstated. For example, in evaluating benefits of crop irrigation, if all or some of the costs of labor are omitted from the calculations, the omitted contribution of labor is implicitly added to the residual attributed to water, thereby biasing the estimate from the "true" value.

An additional problem in specifying the role of water in a production function is the difficulty of empirical measurement, particularly where water contributes a relatively minor portion of the total value of product. Potential errors in assigning opportunity costs to nonwater inputs may cause a serious error in the residual assigned to water. For example, in valuing water used in industrial production, analysts employing the residual method must assign opportunity costs to other inputs. A small variation in the assumed costs of these other inputs, particularly inputs owned by the firm, such as the opportunity cost of stockholder financial capital or of entrepreneurial skills, can have a large impact on the residual derived for water (see Section 3.7).

3.6.3 Estimating Prices of Inputs and Outputs in a Residual Analysis

Assigning prices to inputs and outputs is also a challenging task. Incorrect input prices obviously translate directly into biased estimates of the value of the residual claimant, but with opposite sign. In other words, underpriced inputs yield overestimates of the residual, and the converse leads to an underestimated residual. Errors in estimated output prices translate into errors in the residual with the same sign: if outputs are over- (under-) priced, the residual is also over- (under-) estimated.

For short planning periods, this portion of the analysis usually begins with current or recent observed market prices for outputs and inputs (other than the residual claimant). Adjustments for general price level changes (inflation) may be called for. For markets which exhibit substantial year-to-year variation in prices, like agricultural commodities, an inflation-adjusted average of several years' prices may be desirable. For very short planning periods, using the prices currently facing the producer will suffice for analyses from the private or even regional accounting stances.

For long planning periods—frequently encountered in water policy analysis—the forecasting of prices of inputs and outputs is one of the most difficult tasks. When the planning period extends several decades or even indefinitely into the future, the analyst needs a very accurate crystal ball to extrapolate both input and output prices. To understand the limitations of long-term economic price forecasting, one only needs to look back at the price fluctuations observed over the past half-century and consider how far off the mark were price prognostications made at the beginning of that time. Technological improvements, institutional changes (such as the adoption of a more open international trade regime), and resource scarcities are among the important factors influencing both input and output prices. These limitations imply that conclusions reached in residual measures of benefits in the production context need to be taken only as seriously as the estimates of future input and output prices. Even forecasts made with the best available data and the most elaborate deductive techniques have frequently missed the mark, sometimes by wide margins. It is always good practice to acknowledge this uncertainty and to use formal sensitivity analysis to test how the results vary with alternative assumptions about output and input prices.

The interdependence of technological advances, levels of investment, and product prices over an extended future period is another issue warranting emphasis in the longer planning period case. At the national economy level, technological advances in production typically bring reductions in prices for the associated products. Any analysis which assumes technological gains in production over the future planning period should also include a forecast of the consequent reductions in real prices over the same planning period. Harberger (1974, *19*) early on made the general point:

> Almost any investment made today would become profitable if no competing investments were made in the future... The "profitability" of today's investments should be estimated on the assumption that all "profitable" future investments will also be made... Here, of necessity, the project analyst himself has to estimate an expected time path of prices—not on the assumption that his project will stand alone, nor on the assumption that future projects will be held up in order to "protect" his current project, but on the much more rigorous assumption that future investments will be made on their own merits.

Harberger's comments are equally applicable to evaluating water projects supplying agricultural or manufacturing activities. Important types of alternative investments in these cases would include public or private research programs to increase agricultural or manufacturing productivity, which help to expand output per capita and to lower real prices for food and manufactured products. Evaluations of public irrigation projects have on occasion forecast a steady increase in output per unit water used, while holding output prices constant at the levels experienced during the period immediately preceding the development of the evaluations. Under such assumptions, the estimated residuals increased steadily over the life of the project, but in retrospect, since real commodity prices fell, overly favorable estimates of benefits were the result (Young 1978).

Choosing the correct *accounting stance* is very important in selecting prices for a residual analysis (see Section 2.3.4). Some adjustments may be necessary when approaching the problem from the social accounting perspective. If government intervention or market failures lead to prices for input factors and products which deviate from what might be the competitive equilibrium prices, then the imputed value of the residual, while reflecting the private perspective, will be an inaccurate reflection of society's interests. Issues of choosing the correct accounting stance are frequently encountered in water resource planning: governments regularly intervene in the workings of markets to raise or lower prices of either products or inputs. Some developing countries, for example, have maintained agricultural commodity prices below world market prices with policies designed to keep food prices low to urban consumers. When artificially depressed prices are lower than market equilibrium, then the imputed values of irrigation water are accordingly lower than they would otherwise be. Conversely, in many developed countries, agricultural policies raise prices for a number of commodities to a level above what would exist under unregulated market conditions. In this case, the residual value of water is overstated from the social accounting perspective. On the input side, wage rates may be raised by minimum wage regulations. Capital costs are affected by government credit programs and macroeconomic policies influencing interest rates. From the social accounting stance, an understatement (overstatement) of input costs yields a higher (lower) residual value than should be the case.

Specifying the *length of run* is another consequential choice, since the product prices and input costs used in a residual analysis depend on the planning period (see Section 2.4.1). Long-run and short-run models yield markedly different results. Some expenditures may be considered to be sunk costs in the short run and therefore rightly ignored in that context. These same costs should be counted (i.e. deducted) in long-run planning.

3.7 The Special Problem of Owned Inputs in Residual Imputations

Empirical grounds suggest that typical application of the residual method yields overly optimistic predictions of realized benefits, especially in the case of agricultural irrigation (see Chapter 5). Some of these erroneous forecasts may be due to the incorrect application of the method (omitting cost variables, using overly optimistic prices and yields, and applying short-run models in instances where long-run formulations would be appropriate) as discussed in Section 3.6. However, some biases seem to be due to a more systematic misapplication of the residual method. To sum up the evidence, there are a number of econometric findings from the United States and Asia that investments in irrigation projects fail to yield an adequate return on the public's investment when the return is measured by economic impacts registered at the state or regional level. Returns are too often less than the opportunity cost of capital and, in Asia, agricultural research, rural roads, and education have been found to yield much higher returns on public investments. A second, related observation is that farmers are unable or unwilling to repay more than a small fraction of the costs of developing new water projects or improving and rehabilitating existing projects. Finally, the values predicted by the residual method tend to be significantly higher than those found by the few formal applications of land value and hedonic property value methods to irrigation water, even after adjusting at-source values to derive at-site values.

These findings suggest other reasons why the residual method often results in higher estimated values than do econometric methods and observations on land and water markets. One possible source of the discrepancy is inadequate accounting for "owned" or noncontractual inputs.

3.7.1 Are Owned Inputs Inadequately Represented in the Residual Method?

The residual method, as shown in equations 3-7 and 3-10, means finding an estimate of water-related rents (or equivalently, an estimate of the value marginal product of water) by deducting the costs of all nonwater inputs from the estimated total value of production. The textbook derivation (e.g. Heady 1952, *402–414*), via either the product exhaustion theorem or the theory of rents, assumes that prices of all inputs but one (the residual claimant) are readily observable on competitive markets, so that the residual income can without difficulty be imputed to the unpriced resource. However, in practice we recognize that firms may employ, in addition to water, other inputs not regularly purchased on competitive markets. A more realistic model of the firm acknowledges that some inputs are not purchased, but are *owned* by the firm. Determining prices for owned (also called noncontractual) inputs in a residual analysis calls for special strategies.

Although never a major concern in most mainstream microeconomics textbooks, the distinction between owned and purchased resources has a venerable history in economic theory, going back at least to the classical period. Contractual inputs are those purchased by the firm at known prices. They typically include materials and services procured from other firms and individuals, as well as hired workers, supervisors, and managers, plus borrowed capital, insurance, and other inputs whose costs are known. As explained by Friedman in the context of the definition of cost (1976, *149*):

> ...the best procedure seems to me to define total costs as identical with total receipts—to make the totals of two sides of a double entry account. One can then distinguish between different kinds of costs, the chief distinction in pure theory being between costs that depend on what the firm does but not how its actions turn out (contractual costs) and the rest of its costs on receipts (noncontractual costs). The former represent the costs of factors of production viewed solely as "hired" resources being capable of being rented out to other firms; the latter represent payment for whatever it is that makes identical collections of resources different when employed by different firms. ...Actual noncontractual costs can obviously never be known in advance, since they will be affected by all sorts of accidents, mistakes and the like.

Two essential points must be brought out regarding the role of owned inputs for residual analyses. First, their prices are uncertain because they are determined by the outcome of previous management and investment decisions. Although finding the appropriate prices of inputs purchased on markets outside the firm brings up many problems, pricing owned inputs presents even more of a challenge.

Second, even though owned inputs are not purchased on markets, for the individual firm they have opportunity costs and therefore are scarce and valuable. Hence, for long-run evaluations of additions to or reductions in input (i.e. water) use from an initial situation, noncontractual costs other than for water should be considered along with the standard purchased variable costs. Similarly, for the society or economy as a whole, owned inputs have opportunity costs and should be costed as part of any analysis from the social perspective.

Little literature precisely addresses these points. Conventional agricultural economics textbook treatments of costs and returns from the private firm's perspective, particularly those relating to the allocation of land and other resources in the agricultural sector, do not typically price such inputs. In such contexts, the residual to the firm is assumed to be the sum of returns to certain owned inputs, such as return to "risk and management" or, for farm appraisal studies, perhaps the returns to land. These are reasonable simplifications in a situation where the issue is optimizing returns to all of the firm's owned inputs. Also, in short-run decision contexts, there is no need for debate. For evaluating short-run decisions, the costs of owned inputs can properly be treated as sunk costs and ignored.

Although owned inputs have long been recognized by economic theorists, the fundamental issues concerning how to define and price them in a residual analysis remain contentious. Many viewpoints are expressed on the nature and existence of various types of owned inputs, and the differences among these are not entirely resolved. Below, some of the areas of controversy are presented as they bear on the application of the residual method, but no pretense is made of solving the main issues, or even of advancing the theoretical debate.

In practice, the distinction between contractual and noncontractual inputs is often vague or indeterminate. Some types of inputs may be both hired and owned, even in the same firm. For example, some financial (equity) capital is owned by the firm, and part of the required capital may be hired (borrowed) via bank loans or the issuance of interest-bearing notes or bonds. For another example, some business risks can be contractually avoided by purchasing insurance or by hedging, but the owners of the firm's equity capital must bear some irreducible degree of price and production risk. Another instance arises with the managerial input. In small family firms, management is typically an owned resource, but in larger firms it is usually mostly hired. Other models recognize that the firm may possess special technological advantages which contribute to its net return. Rents to land and other natural resource inputs may constitute a major element of owned inputs. These types of owned inputs are discussed in more detail below.

When applying residual analysis in long-run planning, the goal is to estimate returns to "ownership" of water, not simply the total returns to ownership of the firm (the entity that owns the water). In addition to quantifying and pricing contractual inputs, one would thus need to put a quantity and a price on each of the noncontractual claims other than water. Consequently, the cost model must be elaborated on. What are the constituents of the list of noncontractual inputs, and how are their contributions to output to be determined (i.e. quantified and priced) in a residual imputation exercise?

3.7.2 Owned Inputs and the Concept of Profit

One place to launch the discussion is from the concept of "profit." In common business parlance and everyday language, the returns to owned resources constitute what are usually called profits. The concept of profit in the theory of the firm has had a turbulent and controversial history. In the most recognized theory of static general economic equilibrium, stemming from the writings of Leon Walras, profits are zero in the long-run equilibrium. (In the Walrasian model, the return to capital is fully subsumed in interest payments.) However, such a finding conflicts with observed reality in market economies. Some payments to owners of the firm—conventionally called "profits"—do exist in the modern market economy. Although definitions and understandings of the term are many and diverse, profits are one of the distributive shares in a modern mixed economy. To paraphrase Bronfenbrenner (1971), profits are measured by accountants, sought by investors, and taxed by governments. Hence, a more realistic residual analysis will account for profit as one of the elements of economic returns to business enterprises. I assume in the subsequent discussion that any attempt to seriously consider pricing of owned inputs for a residual analysis necessarily takes the discussion beyond the unrealistic simplifications of zero-profit equilibrium models.

Bronfenbrenner (1971, *372*), elaborating on Knight's (1921) theory of profit, proposes to formally define profit as payments for *all* owned resources. In his view, profits are:

> ...compensation for merely that subset of uncertainties arising from *lack of any contractual claim* to recompense either per hour of labor, per piece of output, or per unit of land or capital supplied. We concentrate, in other words, upon the incomes of persons who accept, as residual claimants, part or all of whatever is left after contractual claims are honored and contractual claims are paid [emphasis in the original].

Bronfenbrenner's definition seems to fit both everyday and formal accounting understandings of what is meant by profit. Nonetheless, although Bronfenbrenner acknowledges several types of noncontractual inputs, his solution for implementing the product exhaustion theorem is to simply lump all types into a return to owners' equity capital. His approach permits an implementation of the product exhaustion theorem in a broad macroeconomic context. However, in the context of developing a microeconomic model to account for all nonwater elements of returns to owned inputs, a more detailed approach is needed. Because water use by producers ranges from relatively simple agricultural production of staple crops through risky and technically demanding production of perishable fruits and vegetables to capital-intensive industrial processes, our problem calls for a broader conceptual framework to account for the potential roles of owned inputs under the widest variety of production conditions.

3.7.3 Types of Owned Inputs

Following Baumol (1993) (who acknowledges the influence of Joseph Schumpeter), we can divide owned inputs into several types. The first is the firm's financial or equity (or risk) capital. Then there are several types of human inputs, including owner labor, entrepreneurial creativity, and management. The last type includes land and other natural resources. The role of each type is understood to be separate and distinct. Each is likely to be economically scarce and require a payment to call it into production. Hence, for long-run analyses, each must be priced and deducted from revenues in the process of estimating an accurate residual value. To elaborate on these distinctions, consider some of the ideas that have been expressed on the various aspects of the general problem.

Equity Capital. Knight's influential treatise (1921) proposes a theory in which profit is a special return for risk-bearing. Putting a label on the function, we can say that the *capitalist* earns income from advancing capital in risky situations and gains a return when the production process yields returns in excess of contractual costs. As Friedman (1976, *149*) states:

> It is important to further distinguish between *expected* and *actual* non-contractual costs. ...The difference between expected and actual noncontractual costs is "profits" or "pure profits"—an unanticipated residual arising from uncertainty [emphasis added].

Entrepreneurship. However, others expressed different views of the sources of profits to firms. An even earlier line of reasoning emphasizes innovative activity as a crucial aspect of the growth of modern economies. Schumpeter (1936) notes that capital may be advanced to the firm by lenders such as bankers, who take some of the risk of business enterprises, so the firm's owners are not the only capitalists. In contrast to Knight, Schumpeter emphasizes the role of the entrepreneur as the source of profits. For Schumpeter, the entrepreneur is an innovator—the person who puts an original and unique idea into operation and brings it from the conceptual stage to the market. Schumpeter attributes the returns to the firm, beyond the opportunity cost of capital, as springing primarily from innovative activity. As the economics profession increasingly recognizes that economic growth has stemmed primarily from innovation in production, Schumpeter's approach has gained wider support.

Makowski and Ostroy (2001, *484–485*) remark that the zero-profit conclusion of the Walrasian general equilibrium model stems from an assumption that all technologies are freely reproducible. This means that ownership of technologies is not scarce, and so there is no cost of entry to new firms. Since incomes must be assignable to scarce resources, and the ownership of technology is assumed not to be scarce, profits are necessarily zero in equilibrium in the static Walrasian system. For a more realistic conceptualization, Makowski and Ostroy point to Alfred Marshall. In contrast to the Walrasian tradition, Marshall posits that firms *can* own and control unique technological skills and abilities. (See Marshall 1920 or the entry "Alfred Marshall" in Eatwell et al. 1987.) In such cases, technologies are not freely reproducible and free entry may not be possible. Although this type of scarce input may not be immediately identifiable or measurable, the firm's owners may earn returns (profits) to scarce technological knowledge. This theme thus integrates with the subsequent contentions of Schumpeter, which holds that profits arise from the successful search for better methods of production or for new products altogether.

Significantly for residual analysis, entrepreneurship is not measurable in any quantity metric. This means that it cannot be readily priced in money terms.

Management. In contrast to the capitalist or the entreprenuer, another potential contributor to the returns to the firm is the manager. This role includes decisionmaking, superintendence, coordination and control of the firm, and the application of specialized knowledge. In Baumol's (1993, *3*) words:

> We may define the manager as the individual who oversees the ongoing efficiency of continuing processes. It is the manager's task to see that available processes and techniques are combined in proportions appropriate for current output levels and for the future outputs already in prospect. The manager sees that inputs are not wasted, that schedules and contracts are met, that routine pricing and advertising outlay decisions are made, that simple growth processes entailing no novel procedures take place, and so on. In sum, the manager takes charge of the activities and decisions encompassed in the traditional models of the firm.

This definition distinguishes the manager from both the entrepreneur and the capitalist. Entrepreneurs generate a return from innovation and scarce technical knowledge, and capitalists are rewarded for providing funds to risky ventures. Only if the manager has equity capital at risk will they be a capitalist. Conversely, only if the manager performs the creative functions of putting unique and original ideas into operation will they be called an entrepreneur. Management is often hired, particularly by larger firms; but in smaller ones, such as family farms, it may be an owned input, the payment to which is implicit in the combined returns to owned inputs.

Marshall, as usual, has something to say on this point. The owners of Marshall's firms have sufficient training and ability to provide the required "business power" (by which he apparently means managerial ability) to operate the firm. Marshall believes that the necessary managerial abilities are available throughout the economy, so managerial ability is simply a type of skilled labor that receives a premium wage. However, Marshall also recognizes that exceptional individuals will receive rents or surpluses in addition to the normal return to managerial ability. This rent can be paid to them as hired managers or received as a noncontractual residual by owners of (typically smaller) firms.

Land. The final type of owned input is land (or, more generally for our purpose, nonwater natural resources). In water valuation, land will, of course, be much more significant as an input to agriculture than in industrial uses. In the terminology of rent theory introduced earlier, where land is an owned input, it may accrue differential or locational rents and contribute to the generation of composite quasi-rents. These incomes or rents to land or nonwater natural resources would be included in the accountants' definition of profit (or more broadly, in the return to equity) but would need to be isolated in estimating a long-run return to the water resource.

No one theory seems to account for all the potential sources of returns to owned inputs, although Marshall's seems to come closest. But it is appropriate to recognize that risk-bearing, innovation, technological skills, management, and nonwater natural resources all represent scarce resources that are typically owned by the firm and will be considered for pricing in a complete residual analysis, particularly in long-run planning.

3.7.4 Estimating Prices for Owned Inputs

Functions such as bearing risks, managing, and innovating need to be effectively performed for the firm to survive in a dynamic economy, so all will require a return or payment to summon them into production. In some cases, owned inputs can be priced by appealing to opportunity cost or reservation price. Opportunity cost of an owned input is the forgone benefit in the best alternative use. If the input is to some degree marketed, the prevailing or expected market price can be considered an appropriate measure of opportunity cost. If competitive markets are absent, the problem will be more complex. That is not to say that the markets for capital, managers, and land are irrelevant; factor owners are assumed to consider their own attributes (such as entrepreneurial and management skills, amount of capital, and aversion to risk) in deciding whether to offer their resources on markets (to be hired by other firms) or risk these resources by forming a firm and engaging in private production. Hence, the market rates will provide some guidance as to the opportunity costs of nonwater inputs. The second, related concept is the reservation price, the price required for the resource owner to offer the service or input to the enterprise in question. The reservation price concept applied to owned inputs seems clear enough in theory, but in application is likely to be subjective. Some ingenuity will be required to quantify it in practice for applied residual analyses.

Measuring noncontractual inputs can be difficult because they tend to be *specialized*. This means that they are unique to the firm, and their prices may not precisely reflect the market for similar services. That is, since their values depend largely on the outcomes of prior managerial decisions, they differ from location to location, from firm to firm, and from industry to industry, and prices cannot necessarily be accurately drawn from observing market transactions. Friedman (1976, *147*) notes that the existence of specialized resources

> …makes it impossible to define the average cost of a particular firm for different hypothetical outputs independently of demand. The returns to the specialized factors are now "rents" at least in part, and in consequence, do not determine the price, but are determined by it.

Given these considerations, let us now consider pricing of each of the four major types of owned inputs.

Equity capital. Probably the most important owned input is equity capital. Aside from the dot-com wonders of the 1990s financial bubble, any operating firm must have some equity or working capital, and for a residual analysis this resource needs to be priced. It is a challenge to convert the uncertain return to equity capital (itself usually calculated as a residual) to a known quantity so that a residual value of water can be derived. One of the functions of stock markets is to price equity capital. It is observed that the market price of each individual firm differs according to the market participants' perception of the risk and extent of future net income possibilities relative to other opportunities for investment (such as fixed income securities markets). Pricing individual firms becomes regularized for successful firms as the public's anticipations of risk and growth opportunities become refined. Nonetheless, observations of prices of individual common stocks demonstrate that agreement is still lacking on how equity capital is priced. Some standard theories of securities valuation hold that prices of stocks are based on anticipated earnings streams. Or are they perhaps reflective of anticipated future dividend payments? Pricing of equity in new firms on the new issues market seems to be particularly capricious because of the uncertainty of returns.

The financial capital of nearly all firms is a combination of owned and borrowed capital. For purposes of implementing the product exhaustion theorem for distributing income among factors of production, Bronfenbrenner (1971) suggests using a weighted average of the cost of borrowed capital and the reservation price of owners' equity capital as the opportunity cost. However, the reservation price applicable to owner's equity is not readily observable, but typically is higher the higher the risks undertaken by the firm (and the greater the financial leverage assumed by the firm). An estimate based on returns to investments of commensurate riskiness seems appropriate. However, given the variety and differing risk of production and market situations across industries, there is no clear choice of reservation price of the firm's capital. Assuming that the water-using sector must compete with the remainder of the economy for capital, an approximation might be the average *pre-tax* rate of return on equity among business firms in the national economy. For social analysis, in the United States this would often be in the neighborhood of 10% to 12% per annum. (For after-tax rates of return, see U.S. Department of Commerce 2000.) A lower bound would be the cost of borrowing funds for business operations of equivalent risk from the private banking system. Where the government subsidizes credit, as may be the case for farms and small businesses, the market rate rather than the subsidized rate would be applicable for a social analysis.

Entrepreneurship. According to Schumpeter's (1936) extension of the neoclassical model of the firm, profit is the return to specific innovative activities, distinct from returns to risk, equity capital, or management. Because entrepreneurship is not applied in doses that can be measured in hours or even as a percentage of the value of output, and because it is non-standardized and its value is measured only *ex post* as the result of prior production decisions, I see no obvious way to incorporate a direct measure of entrepreneurial contributions in a business budget. For water-using industrial activities, it could be assumed that entrepreneurial inputs are embodied in the contractual return to paid corporate executives and their research staffs, and no further attempt to price it separately would be warranted. For purposes of valuing irrigation water, one could hypothesize that innovation occurs mainly in public and private agricultural research organizations and, on the average, the earnings of innovative activities is negligible for average or representative (noncorporate) farmers and can be safely ignored. To the extent that these assumptions are incorrect, as both might be for some specialty agricultural crop producers, the residual assigned to water would be overstated. Nevertheless, because of the indeterminancy of the concept, I do not advocate any attempt to value innovative entrepreneurship in order to derive a residual value for water.

Management. As with entrepreneurship, assigning a charge to management *per se* is difficult in practice, because management is not always quantifiable as an input in terms such as hours of work per unit of output. However, this task may be less difficult in practice for larger firms with a corporate structure than for smaller, family-owned businesses. This is because management tasks are mostly hired or contracted in larger firms, and thus the costs of management appear among the contractual costs. However, in family-owned businesses such as farming, management is likely to be a contribution of the owners and hence unpriced except as a residual to the business. Consulting firms that provide managerial services are found in many industries. In such cases, the approximate cost of hiring the equivalent services from experienced consulting firms may provide a solution to the problem, and this approach is often observed in standard budgeting exercises.

Land. Assigning an opportunity cost to land is relatively unimportant in calculating benefits of industrial water use but it is, of course, a significant issue when valuing agricultural water use with a residual method. Land also is often nonhomogeneous in location or fertility of individual parcels, so the forgone benefit may be difficult to isolate. Nevertheless, both rental and sales markets for land do exist, and they can be examined by either formal statistical methods or less formal means to estimate the opportunity costs of land in residual analyses. (See Chapter 5.)

3.7.5 Further Remarks on Owned Inputs in Residual Analyses

Using the residual methods that are appropriate for analyzing private resource allocation decisions—those traditionally taught in farm and business management courses—will lead to erroneous valuations of water resources. Typical models of private decisions (particularly in a short-run context) calculate a residual that combines returns to several owned inputs, and seldom provide a formulation designed to isolate returns to a single resource. Imputing the returns earned by all owned inputs to only one input is inappropriate in public planning, especially when the object is to estimate the residual value of a single owned input such as water.

These considerations identify a serious limitation on the precision of residual methods for valuing water as a producers' good, a limitation exacerbated by the fact that water in most producers' good contexts contributes but a small proportion to the value of the firm's output. Owned resources other than water are significant inputs to most water-using firms and, therefore, failure to account for their opportunity costs will bias results in favor of the residual claimant. So some attempt to account for owned inputs will be necessary. But even if an estimate of normal opportunity costs is included (say for typical managerial abilities or normal risks to capital), if the business under study warrants special rents to uniquely skilled managers or premiums on capital for special risks, these premiums will be incorrectly credited to the residual claimant.

For most water-using manufacturing industries the input of water to production processes is a minor contributor to the total value of output, while the relative value of other owned inputs, particularly capital, is often quite large. Any residual estimated for water benefit will be overwhelmed by the variation in the plausible assumptions regarding the required reservation price to equity capital, as well as the appropriate payments to management, entrepreneurship, and land. (Think of the problem of finding a residual value of water used by a large manufacturing corporation using advanced technologies, such as the Intel Corporation, the well-known maker of semiconductor chips.) Therefore, the larger the role of nonwater owned inputs, the more chance for error in finding a residual value of water, and the less appropriate is the residual method for this purpose.

Conversely, given the sensitivity of the results to assumptions regarding owned input costs, the residual approach is most suitable for cases where the residual claimant contributes a significant fraction of the value of output and the other types of owned inputs—management and entrepreneurship—are smaller. In the case of water, the simpler types of agricultural production fit this prescription.

To sum up the implications for the role of owned inputs in residual valuation of water: even aside from uncertainties regarding future technology and prices, any residual value assigned to water is to some degree arbitrary. Since there is no precise market price from which the estimates of opportunity cost or reservation price can be obtained for the nonwater owned inputs such as equity capital, management, innovation, and land, the derived residual will necessarily depend on the judgments made regarding the opportunity costs or reservation prices of these other owned inputs. This issue will matter to the degree to which various specialized owned inputs contribute to the firm's output.

3.8 Extensions: The Change in Net Rents Method and Mathematical Programming Models

The treatment of the residual method so far has considered only the basic (and somewhat special) case of finding a point estimate of producers' willingness to pay for the optimally applied input water used to produce a single product. That approach provides the building blocks for more complex approaches. The discussion now turns to some more realistic cases, such as discrete increments and decrements of water and the multi-product firm. The methods which can be applied in such cases include the Change in Net Rents (CNR) Method and the more elaborate mathematical programming models.

3.8.1 Change in Net Rents Method

Often the task is to estimate the value contributed by a discrete but partial change in the water supply, rather than that for a single point on the value marginal product function. In such a case, it may not be appropriate to assume that the amounts of other inputs are held constant. Analysts typically also want to estimate the value of water for a multiproduct firm, since few firms, even farms, produce only a single product. A method developed for such situations is what I will call the *Change in Net Rents* method. (The U.S. Water Resources Council, 1983, without labeling the concept, recommends a process of calculating a "change in net income" for irrigation benefit evaluation, which is essentially the Change in Net Rent method.)

The Change in Net Rents concept likely traces its origins to Alfred Marshall's notion of "marginal net product." His theory of factor demand is at once more realistic and more complex than that found in the basic neoclassical model of his time. Marshall emphasizes that when the amount of one productive factor is changed, it may be profitable to change the amounts of other productive factors. (This is in contrast with the more customary neoclassical textbook approach, which, using the differential calculus, varies one input while holding all others constant.) For example, a farmer who is adding a consequential increment of irrigation water to their production mix will likely find it in their interest to increase the amount of other inputs, such as fertilizer, pesticides, or labor. Marshall (who, contrary to present-day terminological practice, omits the term "value" from his label) allows for a simultaneous variation of the amounts of all inputs in his formulation of a concept similar to what we now call VMP. In Marshall's words (1920, *406*):

> [Every business man] estimates as best he can how much *net product* (i.e. net addition to the value of his total product) will be caused by a certain extra use of any one agent; *net* that is after deducting for any extra expenses that may be indirectly caused by the change and adding for any incidental savings [italics in the original].

If we invoke the willingness to pay principle to define the welfare change measure in the case of discrete changes in an input, the producers' willingness to pay for an increment of an input is the change in net producer income or value of net rent associated with that increment.

This approach can be implemented by a process similar to that used for the residual method. It also requires combining knowledge of the production function(s) and estimates of prices of products with the prices and opportunity costs of nonwater inputs in a budgeting procedure.

In most applications, the analyst assumes that factor and output markets are unaffected by the policy intervention or investment under consideration, so product price and input prices are assumed unchanged between the "with project (or policy)" and the "without project (or policy)" scenarios. However, outputs and nonwater input quantities are allowed to vary as called for by profit maximization according to the level of water input.

More formally, the net income (Z) from producing a single product at specified input levels can be represented by:

$$Z = (Y \cdot P_y) - \sum_{j=1}^{n}(X_j \cdot P_{x_j}) \qquad (3\text{-}11)$$

where P_y refers to the product price and P_{x_j} to the price of the jth input (X_j). For evaluating an increment of water supply, define the Change in Net Rent as:

$$\Delta Z = Z_1 - Z_0 \qquad (3\text{-}12)$$

where the subscripts 0 and 1 refer to the "without policy or project" and "with policy or project" water use situations, respectively. Then,

$$\Delta Z = \left[(Y_1 \cdot P_y) - \sum_{j=1}^{n}(X_{j_1} \cdot P_{x_j}) \right] - \left[(Y_0 \cdot P_y) - \sum_{j=1}^{n}(X_{j_0} \cdot P_{x_{ij}}) \right] \qquad (3\text{-}13)$$

The imputed at-site value or net income per unit of water (ΔW) is:

$$\frac{\Delta Z}{\Delta W} = \frac{\left[(Y_1 \cdot P_y) - \sum_{j=1}^{n}(X_{j_1} \cdot P_{x_j}) \right] - \left[(Y_0 \cdot P_y) - \sum_{j=1}^{n}(X_{j_0} \cdot P_{x_{ij}}) \right]}{\Delta W} \qquad (3\text{-}14)$$

which is the change in net rent associated with an increment in water use. Note that for deriving an at-source value in analyses of intersectoral water allocation issues, the costs of water in both the without-change and the with-change conditions must be further deducted.

As with the basic residual method, the CNR method is readily solved via a budgeting procedure with conventional spreadsheet software. Needed, once again, are reliable estimates of applicable input and product prices and accurate knowledge of the pertinent production functions.

Further, for a multiproduct firm, it is an elementary extension of the analysis to perform these calculations for each of a number of products of a representative firm and determine a weighted average value of the residual claimant, water.

Finally, a reduction in producers' output (damages) can result from natural causes, such as from water shortages (droughts) or excess waters (floods). Water pollution is another common source of damages to production. As long as the assumption can be maintained that input and product prices remain unaffected, the reduction in output can be estimated by the formula given in equation 3-14. The only difference is that the changes in output (Y_1 minus Y_0) is negative, rather than positive.

3.8.2 Mathematical Programming Models

The simplicity of the basic residual model is an advantage, but one that sacrifices some degree of generality. Attempting as it does to find only a single, point equilibrium value marginal product or an estimate of net economic rent, the basic residual method encounters difficulty in providing a more elaborate functional relationship to represent the value marginal productivity of water. One might wish to evaluate the effects of potential changes in product mix or in technology of water use. A number of models of producers' water use have been developed to deal with such issues.

Mathematical programming models are a particular type of optimization model that can represent the profit-maximizing or cost-minimizing allocation of resources by a producing firm. Mathematical models in operations research consist of a set of equations, inequalities, and logical dependencies that can be given empirical content to correspond to real-world relationships. Mathematical programming covers a range of special types: linear and quadratic programming are the most-frequently used types, depending on the form of the objective function.

In water economics, mathematical programming models are often employed to measure benefits of changes in water supply or quality for agricultural or industrial production. They have often been developed to represent the optimum allocation of water and other resources so as to maximize net income, subject to constraints on resource availability or to institutional arrangements. Models of this type can be a sophisticated way to estimate Change in Net Rents: willingness to pay for an increment or decrement of an unpriced producer's input. Further, mathematical programming models can approximate a producers' demand function for water. (See Williams 1999 for a general discussion of how to develop applied mathematical programming models.)

Mathematical programming models may be characterized by an *objective function* and a set of *constraints*. The objective function is key to the model's use in resource valuation, as it defines willingness to pay for the constrained input.

The objective function for a mathematical programming model may be written in matrix notation:

$$\text{Max} f(\pi, \boldsymbol{X}),$$

subject to a set of constraints:

$$A'X \leq B$$

where π_i represents net income or rent per activity i; X_i is a vector of production activities; the elements of the A matrix are production coefficients; and B is a vector of constraints on production inputs such as labor, capital, and natural resources. The objective function can be linear or nonlinear (e.g. quadratic).

In interpretations of mathematical programming models for purposes of water allocation, the parameter π_i is usually a measure of the marginal net rent to water in activity X_i, calculated according to the residual method. Mathematical programming is advantageous where a wide range of alternative productive technologies (formulated as alternative activities) is to be studied. These options can include alternative levels of inputs (particularly water) to produce a given output, alternative products, alternative production technologies, or all of the above. The model can be solved to find the net income maximizing set of activities (X^*) given the constraints on resources. The value of the objective function in the optimal solution reflects the benefits to water from that optimal set of activities. Solutions of a mathematical programming model for a range of water supply constraints trace out a set of net total benefit points, from which a set of net marginal benefit points can be then derived.

In developing the model, the value marginal productivity represented by the net income coefficient π_i must be accurately calculated according to the comments on the residual method in Sections 3.6 and 3.7. As in that discussion, the model formulation must accurately reflect the type of decision problem being studied: short-run versus long-run, private versus public, and at-site versus at-source valuation. Analysts sometimes give more attention to the mathematical formulation of the overall allocative model and its solution than to the less exciting but equally important work of specifying the correct valuation model and calculating the appropriate empirical parameters. A particular concern is that mathematical programming models of producers' water demands have sometimes been formulated with a short-run objective function to address a long-run issue, yielding shadow prices which ignore the opportunity costs of owned inputs and thereby over-estimating the value of water.

The main use of mathematical programming models in water valuation is in agriculture. Section 5.6.6 mentions some aspects of mathematical programming models in agricultural water valuation.

3.9 Misconceived Water Valuation Methods with Versions of the Residual Method

As mentioned earlier, applied methods of valuing water in producers' good uses have not received the same intensive critical scrutiny as environmental and nonuse values. In consequence, some less frequently used approaches that greatly overestimate actual willingness to pay for intermediate goods are still encountered in the literature. Two of these are discussed next. One approach derives from regional economic models; the other from a simple budgeting method.

3.9.1 Valuing Water via the Input-Output Model

Water in production is sometimes valued by directly using the value-added calculations that are a prominent part of regional input-output (or interindustry) models (Miller and Blair 1985). The general modeling methodology is also called, after its originator, Leontief input-output analysis. Input-output (I-O) models are relatively simple representations of a regional (or, less frequently, a national) economy, formulated to portray the sales of products to final users such as households, the flow of products among industries, and the use of inputs (materials, capital, and labor) by industry. Such models may be simple, with production aggregated into only a few industries or, in more ambitious efforts, the economy can be broken down into numerous (several hundred) producing sectors. Input-output models are designed primarily to estimate the region-wide effects of changes in demand for outputs. They are less adapted to measuring impacts of changes in resource supply.

Value-added is a technical term applied in certain specialized models in regional and national economic accounting systems. It refers to the combined payments to primary resources, including labor, natural resources (such as land), and capital (interest and profits) and to government (as taxes). The term has induced some, many of whom are not very familiar with applied welfare economics, to apply it to regional water valuation as a measure of willingness to pay. This misconception may arise from the terminology, since value-added sounds as if it has the same meaning as the appropriate welfare measure: value marginal product.

Assembly of an empirical input-output model of a region can be a challenging task, requiring resources for data collection and skills at modeling and computer use. Nevertheless, input-output models have come into frequent use among natural resource policy analysts interested in regional economic impacts of policy initiatives, in no small part because they can be readily constructed from off-the-shelf or synthesized input-output (SIO) models, which use national input-output accounts to represent a particular region. By making what some feel are questionable assumptions, the national database can be adapted to represent counties or multi-county regions, and to estimate the direct, indirect, and induced economic impacts of alternative policy options or resource management plans. One of the best-known synthesized input-output formulations is called IMPLAN (IMpact analysis for PLANning), which was originally developed by staff economists of the U.S. Forest Service for assessing the role of forest activities in regional economies. The basic IMPLAN model is a detailed representation of the United States economy, broken down into over 400 sectors, and continually updated. IMPLAN is now commercially available (Minnesota IMPLAN Group 2003). McKean et al. 1998 point out the limitations of synthesized I-O models for portraying small regional economies, particularly those based on agriculture and natural resource extraction, as is often the case in the evaluation of water policies. Although more expensive and time-consuming, a model based primarily on an interview survey of a random sample of firms in the study region is a preferable alternative approach.

Below, I demonstrate that from the generally accepted applied welfare economics perspective, water valuation employing a measure of value-added will greatly overstate the appropriate measure of willingness to pay for water as a producers' good. This misconception has had lasting policy impacts; in the initial stages of developing methods for shadow-pricing of water several decades ago, the value-added approach was unfortunately adopted by a number of influential analyses (e.g. Wollman et al. 1962; Lofting and McGauhey 1963; Bergman and Boussard 1976; Bell et al. 1982). These publications conveyed to nonspecialists what I believe to be serious overestimates of the actual rents or willingness to pay for water as a producers' good, misconceptions which have not entirely disappeared.

In that it involves estimating a residual by subtracting certain costs from projected revenues, the value-added approach appears, at first glance, to be similar to the residual method described earlier. However, it differs in certain key respects. (The critique outlined below is developed more fully by Young and Gray 1985. See also Hamilton et al. 1991 for a more general discussion of the complexities in deriving measures of economic benefits from input-output models.)

A Sketch of the Input-Output Model. The input-output model is a static model of production, ordinarily used to portray a geographic region or political subdivision for purposes of understanding the structure of the regional economy, and for making short-run predictions of the effects of exogenous changes in final demands on such economic variables as output, employment, and income. Input-output models can predict such variables not only in the aggregate, but for each sector of an economy. The conventional input-output model is characterized by a production function exhibiting constant returns to scale.

A number of theoretical limitations characterize the class of input-output models. Input and product prices are constants in the conventional input-output model (as they are, of course, in most residual analyses). There is no provision for product substitution in consumption or input substitution in production due to changes in prices or technology. The model does not proceed from the constrained optimization assumption common in the theory of the firm, and it lacks constraints on resources (i.e. input supplies are assumed to be unlimited). Hence, impacts tend to be overestimated.

A standard input-output model representing a region (usually for a period of a year) views the economy from two perspectives (Miller and Blair 1985). The first is based on the five ways that the annual outputs of its industries are distributed: to household consumption, to investment in capital goods, to consumption by government agencies, to inputs used by other individual industries, and to exports beyond the regional economy. The second perspective—which is our primary interest here—breaks out payments to regional suppliers of inputs: to wages and salaries for the work force, to annual rents paid to land and other natural resources, to interest on borrowed capital, to annual depreciation on durable material inputs, to profits, to taxes, and to any resources imported from outside the region.

This latter formulation can be expressed (for industry i) in terms of the total outlay (X) of industry i:

$$X_i = \Sigma_{i=1...n} \, x_{ij} + (W_i + L_i + K_i + \Pi_i + S_i) + M_i \qquad (3\text{-}15)$$

where:

$x_{ij}=$ the amount of industry i's outputs purchased as inputs by industry j
$W_i=$ wages and salaries paid to workers in industry i
$L_i=$ rents paid to land and other natural resources used in industry i
$K_i=$ interest and depreciation on capital used in industry i
$\Pi_i=$ profits paid to capital owners in industry i
$S_i=$ taxes paid to government by industry i
$M_i=$ payments for inputs imported from outside the region

Consider the terms inside the parentheses in equation 3-15: W_i, L_i, K_i, Π_i, S_i. This subset of total payments constitutes what is conventionally termed in aggregate I-O models the *value-added*; in some presentations, the concept may also be termed gross regional income. Value-added represents the payments to primary factor owners and to government in the regional economy represented by the model. Another equivalent approach defines value-added (Gittinger 1982, *503*) as the difference between the value of the output of the firm and the value of all inputs purchased by the firm. But, significantly for our purposes, in this formulation the value of "capital and labor used by the firm are considered internal inputs, not externally purchased inputs."

The value-added approach of imputing a value to water in a specific sector can be represented as follows, employing a sectoral production function similar to that shown in equation 3-15. Individual sectors typically are defined to represent an aggregate of producers in a particular industry, such as agriculture, food processing, or energy. In the usual procedure,

---

Classification of Inputs in a Regional Input-Output Model

Purchased Goods and Services, Including Imports
- intermediate products
- raw materials
- energy
- transportation
- other goods and services (spare parts, insurance, packaging)

Value-Added
- salaries, wages
- rents accruing to land, water, and other natural resources
- interest
- profits
- depreciation
- certain taxes

---

imputation of the value-added per unit of water withdrawn (denoted as P'_w) is accomplished by rearranging (3-15):

$$V\Pi_i = \mathbf{X}_i - \sum_{i=1}^{n} x_{i_j} - M_i = W_i + L_i + K_i + \Pi_i + S_i \qquad (3\text{-}16)$$

and dividing $V\Pi_i$ by the quantity of water withdrawn (W_i) for use in sector i:

$$P'_w = \frac{V\Pi_i}{W_i} \qquad (3\text{-}17)$$

Interpreting the "Value of Water" Derived from Value-Added. Initially the imputation process shown in 3-16 and 3-17 appears to closely resemble the basic residual approach. An accumulation of costs is deducted from estimated revenues. However, a closer examination shows that rather than isolating only the contribution of one input (water), the process imputes the productivity of *all* primary resources (labor, management, entrepreneurship, capital, land and other natural resources, taxes, and even depreciation) to the residual (value of water). Value-added has perhaps a useful descriptive meaning from a narrow regional accounting stance, representing the payments to the primary inputs "possessed" by factor owners in the region. But it is problematic as a normative representation of net rents for a firm or an industry in either private or public accounting stances, which are the contexts of concern here. Clearly, since the calculation of value-added does not subtract opportunity costs of nonwater primary inputs, value-added per unit water is much larger than the water-related rents (or value marginal product) of water that were derived above as measures of producer welfare changes. Consequently, dividing a sector's value-added by its water use yields a figure which greatly overstates the conceptually valid marginal value of or willingness to pay for water used in production.

This point can be illustrated by a thought experiment: Consider a representative self-interested farmer contemplating an investment in water supply to begin or augment an irrigation system. How much would they be willing to pay for that increment of water? Because the farmer would have to pay for purchased inputs (materials, equipment, and labor needed to conduct the business) and, in order to be willing to undertake the investment, would need at least an opportunity return on their own labor, land, and capital, this farmer would be willing to pay for the investment in water supply only the amount represented by the net rents to water: the returns after all other costs and opportunity costs are deducted. Since value-added includes (rather than deducts) wages and salaries, interest, profit, taxes, depreciation, and rents, the farmer's true willingness to pay for water is much less than (actually, a small fraction of) the value-added for their business.

To further illustrate the bias in the value-added approach, note that each of these primary resources other than water is implicitly assigned a zero opportunity cost or shadow price, and their contribution to output is thereby credited to water. Although there may be cases where some primary resources might appropriately be shadow priced at other than market price, to assume that the opportunity costs of *all* primary resources other than water are zero and thereby attribute all primary resource productivity to water clearly yields a large overstatement of its correct value. Another way of expressing this critique is to note that in the value-added approach, certain payments to (costs of) capital and labor are treated incorrectly as income or benefits. Instead, they should actually be understood as opportunity costs. For the water policy issues of primary interest—intersectoral transfers and public investment in water supply—value-added is not a measure commensurate with, respectively, the benefits of transferring water from low-valued to high-valued uses or the costs of supply investments.

In my view, it would be better if regional economists were to drop the term value-added entirely. If value-added were to be replaced by a term that better reflected the real meaning of the concept being measured, the temptation to use a descriptive concept in normative contexts might be avoided. "Primary factor incomes" would be a term more descriptive of the meaning of what is measured by value-added and certainly less confusing to noneconomists.

Finally, another instructive tactic for understanding the limitations of the value-added concept as a measure of producers' benefit for a changing input level is to compare value-added with the concept of producers' surplus. From the discussion of welfare concepts applied to producers in Section 3.2, recall that a change in producer surplus is often used as a measure of producer welfare gains or losses in short-run contexts. Producer surplus is defined as the difference between revenues and variable production costs, so it excludes payments to several variable cost items not deducted from total outlay to estimate value-added. In any given circumstance, the concept termed value-added is thus even larger than producers' surplus. The most notable element included in the value-added measure that is subtracted from revenues to infer producer surplus is hired labor (usually a variable cost). Other items usually encompassed in value-added that are excluded from producers' surplus include interest on variable operating cost and that portion of depreciation reflecting use of or wear and tear on machinery and equipment. Payments to local government as taxes or user fees are included in counting value-added, but in some cases—such as when assessing a proposed new water supply project—should be counted as a variable cost of production from society's viewpoint.

Thus, evaluating regional water resource development projects on the basis of value-added from an input-output model would greatly inflate the estimated returns to a public investment program. Similarly, value-added would greatly overestimate the benefits of transferring water to an industrial sector (which exhibits a high value-added per unit of water used) from, say, agricultural production (which displays a relatively low value-added per unit of water used. See Mills 1993 for a more general critique of the tendency to ignore cost considerations in applications of regional economic models to economic evaluation of local or regional policy interventions.

Finally, as an example of estimating forgone producers benefits from an input-output-based model, consider Berck et al. 1991, an early application of the *computable general equilibrium* (CGE) modeling technique to water policy analysis. The model, which portrayed the economy of the San Joaquin Valley in central California, was designed to study the effects of removing increments of up to 50% of the base irrigation water supply from the region. CGE models are a considerable advance on the input-output models, in that they determine domestic prices, supplies, and incomes jointly via a system of nonlinear simultaneous equations. The model developed by Berck, et al. accounts internally for opportunity costs of land and labor, thus overcoming some of my objections to using value added as a measure of economic benefit (although only one quality of labor is represented).

Recent Applications of Value-added Measures to Water Policy Evaluation. The value-added approach is occasionally reinvented to measure economic value or benefits of water use, particularly in developing country contexts. For example, Schiffler et al. 1994 (quoted in Merrett 1997), conceptualizing a study of water use in Jordan, proposed a concept they termed "water productivity." This is equivalent to sectoral value-added divided by water intake, which is identical to the concept in equation 3-16 and shown to overstate the willingness to pay for water. The average "water productivity" in industry was, of course, found to be many times larger than in agriculture. Although the authors' policy conclusions that (given Jordan's limited per capita water resources) marginal agricultural consumption of water needs to give way to other uses is likely correct, their method of reaching this conclusion leaves something to be desired. In particular they claim that the value of water measured by "water productivity" is the opportunity cost of not using water in a sector, but this would be true only in a very unlikely scenario, in which *no* water is available to the industries making up that sector; the input factors (such as labor and capital) making up value-added have no value in alternative uses; and no technical possibilities are available to substitute other resources for water or to adopt alternative, water-saving technologies. Note that one could make exactly the same assumptions with regard to other inputs, such as labor, and impute the entire value-added to that input.

Another recent example is found in Bouhia's (2001) study of the water economy in Morocco. The author develops a national input-output model of Morocco with an emphasis on the role of water. Value-added (i.e. primary factor income) per unit of water is given a key role as a measure of economic benefits in the various sectors. The input-output model is recast as a linear programming model, and "shadow prices" for water are derived and used to draw implications regarding national policies on water pricing and investments in incremental water supply. Bouhia seems to say that because water charges are less than ability to pay (measured by value-added) for all the agricultural sectors, water is underpriced, and that because a large amount of water could be developed for a unit cost less than value-added per unit, additional investments in water supply are warranted. The implicit assumption is that there are no opportunity costs to the labor, land, and capital inputs associated with water use in Morocco.

Concluding Remarks on the Value-Added Concept of Producer Benefits. It is important to keep in mind that value-added derived from an input-output model is a *descriptive* measure created for a particular type of regional economic modeling. It is *not* by usual standards a valid *normative* or economic efficiency-based measure of willingness to pay, as expressed by water-related rents or value marginal product as derived from applied welfare economic theory. It is one of the latter concepts that we wish to measure in deriving conceptually valid estimates of the value of water. Using regional value-added to impute value marginal product or net rent to water resources used in production will not yield a measure compatible with other measures of water value, and will greatly overstate the "correct" value for economic analysis for public policy.

This is not to say that input-output models could never be an initial stage in the process of estimating the value marginal product of water in long-run planning contexts. With some careful additional analysis, a more accurate measure could be derived. One could begin by measuring value-added from an input-output model, then deduct the opportunity costs of all nonwater primary inputs (e.g. labor, management, financial capital, and natural resources) to obtain the appropriate measure of the residual return to water. Nevertheless, as discussed above in connection with the residual methods, estimation of opportunity costs of owned inputs is not an easy task.

A Digression on Regional "Water Multipliers." One of the measures of economic impact frequently derived from regional input-output models focusing on water is *multiplier effects* of public investments. These effects are mainly of concern when the benefits of project investments are localized but costs are paid for by a national government or international donor. During and following a water project's construction, demands for services of local businesses and workers will rise. These businesses and workers will, in turn, spend their new revenues nearby, yielding further gains to the local economy; the subsequent gains in secondary markets are called the multiplier effects. Multiplier effects are usually measured as the value-added in secondary markets. They are the primary factor incomes in those sectors that sell to or buy from the businesses who are the direct beneficiaries of augmented water supply. The importance of multipliers is emphasized in the Neo-Physiocratic tradition that holds that regional economic development derives primarily from natural resource development and the multiplier effects arising therefrom.

The conditions under which pecuniary externalities are properly included in measures of project benefits continue to be debated, but the mainstream neoclassical position has been generally agreed to for nearly a half century (e.g. McKean 1958). Since water projects are classic "pork barrel" cases of concentrating benefits to a local region while dispersing costs to the national economy, the main critique has been the focus of planning agencies and local political interests on only the revenue side in the impacted region. Mainstream economic writers on the issue contend that secondary costs, which are likely to be spread across the national economy and usually represent the elusive opportunity costs or potential returns to alternative investments, are not given equal consideration by proponents of the multiplier analysis.

In a properly functioning competitive economy, with fully employed resources, a new investment yields no net benefits beyond its own net income. Any expansion in secondary sectors in one region is offset in the long run by a fall in activity and profits elsewhere. Moreover, potential alternative public investment projects would be expected to have similar effects. Thus, there is little reason to award special treatment to water supply projects (by adding multiplier effects only for water projects) in the broad context of planning public investment projects.

Cost–benefit analysis conducted from a national perspective will therefore recognize that any alternative public investment will have similar multiplier effects on the economy. Investments in areas such as education, transportation, health, and research will also yield secondary effects. (The secondary effects of these other investment options will typically be spread more widely through the economy, and, not incidentally, will be harder to empirically estimate.) Thus, from a national perspective, the multiplier effects of water supply projects would be offset by the multiplier effects of forgone alternative public investments. Unless there is reason to assume that water projects yield larger secondary effects than do alternative public investments, which is doubtful, the effects can be presumed to "wash out," that is, to offset each other. As Boardman et al. (2001, *114*) remark: "From the broader social or national perspective, they [the regional multipliers] simply represent a transfer from nonresidents to residents because they only occur as a result of consumers shifting their spending from one geographic area to another."

Cost–benefit theory does recognize cases where local conditions may warrant recognition of secondary economic effects of local developments as real economic impacts (Boardman et al. 2001, Chapter 5). Departures from competitive conditions, such as long-term unemployment or immobility of certain resources, can lead to real economic impacts in secondary markets (Howe and Easter 1971). In such cases, some careful adjustments of market prices to reflect social opportunity costs of inputs may be justified. However, adjustments such as these do not extend to assuming a zero shadow price for all labor, capital, or land, as would be the case if multipliers were measured by value-added in secondary markets.

Under some special conditions, such as excess production capacity, immobile resources, or unemployed family labor, some secondary WTP for water might exist for the firm (Howe and Easter 1971). However, in my view, secondary WTP in these conditions would probably be very small relative to total outlays or even relative to value-added, and would be unlikely to persist for more than a short initial segment of a long-term investment planning period.

This point can be further demonstrated by performing the same type of thought experiment as before, but this time for a business in a secondary market. Consider, for example, a firm that sells fertilizer to farmers who actually use the project-supplied irrigation water. Such a firm would not demand or receive any appreciable amount of project water and so is not itself a direct beneficiary. In other words, water is not a significant component of its production function. But that firm must pay for materials (bulk chemicals, bags); pay taxes, insurance premiums, and interest on borrowed capital; pay wages and salaries for skilled and unskilled labor; and account for depreciation on mixing equipment, vehicles, and buildings. Moreover, to stay in business in the long run, in addition to covering out-of-pocket costs, it must generate at least an opportunity return to the owner's labor and management plus a return on equity capital commensurate with the anticipated risks. The elements of value-added (wages, interest, profits, taxes, land rents, depreciation) must be paid to input suppliers, to owners of noncontractual inputs, or to governments to keep the firm in operation. Under competitive market conditions in the long run, that firm would have *zero* willingness to pay for the water supply project that serves its customers, since all revenues must be allocated as input purchases or opportunity costs of owned inputs.

Considering further the public point of view (since water supply investments or bail-outs of water transfers are often proposed with public funds in mind), we might perform another thought experiment on willingness to pay, this time from the perspective of a fully-informed, representative taxpayer in the region affected by a water policy choice. While such a taxpayer might be willing to pay up to the value of the forgone water-related rents, would that taxpayer be willing to pay an amount including the entire wages and salaries of farm workers, the interest and opportunity costs on the private farmers' investments, and the opportunity costs of other noncontractual inputs to insure the water supply investment or to avoid a water rights sale? This is the implication of using value-added multipliers as measures of regional willingness to pay. However, that strong a conclusion would be doubtful, so the use of value-added multipliers for policy analysis for either increments or decrements of water supply should be avoided except in special cases.

To sum up, the economic multiplier effects of a water supply project, measured by value-added in secondary markets, do not normally represent a willingness to pay for water or, therefore, a national economic benefit of increments in water supply or a forgone benefit of decrements of water supply.

This analysis and conclusion, appropriate for evaluating water supply investments from a national perspective, may not hold for policies and issues calling for a short-run point of view. An example of such a case might be that of evaluating secondary economic impacts of droughts from the perspective of a sub-national region. Regional secondary costs occur during serious droughts, and corresponding offsetting regional gains seems doubtful. The conceptual framework for such cases needs to be better developed. Similarly, for the case of water transfers from low-valued uses to higher-valued uses, those inputs that are completely immobile—such as buildings or irrigation canals—represent a forgone real value that should be counted. Even here, the forgone productivity should be measured only by the undepreciated value of the asset, rather than by the equivalent annual cost as of the time of the initial investment.

In addition to the debate over the normative significance of value-added multipliers for the evaluation of water supply changes, there is a separate dispute over the empirical accuracy of such multipliers calculated from input-output models. This critique is particularly forceful when the multipliers are derived in a supply-driven form, rather than from demand-side changes, the purpose for which they were originally designed. (See Oosterhaven 1989 and the references cited therein.)

3.9.2 Finding a Producers' Water Value by Dividing Total Value of Product by Water Use

Although this method is rarely applied, some nonspecialists have proposed estimating a "value of water" by taking the total value of product and dividing by some measure of water use (withdrawal or consumption). For example, Omezzine et al. 1998 took this approach in studying water policy in the Sultanate of Oman. This tactic for measuring benefits of water in production is not strictly a residual method. It actually has little basis in microeconomic theory, but warrants brief mention and is most easily discussed in connection with the residual method. Where TVP_w and Q_w are used as before, the calculation takes the total value of product and divides it by the amount of water used to derive a new measure that can be denoted P''_w (the second prime distinguishing this measure from value added per unit water, P'_w):

$$P''_w = \frac{TVP_w}{Q_w} \tag{3-18}$$

Comparing equation 3-18 with equations 3-7 or 3-10, it is clear that 3-18 fails to subtract the value of *any* nonwater inputs from the total value product. In effect, it assigns the entire value of output to water. Put another way, this approach can be said to implicitly assign a zero shadow price to all purchased and owned inputs other than water. The formula thereby greatly overstates the correct welfare measure, the value marginal product, or the value of water-related rents. The necessary assumptions are both empirically and theoretically invalid, so this method must be deemed an unacceptable procedure for deriving a measure of benefits of water as a producers' good or for evaluating policy.

3.9.3 Distortions in Water Development Agencies' Procedural Manuals

As emphasized above, if an input that should be represented in the production function is omitted in the residual analysis, this will result in the contribution of that input being attributed to the residual claimant, thereby overstating the benefit assigned to that residual input (in this case, water). Nevertheless, the procedural manuals of some major water development agencies have historically recommended that crucial inputs be omitted from the calculation of residual water values. For example, U.S. Bureau of Reclamation, the primary federal agency in the United States involved in irrigation water development, for many years made no provision in its irrigation benefit calculations for the opportunity cost of labor or management inputs provided by the owner and household (Young 1978). While this approach might be acceptable in short-run (annual) private crop selection settings, it is inappropriate in long-run public investment contexts.

Gittinger (1982, *19*) writing for the World Bank in the broad context of evaluating agricultural investments, indicates that an opportunity interest on equity capital "is never separated and deducted from the gross total return because it is part of the return to the total capital available" in evaluating agricultural projects.

Bergman and Boussard's (1976, *59*) Organization for Economic Cooperation and Development (OECD) manual for irrigation evaluation went even further, recommending that social economic benefits be measured according to the regional economists' value-added concept critiqued above. Since value-added comprises several factor incomes other than rents attributable to water, the approach ignores the opportunity cost of such resources.

According to the model developed in equation 3-10, these recommended procedures assign a zero shadow price to one or more nonwater resources that are scarce and valuable to society. *Labor and capital input costs omitted from a residual analysis are treated as benefits rather than opportunity costs to society.* The estimated value of the residual claimant, water, is correspondingly increased (i.e. overestimated). More generally, the omission of any important input from the costing process can lead to drastic overstatement of the benefits to society, since the residual is normally a relatively small portion of the total revenue.

A further consequence is that systematic omission of opportunity costs of one or more resources in an evaluation of a class of proposed public expenditures for water leads to systematically biased results, thereby tending to favor water-related public investments over more valuable alternative private (and public) uses of scarce capital funds.

3.10 Concluding Evaluation of the Residual Method

Some of the principal advantages and limitations of the residual method are reviewed below. The comments are directed to both the basic residual method which aims at a point or single-valued estimate of water-related rents and the extensions via the change in net rent method and mathematical programming models designed to estimate input demand or value marginal product functions.

3.10.1 Advantages

The basic residual method with recommended techniques as sketched above yields a result that satisfies many needs for private and public evaluation of proposed water policies: a single surrogate shadow price or willingness to pay per unit of water that is comparable to and commensurate with prices observed for other goods and services in the economy and, when suitably adjusted for costs of water, an estimate that can be compared with estimates of costs or opportunity costs (per unit volume) of the policy proposal. The results are easily understood by nonspecialists and lay persons.

Another principal advantage of the basic residual method is its ease of application and its flexibility as a planning tool. The arithmetic and accounting principles seem simple to understand and are easy to perform, even for nonspecialists. Before the recent advent of more advanced production models and computing systems, the residual method represented about the maximum sophistication that could readily be implemented in practical planning situations. Particularly in developing countries, the agency staff charged with implementing applied water planning exercises (as opposed to university researchers with advanced training) seldom have the time, resources, and skills to attempt the more realistic but more theoretically and computationally demanding deductive methods.

A third valuable feature, shared with other more advanced deductive techniques, is the ability to estimate benefits not only for observed situations, but for hypothetical scenarios. Depending on the problem at hand, and subject to data availability, the analyst can estimate long-run or short-run, private or social, at-site or at-source values of water to producers. The inductive alternatives (usually market-based measurements) which rely on observations of past behavior under previously existing production, market, and policy scenarios, are often of limited applicability for studying hypothetical changes in water supply conditions, such as those resulting from public water supply investments or intersectoral reallocations.

In the agricultural sector, where the residual approach to water valuation finds its major application, suitable data is often readily available. Information on prices (or opportunity costs) together with estimates of typical total production and input use (usually on a per unit land basis) can in most countries usually be obtained from government or international donor agencies or university researchers working in the study area (although the quality of such data needs to be carefully scrutinized). As a preferable alternative, a survey of producers can be conducted in the region of interest. Given the availability of data, the residual approach is adaptable to evaluating the impacts on producers of a wide variety of proposed future policies or programs.

3.10.2 Limitations

Issues in the application of residual methods center on the assumptions of the product exhaustion theorem or the net rent model, and on the planning contexts in which they are implemented. The assumption of optimization by producers (equating incremental revenues with incremental costs) is likely to be reasonably approximated in most real-world circumstances. The constant returns to scale and the static equilibrium hypotheses, where firms are assumed to operate with perfect knowledge, seem to be more problematic. In a world where technologies, markets, and policies seldom stand still, results depending on these assumptions should be treated with appropriate caution. Because of the complexity of dynamic models, few practical water policy analysts have chosen to go beyond the static models for estimating future benefits.

Even a direct application of the basic residual method encounters a number of difficulties. One of the advantages listed above was the simplicity of the basic method. However, its transparency can be deceptive: application without understanding the strict assumptions of the approach and the applicable data can yield incorrect results. Analysts may inadequately account for costs of all inputs, thereby overestimating the "correct" value. Those adapting the technique to short-run private farm management decisions may mis-quantify or even omit inputs. Accurate pricing of inputs and outputs is a challenging task, particularly owned inputs. The use of regional economic models (such as the input-output model) for water valuation is prone to serious overestimation because of inadequate accounting for opportunity costs of nonwater inputs. Applying the residual approach to industrial manufacturing processes, while not often attempted, may require detailed surveys to develop the input and output coefficients and particularly to estimate opportunity costs of owned inputs.

The basic residual method and its extensions, in spite of their long history of use and apparent adaptability, simplicity, and flexibility for use in evaluating both *ex post* and *ex ante* policy alternatives, should be treated with appropriate caution. The methods must be applied with careful acknowledgment of the full theoretical apparatus and with relevant, accurate data. The methods are best adapted to cases like production of staple agricultural commodities, where the production process is simple, standardized, and stable over time, and water represents a significant contributor to the value of production. In agricultural enterprises where the production process is complex and risky—such as perishable crops—problems of adequately pricing owned inputs such as management, scarce production skills, and equity capital are more frequent and estimates of water-

related rents more subject to error. Manufacturing enterprises characterized by high capital requirements and experiencing rapid technological
changes, where water contributes a small portion of the value of output,
and where equity capital and other owned inputs account for a significant
fraction of output are the most difficult subjects for residual water valuation, and the method is of doubtful utility in such cases.

3.11 The Alternative Cost Method and Other Less-Used Deductive Techniques

Beside the residual method, there are a few less used deductive techniques
for valuing water in producers' uses. This section focuses on the alternative
cost method, but mentions the benefit transfer method.

3.11.1 The Alternative Cost Method

The alternative cost method, which can also be used for consumption goods,
is another deductive approach appropriate to evaluating water-related producers' benefits. The method is attractive under the assumption, valid only
in certain limited instances, that if a given project of specified output costs
less than the next-best public or private project which can achieve the same
output, then the cost of the next best project can be assigned as the gross
benefit to the public project under consideration. However, the analysis
must verify that the higher cost alternative would actually be constructed in
the absence of the project under consideration. Put another way, the effective demand must be established for the alternative product.

Water resource planners have employed the alternative cost method for
evaluating many types of benefits, including industrial, hydroelectric
power generation, and waste load dilution. When estimating a direct
demand or value marginal product schedule proves difficult because of a
lack of data or other reasons, the alternative cost method may provide a
solution. However, the method has its limitations and should be used only
when its applicability is assured. Herfindahl and Kneese (1974, *267–280*)
provide an authoritative exposition, illustrated with examples from cost–
benefit analysis applied to inland waterways navigation and water quality.

The alternative cost method can be understood as the principle that,
from a social accounting stance, maximum willingness to pay for a publicly
supplied good or service is not greater than the cost of providing that good
or service via some other process or technology. The alternative, which
may be produced from either the public or private sector, should be a substantially different means of producing the same output.

Consider a situation in which a private alternative to a public investment
can be identified. This might be a fossil fuel-powered electricity generating

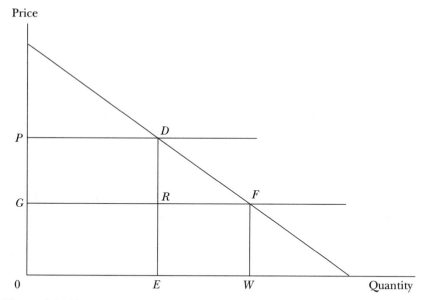

Figure 3-3. Alternative Cost Method of Evaluation

plant as an alternative to a proposed hydroelectric facility. Assume that the two alternatives provide the same service or commodity in equal amounts. In Figure 3-3, output level *E* is the amount that would be yielded by each of the alternatives. Further, let *P* and *G* identify, respectively, the costs of the private and the public alternative. (The approach is also applicable if both alternatives are publicly supplied.) For simplicity of exposition, costs are assumed constant. In this case, assume a completely inelastic demand for the output at *E*, so the issue is only one of comparative costs. Because *E* units of output are to be provided, no matter which alternative technology is selected, the problem is simply to provide the good or service at least cost. In Figure 3-3, gross benefit or willingness to pay is shown as the area bounded by *OEDP.* The net benefits are the difference between the costs of the two alternatives, being the *reduction in costs associated with the cheaper alternative:* namely the rectangle *PDRG.* If any cost saving is found, it can be interpreted as a net rent attributable to the water used by the less expensive alternative.

A more realistic case exists where a higher cost private alternative can be identified which would be implemented in the absence of the public alternative. If neither alternative must be built to a fixed scale, and if the demand schedule is not perfectly inelastic, then the optimum level of provision of the good or service is *W* in Figure 3-3. In this case, the demand function would need to be estimated between the points *D* and *F.* The benefit would be *PDFG,* because of the higher output demanded at lower cost.

The alternative cost method is easily misused and should be applied only with considerable caution. The main weakness is that some alternative can always be conceived which would be more expensive than the project being evaluated, thereby inevitably producing an estimate of cost savings and positive net benefits. Therefore, the alternative cost method must be supplemented by a study to confirm that the demand for the alternative is sufficient to justify the alternative expenditure, i.e. that the alternative under question is itself economically feasible.

Implementing the alternative cost method is not difficult in concept, although accurate, detailed empirical analysis typically requires considerable time and effort. In costing a long-lived capital investment, the method can be recognized as an application of discounted cash flow or investment analysis. The present values of costs of each alternative are calculated on the basis of a commensurate planning period, price level, and discount rate. Questions quite similar to those arising with the residual method must be addressed, including specifying the production function for each alternative, selecting the long-run or short-run context, accurately pricing other owned inputs, and carefully forecasting trends in technology and prices over the planning period for each of the alternative investments.

Some analysts have dismissed the alternative cost method as merely a form of cost-effectiveness study, which should be performed in the course of any competent economic evaluation and does not warrant special treatment as a separate method. That each proposed plan should be tested to assure that it is the least-cost alternative is of course undeniable. However, the alternative cost method can play a useful additional role in measuring benefits of water-related projects and programs, particularly for the assessment of transfers of water between water use sectors.

The alternative cost approach provides a tool for estimating a shadow price of certain unpriced benefits that, when combined with residual imputation calculations, is advantageous for imputing benefits of water use in hydroelectric power and waste load dilution. In the hydroelectric power case, any cost saving from the water-intensive hydropower alternative can be imputed as the rent or value of water in that use. (See Chapter 6 for a case example.)

Because of its computational demands, one would expect this process to be formalized for solution within the framework of optimization modeling. One of the few examples in the context of water planning is Stone and Whittington's (1984) analysis. They developed an elaborate cost-minimizing optimization model of electricity generation representing a region in southern Poland, focusing on the effect of varying costs of alternative cooling technologies on the optimal annual pattern of water withdrawals. In their study, the main determinant of water demand was the configuration of the cooling system. Cooling water withdrawals would depend on river flows, temperature, standards regulating heat discharges back to the river, and potential charges for water withdrawals. Alternative cooling system specifications would be optimal under alternative hypothesized water charges, permitting the tracing out of a demand function for cooling water.

3.11.2 Benefit Transfer Methods

Benefit transfer refers to a class of procedures by which benefit assessments or demand functions estimated for one or more sites or policy proposals are employed to assign benefits or value to other sites or policy proposals. The main goal of benefit transfer is to find demand estimates for situations where limitations on time, resources, and perhaps technical skills do not permit a full empirical analysis. Benefit transfer takes value or demand parameter estimates from a "study site" and shifts them to a "policy site," the latter being the situation for which benefits are needed. Where sites differ in location, environmental attributes, and nature of the user population, the study site estimates may be adjusted to better reflect the conditions anticipated at the policy site. This class of methods which employ data from secondary sources may include expert opinions, generalized estimates provided in tables developed by relevant government agencies, or more systematic methods for statistical winnowing of general conclusions from earlier studies of similar relationships.

Benefit transfer methods have received most attention in connection with evaluating proposed improvements in environmental or recreational quality (Florax et al. 2002). However, they are also employed in other circumstances, such as estimating demand functions for withdrawal uses of water in river basin models. For example, (although neither team used the term benefit transfer), Vaux and Howitt (1984) and Booker and Young (1994) applied this approach by drawing on estimates of price elasticities of demand for municipal and industrial water uses from other published sources to estimate the industrial demand for water in other study regions. Together with an observed water charge and corresponding water use data from the study area, the process involved extending the demand curve from the known price–quantity point by drawing on the transferred elasticity estimate and an assumption about the form of the demand function. The extended demand function was then used to derive corresponding at-source (raw water) values for intersectoral water allocation comparisons in regional water allocation modeling exercises. (See Chapter 7 for a municipal case example.) Because the benefit transfer methods have found most use in consumer demand studies, further discussion of the method is reserved for Chapter 4.

3.12 Valuing Producers' Water Using Inductive Techniques

Besides the deductive techniques, a number of inductive techniques are used to estimate the value of water and water quality. Statistically estimating values of water as private producers' goods deals with the same problem as deductive techniques: to find or approximate a value marginal product function or a measure of producers' rents for various quantities of the water resource in specific uses. These analyses are typically based on applying statistical methods to empirical observations of actual or reported water user behavior or of water and water-related markets. The observations may come from a variety of sources: reports from government agencies, a sample of price–quantity observations on producers' transactions in water or land markets, or responses to survey questionnaires.

In the producers' case, inductive techniques are used less than deductive techniques for valuing water. The primary reason is perhaps that in the absence of markets to register values, it is difficult and costly to find adequate data. Another may be the skills in statistical and econometric analysis required for such analyses. Finally, using observed past behavior is less flexible than constructing models for evaluating benefits of proposed policies.

Several approaches to valuing water as a producers' good via inductive methods are in use:

- Production functions have been estimated statistically (via regression techniques) from primary data (surveys) or secondary data (such as censuses or other government reports) and demand functions derived.
- The most attractive approach is the direct statistical analysis of actual transactions in water rights between willing buyers and willing sellers in free markets. But, in practice, this approach is of limited applicability because of the sparsity of markets where unfettered supply and demand come into play, as well as the scarcity of carefully-collected data where water market transactions do exist. It is also possible to analyze purchases from water utility suppliers (which are more or less monopolies) by buyers facing a fixed price. When a cross section differing in the cost of water and other measurable factors can be obtained, a demand curve can be inferred by advanced statistical analysis. This method has been exploited in study of industrial, commercial, and residential water demands.
- The hedonic property value method analyzes transactions (usually for agricultural real estate) in which water quality or water supply differs across transactions. The contribution of water rights to the sale price can be isolated via statistical analysis.

3.12.1 Production Functions and Derived Demand Functions

Although these approaches are infrequently used, production and demand functions are sometimes fitted to production data with econometric techniques as a basis for estimating the value of water.

A production function of the general form of:

$$Y = f(M, H, L, K, W)$$

where *M* is materials; *H* is labor; *L* is natural resources and land; *K* is capital; and *W* is water) can be fit to empirical data with econometric techniques. Value marginal product functions can then be derived to provide measures of water demand and hence value. The approach has mainly been used to study agricultural water productivity. Water represents a small element of costs in industrial enterprises, and data are hard to obtain, so few nonagricultural estimates of water value via the econometric production function approach have come to the writer's attention. One exception is a study of Chinese industries by Wang and Lall (2002). (See Chapter 6.)

Empirical production functions for agricultural crops where water is an explicit input can be placed in three categories. First, controlled crop experiments performed by agronomists (with or without collaboration with economists) are the most common source of data. Probably the most extensive study is that by Hexem and Heady (1978), who report on an elaborate series of crop experiments that studied the effects of varying irrigation water application levels on yields of several important crops. The experiments were conducted at several localities in the western United States, so climate and soils differed among the experiments. Most other production practices and input levels are typically held constant in such experiments, although fertilizer levels (e.g. nitrogen, phosphorus) may sometimes be varied. Even more complex models examine the effect of timing on crop yields. The high cost of experiments and the restrained interest of agronomists in the economists' concept of the production function have limited the approach to a few examples.

Second, observations from interview surveys emphasizing use of water and other inputs and production have also been used as data for econometric agricultural production function analysis. Farmers in a random sample are typically asked to recall their input quantities and costs (including water) and revenue levels for a previous cropping season. Such studies usually are performed for multiple crops, but individual crops are sometimes studied. Survey responses are fitted to hypothesized production function forms with econometric methods to yield marginal values of water (and other inputs). Frequently the Cobb-Douglas or log-log equation is the chosen form. Such studies must acquire data covering a wide range of water applications to obtain a suitable measure of the value marginal product of water. Examples from sample surveys of irrigated crop farms from Pakistan are described in Chapter 5.

A third category of water input demand studies directly investigates the demand relationship (quantity taken as a function of price) rather than deriving a value marginal product from the production function. A model for producers' demand (denoted Q_w) for water can be expressed as:

$$Q_w = f(P_w, P_a, \boldsymbol{P_i}, X, \boldsymbol{S})$$

where P_w and P_a represent the price of water from the given system and from an alternative source; P_i represents a vector of prices of inputs (capital, labor, and materials); X stands for the quantity of output to be produced and S represents a vector of other factors, such as technology and climate. (See Renzetti 2002a or Spulber and Sabbaghi 1998 for more complete theoretical developments.) The main drawbacks of this approach are the cost of data and the wide variation in production technologies among industries. Surveys of representative firms within an industry have been occasionally reported, but need large, expensive samples to implement statistically. Considering econometric analysis of data from secondary (published) sources, Renzetti (1992) initiated a research program on Canadian manufacturing industries that represents perhaps the most extensive body of econometric studies of industrial water demand. (See also Renzetti 2002a and 2002b).

3.12.2 Direct Observation of Water Markets

Willing buyer-willing seller transactions involving intersectoral exchange of money for water rights are relatively uncommon in most of the world. This may be mainly because of the general lack of both market rules and publicly sanctioned property rights necessary for market transactions, or a dearth of situations where the willingness to pay in nonagricultural uses exceeds the cost of completing transactions, including checking for and possibly compensating for third-party effects of transfers (Young 1986). However, water rights transactions are increasingly occurring, particularly in the arid and semiarid western United States, where transferable water rights allow market transfers of water from agricultural uses to meet growing urban demands. For several southwestern states, Saliba and Bush (1987) examine a series of cases, describing how water market institutions function and identifying trends in prices. Easter et al. (1998) report examples of water rights markets elsewhere in the world. Since water markets almost always involve agricultural rather than industrial water, the valuation of irrigation water from various forms of transactions and exchanges is mainly discussed in Chapter 5. However, an introduction is provided here.

Lease Markets for Water Rights as a Source of Water Values. Lease (or rental) markets for water, both official and informal, are observed among agricultural water users in many parts of the world (Easter and Hearne 1995). Lease markets serve to exchange rights for a limited period, ranging from one irrigation cycle to a season. Most lease markets are among agricultural water users, typically among neighbors and where transactions costs and conveyance expenses are not large. However, some examples of intersectoral leases can be identified. In the western United States, some urban water supply agencies—anticipating rapid future growth in water demand—have purchased an inventory of perpetual water rights larger than currently needed under typical water supply conditions, and annually lease their excess supplies back to the agricultural sector. Increasing interest is also found regarding the opposite possibility of urban water users arranging to lease irrigation water rights via dry-year options from agricultural interests during occasional drought periods.

Lease prices can be characterized as mainly short-run, private, at-site, per period values. Although some leases may run for longer than one year, the pricing is usually in annual terms, so the value is a per period price. The prices observed typically reflect demand in the Marshallian short-run sense, as the participants do not have the opportunity to adjust fixed inputs. Lease market prices reflect the private perspective rather than the public point of view (which ignores subsidies or other market interventions). As to the difference between at-site and at-source measures of value, lease prices appear to generally represent an at-site value, because the buyer typically does not have to pay the charges for providing water assessed by the water supply agency, costs the seller normally must pay to maintain a water right. This practice is likely due to the fact that the seller—the water right owner—will have paid the annual assessment costs prior to deciding to offer water for lease. Of course, lease transactions could reflect at-source considerations, with the understanding that the buyer would pay the delivery charges. Observed water lease rates tend to vary widely with current rainfall and water supply, so, while providing interesting observations on short-run private demand and supply for irrigation water, in the absence of longer time series of observations they may be of limited value for long-term public planning purposes.

Observed Market Prices for Perpetual Water Rights. With markets for perpetual water rights increasingly seen (Saliba and Bush 1987), some time-series data on prices for perpetual water rights are available for analysis. As are lease rates, prices for perpetual water rights reflect the private (rather than social) accounting stance, but they differ on other grounds. They are long-run, at-source values, because buyers and sellers presumably account for all production, processing, and conveyance costs in their calculations of willingness to pay and to sell. Unlike lease rates, transactions for perpetual water rights are capitalized values, reflecting the anticipated present value of future net benefits. Observation of prices on markets for perpetual water rights can be regarded as a more appropriate basis than rental rates for estimating values in long-run planning, but caution is still required.

The value conventionally used in water planning and policy analysis is an annual benefit measure. An initial step is to convert market values for perpetual water rights into estimated annual net rents. The observed price for a perpetual water right is for a capital asset. Applying a conventional model of asset valuation, an annual value can be obtained by converting the asset price to equivalent annual value terms. The analyst selects a capitalization formula to convert the water right price, along with the appropriate planning period and interest rate.

Here I digress to describe some of the basic economic models of capital asset valuation. The conventional approach, via what are sometimes termed the "capitalization of income" models, relate the market price of a capital asset to its expected future stream of net income. Where water rights can be readily marketed in a willing buyer-willing seller setting, a share of a water right is an asset essentially like a share of stock in a publicly traded corporation. Expenditures to purchase a water right are an investment made at present with the anticipation that income will be received from the asset in the future.

The value of the asset (e.g. a water right) is the willingness of a buyer to pay for the asset. In keeping with capital asset pricing theory, this price is linked to the future stream of income or payments the asset is expected to yield. However, because of the time value of money, income received at present is worth more than income received in the future. The interest or discount rate (denoted r) reflects the tradeoff buyers make to convert future income to value at present, or the rate at which the market discounts future income (Barry et al. 1995). The present value of net returns (*PVNR*) represents the sum of all future income earned, each year's expected net income (denoted A_i) properly discounted to reflect the time value of money. In symbols:

$$PVNR = \frac{A_1}{1+r_1} + \frac{A_2}{(1+r_2)^2} + \frac{A_3}{(1+r_3)^3} + ... + \frac{A_t}{(1+r_t)^t} \qquad (3\text{-}19)$$

Because of the difficulty of empirically implementing a formula such as equation 3-19, economic analysts often follow a streamlining convention, one which has frequently been used by real property appraisers. For simplicity, assume a constant interest rate and a constant annual net income or rental value, each holding over a very long planning period (approaching infinity). Under such assumptions, the present value formula in equation 3-19 reduces to the expression:

$$V = \frac{A}{r} \qquad (3\text{-}20)$$

where V is the present value of a stream of equal annual values A capitalized at a constant interest rate r (Barry et al. 1995). If V is the observed market price of a water right and r is known, the expression can be solved for A, the unknown annual value. The choice of interest rate is key in this derivation; the private market rate of interest which determines V may be influenced by expectations of inflation or by government policies which affect real interest rates. Note that the simple formula represented in equation 3-20 permits an easy mental calculation of the annual income associated with any given asset value and interest rate. For example, if $r = 0.05$, then $A = 0.05V$, or $V = 20A$.

The static world assumed by equation 3-20 may not be realistic. The observed sales prices (V) may also reflect anticipated appreciation due to growing demands from other use sectors. Therefore, although it may be plausible to accept that the real value of water in agricultural uses is stable over time, in the many cases where nonagricultural demands for water rights are growing, assuming that the annual value (A) is constant over a long planning period may not reflect actual expectations of market participants.

In the case where investors expect returns to grow, an adjustment to equation 3-20 can model the conversion (which could arise from expected growth in either income or capital gains, e.g. from growth in the value of water rights). If market participants expect annual returns to grow at some constant percentage rate (g), and if the assumption of a constant rate of discount r is maintained, then the value of the asset can be shown to be (Barry et al. 1995):

$$V = \frac{A}{r - g} \tag{3-21}$$

If annual incomes are expected to grow even minimally, the corresponding value of the capital asset is substantially affected. Conversely, a derived annual value is greatly changed by a small hypothesized annual increment in income. Extending the above example, now using equation 3-21, leave $r = 0.05$ and assume $g = 0.01$; then $r - g = .04$ and $V = 25A$. Thus, an expectation of only a 1% growth rate in annual income can increase the capital value by 25%.

The market value of private rights to water may in fact reflect expectations of increasing values of future income streams. These changes may be due to broad inflationary forces in the national economy. Or they may be due to regional conditions such as increasing real values of water due to growth in urban demands. Michelsen (1994) describes historical variations in real water right prices for one of the best-known water rights markets— that operating in the Northern Colorado Water Conservancy District in the western United States. The semi-arid area, initially settled by farmers, has experienced a relatively rapid rate of nonagricultural economic and population growth for the past several decades. With all water supplies claimed for one or another offstream use, water rights sales mostly go from agricultural water users to urban water agencies. *Real* prices for perpetual water rights were seen to have increased from about US$1,000 per annual acre-foot (1,233 cubic meters) to about US$6,000 in the decade from approximately 1970 to 1980, but by 1985 had fallen back almost to the real 1970 level. Although there were steady changes in both urban and agricultural demands (and these particular water rights are valuable for their reliability), the changes in underlying demand factors do not appear to be extreme enough to account for this wide fluctuation, at least not using as simple a model as represented by equation 3-21. (However, interest rates were rising sharply during that time.) This impressive price movement appeared to repeat itself at the end of the 1990s. Water right prices in the Conservancy District again increased six-fold from 1995 to late 2000, paralleling the behavior of financial markets elsewhere and likely reflecting sharply falling interest rates plus a record period of drought.

Such patterns of highly variable capital asset prices are similar to those observed in other speculative asset markets. An example is the "bubble" market for common stocks associated with anticipated profit growth from improved technologies in computers, telecommunications, and the Internet in the late 1990s. These fluctuations in capital asset prices are partly due to apparent fundamental factors, such as anticipated increases in corporate earnings and declining interest rates. However, capital asset markets seem to behave at times as if participants are reacting to prior price changes for the asset in question, rather than to the underlying fundamental expectations of future annual incomes. Proponents of the emerging field of behavioral finance (Schleifer 2000, Chapter 6) call this type of asset market behavior "positive feedback trading." Positive feedback traders buy assets following price rises and sell following price declines. This behavior tends to for a time accelerate whatever is the prevailing short-term trend. However, as asset prices depart too far from the basic worth of the asset—as measured by the expected actual dividend or income streams—these short-term trends are eventually reversed. The evidence suggests that sooner or later enough investors consider the underlying fundamentals. Positive feedback trading leads to a range of asset price fluctuations that is much wider than information on income and interest rate expectations would warrant.

Michelsen et al. (2000) employ advanced econometric techniques to explain the extremely wide historical variations observed in real prices for rights to Northern Colorado Water Conservation District water. They hypothesize that the price fluctuations can be explained by a two-equation rational expectations model (of the type originally developed for macroeconomic analysis of business cycles). Their model incorporates historical data into a distributed lag structure with future-value expectations of sale values to account for the speculative pressures. The model also includes more conventional underlying factors reflecting demand for this type of capital asset, such as regional income, housing starts, and interest rates. The econometric analysis yields a very good statistical fit, confirming that water rights prices in this region, once a trend is set in motion, tend to continue the trend, then accelerate and eventually peak, and then cycle the other direction. However, in trying to use such a data series to estimate the future social value of water supplies for urban uses or for forgone benefits in agriculture, it is not clear just what point in the cycle to choose, or how representative any choice selected at a random point in time would be.

When market prices for water rights are used in social cost–benefit analysis, the water right markets may be distorted by public intervention such as agricultural policies designed to influence commodity prices. When, as has been the case in the United States and many other developed countries, crop prices are supported by government programs, agricultural water right prices will likely overstate the social value of irrigation water. As an example, consider the production of cotton, the major irrigated crop in central Arizona. There is an active market for crop land in the region, and land prices have increased steadily during the 1990s. However, recent estimates (Teegerstrom and Husman 1999) indicate that without federal subsidies, net returns to owned inputs and management in cotton production in central Arizona would be minimal and perhaps negative, and therefore social returns to irrigation water would also be small to negative.

Although prices observed for actual transactions in perpetual water rights, where available, will provide important market evidence on the economic value of water, the limited number of actual markets and the wide fluctuations in asset prices suggest caution in applying the observed water prices for public planning purposes in the producers' context.

3.12.3 The Hedonic Property Value Method for Water as a Producers' Good

Another inductive technique occasionally used for inferring producers' valuation of water is called *hedonic property valuation* (a case of the more general *hedonic pricing model*). This method, a type of revealed preference approach, applies to situations in which observations of market transactions can provide data that can be used to indirectly measure willingness to pay for changes in water supply or environmental quality.

General Approach. Hedonic pricing methods were developed to analyze markets for goods with several attributes that are recognized by purchasers but cannot be unbundled when purchasing the good. This approach assumes that the price of some marketed good is a function of its characteristics, and an implicit price exists for each of the characteristics. Examples of characteristics identifiable by market participants are supply or quality of water associated with a marketable productive asset such as land. The method posits that an increment in price due to an increase in any characteristic will equal the buyer's marginal willingness to pay for the characteristic, as well as the sellers' marginal cost of producing the characteristic. When buyers and sellers have time to adjust their responses, the equilibrium marginal hedonic price equals the marginal value to buyers and the marginal forgone benefit to sellers. From a sample of similar marketed goods, an implicit price exists which reflects the value of the different characteristics of that good. The contribution of alternative characteristics can then be identified with statistical techniques.

Typical sources of data are observations of real property transactions which include implicit or explicit rights to water supply. In the quality dimension, the observations might represent exposure to various qualities of water as part of the bundle of property attributes being sold. Buyers and sellers must be able to recognize the actual physical differences in the level of characteristics to be valued. Hedonic property value methods are econometric means of isolating the contribution of the water supply or quality differences to the total price of the real property.

In natural resource and environmental economics, hedonic property value methods have been used mostly in the case of measuring consumers' valuations of public environmental amenities (such as air quality), but also in a few producers' goods situations, all in agricultural contexts; they will be discussed in more detail in Section 5.4.3. Palmquist (1989) developed a conceptual model of the farm land rental market that is suitable for applying the hedonic property value method to the valuing of water supply or quality for farm producers. See Freeman (2003) or Taylor (2003) for recent concise general discussions of the theory and econometrics of applying the hedonic property value method.

Hedonic estimates yield an at-source rather than an at-site value. The expected costs of water, as a charge for receiving surface water (typically supplied by a government agency or a nonprofit cooperative organization) or as the private cost of pumping groundwater, are assumed accounted for in the price negotiations of the rational, fully informed buyer and seller of land. Hence, the estimated marginal contribution of irrigation water yielded by a hedonic property value study will be a "cost-adjusted value," which will be less than the standard at-site measure of water-related rents. The estimated net income converted into land values by land market participants will be the expected rents *net* of the estimated costs of bringing water to the point of use. This concept can be represented by taking equation 3-7 (or equivalently 3-10) and subtracting the costs of delivering water to the property. Conversely, to estimate an at-site value from one derived by the hedonic property value method, the analyst must add an estimate of the cost of water to the producer.

In a producer-based hedonic valuation the initial estimate is a capitalized asset value rather than a per-period value. The hedonic property value method measures the implicit asset price of the characteristic; to convert to an annual value requires realistic assumptions regarding interest rates and planning period.

Of course, a valid data set reflecting enough variation in the characteristic of interest must be obtained. Further, the market participants must be able to recognize differences in the environmental characteristic of interest. If, in the market for land parcels, transactions are infrequent or adjustments to new equilibria are slow, then the derived implicit prices may not accurately measure producers' willingness to pay.

In its favor, the hedonic pricing method is based in actual conduct of market participants, providing reasonable assurance that the valuations are connected to actual economic behavior. This is not attainable using the deductive techniques discussed earlier. However, the hedonic study of a natural experiment or a policy initiative characterized by variations in the supply or quality of water may apply to the situation represented by the database, but not to alternative policy proposals applicable to other places or times. For example, hedonic valuations of irrigation water measured under normal conditions would provide serious understatement of short-run damages from a drought. In cases characterized by public intervention in product markets (often true of agriculture commodities) a social value is not obtainable from hedonic techniques. Also, real property represents a capital asset, and the real estate markets studied with hedonic methods are themselves subject to fluctuation with changing macroeconomic policies and their effects on such factors as interest rates and the general price level. Outside the developed nations, real property markets may not function well enough or data may not be available to accurately distinguish water rights or water quality benefits. The writer is aware of few formal applications of hedonic methods to developing country water values, and none in a producers' good context. In spite of these limitations, hedonic valuation in the producers' context can provide useful evidence of how the market participants actually value water, evidence that can be used to assess the reliability of results derived from the more flexible deductive methods.

3.13 Concluding Comments on Valuation in Producers' Uses

Producers' good types of water uses represent the largest offstream uses of water in the world. The largest single consumptive use class is irrigation of agricultural crops; industrial uses represent another large portion of withdrawals, but a lesser, though still significant amount of consumptive uses. Demands in these sectors continue to grow. Thus, producers' uses of water are the primary competitors for water versus growing consumers demands, such as residential uses and environmental public goods.

Deductive Versus Inductive Methods. Deductive approaches deduce benefit measures from constructed models of producer behavior, usually assuming profit maximization. They use methods ranging from simple accounting budgets to complex optimization models of firm behavior. In contrast, inductive techniques rely on observed economic behavior, employing statistical (usually regression) methods to fit data to models of producer behavior.

Deductive models have advantages of simplicity, flexibility, and the ability to analyze hypothesized future policy options. They can, in principle, incorporate alternative assumptions about prices, interest rates, and production technology, permitting tests of the influence of assumptions about unknown future conditions on the results of the analysis. However, the simplicity brings with it some drawbacks. The residual method, on which most of the deductive strategies of water valuation are based, estimates value by deducting costs from predicted revenues. Omitting costs of some inputs, leading to overestimates of benefits, is a frequent trap for the uninitiated. Some input elements, such as those owned by the firm (e.g. risk-bearing, management, and entrepreneurial capacity) are not priced on markets, but are themselves residuals, so finding appropriate prices is at best complicated, and a certain degree of arbitrariness is difficult to avoid. A general conclusion is that the more complex the firm and the smaller the role that water plays in the production process, the more prone to error and the less applicable will be deductive techniques. Hence, the residual and related approaches are best suited to simple agricultural production, and industrial uses may not be sufficiently accurate. Although they may seem simple to use, deductive techniques require appropriate data, familiarity with the conceptual model of the firm, and quantitative skills. More advanced mathematical programming procedures require special training.

Inductive techniques for determining producer benefits are preferred by many analysts, being based on observations of behavior in actual production situations. Hedonic price analysis uses data on real estate market transactions, while production function analyses may be based on actual experimental data, interview surveys, or secondary reports from government agencies. They can be used to analyze previous policies and natural experiments in some cases. But evaluations of hypothetical policies may involve assumptions that do not reflect the available historical observations.

There are various reasons that even for a particular site and production process, the empirically estimated value of water can vary according to the policy issue:

- Much of the literature on producers' water valuation takes an implicit short-run perspective, but most policy decisions (such as investment in water supply or reallocation among competing uses) call for a long-run perspective.
- Water may be best regarded as a fully variable input or as a specialized fixed input in production. For the former (most often observed for industrial water users) a value marginal product (VMP) model of welfare change best fits the situation. Where water is a specialized input in

inelastic supply, as often occurs in agriculture or hydroelectric power generation, a residual rent model is more appropriate.

- An at-site value or at-source value may be needed. An at-site value of water is frequently used in investment evaluations, to be compared with costs of supply to the site. The at-source value of water represents a derived demand less than at-site value by any costs of capture, transport and treatment enabling it to be put to use by users. At-source values are those calculated for evaluations of intersectoral allocation proposals, so that values of each sector are comparable in place, form, and time dimensions.
- Analysts must decide whether the prices used in the analysis should be private prices or the accounting stance is such that public prices are appropriate.

CHAPTER

4

Applied Methods of Valuation of Water as Environmental Public Goods

This chapter takes up methods for valuing water-related environmental public goods, where the good in question is nonrival and nonexclusive. Where water yields a public good, and neither diversion for production nor prices for private purchases exist, special data collection and demand evaluation methods must be adopted. These instances are often associated with both use and nonuse (or passive) values for outdoor recreation, aesthetic enjoyment of water in its natural surroundings, water quality improvement, and other environmental benefits.

Several methods for measuring benefits of environmentally-related water uses are commonly employed. *Revealed preference* methods rely on actual expenditure choices for environmentally-related private goods made by consumers from which their preferences can be deduced via statistical analysis. *Expressed preference* (or *stated preference*) methods involve asking people directly about the values placed on proposed or hypothetical improvements or reductions in environmental services. In the terminology introduced in Chapter 2, both approaches are inductive, in that they use statistical or econometric methods to infer willingness to pay for environmental services from behavioral observations or consumer surveys. *Benefit transfer* is often used where limited study resources prevent application of the other methods. It uses benefit or value estimates derived from earlier similar studies to provide estimates for new cases. *Meta-analysis*, a statistical technique for studying previous research results, can be also be used as a basis for benefit transfer.

4.1 Revealed Preference Methods for Environmental Valuation

Revealed preference methods infer net willingness to pay (WTP) for a non-marketed environmental benefit from differences in expenditures on some private good. When expenditures on a private good vary with levels of environmental amenities, under certain conditions a valuation of the environmental amenity can be derived. For example, if the potential use of water-based recreational services influences the demand for any marketed commodity, purchasing behavior related to the marketed commodity can be analyzed to derive information on the preferences and willingness to pay for the environmental amenity. (See Bockstael and McConnell 1999 for a valuable restatement and evaluation of the welfare theory underlying revealed preference models.)

Several conditions must be met for revealed preference methods to be successful:

- Changes in the level of some good or service will influence some observable behavior. For example, it might be expected that the number of recreational visits to a body of water—a steam, lake, or reservoir—would vary with the flows in the stream or levels of the lake, in which case values of recreational demand might be inferred. However, changes in some valued environmental amenities, such as a reduction in population of an endangered fish, might not prompt any observable behavior changes.
- The analysis rests on paired observations of levels of the environmental attribute and human behavior, often expressed as prices.
- The behavioral alterations are in fact responses to changes in the environmental good and not reactions to other stimuli. This condition is often untestable because data on other motives is seldom available.
- The private good is nonessential, i.e. there is a "choke price"—which can be very large—a point at which the demand for the good becomes zero.

Put more formally, application of the revealed preference approach requires that the environmental good and the private good must be *weak complements* (Mäler 1985; Bockstael and McConnell 1999). This means that whenever the consumption of the private commodity is zero, the marginal utility received from the public good must also be zero. Consider a consumer whose utility depends on the consumption of an environmental attribute (such as the surface level of a body of water) denoted w plus a set of n private market goods (y_i; $i = 1,2,...n$). That consumer's utility function can be written:

$$u = u(w, y_1, ..., y_n) \qquad (4\text{-}1)$$

If a commodity y_1 can be identified such that u is independent of w if that commodity (y_1) is not consumed, then y_1 and w are said to be weak complements. Weak complementarity can be written as:

$$u_w \, (w, 0, y_2, \ldots, y_n) = 0 \tag{4-2}$$

where u_w refers to marginal utility with respect to w. In the above expression, w and y_1 are weak complements; if y_1 is not consumed, the marginal utility of w is zero. For example, a recreationist will not ordinarily assign any value to changes in the water level in a reservoir if the cost of travel is too high for them to visit the reservoir.

Two principal types of revealed preference methods are applicable to environmental valuation. One is the group of recreational demand models, exemplified mainly by the *travel cost* method, which infers the value of a recreational site from data on the varying expenditures incurred by consumers to travel to the site. The other is the *hedonic property value* model, which usually measures the difference between real property prices (usually residential housing) exhibiting varying environmental qualities to infer value placed on improved environmental quality. The principal attraction of the revealed preference approaches is that they reflect actual consumer choices. Most economists believe that, when possible, this is preferable to methods which rely on responses to questions regarding hypothetical scenarios. However, for evaluating policies whose outcomes are yet to be observed, actual past behavior may be of limited relevance.

4.2 Travel Cost Methods

The environmental economics literature typically calls approaches employing the cost of travel or access to a recreation site as a measure of price *travel cost* methods (TCMs). (Many other models outside of environmental economics—for example, the transportation economics literature on commuting to work—employ cost of travel in demand studies.) The label is sometimes further qualified as *travel cost models of recreational demand.* Travel cost models are the most fully developed and widely used examples of revealed preference methods of valuing nonmarketed environmental commodities. Ward and Beal (2000) present a complete and accessible treatment of the assumptions, procedures, and limitations of the approach.

4.2.1 The Continuous Travel Cost Method

The original travel cost method was developed to measure demand for annual visits to outdoor recreational sites. It has been widely applied where no fee or only a nominal fee is charged, and that fee is the same to all visitors at all times. Under such conditions, a normal demand curve is not derivable solely from data on the number of site visits.

The travel cost method originated with a letter sent by the eminent economist Harold Hotelling to the U.S. National Park Service in 1947 (reproduced in Ward and Beal 2000, *217–18*). Hotelling observed that the absence of variation in fees for recreational and amenity sites precludes estimating directly the demand for such sites. However, he pointed out that if the cost of travel to a recreational site varies widely among consumers, and if these consumers respond to higher travel costs in the same way that they would respond to higher entrance fees, a demand schedule for recreation at the site can be derived from an analysis of the costs of travel. From this demand schedule, a measure of consumer surplus enjoyed by recreationists could be derived. Freeman (2003) provides a characteristically rigorous discussion of the conceptual foundations of the travel cost method, while Parsons (2003) introduces applications.

In a travel cost model, two alternative measures of recreational demand are commonly employed. The *individual* travel cost method uses the annual number of visits *per person* to the recreation site. The *zonal* travel cost method measures quantity as the annual number of trips *per capita* from a specified geographic zone. Zones are defined by dividing the area around the site so that the average cost of travel is the same for each zone. This may be accomplished on the basis of a straight-line distance from the site so that the zones are a series of concentric rings extending away from the site, or the zones can be defined by road distances or travel times. Counties or other political subdivisions are often convenient zones because data on population is more readily available. In either case, the number of visits is assumed to be influenced by the cost and time of travel to the site, as well as other factors, including the quality of the recreational site, the amount of discretionary time available to the recreationist, income, opportunity cost of time (as reflected in the wage rate or some fraction thereof), and the availability of substitute sites. In the case of water, the site quality variable may represent water quality or quantity. For example, in white-water boating, the rate of flow (in cubic feet or cubic meters per second) is an important component of the value of the site and of the recreational experience. This approach has mainly been used to estimate consumer surplus for access to a specific recreational site, and to determine benefits associated with developing or maintaining such a site.

The Basic Travel Cost Model. Consider first the basic or simple travel cost model (Freeman 2003, *419–32*). The travel cost approach assumes, as noted above, that recreationist behavior related to increasing costs of travel corresponds to the changes in demand for the activity which would occur if prices changed.

The basic model also assumes that recreationists derive no utility or disutility from the time spent journeying to the site. The existence of utilities or disutilities from travel would bias the estimates of costs; for example, net demand for a site would be overestimated if enjoyment were obtained from driving to the site, such as through attractive countryside.

Third, it assumes that no alternative recreation sites are available, and that there is no purpose for the trip other than visiting the site. Should the trip involve other sites or any nonrecreational (e.g. family- or employment-related) purposes, part of the travel cost would need to be attributed to them.

Fourth, for any individual, all visits are assumed to involve the same amount of time on the site. This condition makes it possible to measure usage of the site as a scalar value: the number of visits. The cost of a visit can thus be treated as a constant for the individual recreationist.

Fifth, it is assumed that part of the cost of travel is the opportunity cost of the recreationists' time. Travel cost analysts often further presume that the wage rate or some fraction thereof is the relevant measure of that opportunity cost.

Given these assumptions, data on costs and time of travel to the site and other relevant characteristics of the recreationist population can be collected from a sample of visitors to the study site. Statistical analysis can then yield a demand curve for the recreational experience at that site. Note that the costs of travel themselves are not a measure of the site value; those costs are used only to infer the desired consumer surplus measure.

This basic travel cost model may be represented by a *trip generating function*:

$$Trips_i = \beta_0 + \beta_1 (TC_i) + \beta_2 (TravTime_i) + \ldots + \beta_n (X_{ni}) + \varepsilon \qquad (4\text{-}3)$$

where $Trips_i$ represents the trips per year (visit rate) person i takes to the site, TC_i is the round trip cost of travel to the site from the residence of individual i, $TravTime_i$ is the time required from the residence of individual i to the site; X represents a vector of socioeconomic characteristics (e.g. income, education, age) of the population of recreationists, ε_i is an error term and the β are parameters to be estimated.

Implementing the Basic Travel Cost Model. To derive a measure of consumer surplus or economic benefit via the travel cost analysis calls for three basic steps:

1. Assemble an adequate data base. The distance traveled must ordinarily be obtained on-site from a sample of recreationists, preferably from actual interviews. An alternative, less desirable source of travel data might be from addresses or postal codes found on permits to visit the site. The other socioeconomic data may also be obtained directly from the recreationist population or, if necessary, estimated from secondary published sources. All the requirements of collecting an accurate data base—defining the population; specifying the sampling procedure,

including setting the size of the sample; designing the questionnaire; training observers; and tabulating data—must be carefully observed. (See, for example, Salant and Dillman 1994; Rea and Parker 1997.)

2. Estimate by multiple regression the individual recreationist's demand for the resource. An equation such as 4-3 relating annual trips per zone of origin or per individual to the cost of travel and other socioeconomic characteristics of the recreationist population is fitted to the relevant data set. The analyst statistically derives the relevant aggregate resource demand curve. Haab and McConnell (2002) rigorously treat the econometric issues that arise in environmental demand studies, including that of travel cost models of recreational demand.

3. Use the results of the statistical analysis to calculate the demand of the overall population. The trip generating function is interpreted as a demand function. For the zonal model, estimate per recreationist consumer surplus for a given zone by integrating the demand function between the price at which visits are made and the price at which the number of visits drops to zero. Multiply consumer surplus per household by the number of households in the zone to obtain an estimate of total consumer surplus per zone. Then the aggregate consumer surplus for the site for all zones is obtained by adding up the surplus estimates for all zones.

Choices Faced in Applying Travel Cost Methods. In any empirical application in economics, complications call for judgment. The analyst must choose whether to use zonal data or individual observations. For analytical simplicity, computational ease, and reduced cost of data collection, early applications placed each of the observations in one of several zones defined by concentric circles around the site. For convenience, a political subdivision (e.g. county or postal code region) is often used in practice. The dependent variable in the zonal travel cost model is the annual visits *per capita* from each zone of residence. Visits per capita are regressed on the average cost of travel from that zone to the study site. For simplicity, the travel cost assigned to individual visitors from the same zone is assumed to be equal for all individuals.

The alternative to the zonal model is individual observations, which is preferable for statistical precision. Each observation represents a different individual, and that person's travel costs and time and socioeconomic characteristics are in the database. The dependent variable in this case is the number of trips per year by individual visitors to the site. However, the individual observation approach requires that most visitors to the site make more than one trip per year. A demand curve cannot be estimated if most recreationists visit only once, as they might for distant or unique sites with high costs of access, because of the lack of variation in the dependent variable. Also, the individual observation method requires a survey to ascertain the number of trips per year. Individual trip data are seldom available from secondary sources such as such as camping or boating permits. Hellerstein (1995) contends that the individual observation approach is more open to statistical flaws such as using an erroneous functional form than is the zonal approach. The choice between the two will depend on balancing advantages and disadvantages in the specific situation.

How an analyst using the travel cost method should define travel costs may not be immediately obvious. The eventual measure of benefit varies directly with the assumed cost of travel: that is, the higher the cost of travel, the higher the imputed site value. The actual cost is usually not readily obtained from recreationists. Hence the research team usually calculates the travel cost based on distance and mode of travel reported by respondents. Most studies, particularly in the United States, use costs of automobile transportation. Some visitors have alternative means (bus, train, bicycle, walking). Even among automobiles, actual costs vary greatly according to the make and model of vehicle. Should the cost of the automobile reflect only the variable costs of the trip (gasoline, oil, etc.) or should full running costs, including an estimate of maintenance, depreciation, licenses, and insurance be included? Garrod and Willis (1999, Chapter 3) point out that the derived consumer surplus estimates are quite sensitive to the particular judgments adopted. They report estimates from the United Kingdom in which consumer surplus measures are two to four times higher when full running costs are used than when only expenditures for gasoline are used. Different analysts have made different assumptions. Some likely reflect convenience for the researcher, as estimating full costs requires considerably more data collection and calculation by the analyst team. Garrod and Willis report that recreationists themselves recognize that their travel costs are larger than just the cost of gasoline, which supports including full running costs. Finally, the travel cost must be adjusted to reflect the number of persons per automobile, and the costs expressed for a round trip, not one-way.

Another dilemma is how to measure the recreationists' opportunity cost of travel time, and whether to include it directly in the transportation cost or treat it as a separate variable in the statistical analysis. Travel time must ordinarily be estimated (or more often assumed) by the analyst, not obtained directly from recreationists. The higher the assumed cost of travel time, the higher the estimated consumer surplus or benefit. The meta-analysis by Walsh et al. (1992) indicates that if the opportunity cost of recreationists' travel time is omitted, benefit estimates are about 30% lower. Some analysts have contended that leisure time should have zero opportunity cost, but most adopt an assumption that the marginal utility of a visit is in fact affected by the opportunity cost of time taken to reach the site. The typical measure assumes that the recreationist faces a tradeoff between work and leisure, and that the wage rate can be the basis for estimating the opportunity cost of recreation. Drawing on early transportation planning literature, the U.S. Water Resources Council (1983) recommended using one-third of the wage rate and, given the estimated time of travel, converting the travel time into monetary terms and adding this to the transportation cost. Others (e.g. Smith and Desvouges 1986) have suggested that the opportunity cost should be the full wage rate. Other analysts have disputed any connection between opportunity cost of recreational travel time and the wage rate. Bockstael et al. (1987) developed a site demand function based on the labor market situation of individual recreationists, in which travel costs and time are separate independent variables as in equation 4-3 above. McKean et al. (1995), noting the usual working time requirements of paid employment, proposed time rationing. They concluded that assuming all time costs to be related to income would bias the results and that more survey information would be needed to deal with this problem.

In a zonal model, there is a high correlation between travel cost and travel time. This leads to a multicollinearity problem in the statistical analysis, suggesting that the time cost be directly added to the transportation cost. How to measure the opportunity cost of travel time in travel cost models remains controversial. Further discussion can be found in Ward and Beal 2000 and Freeman 2003.

Another dilemma in the travel cost method is the treatment of *substitute sites*. As with any economic good, availability and cost of substitutes are significant determinants of the demands for particular recreational sites. If relevant substitute recreational activities are not accounted for in the analysis, the estimates of consumer surplus will be biased upward. Evaluating the recreational benefits of a proposed U.S. Army Corps of Engineers reservoir, Burt and Brewer (1971) first formulated a multiple site travel cost model to account for substitute reservoir sites. Rosenthal (1987) used travel cost data from reservoirs in Kansas and Missouri to test for the importance of substitute sites. Statistical tests showed that benefit estimates were significantly higher when the substitutes were ignored, signaling the potential for bias. The meta-analysis by Walsh et al. (1992) found that estimates that omitted a cross price term for substitutes were about 30% higher. Most recent studies incorporate substitute sites, or ignore them only when unique experiences are being valued.

When performing and interpreting statistical analyses for travel cost studies, the functional form chosen to represent the relationship between travel costs and visits is of considerable significance. The log-linear functional form is probably the most commonly used:

$$\ln \textit{Trips} = a + \beta TC + \gamma S$$

where *Trips* = number of visits; TC = cost to travel to site; S = cost to travel to substitute site, and a, β, γ are constants to be estimated. The log-linear form yields results consistent with theory and observation, in that it does not ever predict negative visits and implies a finite number of visits at zero cost. Linear, double log, and other forms may also be used. However, the double log form implies an infinite number of visits per person at zero costs. Morever, it indicates infinite consumer surplus whenever estimated demand is inelastic. The linear form predicts that negative visits will occur above some critical cost.

Tests of the sensitivity of consumer surplus estimates to alternative functional forms but using the same data have found large differences depending on the functional form chosen. For example, from a single data set reported in Garrod's and Willis's (1999, *65*) study of visitors to canals and waterways in the United Kingdom, the double log model predicted infinite consumer surplus and the log-linear form yielded an estimate of 124 UK pounds per visit, much larger than other estimates (from contingent valuation methods, for example) or intuition. The linear model generated an estimate of about 0.50 UK pounds per visit. It is not clear which of these estimates should be accepted for policy analysis.

Water is likely to be only one of many attractions of a site. People travel to rivers and lakes for a multitude of reasons, some of which may be unrelated to water supply or quality. To isolate the value of the water or of a water quality improvement, some method must be devised to segregate the contribution of water to the total estimated site value. One solution is *multiple site* analysis. If the sites vary according to water quality, it is possible to infer the incremental value of the improved quality from a travel cost analysis. In a study notable for its conceptual and statistical rigor, for its careful documentation of procedures and results, and for the large amount of resources invested over a five-year period, Smith and Desvousges (1986) developed estimates of the value of improved water quality on a sample of U.S. Army Corps of Engineers reservoirs. They also employed, for comparative purposes, the contingent valuation method to estimate values for the same reservoirs. They developed a general travel cost model to infer the value placed on water quality improvements by recreationists. However, the resulting benefit estimates were implausibly large, illustrating the problems of extrapolating beyond the range of the site characteristics for which the model was estimated.

In a recent study of recreational salmon anglers on Lake Michigan, focused on heterogeneity of preferences, Provencher et al. (2002, *1074*) introduce a new issue, remarkable for the fact that in over four decades of perfecting the TCM it has not been brought up before. They point out that their basic reported recreation values

> ...are not Hicksian consumer surplus measures. To get Hicksian values would require that seasonal fixed costs be subtracted from the values given. Such fixed costs would involve such items as deprecia-

tion on boats, motors, trailers and major equipment items; boat storage; insurance; seasonal launch fees; and miscellaneous fishing equipment such as lures.

They remark that these fixed costs may be so large that some user groups may enjoy relatively small net benefits. The authors did not estimate these fixed costs for their sample. Nevertheless, the point appears to be valid, and deserves further discussion.

4.2.2 Site Choice (Discrete) Travel Cost Models

As the name implies, *site selection* models seek to understand how recreationists choose among alternative sites. Each recreationist is assumed to compare the net value (satisfaction or utility minus travel costs) of visiting each site and to choose the one that provides the largest net value. The distance and time costs of travel reduce the net value. An increase in quality increases the value. Recreationists balance these competing forces to select a site. This class of models, rather than having a continuous variable (annual visits) as the dependent variable, represent the dependent variable as a discrete choice: the decision to visit a site is a yes/no choice, coded as a 1 if the site is visited or a 0 if the site not. Data on attributes of the sites (such as fish populations, water quality, visitor facilities, and congestion) together with travel cost and recreationists' attributes (income, age, education) can be subjected to statistical analysis to estimate the value assigned to various quality characteristics of the sites.

A number of analysts have adopted the Random Utility Maximization (RUM) model of discrete choice developed by McFadden (1974; 2001). Random utility maximization theory was originally developed to study travel choices in transportation economics. The term random utility reflects the fact that while recreationists presumably know all the considerations going into their choice, the analyst or researcher cannot model all of them. Hence, to the analyst, the choices contain a random element. Recreationists' choices, however, can be modeled as the probability (between 0 and 1) of choosing a particular site as a function of site attributes and costs of travel plus a random error component.

The RUM model predicts the probability of choosing a given site among many alternatives. The multinomial logit is the functional form generated by the basic RUM model. Maximum likelihood methods are typically required to estimate the model. Because travel cost is the price variable in the discrete choice recreational site selection models, procedures are available to derive the recreationists' net WTP for a site or to improve its quality for recreationists from the multinomial logit model (Hanemann 1999b). Mittelhammer et al. (2000) is one of a number of advanced econometric textbooks that contain a treatment of binomial and multinomial response models.

The method is most useful for evaluating sites that most visit once a year or not at all. It does not replace the standard continuous travel cost model in predicting how many trips will be taken each season nor how these trips are allocated across sites. Nor does it measure benefits per visitor day, which are often useful to recreational site managers in making budget allocations for expansion of the number of sites or enhancement of existing sites.

For more detailed discussions, see Herriges and Kling (1999), who assembled a number of papers by leading authorities on the theory and econometric implementation of the travel cost and related models of recreational demand, with an emphasis on site choice studies.

4.2.3 Advantages and Limitations

Because of their basis in actual consumer behavior, travel cost models of recreation demand are among those in which environmental economists have the most confidence. Nevertheless, as emphasized by Randall (1994), Ward and Beal (2000), and others, a considerable amount of judgment is involved in completing a travel cost model. Although the travel cost model has the advantage of effectively measuring revealed preferences, wide ranges of estimates can be obtained. Assumptions and choices must be made on how to treat the various elements that go into a travel cost study:

- how to measure the cost of travel (e.g. variable or full costs, the opportunity cost of time),
- how to account for substitute sites,
- how to handle instances where recreationists have more than one destination in mind,
- the length of visit,
- whether to use aggregate or individual trip data, and
- what functional form to use.

The profession has not come to firm agreement on these matters. (See Ward and Beal 2000, Chapter 9.)

Travel cost methods can measure historical experience, but the results are not always immediately useful for evaluating proposed projects or allocation decisions. Although some studies in developing countries have been successful, their applicability is likely to be limited for some time. In addition to the unresolved matters of judgment, to accurately estimate the contribution of site characteristics requires special skills in data collection and applied econometric methods and a sizable study budget. Its use remains problematic for many applications in water resource valuation. However, an interesting case study of the value of water level in reservoirs under drought condition will be discussed in Chapter 8.

4.3 The Hedonic Property Value Method Once Again

The hedonic property value model, another revealed preference approach to nonmarket valuation, observes consumers' market activities to indirectly measure WTP for changes in water supply or quality. Although introduced in Section 3.12.3 among the methods for valuing producers' goods, it has been more often used to value public environmental goods.

The hedonic pricing method was originally developed to analyze and exploit observations on markets for differentiated products. Differentiated products possess several attributes which are recognized by purchasers, but the attributes cannot be unbundled when purchasing the good. The term *hedonic*—which is not exactly self-explanatory, even to economists—refers to the pleasure experienced from the attributes of a good. The term was adopted to describe the behavior of self-interested, utility-maximizing market participants selecting goods or assets with a preferred balance of characteristics.

Hedonic valuations of consumer behavior are empirical manifestations of the household production function model, an elaboration on neoclassical consumer theory, which posits that goods and services, rather than being homogeneous, comprise a particular bundle of characteristics and attributes, and prices for goods and services vary according to these differences. The hedonic pricing method rests on the specific assumption that the price of some marketed good is a function of its different characteristics, and an implicit price exists for each of the characteristics. Examples of characteristics identifiable by market participants are the health or safety risks of jobs, horsepower of an automobile engine, the number of rooms in a house, or the air quality surrounding a residence.

Most contemporary versions of hedonic pricing descend from Rosen's (1974) model of the market for a differentiated product. Rosen begins by modeling the interaction of individuals or firms that supply the differentiated goods and the consumers who purchase them. Suppliers exhibit offer prices that depend on the characteristics of the differentiated product and other factors. Similarly, because consumers receive utility from the characteristics of the differentiated product, they are willing to pay different amounts for products possessing different characteristics. Their bids will also depend on their income and the particular level of utility they derive from consumption of the differentiated product. The model posits that an increment in price due to increases in any characteristic will equal the buyer's marginal WTP for the characteristic, as well as the sellers' marginal cost of producing the characteristic. When buyers and sellers have time to adjust their responses, the marginal hedonic price equals the marginal value to consumers and the marginal cost to suppliers. Within a sample of similar marketed goods, a set of implicit prices exists which reflects the values of the different characteristics of that good. The contribution of alternative characteristics can then be identified with statistical methods. See Freeman 2003 and Taylor 2003 for recent reviews of the theory and practice of hedonic property value for environmental attributes.

For valuing environmental attributes, hedonic pricing is used most often to analyze data from the residential housing market. This analysis tracks prices of real property (land) that exhibits varying environmental characteristics (e.g. water qualities, water supplies), so it is usually called the hedonic property value method. The model hypothesizes that the utility of consumption of housing services depends on the structural characteristics of the dwelling, a vector of neighborhood characteristics (accessibility to jobs, shopping, and parks; crime rates) and location-specific environmental amenities. Water quality and water level in lakes or reservoirs adjacent to residential or recreational homes are of interest here. Econometric methods are applied to isolate the incremental effect of the environmental variable on the market value of real estate, with the incremental effect being a measure of the environmental value sought.

4.3.1 The First Stage Hedonic Price Equation

Application of the hedonic property value method to the evaluation of environmental quality is a two-stage process. The first yields an estimated *hedonic price equation*, which posits that market outcomes for a differentiated product can be modeled as follows:

$$p_i = g(S_i, N_i, Q_i) + \varepsilon_i \tag{4-4}$$

where:

p_i is the sales price of the ith marketed item;
S_i is a vector of the structural characteristics of the ith item;
N_i, a vector of neighborhood characteristics;
Q_i represents the location-specific environmental attributes of interest;
g is a function to be estimated with best-fit (regression) methods; and
ε_i is an error term.

For the housing market, in addition to Q_i: representing, say, water supply, water quality, or distance to a lake or stream, the relevant characteristics of the ith dwelling (S_i) might include square footage, age, number of rooms, quality of construction, and size of the lot. In the list of neighborhood characteristics might be found: accessibility to jobs, shopping, and parks, or crime rates. The hedonic price equation represents not a behavioral equation reflecting the market participants' demands, but a market equilibrium price schedule.

The functional form of the hedonic price equation should be chosen with care, and is best determined empirically. Although in certain situations the function g might be linear, the nonlinear case is thought to be more likely. The partial derivative of the hedonic price equation with respect to the characteristic of interest ($\partial g / \partial q$) yields a measure of the marginal value of the characteristic q. See Freeman 2003, *363-365* for a discussion.

4.3.2 The Second Stage

In the first stage a hedonic price equation is estimated, and from the parameters the marginal prices for the characteristics can be calculated. These marginal prices do not yield the consumers' demand or inverse demand equations for the attribute. But in a second stage they can be used, together with measures of income, wealth, and other socioeconomic attributes of the transactors, to estimate the parameters of the consumers' demand equations.

The second stage presents difficult econometric problems, particularly identifying the model and distinguishing the demand equation from the hedonic equation. The result of the first stage can often itself provide useful information. Palmquist (1992) shows that when the environmental effect under study is "localized"—meaning it affects only a small number of properties in the market—the hedonic price equation can be sufficient to estimate WTP for an environmental change. This condition is sometimes met in water quality or water supply studies and, because the data and econometric requirements for the second stage model are more demanding, it is often critical. Of course, there is the possibility of error due to mis-specification of the model. If important variables are omitted, the estimated coefficients for the measured variables will capture effects of other, unmeasured factors, and upwardly biased value estimates are the likely result. On the other hand, there is reason to believe that some studies estimating benefits of both environmental and recreational improvements may capture only a part of the total benefits. Gains that would also likely accrue to others beside property owners—day-visitors who travel to a reservoir from elsewhere—are not captured by the hedonic technique. Benefits enjoyed by households that rent rather than purchase may not be fully captured.

The hedonic property value method has not been applied as extensively as the travel cost and expressed preference methods. (See, however, the application to specific water uses discussed in Chapter 8.) Lansford and Jones (1995) analyzed residential house sales surrounding a lake near Austin, Texas. The value of proximity to the lake was found with the standard hedonic price analysis approach. More interestingly, the authors showed that prices varied systematically with the level of the lake at the time of sale, which permitted an estimate of the marginal value of water to purchasers.

4.3.3 Further Remarks

Hedonic pricing methods rest on assumptions that may often be unrealistic. Of course, the method only works with a valid data set reflecting enough variation in the characteristic of interest. Further, the market participants must be able to recognize differences in the environmental characteristic of interest. If the market for land is such that transactions are infrequent or adjustments to new equilibria are slow, then the derived implicit prices may not accurately measure producers' willingness to pay.

Collection of adequate data and statistical analysis are primary challenges of applying the hedonic pricing method. Selling prices may be obtained by consulting public tax records. If not, then prices must be found in some other way, such as a survey of real estate professionals or land appraisers. (Tax data and appraisals may not reveal the actual sales prices.) To obtain estimates of the water supply or quality, the neighborhood variables, and the productive characteristics associated with each of the price observations may require a mail or personal interview survey of the buyer or seller of each parcel.

Familiar econometric issues commonly arise in estimating the price function. Errors introduced by omitted variables, potential multicollinearity in explanatory variables, and choice of functional form are among these concerns.

The hedonic property value method has documented that market participants exhibit a significant WTP for some of the less tangible environmental aspects of real property ownership, supporting the applicability of the neoclassical economic model to environmental policy evaluation. Moreover, if the range of the environmental variable of interest (e.g. water quality) is wide enough to encompass both "with policy" and the "without policy" conditions, the method is quite useful for evaluating proposed policy initiatives. The study by Boyle et al. (1998) summarized in Chapter 8 illustrates this point.

However, the value of water supply or quality attributes—whose nature, future status, and impacts may be imperfectly perceived by market participants—may be difficult to isolate. Buyers and sellers must be able to recognize the actual physical differences in the level of characteristics to be valued, which may be difficult when water supply and quality are highly variable.

Furthermore, estimation of economic values of water and environmental resources with hedonic property value methods requires considerable time, resources, and applied econometric skills. Data requirements for a valid and reliable hedonic analysis are quite demanding. A large enough sample of relevant real estate transactions may be difficult and expensive to obtain. A mail or interview survey of parties to the individual transaction will usually be necessary to estimate other characteristics of the property parcel (size, age, and quality of dwelling, for example). Other data, such as water quality, supply, and distance from the dwelling, must be obtained from yet other sources. The hedonic property value method will be difficult to implement in jurisdictions—such as developing countries—where real property markets do not function effectively, occurrences and prices of transactions are not publicly recorded or otherwise available, or data on property characteristics and neighborhood attributes are difficult to obtain.

4.4 Defensive Behavior and Damage Cost Methods

Two less frequently used approaches are the *defensive behavior* method (often called *averting behavior*) and the *damage cost* method. Both apply to measuring WTP in order to avoid some adverse environmental effect, such as pollution of water supply. The defensive behavior approach examines expenditures made by people to reduce exposure to pollutants or to offset the adverse effects of exposure. From these expenditure patterns, a measure of their willingness to pay can be inferred. Damage cost methods, on the other hand, measure the resource costs imposed by the biological or chemical contamination of water, for instance, increased costs of production or medical costs associated with waterborne illnesses.

4.4.1 The Defensive Behavior Method

The defensive behavior method infers values from expenditures that households make to avert being subjected to an environmental pollutant. People are considered to combine purchased inputs with time in order to improve health by reducing exposure to the disamenity. The underlying premise is that a rational person will adopt defensive behavior as long as the value of the damage avoided is greater than the cost of the defensive steps. Accordingly, decisions made avoid damage from environmental or water pollution can be studied to reveal how consumers value the avoidance of environmental damage. Bartik (1988) developed a model showing the complex role that defensive expenditures play in measuring welfare changes. The marginal value of pollution reduction is not measured by marginal changes in defensive expenditures, because the quality of drinking water does not remain constant. The saving in defensive expenditures is only a lower bound for exact willingness to pay.

Defensive behavior models have mainly been applied in the context of human health. Although there is not yet an extensive literature on water quality, several studies, mostly using survey research tools, have addressed valuation of water quality improvements to protect against polluted drinking water. For example, Harrington et al. (1991) investigated responses to contamination by a water-borne microorganism. Abdalla et al. (1992) studied consumer responses to organic chemical (trichloroethylene) contamination of groundwater. McConnell and Rosado (2000) used discrete choice methods to study how the costs of boiling or filtration of tap water or purchase of bottled water affected willingness to pay for safe drinking water in a city in Brazil. For a recent rigorous statement of the conceptual framework and a review of the appropriate literature on the defensive expenditures model, in conjunction with the damage cost method, see Dickie 2003.

4.4.2 The Damage Cost Method

Damage cost methods measure the resource costs brought on by an environmental change. Examples include effects of water contaminated with microorganisms or chemicals. On the producers' side, increases in costs and reductions in output caused by contaminants are included as damage costs. Damages caused by floods are often used as measures of benefits of policies aimed at reduced flood risks.

The general premise of damage cost methods is that the affected individual or household is willing to pay up to the amount of expected damages to avoid them. Hence, the cost of damages can be used as a measure of benefits of proposed policies to reduce or mitigate potential damages from the environment. When applied to the effects of waterborne pollutants on human health, the damage cost approach is called the "cost of illness" approach, measuring the resource costs imposed by the biological or chemical contamination. The cost of illness method is not based on analysis of individual decisions. Instead it sums the cost of medications, visits to doctors, and the time lost from work associated with waterborne illnesses. The level of care provided influences treatment costs, and reflects individual and social decisions. Only a lower bound estimate of WTP is expected from estimates of damage costs.

Assessment of the effects of pollutants on producers' welfare and on producers' and households' willingness to pay to reduce risks of flood hazards is described in Chapters 6 and 8.

4.5 Expressed Preference Methods

In many environmental evaluation problems, economic value measures cannot be derived from individual market choices. Some goods and services provided by public policy or the environment contribute to satisfying consumer preferences but are not or cannot be yet valued via market transactions. When a policy is potential rather than actual, or when nonuse (or passive-use) values are involved, market transactions are difficult to identify. But unlike the revealed preference methods, which require some sort of natural market experiment to provide data, members of the population can be questioned directly for preferences regarding proposed environmental policy.

Although the terminology is not yet fully settled, the group of methods developed to measure environmental values in such cases have mostly come to be called *expressed preference* methods. A sample of respondents are presented a description of conditions simulating a hypothetical market in which they are asked to express WTP for existing or potential environmental conditions not registered on any market. The original and still most common form of questioning to ascertain individual valuations of hypothetical future events is called the *contingent valuation method* (CVM). Respondents are asked to provide WTP for moving from a given state of affairs to a supposedly more desirable one. *Choice modeling* (CM) analysis (or stated preference, or conjoint analysis) involves presenting the respondent with a set of policy options, each described by a cost and a complete set of attributes or consequences of choosing that option. The respondent is asked either to rank the options or to choose the preferred one. Statistical analysis, usually within the random utility maximization (RUM) modeling methodology, is then applied to infer monetary WTP for various attributes of the policy options.

4.6 The Contingent Valuation Method

The oldest method to elicit consumers' WTP for nonmarketed environmental goods is the Contingent Valuation Method (CVM). It involves asking people directly what they would be willing to pay *contingent* on some hypothetical change in the future state of the world. The technique originated from a suggestion by S. V. Ciriacy-Wantrup (1947) in an article about the public economics of soil erosion abatement. Noting that some of the beneficial effects—such as reduced pollution in watercourses—were public goods and market valuation was not feasible, Ciriacy-Wantrup proposed that interview surveys could be employed to ask people "how much they would be willing to pay for successive additional quantities of a collective extra-market good." However, Ciriacy-Wantrup did not follow up on his own proposal. The prevailing belief that free-riding and strategic behavior by self-interested individuals would frustrate attempts to elicit reliable estimates of individual valuations of public goods discouraged exploration of this avenue for some years. Davis's (1963) study of recreation in the Maine forests in the northeastern United States was the first academic implementation of contingent valuation. A number of CVM studies were reported in the 1970s, most notably Hammack and Brown (1974) on wetland preservation and Randall et al. (1974) on air pollution and visibility in the southwestern United States (considered to be the first study to explicitly measure nonuse values). By 1979, the U.S. Water Resources Council's planning procedures recommended CVM as an acceptable method for estimating benefits of water and related land resource projects. Loomis 1999 describes how the use of CVM by federal agencies in the United States evolved.

Since these early studies, many hundreds of investigations employing CVM have appeared, both in technical journals and in government and consulting reports. The method has aroused enormous interest among economists, on balance favorable, but some of it highly distrustful. Since its first applications, several book length expositions and assessments have traced the various stages of development. Cummings et al. (1986) and Hausman (1993) exemplify the skeptical perspective. Mitchell and Carson (1989) provide a still valuable general assessment. The papers collected in Bateman and Willis (1999) give an exhaustive and balanced evaluation of the contingent valuation technique. Other recent treatments include Kopp et al. (1997), Bateman et al. (2002), Garrod and Willis (1999), and Boyle (2003).

4.6.1 General Approach

Consider a questionnaire submitted to a recreationist (fisher or boater) to value a policy which would change the level of river flows. It would ask a WTP question and solicit socio-economic data to describe the respondent. The contingent valuation question in this situation might be expressed as follows:

> Suppose the management of the _____ River is changed so that the flow during the month of _____ is increased by an average of ____ cubic feet per second to ____cubic feet per second in the part of the river between _____ Campground and _____ Town. This increase in flow will require diversion from other valuable uses. It is proposed that the new policy be paid for by an access charge on all river recreationists. What is the maximum amount you would be willing to pay for this flow increase?

A CVM questionnaire designed to value a water-related policy initiative typically has three components:

- A description of the water resource or water-based amenity to be valued and the conditions under which some policy change is being undertaken. Data, graphics, and photographs may be provided to help visualize the alternatives.
- Choice questions used to infer values of the amenity or policy change. The several alternative forms by which these questions might be expressed are discussed in the next section.
- Questions about the respondents. The reliability of a CVM study will, as with any study of economic demand, be improved by including the usual demand shift variables, primarily socioeconomic characteristics such as age, education, income, and gender. Also in this category are

questions on attitudes and beliefs, such as attitudes toward environmental policies. These data are used as shift variables in the subsequent statistical analysis.

The primary attraction of CVM is that it can measure the economic benefits (or damages) of a wide assortment of beneficial (or adverse) effects in a way consistent with economic theory. One major advantage is the ability to evaluate proposed, in addition to already available, goods or services. This is important in numerous cases where the impacts of potential changes in water supply or quality cannot yet be observed.

Second, CVM can address values that cannot be dealt with any other way, such as nonuse or passive-use values. In developing economies, the CVM has been successfully used to study demand for domestic water and sanitation improvements in rural villages (described in more detail in Chapter 7).

4.6.2 Methodological Issues in Designing a CVM Study

Target Population. For studies of direct use values, the sample population will be direct recreational water users. In contrast, to estimate nonuser values like existence, bequest, or option values, the study must address a regional or even larger population. Sampling procedures ensure that the sample represents the target population (Rea and Parker 1997; Salant and Dillman 1994).

Product Definition. The resource flow being studied must be clearly described to respondents. The nature of proposed interventions, such as changed flows or improved water quality, are often difficult to communicate. Some researchers have employed charts or photographs as part of a personal interview survey, while others rely on verbal descriptions in telephone or mail questionnaire surveys.

Payment Vehicle. The amenity will have be paid for, with taxes or site fees, for example. The vehicle should be a realistic, plausible, and noncontroversial way of collecting revenue.

Data Collection Technique. Data can be gathered by personal interview, telephone interview, or mailed questionnaire; there are tradeoffs in accuracy and cost. Personal interviews are usually preferred, but training, time, subsistence, and transportation costs for interviewers can mount. Less expensive telephone or mail surveys are most frequently used. One must also decide who will actually contact respondents. Although members of the research team, particularly the student assistants or temporary hired staff, are the usual interviewers, researchers often choose to contract with a professional surveying organization.

Question Format. The questions may be open-ended, iterative bidding games or discrete choice forms. These options are discussed in the following sections.

Method of Statistical Analysis. The appropriate statistical method depends on the question format. Standard regression methods usually apply, but the discrete choice questions favored in recent years require discrete choice statistical models such as the logit approach.

Supplemental Data. Shift variables incorporated into the demand analysis typically include socioeconomic factors such as income, age, or education, and other variables which should be controlled for in the valuation effort.

4.6.3 Traditional Approaches to Questionnaire Design and Potential Sources of Bias

Early CVM surveys requested a direct expression of value for the good in question. In the *open-ended* (or *direct question*) approach, the analyst poses a simple question: How much would you be willing to pay for ____? But in familiar market settings, people are presented a listed price that they can accept or ignore. High rates of nonresponse and implausibly high or low valuations have been experienced with the open-ended approach.

In the *iterative bidding* (or bidding game) approach, respondents are asked if they are willing to pay (bid) a specified amount—call it B. If the answer is "yes" the question is repeated, increasing the price until a "no" response is received. Conversely, if the initial response to B is "no," the questions iterate downward until a "yes" is recorded. The iterative bidding approach was tested to determine whether the starting value B had any influence on the bid. The final bids did in fact tend to correlate with the initial value. Therefore, it appears that "starting point" bias can be a problem with iterative bidding (Cummings et al. 1986). However, starting point bias is typically not large, and can be reduced with pretests to determine the likely range of response so the initial bid can be set near this amount.

A *payment card* visually lists an array of potential bids of annual WTP, ranging from zero to some very large number. Respondent is asked to choose the one that most closely reflects their valuation of the policy. It was first used by Mitchell and Carson (1989, *100–101*) in the early 1980s as an alternative to iterative bidding. They supplemented the list of potential annual payments by also identifying the amounts already being paid through taxes for households in the respondent's income group for other, unrelated public goods (such as police and fire protection, national defense, roads and highways, and public education). The payment card approach has been found to reduce but not eliminate the potential for starting point bias.

Critics are concerned about the overall validity of CVM, exemplified by the title "Is Some Number Better Than No Number?" (Diamond and Hausman 1994). The debate has been fruitful in that it has brought out a number of potential sources of bias or error, and encouraged researchers to test for their presence and formulate approaches which minimized or eliminated the problems.

A questionnaire may provide an incentive for respondents to misrepresent their true preferences. It may encourage *strategic behavior*—responses deliberately chosen to influence future availability of the amenity being valued. Despite misgivings of early critics of CVM, the evidence suggests that properly designed questions can avoid or minimize this risk. A plausible payment obligation seems to be key. When the purpose is properly explained, respondents seem to make a serious effort to convey their own feelings (Smith and Desvousges 1986).

Compliance bias is a tendency of respondents to fit their answers to the perceived preferences of the interviewer or the surveying organization. Interviewer effects are an issue in many types of surveys, not only with expressed preference studies. Careful training and supervision of interviewers—and, where possible, the use of experienced interviewers—is the path to minimizing the problem.

Questions may provide *implied value cues* to the respondent about what an appropriate response might be. One example, starting point bias, was mentioned above. *Relational* bias is caused when the amenity to be valued is linked to other public goods. The payment card method, which provides explicit statements of the cost of alternative public goods, is thought by some to be subject to relational bias. However, tests by Mitchell and Carson (1989) do not support this concern. *Importance* and *position* biases arise from the way the amenity is presented in the questionnaire. The respondent should not be led by the fact of the survey itself or by the position of the WTP elicitation in the questionnaire to infer an extra value to the amenity. Reassurance that some people will vote no and others yes can make respondents comfortable with zero responses when that is their actual valuation.

A questionnaire may be worded so poorly that respondents do not comprehend the scenario intended by the researcher and systematically over- or understate their responses. This is called *scenario mis-specification*. Survey researchers have long been aware that small variations in wording can greatly affect responses. The antidote in this case is careful questionnaire design, including the use of focus groups and extensive pretesting of questionnaires to assure that the intended meaning is conveyed. Respondents may exhibit *insensitivity to scope*: that is, their WTP may not be sensitive to the amount of a good being valued. Suppose that environmental good A refers to improved water quality in a river basin, and subset a_1 to a similar degree of improved quality in only one branch of the river. It would be expected that the value assigned to a_1 would be less than the value of A. Some studies, however, assert that if a sample of respondents is asked to value an improvement in a_1, the elicited values will be quite similar to values elicited from another group for the larger set A, a result not observed if one group is asked to value both a_1 and A. Critics cite these anomalies as strong evidence that CVM can not be relied on for valid measures of potential welfare from proposed environmental changes. Kahneman and

Knetsch (1992) offer the hypothesis that respondents are purchasing the "moral satisfaction" of contributing to the supply of public goods, meaning that respondents may permit themselves to express values higher than their "true" WTP in order to appear to be magnanimous toward a good cause. They argue that responses to CVM questions, since they don't require actual money exchange, lead to estimated WTP much larger than actual WTP. However, although the concept of moral satisfaction has achieved considerable renown, Carson (1997) notes that Kahneman and Knetsch (1992) have not statistically tested the insensitivity to scope hypothesis, nor do the data offered in support of their critique actually show insensitivity to scope. From a review of over thirty tests, Carson concludes that this supposed limitation of the CV method has little empirical support, and that those studies that purport to show insensitivity to scope are characterized by small samples and other problems of inappropriate survey design. Smith and Osborne (1996) reach similar conclusions with a meta-analysis of national park visibility studies. Moreover, Randall and Hoehn (1996) submit that due to consumers' budgets and to order, scope, and scale effects in questions, WTP for a good will be larger when the good is valued alone than when it is included within a larger set of goods.

4.6.4 The NOAA Panel Recommendations and Contingent Valuation

An important landmark in the debate about the use of CVM occurred in connection with the well-publicized spill of crude oil from the supertanker Exxon *Valdez* in Prince William Sound, Alaska in 1989. The Comprehensive Environmental Response, Compensation and Liability Act of 1980 (CERCLA), also known as the Superfund Law, established procedures by which parties responsible for environmental contamination could be made to pay costs of cleanup and government agencies could sue for damages to environmental resources entrusted to their care. Interior Department regulations declared that lost nonuse values could be recovered under CERCLA and that, in certain situations, contingent valuation was acceptable as a method of measuring such damages. (A more detailed recounting of the conflicts over the regulations implementing CERCLA is found in Kopp et al. 1997.)

Under Interior Department regulations, the Exxon Corporation would have been liable for damages over and above the out-of-pocket losses to the direct users of the resource, the fishing and recreation industries. However, because of the location of the spill, assessment of the Exxon *Valdez* disaster fell to the National Oceanic and Atmospheric Administration (NOAA), a branch of the U.S. Department of Commerce. In subsequent legislation, Congress directed NOAA to prepare its own regulations concerning damage assessment under CERCLA.

In view of the high stakes involved and the conflicting views of using CVM to measure nonuse values, NOAA asked Nobel Laureates in Economics Kenneth Arrow and Robert Solow to lead a panel of experts to assess the reliability of CVM. The validity of the concept of nonuse values, although questioned by many at the time, was apparently not at issue in this case. After lengthy deliberations, a review of written submissions, and oral comments at a public meeting, the NOAA panel delivered its report (Arrow et al. 1993). Their main conclusion was that "CV studies can produce estimates reliable enough to be the starting point of a judicial process of damage assessment, including lost passive use values."

However, the panel members were not entirely enthusiastic in their support for CVM as practiced as the basis for actual damage awards (Portney 1994). They therefore went on to recommend guidelines for future applications of CVM for reliable estimates of lost passive use values for damage assessment. According to Portney, the panel developed the guidelines because they felt that casual applications of CVM method should not be used for damage assessment. The six most important of these guidelines (Portney 1994) are noted below:

- CVM should rely on the *discrete choice* format. Respondents should, in other words, be questioned on how they would vote ("yes" or "no") if offered a choice regarding a program that would involve higher taxes or payments but yield a specified environmental benefit. The yes/no decision is similar to that frequently experienced in actual purchase decisions or in voting for public programs, and responses to discrete choice questions are closer to actual valuations.
- Personal interviews are preferable to telephone surveys, which in turn are better than mailed questionnaires.
- CVM applications should contain a scenario that accurately and clearly describes the expected effects of the policy or program being valued.
- Questionnaires should include reminders that any expressed WTP for the policy in question would reduce the amount available for other goods and services.
- CVM applications must include reminders of the substitutes available for the improved good or service in question. For example, if asked to vote on a proposal to improve reservoir recreation, the respondent should be reminded of existing reservoirs or other reservoirs being created independent of the proposal in question.
- Surveys should include follow-up questions that ensure that respondents comprehend the decision they are asked to make and help the analysts understand the basis for their responses.

In spite of the panel's conclusions, or perhaps because they were equivocal, a vigorous debate continued over the validity of valuations obtained via contingent valuation.

4.6.5 Discrete Choice and Related Approaches in Questionnaire Design

Because of the perceived limitations of traditional questioning formats, two additional refinements were developed, *discrete choice* (or *dichotomous choice*) and the *multiple bounded referendum*. These formats ask the respondent to make a judgment similar to those made by consumers in market contexts. Because the method resembles voting in a referendum election, the term *referendum* is has also come into use to identify the method (Freeman 2003).

Fairly early in the history of CVM, Bishop and Heberlein (1979) adopted what is now called discrete choice in a study of WTP for goose hunting in Wisconsin. They predetermine a number of prices, which are expected to include the entire likely range of WTP. The potential respondents are grouped into an equal number of subsamples; members of a given subsample are presented with the same price, and asked whether they would be willing to pay that amount for the amenity. The approach is simpler for respondents than the bidding game, and is thought to exhibit what is called "incentive compatibility"—the respondent has no incentive to strategically bias answers toward desired outcomes. With a sufficiently large sample, a special form of statistical analysis of the pattern of yes and no responses permits the inference of WTP. The yes/no answers are converted to ones and zeros for statistical derivation of the probability of accepting an offer as a function of the expressed bid and of socioeconomic variables. Responses to discrete choice questions yield a lower bound (for a yes) and an upper bound (for a no) on the applicable welfare measure.

Discrete choice approaches are also subject to a form of starting point bias, what Mitchell and Carson (1989) called "yea-saying": the tendency of some respondents to agree with the interviewer, no matter what their own opinions might be. And under discrete choices the responses may not show the respondent's maximum WTP, so a larger sample size is required to measure the WTP function.

Take-it-or-leave-it with follow-up (Mitchell and Carson 1989, *103*), or, as it more often called, *multiple bounded referendum*, is proposed as a way to circumvent the large sample size needs of the basic referendum method. It calls for a second question (or even a third) to follow the first. If the first response is "no," a randomly selected second lower bid is posed; if the first response is "yes," a randomly selected higher second question follows. Gains in the information content per response are achieved because the follow-up more often brackets the true WTP.

Observed Differences in Estimates Between Open-ended and Discrete Choice Questionnaires. Even though it was recommended by the NOAA panel (Arrow et al. 1993) and has been subject to much refinement and testing, discrete choice has not avoided controversy. Several studies have reported unexpected large disparities in the results of discrete choice and open-ended questioning. Studies which compare the two formats find that discrete choice questions yield values much larger than estimates under similar conditions using the open-ended method. However, some of these differences can be attributed to the survey method (e.g. telephone vs. personal interview). Of more concern is the contention that discrete choice significantly overestimates willingness to actually pay cash for market goods (Brown et al. 1996; Loomis et al. 1997). Loomis et al. (1999) hypothesize that some respondents think that a good is worthwhile, but only at a price less than the bid amount given to them on the questionnaire, so they must choose between a truthful response ("no") and a response that registers their support for the public good. In the face of this quandary, some may opt for a "yes" response and bid in excess of their actual WTP. The authors propose a "trichotomous" choice, which gives the respondent the opportunity to select "yes, but at a lower price." This approach yields a reduced proportion of "yes" responses and significantly lowers mean WTP.

Nevertheless, although questions remain as to the validity of discrete choice question formulation, recent meta-analysis of CVM studies (e.g. Rosenberger and Loomis, 2000) does not confirm that discrete choice or referendum questions generally yield significantly larger estimates than do open-ended questions.

Statistical Analysis of Discrete Choice Responses. The statistical procedures used to analyze referendum-type (discrete choice) questions differ from the simpler Ordinary Least Squares (OLS) methods applicable to standard CVM questions. Because discrete choice responses are binary (i.e. answers are either yes or no), a statistical model appropriate to a discrete dependent variable is required. Further, because the mathematical expectation of a dependent variable is essentially nonlinear, data from a discrete choice survey must be estimated with a nonlinear approach. Logit and probit models are the usual choice. The logit model is appropriate if the error term in the model is distributed according to a logistic distribution. If the error term is normally distributed, the probit model applies. The logistic function is mathematically less demanding, and discrete choice data often seem to match a logistic distribution, so logit models are used more frequently. In any case, since the logistic and the normal distributions are fairly similar, the two versions yield similar results. Logit and probit models are estimated using maximum likelihood estimation (MLE) methods, and may require more sophisticated software than does the OLS technique. See Hanemann and Kanninen 1999 for a detailed and rigorous treatment of the statistical issues inherent in analyzing discrete response contingent valuation data. Many advanced econometric textbooks, e.g. Mittelhammer et al. 2000, contain treatments of binomial and multinomial response models.

4.6.6 Divergences Between WTP and WTA in CVM Studies

In early applications of CVM, analysts expected that WTP and WTA ("willingness to accept") for the same good would be similar, so either measure would be acceptable. Willig (1976) demonstrated for price changes that under plausible assumptions (the environmental good is not unique—i.e. it has close substitutes—and there are no large income effects) the divergences between WTA and WTP would be small and the Marshallian consumer surplus would lie between them. Randall and Stoll (1980) reported similar findings with *quantity changes*. (For a detailed review of the controversy, see Hanemann 1999a.) However, as CVM studies have accumulated, WTA measures have consistently been several times as large as WTP for the same environmental good. Many individual responses to WTA questions seem implausibly large. WTP measures are for the most part easier to obtain from respondents than WTA formulations. If these anomalous results stand up to further tests, there will be major implications for both microeconomic theory and environmental policy. A systematically greater WTA than WTP for the same choice alternative seems to call for a richer microeconomic model of consumer behavior. If WTP measures are used in environmental policy analyses where WTA is the appropriate measure, an inadequate level of environmental protection may be recommended. The issue also has a bearing on how much property owners should be compensated when their property is condemned for public use under eminent domain statutes.

Several explanations for this anomaly have been offered. Mitchell and Carson (1989) observe that the choice of measures can be regarded as an issue of property rights. If the person has the right to sell the good or service, then WTA is the proper measure. Conversely, if the person has to buy it to enjoy it, then the appropriate measure is WTP. However, with environmental public goods it is often not obvious what the property rights are and who possesses them.

Critics of CVM view the disparity as evidence that CVM cannot generate reliable and consistent responses. In particular, WTA may be an inappropriate form for the valuation question. Respondents may, in effect, be rejecting the property right embedded in a WTA question, i.e. the implication that they might be "selling" the right to the environmental improvement. For example, monetary compensation may not be seen as a legitimate reaction to the loss of some environmental goods, such as endangered species. Reflecting that attitude, respondents' higher WTA bids might represent a protest against the format of the question, rather than reflecting a valuation of an environmental loss. Or respondents may be behaving strategically, in order to encourage adoption of a preferred policy, demanding a greater amount than would actually be required to restore them to their original utility level. Some noneconomists contend that the disparities reflect fundamental behavioral considerations not accounted for in the Hicksian model on which welfare economics is based. Kahneman and Tversky (1979) propose that individuals have different values for losses and gains of the same size. In their formulation of "Prospect Theory," they claim that people often exhibit "loss aversion." That is, they may require much more compensation to give up an object than they would pay to obtain it, preferring the *status quo ante.* Several more recent papers report experimental evidence of an endowment effect—respondents express a willingness to pay less for a commonly available good not in their possession than they are willing to sell the exact same good for. These assertions that a good's value increases once it comes into the possession of an individual contradict a fundamental assumption of economic theory.

Several responses to the endowment effect hypothesis have emerged. Shogren et al. (2001) suggest that more elaborate auction mechanisms may decrease or even remove the effect. They report a laboratory experiment that shows that the endowment effect is evident in the initial bidding in an auction, but can be removed in more complex auction formats such as repetitions of a second price auction or random nth price auctions. (However, it is not clear that this added effort and complexity is practical in a contingent valuation survey.) Others have shown that the assumptions underlying the Willig (1976) and Randall and Stoll (1980) derivations (perfectly divisible goods, zero transactions costs, and large markets) may not hold in the case of environmental goods and services, and that disparities should not be a surprise. Hanemann (1999a) has demonstrated that if substitutes are limited, some disparities between WTP and WTA should be expected. Further, if no substitutes are possible (as with endangered species preservation), large differences are actually likely. The review of methods to compensate for lost nonuse or passive use values by the NOAA panel (Arrow et al. 1993) advocated a conservative stance. They suggested using a question format that underestimates willingness to pay and avoiding estimates based on implausibly large bids.

In their meta-analysis of WTA/WTP studies, Horowitz and McConnell (2002) throw new light on the issue. They include all studies they could identify that value various types of private goods as well as public environmental goods, conducted in laboratories as well as surveys. They conclude that the high WTA/WTP ratios do not appear to be experimental artifacts in that familiarity with the experiment does not systematically lead to lower ratios, that the results are found with student and nonstudent subjects, and that hypothetical experiments do not yield statistically significant higher ratios. Further, the closer a good is to being a private good, the lower the ratio of WTA to WTP. While theory supports a ratio of WTA to WTP greater than 1 for environmental goods, their results suggest much larger ratios on the average. Conversely, List (2003) studied actual markets (in this case functioning markets for sports memorabilia, such as sports cards). Dividing participants into experienced and inexperienced, he found that those without market experience exhibited the endowment effect, but not those who had extensive experience with the particular market, such as sports card dealers. While this result supports microeconomic theory in general, it does not seem to solve the environmental economist's problem of surveying a population on unfamiliar choices. In applied stated preference surveys, the WTP/WTA issue still awaits full resolution.

4.6.7 Hypothetical Bias in CVM Studies

Hypothetical bias means the hypothetical nature of the expressed preference format yields systematically higher bids than would bids requiring actual purchase of the commodity. One of the basic critiques of CVM is summarized in the phrase "ask a hypothetical question; get a hypothetical answer." Is the WTP elicited in survey research when compensation for the good is not actually demanded larger than when the respondent must in fact pay the cost?

In recent experiments on hypothetical bias (e.g. Shogren et al. 2001), two groups of subjects are questioned about their willingness to pay for specific, nonartificial goods, including contributions to an environmental organization, calculators, or candy. For one group of subjects, the "real" treatment, their stated willingness to pay leads to actual payment and acquisition of the good. The other subjects, in the "hypothetical" treatment, are not required to actually pay for the good nor do they receive it. Cummings and Taylor 2001 provide a survey of experimental methods applied to environmental economics.

Laboratory experiments have tested whether the bids made in open-ended CVM studies reflect "actual" WTP for a good, using real (but nonenvironmental) goods. Although some studies show little or no hypothetical bias, Cummings and Taylor (2001) report that WTP in hypothetical markets is significantly higher than in real markets, supporting the hypothetical bias. Brown et al. (1996), Cummings et al. (1997) and Cummings and Taylor (1999) find that the proportion of respondents voting yes is significantly higher in hypothetical referenda than in real referenda.

Cummings and Taylor (1999) devised a "cheap talk" method of avoiding hypothetical bias. In game theory, cheap talk refers to nonbinding communication between players. In CVM survey research, cheap talk is an element of a questionnaire that explains the problem of hypothetical bias in survey questionnaire responses. Cummings and Taylor and others following this approach find that cheap talk is effective in removing or reducing hypothetical bias for persons uninformed about the good being evaluated. Researchers have found that hypothetical bias is rare in consumers experienced with the good in question. Cheap talk appears to be a useful variation on questionnaire design for CVM.

4.6.8 Do Some CVM Survey Respondents Report Other than their Private Values?

Some critiques of CVM argue that individual members of society may adopt more than one role when they consider their valuation of proposed environmental policy. Individuals may see themselves as *consumers* in one situation and *citizens* in another. As consumers they pursue their well-being and their family's. But as citizen they act in an ethical role and are concerned with the public interest. Expressed preferences may differ depending on the role adopted. Given that cost–benefit analysis is based on an individualist perspective, if some participants in a CVM survey take the citizen's role in making responses, their responses may be inconsistent with those reported from the consumer's perspective.

Nyborg's (2000) much-praised essay formalized a model characterized by individuals who have two distinct preference orderings. She dubbed the individual acting in one role as *Homo economicus* and in the other as *Homo politicus.* In the latter role, the individual can make subjective judgments of the well-being of others. Nyborg suggests that willingness to pay from a social point of view depends on ethical views of equity and on the role of public goods in others' marginal well-being, so if respondents take on the *Homo politicus* role, their responses will be affected and their expressed preferences may not resemble those of persons acting as *Homo economicus.* This more general formulation, Nyborg notes, may help explain several perplexing anomalies found in many CVM studies, such as the large difference between WTA and WTP, the frequent presence of outliers in which respondents express a willingness to pay a large proportion of their income, and some cases of scoping effects, where respondents' preferences do not vary with the amount of environmental improvement returned by different policy options. Nyborg conjectures that these unusual responses may simply reflect differences in how the respondents interpreted their role in answering the survey questions.

Nyborg suggests that the questions raised by her model call for a questionnaire design which ensures that respondents understand that they should respond in the *Homo economicus* role. This can be accomplished by careful presentation of the questions, by explicitly requesting personal values, and by including follow-up questions to clarify the respondent's motives.

While CVM has been refined since it was first applied to environmental valuation some four decades ago, many questions remain. Nevertheless, CVM and related methods remain important tools for environmental economists because of their advantage in valuation of nonuse benefits and cases where observed market behavior is not available.

4.7 Choice Modeling

The goal of any expressed preference method for nonmarket environmental valuation is to quantify people's willingness to support a financial levy in order to avoid environmental damage or enhance the environment. Given the criticisms of CVM for these purposes, a number of economic researchers have sought to improve or extend expressed preference. A promising method called *Choice Modeling* (CM) traces its origins to psychologists interested in consumers' preferences among multi-attribute goods and services in commercial markets. The choice modeling method characterizes respondents' utility for the individual attributes of goods or services by examining the tradeoffs they make when choosing among alternatives.

The primary distinction between choice modeling methods and CVM is in how respondents are asked about their preferences. In contrast to the direct questions or dichotomous choice questions of CVM, CM presents the respondent with a set of choices among a number of alternatives, each characterized by multiple attributes. Then each respondent is typically asked to express a series of preferences among "choice sets," each involving a constant "no change" situation plus one or more proposed changes. Economic applications typically include price or costs as an attribute of each of the choice sets, which allows a multi-dimensional valuation function to be estimated for cost–benefit analysis. From the tradeoffs respondents make among the various attributes of the problem, the utility function of the sampled population may be inferred from statistical analysis. Subsequently, money measures of attributes of the utility function may be derived. See Bennett and Blamey 2001 for a full treatment of choice modeling concepts, methods, and applications to environmental issues. Terminology in this subject is still unsettled. In transportation economics, *stated preference* or *stated choice* is often used to describe this class of methods of ascertaining the consumers' utility function. Marketing researchers, who labeled the precursor method *conjoint analysis*, improved the general approach in search of tools for testing consumer responses to varying attributes of commercial products. Conjoint analysis was not originally based on any behavioral model of preferences, being primarily designed with mathematical and statistical considerations in mind. Hence, traditional conjoint analysis has been criticized for its limited ability to contribute to the understanding of basic human choice or to be useful for valuation purposes (Louviere 2001). Environmental economists have joined marketing researchers working in this area, adopting techniques based on random utility theory (e.g. Adamowicz et al. 1994). These approaches are often termed *choice experiments* or *choice modeling* (Bennett and Blamey 2001) or sometimes *attribute-based* methods (Holmes and Adamowiscz 2003). The terminology adopted here is *choice modeling* (CM). See Louviere et al. 2000 for a broad review of theory and practice of choice modeling, together with applications to transportation, marketing, and environmental issues.

4.7.1 A Hypothetical Illustration of CM Questionnaire Design

Consider an environmental policy to be evaluated with CM. The policy problem includes elements of a contentious issue presently under study by federal authorities in the semi-arid High Plains in the central United States, namely management of the Platte River, which originates in the Rocky Mountains of Wyoming and Colorado and flows eastward across Nebraska to join the Missouri River. Under natural conditions prior to European settlement, high spring flows from snowmelt created sandbars and wetlands in central Nebraska. These provided habitat for whooping cranes and sandhill cranes, who stop for several weeks on their spring migration from the Texas coast to summer nesting areas in Canada. Several species of small shorebirds (e.g. terns, plovers) also rely on the wetlands for nesting habitat. Since the early twentieth century, upriver development of storage reservoirs to divert water for crop irrigation has greatly reduced the river's annual flow and, in particular, diminished the natural pattern of high spring flows relied upon by the cranes and shorebirds. For this and other reasons, the whooping cranes and two species of shorebirds are now threatened with extinction. The environmental benefits at stake are largely nonuse values. Policy proposals include purchase of irrigation water rights to augment spring flows together with purchase of wetlands for shorebird habitat and reproduction.

Table 4-1 shows a hypothetical questionnaire that might be used to evaluate alternative proposals to augment water supply and wetlands in this policy context (the numbers are purely hypothetical). Following Louviere (2001), the questionnaire design in CM contains four elements:

- A set of fixed policy or choice options (1...*A*) that may have specific labels (such as augment stream flows or preserve endangered species) or simply generically named Option 1, Option 2, and so on. In Table 4-1, three policy options are shown: retain the *status quo*, and two potential increases in water supply and wetlands.
- A set of characteristics or attributes (1...*K*) that describe potential differences among the choice options. The selected characteristics are those hypothesized to influence the respondent's choice. Attributes in Table 4-1 include the cost to the respondent, the number of cranes migrating, the number of shorebirds surviving, the employment in irrigated agriculture, and the area in wetlands.
- Sets of levels assigned to each attribute to reflect an appropriate range in that attribute. The levels shown in Table 4-1 include tax burden (cost

Table 4-1. Example of One of a Number of Choice Sets in a Hypothetical Choice Experiment Questionnaire

	Policy Options		
	Option 1: *Continue* *current*	*Option 2:* *Increase spring flow* *to river (25%);*	*Option 3:* *Increase spring flow* *to river (50%);*
Outcomes	*situation*	*Buy wetlands*	*Buy wetlands*
Your household's cost (annual income tax surcharge)	No change	$25 increase	$50 increase
Number of endangered cranes safely migrating	150	200	225
Number of endangered shorebirds present	2000	2500	2800
Farm-related employment	5700	5500	5350
Wetlands area (1,000 acres)	15,000	25,000	32,000

Please check one of the boxes below which most closely matches your views.
_ I would choose Option 1
_ I would choose Option 2
_ I would choose Option 3
_ I would not choose any of these options, because I would prefer that the land and water remain in agriculture.

to the respondent), migrating cranes, wetlands, shorebird population, and farm employment.
- A group or sample of respondents contacted (by direct or telephone interview or by mail) to evaluate a subset of choice sets in the overall experiment. Each respondent chooses one option in each set. The researcher analyzes responses with statistical methods and draws inferences on valuation of individual attributes.

The responses to a choice experiment are analyzed within the framework of random utility theory. Random utility theory, originally proposed by psychologists, postulates that utility is a latent construct that exists (if at all) in the mind of consumers, but cannot be observed directly by the researcher. However, if the researcher employs a valid procedure for identifying consumers' utilities, it is possible to explain a significant proportion of the unobservable utility. However, some proportion of the utility will always remain unexplained, i.e. random or stochastic, from the researcher's viewpoint (Louviere 2001).

Repeated observations of choices from a sample of respondents can provide evidence on how the various characteristics affect the probability of choice. The distributional assumptions made regarding the random term influence the choice of analytic technique. For example, the binary probit model follows from an assumption of normal distribution. A multinomial logit model can be applied if the random term takes on a Gumbel distribution (McFadden 1974). Maximum likelihood methods are typically required to estimate the model. Econometric packages are available to perform the statistical analysis. Welfare measures based on random utility theory can then be applied to value the proposed policy changes (Hanemann 1994, 1999b). See Bennett and Adamowicz 2001 and Holmes and Adamowicz 2003 for summaries of the steps in performing a choice modeling experiment.

4.7.2 Advantages and Limitations

The primary advantage of choice modeling for nonmarket environmental evaluation is its ability to provide more detail of respondents' utility functions than CVM. CM can show the relative importance assigned to characteristics and derive estimated values associated with various levels of characteristics. The marginal rates of substitution of characteristics relative to a money cost are particularly useful products of a CM study. Choice modeling avoids the "framing effects" which may bias a CVM study. Because the CM questionnaire includes a larger range of substitute and complement goods, it reduces the likelihood that the respondent confers an excessive level of importance to the study. Finally, CM advocates argue, it reduces the chances that respondents can employ strategic behavior and tilt their responses to encourage their preferred policy option, rather than making responses which reflect their actual preferences.

But the higher degree of representation of the consumers' utility functions requires more of both respondent and analyst. Respondents may be intimidated by the greater complexity of the survey, and may have to struggle with the implications of the alternative proposals and their preferences among them. The analyst may face a more complex statistical analysis procedure.

On balance, however, it appears that choice modeling is an improvement on the general class of expressed preference studies. It will doubtless be increasingly employed in studies of nonuse values and where revealed preference methods are not applicable.

4.8 Concluding Comments on Expressed Preference Methods

Many analysts have applied CVM and related expressed preference methods to water-related issues. For estimating a marginal value for water allocation studies, the questions asked may not relate to *incremental* changes in water supply or quality, but to the value of the site or policy itself. However, questions regarding alternative amounts of water for fishing, boating, or streamside recreation, illustrated with photographs of alternative situations, have elicited plausible and useful estimates of the marginal value of streamflow. These approaches are treated in more detail in Chapter 7.

An expressed preference study can be effective where no other technique applies. However, if one hopes for an accurate result, extreme care must go into design and conduct of the survey. All the problems of sample surveys must be recognized and overcome (Salant and Dillman 1994; Rea and Parker 1997). Questionnaires must be carefully formulated and tested and, if not a mail survey, interviewers carefully selected, trained, and supervised. Statistical analysis of the responses will require advanced skills in econometric methods. CVM studies, properly performed, require a significant research effort, well-trained staff, and a budget to match.

The controversies over the usefulness of the expressed preference methods will doubtless continue. Hypothetical bias, insensitivity to scope, and the differences between WTA and WTP remain of concern, as does the choice between open-ended and discrete choice formats. A number of summaries using only small samples of studies report wide variations in results, and some results that seem implausible. However, several meta-analyses using very large samples of both expressed preference and revealed preference studies (Rosenberger and Loomis, 2000; Carson et al. 1996; Walsh et al. 1992) have found that, on average, reported willingness to pay from expressed preference studies are actually somewhat less than revealed preference measures for similar experiences. Moreover, expressed preference provides the only way to obtain certain important economic benefit measures, particularly nonuse values and values for proposed new policy. We can expect continued progress in research procedures to better use the advantages of expressed preference techniques.

4.9 Benefit Transfer

The resources and time available for careful valuation of a specific site or policy proposal are often limited. This is particularly true for small-scale projects, preliminary assessments, and projects or plans in developing countries. In such instances, analysts and planners have sought less costly approaches which rely in some way on evidence from previous research. These procedures synthesize previous empirical studies so as to generate additional generalized knowledge.

4.9.1 Overview of Benefit Transfer

Benefit transfer is a class of methods in which benefit assessments or demand functions for one or more sites or policy proposals are employed to assign benefits or value to other sites or policy proposals. In water resource planning, benefit transfer involves shifting value estimates from a "study site" to a "policy site," where the sites differ in location, environmental attributes, or nature of the user population. These methods use secondary sources, which may include expert opinions, estimates by government agencies, or conclusions gleaned from earlier studies of similar relationships. Benefit transfer has received the most attention in evaluating proposed improvements in environmental or recreational quality. However, without being so named, benefit transfer methods have long been employed in other circumstances, such as estimating demand functions for offstream water uses in river basin models. For example, Young and Gray (1972) drew on published empirical estimates of price elasticities of demand for at-site residential water uses to derive corresponding at-source values for intersectoral water allocation comparisons. Other examples are shown in Chapter 5.

Bergstrom and De Civita (1999) classify benefits transfer into three types. The simplest and least demanding, *fixed value transfer*, employs standard fixed values (such as values per visitor day for evaluating recreation benefits, or price elasticity of demand for residential water) from previous study sites to estimate total values at a policy site. Because the underlying demand characteristics determining the value of water at a policy site are likely to differ from those at a study site, the fixed value approach risks yielding somewhat inaccurate results. However, because this method best economizes on time and research resources, it is often the only benefit transfer applied to water planning.

Expert judgment bases policy site values on expert opinion. Examples include the "unit day value" method of the U. S. Water Resources Council (1983, *83-87*), in which planners look up judgment values for a site under investigation. This technique provides values in terms of "visitor days" but does not extend to valuation of water. See Loomis and Walsh 1997, *177-78*.

Value estimator models involve explicit analysis of previous studies of similar cases. Less formal methods are called *benefit function transfer*, while the more rigorous approach is termed *meta-analysis*.

4.9.2 Benefit Function Transfer

Benefit function transfer (Rosenberger and Loomis 2003) applies the results of a previous revealed preference or expressed preference study to a new site. Put another way, where a prospective recreational facility closely resembles an existing facility in the type of recreation to be provided, consumer benefits from the proposed new facilities are estimated by adapting the known demand function to the prospective site. Benefit function transfer assumes that the same basic benefit relationship applies to both sites. It requires that the coefficients for the independent variables (income, travel costs, etc.) in the existing benefit function be multiplied by values of the independent variable appropriate to the proposed site.

Consider a stylized zonal travel cost model (Loomis 1992):

$$\frac{T_{ij}}{POP_i} = B_0 - B_1 TC_{ij} + B_2 TIME_{ij} + B_3 SUBS_{ik} + B_4 INC_i + B_5 QUAL_j \qquad (4\text{-}2)$$

where:

T_{ij} = trips from origin i to site j

POP_i = population of origin i

TC_{ij} = travel cost of origin i to visit site j

$TIME_{ij}$ = travel time from origin i to site j

$SUBS_{ik}$ = a measure of the cost and quality of substitute site k to origin i

INC_i = average income of origin i

$QUAL_j$ = recreation quality at site j

A benefit function transfer from a study site to a policy site would insert the appropriate values for the independent variables (population, travel cost and time, substitute site(s), income, and recreation quality) into the equation already available for the study site, and solve to predict the quantity and value of recreational visits at the policy site.

Bergstrom and De Civita (1999) remark that the feasibility of benefit function transfer rests on the assumption that there exists some "grand valuation equation" in which values of independent variables appropriate to alternative sites can be substituted to derive a suitable value for any site. A test of this hypothesis, called a *convergent validity test*, consists of assembling the raw data from a group of study sites similar in recreation type, to see if the estimated coefficients are statistically different from each other. If the coefficients are not significantly different, using one existing equation to transfer benefits from a study site to a policy site will yield reasonably accurate results.

Studies to evaluate benefit function transfer report mixed results, but do not generally support convergence. Loomis et al. (1995) found that benefit transfers showed only small errors when used on general recreation sites within the same region, although, perhaps not surprisingly, unacceptably large errors occurred with an attempt to transfer benefit estimates from the Midwest to the West Coast. Although some authorities profess cautious optimism that benefit function transfer can perform a useful role, many questions remain unanswered. At this time, it is not clear that this approach is a general solution for benefit estimates in resource-limited situations.

4.9.3 Meta-Analysis

Meta-analysis comprises the more elaborate statistical methods to integrate research findings across a sample of studies. It has been called "the analysis of analyses." Meta-analysis investigates whether the reported differences among studies are due to the subject or location studied or the methods employed. Usually employing regression methods, meta-analysis involves formal statistical synthesis of the results of a number of studies of the same phenomenon for the purpose of distilling general conclusions. Each empirical study in a meta-analysis represents an observation in a meta-regression,with the object of reaching summary conclusions about a body of research. Meta-analysis is intended to go beyond the capabilities of conventional literary surveys and analyses of scientific literature. Although the term was coined in the 1970s, the technique originated much earlier with efforts to combine results of experiments on agricultural production techniques. The method has been most widely applied in medicine and psychology, but has attracted increasing interest in environmental economics.

Meta-analysis uses empirical estimates from a sample of studies in the technical literature and tries to explain the variation in these estimates using inter-study differences in a statistical inference framework. The resulting regression model can, in principle, explain the variation in benefits resulting from the differences among explanatory variables (subject, of course, to the *caveat* that the model specification incorporates all the relevant variables in the correct functional form). In an area lacking detailed study, meta-analysis can be the basis for a benefit function transfer by inserting the appropriate values of independent variables into the meta-analysis model and solving for the dependent variable (Rosenberger and Loomis 2003). Florax et al. (2002) present an extensive analysis of benefit transfer and meta-analysis methods in environmental policy.

Applications of meta-analysis to natural resource and environmental problems, although still limited, are increasing. Significant papers in this literature are described at appropriate points elsewhere in this book. Walsh et al. (1992) and Carson et al. (1996) examine extensive databases of recreational studies; they attempt to explain the net economic benefit per recreation day with such factors as the methodology employed (e.g. CVM versus TCM), the nature of the activity studied, and the character of the site. Rosenberger and Loomis (2000) have recently updated the Walsh et al. (1992) database, and performed a similar meta-analysis. Horowitz and McConnell (2002) examine the unexpectedly high ratios of WTA to WTP in contingent value studies. Espey et al. (1997) provide an example of meta-analysis in a study of residential water demand elasticities in the United States.

4.9.4 Assessing Benefit Transfer and Meta-Analysis

Researchers who have performed benefit function transfers and meta-analyses differ in their judgment of the power of these techniques in benefit transfer. Smith and Kaoru (1990), who focus on TCM studies, find support for meta-analysis, but reason that meta-analysis is best reserved for refining research in environmental valuation. This is clearly a valuable output of meta-analysis. However, this writer shares the view of other researchers experienced in benefit function transfer who contend that the method is not overly demanding of time and data, and will yield a more accurate benefit estimate than off-the-shelf values such as an average value per visitor day. Allowing for the effects of functional form, substitute possibilities, payment vehicle, and the like, meta-analysis could also be used for benefit transfer. In many practical applications to water policy or water supply investment appraisals, as well as in university-based research studies, resources will not be available to perform an original study of economic benefits, and benefit transfers are likely to provide a useful way forward.

4.10 General Conclusions Regarding Valuation of Water-Related Public Goods

In the past half-century economists have devoted enormous effort to developing and refining methods of inferring preferences for alternative uses of environmental amenities, including those related to water. This chapter has reviewed and assessed the three most frequently used approaches to measuring benefits for the case of public environmental goods.

Revealed preference (RP) methods are favored because they derive willingness to pay estimates by statistical analysis of observations of actual consumer behavior. RP methods include travel cost models of recreation demand and hedonic property value studies, which infer environmental values from measures of the effect of water supply or quality on real property values. When possible, economists generally prefer to infer environmental policy benefits from people's actual spending decisions in real consumption or business contexts. Travel cost models of recreation demand and hedonic property value techniques are designed to exploit those few consumption activities that relate to environmental quality in a monetary metric. They provide behavior-based estimates of actual valuations to which other techniques can be compared. However, the range of potential application is often limited, data collection and statistical analysis procedures may be demanding, and these methods may be inadequate for assessing proposed new policy initiatives. The empirical advantage of TCM techniques may mask the fact that they require the analyst to make assumptions about cost of travel, substitute sites, and functional form, each of which can influence the final result. Although their number continues to increase, published environmental valuation studies employing revealed preference are much fewer than those using expressed preference. Bockstael and McConnell (1999) point out that a revealed preference study is more difficult than expressed preference. Revealed preference requires some sort of natural social experiment to yield the necessary data. In contrast, expressed preference methods—as with the experimental sciences—permit the analyst to design a specific test of the relevant hypothesis. The scarcity of appropriate natural experiments accounts in part for the paucity of revealed preference analyses.

Expressed preference (EP) methods such as contingent valuation and choice modeling can be adapted to estimate WTP for contemplated water supply or quality changes. Moreover, EP seems to be the only approach for deducing passive or nonuse values. Because they are usually based on responses to questions regarding hypothetical costs to consumers, many are skeptical that these responses genuinely reflect willingness to pay. The results of these studies still vary according to the analytic procedures employed (statistical methods, model specifications, functional forms, and behavioral assumptions). Recent critiques have argued that some respondents may express what they take to be an ethical or *homo politicus* valuation rather than the *homo economicus* perspective required of a economic evaluation.

Because they avoid the need to collect new primary data, the methods generally classed as benefit transfer (including meta-analysis), tend to be less expensive and time consuming. They are favored where the extensive time, budget, and analytic skills necessary for a full-scale research effort are lacking. But this convenience may be more than offset by the rarity of cases where transfer is possible.

Part II

Applications of Valuation Methods

Valuation of Water Used in Irrigated Crop Production

To this point, the discussion has provided background and a conceptual basis for economic valuation of water and water-related policies. Now we turn to the details and complexities faced by economic analysts in application of these concepts and methods. This chapter and the next two take up water as private goods, primarily withdrawal uses, including intermediate or producers' goods (such as agriculture and industry) and municipal water supplies. Then Chapter 8 considers public consumers' goods, mainly non-withdrawal or instream uses, including water-related recreational and environmental issues, water quality enhancement, and flood risk reduction.

5.1 Background

Much of the food and fiber output in the world occurs on irrigated lands. Irrigation permits the production of agricultural commodities where reliance on natural rainfall would limit agricultural output to dryland or rain-fed crop production or only sporadic livestock grazing. Even in regions where annual rainfall is sufficient for productive crop agriculture, timely irrigation can boost annual crop output, as in much of Asia, where lengthy dry seasons are the norm. The world's supply of perishable vegetable and fruit crops is now in large part produced under irrigation. Producers favor climates where untimely rain is least likely to detract from the quality of the product, and also because very dry climates are often characterized by longer, warmer growing seasons, so perishable crops can be grown when the market is most favorable.

The accurate valuation of irrigation water is of special policy interest. In the United States and worldwide, irrigation of agricultural crops accounts

161

for a large portion of water withdrawals and by far the largest amount of water consumed (by evaporation from soil surfaces and transpiration from plants). Public expenditure on irrigation continues to be significant. The limited number of remaining low-cost sites for new irrigation projects has diminished the need for economic feasibility tests, particularly in the United States. However, some such proposals continue to be presented to policymakers elsewhere in the world, especially in Asia but also in the Middle East and Africa. Other policy problems relating to crop irrigation economics deserve attention. Planned investments in modernization of irrigation facilities often call for large expenditures, and these should rest on sound economic evaluation. Empirical estimates of the value of irrigation water provide important evidence of the farmers' ability to pay for irrigation projects. Perhaps the most important use of irrigation water valuations is analysis of economic tradeoffs among water-using sectors in the face of growing demands for water in urban and environmental uses. Although some agricultural uses of water yield high economic returns, low-valued consumptive uses of water are also common, so that intersectoral tradeoff analysis (such as between agricultural and urban demands) almost always considers the irrigation sector as the source to meet growing demands from other sectors. Conflicts between agricultural and environmental demands for water are also increasing. Yet another need for valuing water for irrigation arises with groundwater management. Agriculture is the major source of demand for groundwater, and economic evaluation of proposed groundwater withdrawal regulations is particularly important in the numerous aquifer regions experiencing overdrafts, land subsidence, intrusion of poor quality water, and other adverse effects of overexploitation. Finally, agricultural crop irrigation is both the source and the receptor of water quality problems, primarily that of dissolved mineral solids (more commonly called salinity). As in other uses, water quality influences the productivity of irrigation water. Salinity is to a greater or lesser degree found in all natural streams; evaporation of water diverted for irrigation leaves salts behind in irrigated soils, and drainage from such soils increases salinity concentrations downstream of irrigation diversions. So the economic benefits and costs (in the form of forgone benefits) are consequential in economic appraisal of salinity control programs.

The challenge in assigning an accurate economic value to water in crop production is the complexity of the allocation processes being modeled. The farmer must choose which crops to grow, how much land, labor, and capital resources to allocate to each crop, and what technologies to employ. Irrigated crop production is a dynamic biological process in which input decisions are made sequentially as crops are planted, grown, and harvested, but some decisions must be made months or years before output is harvested. Each decision in this process is contingent upon results of past decisions, past events, and information regarding future events. Farm households must make these multi-input, multi-output choices while facing uncertain input and output prices, uncertain production possibilities, heterogeneous labor supplies, and alternative employment opportunities for family labor and capital, all in a context of uncertain and changing national agricultural policy. It is well to recognize that the models used by economists represent major simplifications from real-world conditions.

This chapter draws on the broad conceptual framework developed in Chapter 2 and the specific measurement methods applicable to producers' goods presented in Chapter 3, and applies them to measuring irrigation water values. Some of the distinctive problems and pitfalls in actual applications are reviewed, important developments in the literature are noted, and conceptual and empirical issues in irrigation water valuation are analyzed.

5.1.1 Issues in Valuing Irrigation Water

Public projects to develop water for crop irrigation were one of the first subjects of nonmarket valuation. The standard methods of estimating values of irrigation water are deductive: estimates of rents to water are derived from models of farm firm behavior, usually based on the residual method, which forecasts revenue and then subtracts expected costs of purchased inputs and the estimated opportunity costs of owned inputs other than water. These models may be just a simple farm crop *cost and return* (CAR) budget of net return for one crop, which assumes a specific input mix and product yield. Or they may extend to mathematical programming models that portray the optimal allocation of farm water and other resources (land, materials, and labor) among several potential crops, and derive water input, crop yield, and net return to water as part of the solution. Irrigation water valuation may also employ statistical techniques to analyze actual water markets or markets for irrigated agricultural lands.

Methods used by public agencies to measure social economic benefits of public irrigation projects have long been controversial in the United States (Eckstein 1958; McKean 1958; Freeman 1966; Young 1978) and elsewhere. Some criticisms center on the implicit conceptual models employed, which, the critics contend, inadequately account for opportunity costs of labor and capital resources in calculating net return to water. Skeptics also observe that the commodity prices used in public project evaluations are not adequately adjusted for farm subsidy programs to more realistically reflect the social value of the outputs from a national accounting stance. Other challenges are empirical, contending that forecasts of future crop prices and yields, and hence revenues, have tended to be over-optimistic.

Factors Influencing the Value of Irrigation Water. When water economists are asked about the value of irrigation water, the answer, as usual in economics (and any other science), is: "It depends." In this case, it depends not only on the physical and market conditions where the production takes place, but also on the context in which the question is posed. Of course, as a component of agricultural production, the value of irrigation water is site-specific. The productivity of the location will vary according to factors such as climate, soil, and quality of irrigation water. Prices for outputs and inputs may also vary enough by region to influence willingness to pay for water. However, site considerations otherwise equal, there are a number of alternative formulations of the economic value of irrigation water. These vary between long-run and short-run values, private and social values, at-site and at-source (cost-adjusted) values, and per-period and capitalized values (see Chapter 2). Estimates of irrigation benefits over long time horizons must consider the potential for technological change and fluctuations in commodity and input prices. Further, a variety of approaches, both deductive and inductive, can be used in applied irrigation water valuation.

Anomalies Among Irrigation Water Valuations. A review of previous estimates of irrigation water value brings out several anomalies. One is an inconsistency between reported valuations based on observed behavior (inductive techniques) and those based on models of hypothesized farmer decisions (deductive techniques). Although the number of behavior-based valuations is not large, and this inference is not based on a formal meta-analysis, the large majority show a much lower (in dollars per unit volume) valuation than do those grounded in the more common deductive models. See Torell et al. (1990), who report very large differences between their hedonic analysis of the value of groundwater stocks in the High Plains region of the southwestern United States and results of farm budgeting exercises in the same region.

Second, the actual economic returns experienced by farmers from irrigation project investments are typically much lower than forecast by economic feasibility studies, even allowing for maturation of the investment. See Section 5.5.2 for case studies.

Water valuations on specialty crops (typically high revenue products, often perishable fruits and vegetables) exhibit a third anomaly. They are typically much higher than those derived for staple products such as food and feed grains, fibers, or forages. Yet the basic equimarginal principle of microeconomics would suggest that in given conditions of water supply and production, rational producers would allocate water so the value of the resource at the margin would be reasonably close to the same for all crops.

One of the goals of this chapter is to resolve, or at least to better understand, these anomalies.

5.1.2   Neo-Physiocratic versus Neoclassical Views on Irrigation

A largely unacknowledged methodological divide separates neoclassical economists (the perspective represented in this book) and many noneconomists and lay advocates interested in public irrigation policy. The latter's conception of the role of water in regional economic growth bears a striking resemblance to obsolete theories of the wealth of nations first developed by economists in mid-eighteenth century France. The "Physiocrats" (so-called because of their belief in the supreme role of physical— i.e. natural resource—inputs to the economy) held that the fortunes of agricultural producers (and more generally, natural resource extraction enterprises) played the key role in the growth of an economy. Revenues matched costs in all other sectors; these they labeled "sterile," meaning they yielded no net contribution or surplus to the national wealth. (See Blaug 1997 for an appraisal of the Physiocratic movement.) Economic policy should focus on expanding or improving the status of agricultural economic activities, which would increase the national wealth and, because of what are now called forward and backward linked effects, would directly translate to enhanced regional and national economies.

Mainstream classical economists, including Adam Smith, focused on the Physiocrats' failure to account for the roles of capital and trained labor in creating economic wealth. Investments in the agricultural sector would yield an economic surplus only if the costs were less than revenue. In modern views on economic growth, natural resource development is believed to play but a small role. Emphasis has turned to the roles of technological progress, a healthy, educated workforce, and institutions that efficiently allocate resources (see Easterly 2001).

Nevertheless, conceptions of a necessary central role for agriculture and natural resources in economic development, remarkably similar to those of the Physiocrats, recur in modern-day discussions of irrigation development policy. Nonspecialists, particularly those from rural areas, believe that agricultural enhancement via water resource development generates large direct and multiplier effects which provide an assured path to regional economic growth. What we might call *neo-physiocratic* views are rarely published in the academic literature of economics, although empirical applications sometimes appear in peer-reviewed but noneconomic journals. Regional input-output models (discussed in Section 3.9) can be adapted to portray linear responses of regional economies to changing agricultural water resource availability, and to use regional value added as a measure of economic surplus. (See Long 1988 and critical commentary by Young et al. 1988.) Mainstream economists criticize the neo-physiocratic approach for inadequately accounting for both direct and indirect opportunity costs, for ignoring the nonlinearities implied by diminishing marginal returns to resources, for disregarding factor substitution possibilities, and for failing to consider that output prices might be adversely affected by increased production. Neoclassical critics find that analysis from the neophysiocratic perspective overstates net social benefits of public resource development policies. The existence and magnitude of economic surplus from proposed additions of areas of crop irrigation is regarded by present-day economists as a hypothesis to be tested, not a given. Although neoclassical economists cannot yet claim to have learned how to deal with these issues in all practical policy evaluation contexts, they object to implicitly assuming them away.

5.2 Recapitulation of the Conceptual Framework for Valuing Irrigation Water

Section 3.5 derived a concept of "water-related net rents" as a sound, workable point measure of welfare gains and losses (in terms of willingness to pay for producers' goods). For the long term, this measure was shown to be calculated by estimating expected total revenue and subtracting from it anticipated costs of purchased inputs and opportunity costs of owned inputs. Consider the single product case where markets are competitive. Begin with a production function:

$$Y = f(X_M, X_H, X_K, X_L, X_C, X_W, E) \tag{5-1}$$

where Y refers to the quantity of an output and X to the quantity of an input. The subscripts M, H, and K refer to inputs that are typically purchased (contractual)—M: materials, energy and equipment; H: labor; and K: (borrowed) capital. The capital and operating costs of the farm's water distribution system (ditches, pipes, sprinklers, and the like, and the energy to operate them) are here treated as part of the materials, energy, and equipment costs. Although they often may also be purchased, the remaining inputs are assumed here to be owned or noncontractual. The owned inputs are specialized inputs, those whose prices, in reality, are determined after the fact by the outcomes of managerial decisions, but in water valuation practice must be estimated *ex ante* by opportunity costs. The subscript L refers to (unimproved or rain-fed) land, C refers to equity capital of the firm, and W refers to water. E stands for opportunity costs of owned skills, management, technical knowledge, and entrepreneurial creativity.

To move from the production function to the long-run rent function, let R represent rents and P refer to price. The superscript W stands for water and the superscript 1 identifies an at-site value. By convention, the net rent formulas are standardized in terms of land, i.e. expressed in per unit land (acres, hectares). Assuming durable input costs are expressed in annual equivalent terms, the basic (at-site) annual water-related rent formula for a single commodity can be written symbolically as:

$$R^{W1} = [Y \cdot P_Y] -$$
$$[(P_M \cdot X_M) + (P_H \cdot X_H) + (P_K \cdot X_K) + (P_L \cdot X_L) + C + E] \tag{5-2a}$$

The formula represents the at-site measure of a long-run welfare change (i.e. the firm's long-run willingness to pay for water for a crop on a unit land area). The firm's receiving point may be either the connection to a canal delivery system or, for a groundwater supply, the wellhead. By convention, this is the value used in irrigation investment evaluations, to be compared with annualized costs of supplying water to the same point of use.

For the at-source (raw water) value, the delivery costs of moving water from the source to the site must be deducted. Because they are commensurate with values computed for instream uses, such as environmental enhancement or energy production, at-source values are most appropriate for use in comparing intersectoral allocations. The delivery costs may be an annual fixed charge per unit land (denoted D) or, less often, a variable charge per unit water volume. Expressing delivery charges as an annual fixed charge per acre or hectare, the at-source water-related rent per unit land is:

$$R^{W2} = [Y \cdot P_Y] -$$
$$[(P_M \cdot X_M) + (P_H \cdot X_H) + (P_K \cdot X_K) + (P_L \cdot X_L) + E + C + D] \quad \text{(5-2b)}$$

Also, equation 5-2b is less than 5-2a by the amount D, so:

$$R^{W2} = R^{W1} - D \quad \text{(5-2c)}$$

Dividing through by W will give the rents and delivery costs in water volume terms.

5.3 The Water–Crop Production Function

The relationship between water use and crop output—the *water–crop production function*—provides the basis for all irrigation water valuation. A production function mathematically, tabularly, or graphically represents the relation between inputs and outputs in a production process. Water–crop production functions describe, explain, and predict the output from a specified level of inputs. They model farmer response to alternative water management policies, and inform public or private decisionmaking related to crop irrigation. Production functions for irrigated crops in applied valuation are derived mainly through expert opinion, but field experiments have been used and computer simulation approaches have recently become important.

Environmental economics tends to treat production functions as a minor issue in benefit estimation. In reality, any biological production process is extremely complicated, outputs being particularly dependent on the timing as well as the amount of the various inputs. More than most production processes, agricultural production is subject to uncontrolled variations and timing of environmental factors (temperature, precipitation, wind, soil, diseases, and pests). The quality of water may be as powerful an influence on productivity as is quantity. The introduction to Hexem and Heady 1978 presents a useful review of economic and agronomic concepts basic to water–crop production function analysis.

Production functions for irrigated agricultural crops can be derived from casual observation, opinions of local experts, field experiments, statistical analysis of survey data, or mathematical simulations based on observation. Vaux and Pruitt (1983) provide an extensive review of early water crop production functions, particularly those undertaken by agronomists. A later survey is given by Boggess et al. (1993).

The simplest irrigation production relationship is a single input-output coefficient that, for a given crop, specifies the annual water input per unit land area (say in acre-feet per acre or thousand cubic meters per hectare) and the corresponding estimated annual output per unit land area. For example, the annual water use in irrigated corn (maize) production at some specified locale and soil texture in the western United States might be characterized as 1.75 acre-feet per acre for a yield of 125 bushels per acre. Levels of all other inputs are also implicitly or explicitly specified. These coefficients are often used for crop budget studies of the net return to water (discussed later in this chapter) and are typically obtained by consulting local experts such as university or government researchers or agricultural extension agents. This is less expensive but less satisfactory than more systematic approaches.

5.3.1 Water–Crop Production Functions from Controlled Field Experiments

Analysts prefer production functions derived from statistical analysis of experimental data because they are more realistic and reliable than expert local opinion. Controlled experiments treat numerous small plots of a given crop with different amounts of irrigation water; the simplest hold all other inputs constant. More complicated experiments may better reflect the complex reality of producer choices by varying the amount of water applied at different growth stages and by varying the amounts and form of other inputs such as fertilizer, pesticides, row spacing, seeding rates, crop variety, and soil texture. Several replications of each treatment are required for a statistically reliable estimate. Of course, the more inputs included as variables, the more realistic will be the results, but the larger the number of treatments will be needed. Because of year-to-year climatic variations, similar experiments over several years will represent the production function more accurately.

The experimental data are fitted with statistical techniques, typically ordinary least squares regression, to estimate the total and marginal productivity of irrigation water. The quadratic form of the function (in which the water variable appears both directly and as a squared term) is often chosen. Such a function conforms to the expectation of diminishing marginal productivity of the water input. The marginal product is linear and thus easy to derive.

Rather than assume that water is a fixed input (as do the rent models), experimental production functions estimate the marginal physical product. When combined with observed or forecast output price data, this permits the derivation of a value marginal product, i.e. derived demand function. When combined with product price assumptions, the experimental production function yields an at-site rather than at-source measure of irrigation water value. That is, it measures standard willingness to pay for water at the farm receiving point.

Yaron (1967, reprinted in Dinar and Zilberman 2002) reported on water input (including rainfall) data in early experiments on sorghum from several years in Israel. The data were fitted with regression techniques to simple quadratic functions of the following form:

$$y = a + b_1 X + b_2 X^2$$

where y is yield per unit area; X is amount of water applied, and a, b_1, and b_2 are constants to be estimated. For multi-year experiments, an additional term representing the year of the experiment was included. Some versions incorporated varying fertilizer inputs. This function exhibits diminishing marginal returns and a linear marginal product function. Research budget constraints and computational limits curtailed the scope of these early experiments.

Hexem and Heady (1978) analyzed water–crop production function experiments conducted in the western United States from 1968 to 1972 by a team of university agronomists and economists funded by the U.S. Bureau of Reclamation. Fifty-two separate experiments were conducted on four crops (maize, cotton, wheat, sugar beet) at sites in five states. Not all crops were studied in each state. Water and nitrogen fertilizer were the variables. Climate and soil varied across the locations. Demand for water was estimated from the marginal product of the estimated function expressed in monetary terms. The Hexem-Heady study provided a state-of-the-art methodology for experimental development of water crop production functions.

A team of U.S. Department of Agriculture economists led by Harry Ayer conducted water crop production function experiments, again at various sites in the western United States (Ayer et al. 1983; Gibbons 1986, Chapter 2). To derive a point estimate of value, they expressed the result as marginal value of output (incorporating an appropriate product price) and then solved at some level of water use. These studies reported valuation results for individual crops in terms of the marginal value derived at a point representing a 10% reduction from yield-maximizing water levels (i.e. 10% below the point where marginal physical product reaches zero). Comparing values via a constant percentage reduction may seem somewhat arbitrary; it gives high weight to product price. A preferable method for comparing marginal values across crops might be to calculate value marginal product (VMP) at some fixed quantity—say one-half an acre-foot—below the point where VMP reaches zero. This latter approach would yield values per unit water that are more comparable across crops.

Although rigorous and detailed field experiments are among the best basic sources of water crop relationships, they have been infrequent for several reasons. The cost of conducting a water crop production experiment is high relative to the scope of generalization possible from the results. Properly measuring inputs to numerous small plots, especially water, demands skilled workers and extensive resources such as land, fertilizer, or pesticides, in addition to water. Measuring yield from each plot also requires care and effort. The researcher must choose a limited number of experimental options from among a formidable set of possible variations in level of inputs, crop variety, and irrigation delivery technology. Still the results may not be generalizable beyond the local experimental conditions. Transferring experimental results directly to field conditions needed for planning purposes may be difficult because actual farm yields on large fields are seldom as high as those found on small, carefully tended experimental plots. Hence, experimental results may need adjustment for applied valuation and policy analysis.

Economists are seldom able or willing to conduct field experiments themselves, so the complexity of interdisciplinary collaboration is another problem. Economists and agronomists work within differing scientific paradigms, and differences of opinion can arise as to the goals of the study. Agronomists tend to be most interested in identifying the input level to achieve maximum yield, while economists focus on finding the output of a range of water input levels to derive a marginal product function. The writer has debated research proposals with agronomists who rejected the notion of studying crop output under less than yield-maximizing conditions, and hence reject the concept of the economists' marginal product function, although these conflicts are no longer common. The Hexem and Heady 1978 data set continues to be useful in these interdisciplinary contexts. A number of agricultural production economists have used it to test the form of the production function, particularly the von Liebig production function—which embodies a nonsubstitution hypothesis—versus the neoclassical economic production function characterized by an input substitutability model. Several earlier analyses agreed with the von Liebig model, but Berck et al. (2000), using nonparametric methods, conclude that the neoclassical approach fits the data better. On the other hand, economists are often willing to simplify and study the yield only as a function of the total annual amount of water applied; agronomists tend to properly insist on the importance of timing in relation to crop growth stages and understanding the influence of other inputs (e.g. fertilizer and pesticides), soil texture and chemistry, and climate.

5.3.2 Simulation Modeling to Derive Water Crop Production Functions

As more precise scientific knowledge of the physical and biological factors affecting crop growth become available and the costs of computing fall, a new generation of mathematically trained agronomists is showing that simulated production functions are often feasible. Simulated production functions are based on models that combine physical knowledge of the effect of water application on soil moisture status (given assumed physical soil conditions) with biological knowledge of the effects of varying soil moisture levels on crops at differing plant growth stages. The soil component predicts soil moisture stress according to weather conditions and the timing, amount, and quality of water. (Letey and Dinar 1986 is a pioneering example.) The crop growth component reflects the effect of soil moisture on potential crop yield, depending on the stage of the plant growth cycle. These models can be adapted for specific soils and climates. For those with the necessary skills in mathematical modeling of soil moisture and plant growth, they provide a flexible, quick, and inexpensive method of producing agricultural production functions for varying local conditions. See Just 1991 and Dinar and Letey 1996.

To determine the effect of alternative irrigation schedules a transient state model, which reflects timing as well as quantity of water applied, is required. Bernardo et al. (1987) developed an irrigation simulation model of the effects of changing water use on net farm income in Washington State.

Building on prior work of Cardon and Letey (1992), Scheierling et al. (1997) developed a simulation model that incorporates the timing as well as the number of irrigations. Farmers apply irrigation water in discrete, more or less equal increments during the crop season, not an annual quantity along a continuously variable annual opportunity set as is often assumed in the abstractions favored by economists. Scheierling et al. posited that there were up to 9 periods (usually 10 days, but varying depending on the stage of the crop season, up to 25 days) in which water could be applied (or not) during a four-month summer growing season in northeastern Colorado. Their model forecast the yield under all combinations of discrete irrigation events in each of the nine periods. For each crop, there are over 500 possible discrete irrigation patterns. In Figure 5-1, following the procedure demonstrated in Scheierling et al. (1997), each dot

Yield (ton/a)

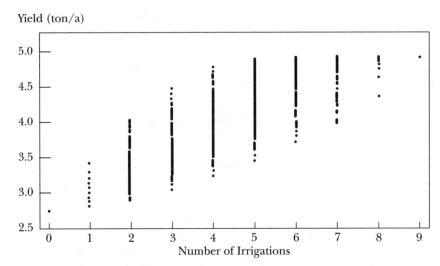

Figure 5.1. Computed Yield of Alfalfa Hay as a Function of the Number and Timing of Irrigations

Source: Scheierling et al. 1997

represents the predicted output of alfalfa hay for a distinct combination of timing and number of irrigations. These results illustrate the wide variation in yields of alfalfa for the range of potential numbers of irrigations (even with such factors as fertilizer application, seeding rate, crop variety, and soil productivity assumed constant) and the complexity of the irrigation production function.

5.3.3 Other Approaches to Developing Water Crop Production Functions

Water crop production function analyses based on secondary data (not originally collected for this purpose) are few because of the scarcity of appropriate data (M. Moore et al. 1992). These studies are valuable for broad scale testing of hypotheses of interest to policymakers but, in contrast to experimental or simulated water crop production functions, they are usually highly aggregated over production regions. They also typically provide marginal value productivity estimates for an aggregate of crops rather than on a crop-by-crop basis. For these reasons, they are seldom suitable for disaggregation into other planning models.

5.4 Inductive Techniques for Valuing Irrigation Water

The inductive (observation-based) methods for valuing irrigation water differ mainly according to the type and source of data and the form of statistical model, if any, used to estimate the productivity relationship. Sources include water rights markets, land markets, farm surveys, and secondary data.

5.4.1 Irrigation Water Valuation from Direct Observations on Water Rights Markets

Direct analysis of transactions in water rights between willing buyers and willing sellers in free markets for both short-term leases and permanent sales can be a useful source of information on water users' valuations of irrigation water. Market observations are of limited applicability in practice, however, because water markets and records of water market transactions are both scarce, and because the prices may not reflect long-run social prices.

Lease Markets for Water Rights. Anderson (1961) studied irrigation water lease markets in northeastern Colorado and noted that the lease prices were quite stable and fairly low (around $20 per acre-foot in current dollars). He also remarked that the price was about the level of the seller's already sunk out-of-pocket expenses—that is, the seller's appropriate share of the water supply agency assessments for operating costs for that year. Anderson suggested that observed water right lease rates may reflect social and cultural factors more than economic considerations (i.e. the marginal value of water). If such factors dominated, it would imply that lease prices are not set by economic forces and may not be appropriate for use for public planning. From a survey of irrigators in the same region, Bash and Young (1993) found that for at least one summer irrigation season with normal water supplies, water rights did mostly lease for about the annual district assessment. However, casual observation over the longer term in the same region by the present writer suggests that when water becomes genuinely scarce due to drought, such as occurred in 2000–2004, water lease prices do rise dramatically above the level of assessment. Denver newspapers in early 2004 reported a one year drought lease of more than 12,500 acre-feet of agricultural water by a Denver suburb for over $400 per acre-foot (Bunch 2004).

These empirical observations are consistent with a properly functioning market. In plentiful water supply, (which has been typical in the northern Colorado region), when reservoirs and groundwater supplement river flows, the equilibrium price would be expected to be low—even at or near the level of the district assessment. Users of water would not ordinarily obtain their full supply on the lease market, and would be willing to pay only a low lease price. Lessors of water might have little need at the margin for their water, but want to recover their sunk assessment costs. But both urban and agricultural irrigation demands would be quite price-inelastic in the short term, so in periods of water shortage such as the drought years following 2000, the lease price could be much higher, above the district assessment but still reflective of short-term buyer and seller valuations at the margin. Griffin and Characklis (2002) indicate that farm-to-farm water lease prices in the lower Rio Grande Basin in Texas were \$10 to \$15 per acre foot in normal years, but rose as high as \$60 per acre foot during dry years.

Saliba and Bush (1987, Chapter 5) describe a lease market for water in the Sevier River basin in southeastern Utah. An electric utility purchased extensive irrigation water rights to support a steam electric power plant, and subsequently leased surplus water back to irrigators at prices that varied with demand. As expected, lease rates varied inversely with river flows.

Annual lease rates for water rights tend to fluctuate widely with local climatic and water supply, reflecting a short-term demand for water that is quite price-inelastic. Hence using lease rates from only a few years to infer long-term valuation is tricky. No systematic application of statistical techniques to water lease prices has come to the writer's attention. In fact, due to the informality of water lease markets, it appears that no archive of water lease data is available for analysis.

Seasonal lease values are mainly short-run values in the Marshallian sense, since the participants have no opportunity to adjust fixed inputs. Lease market prices reflect not a social perspective (considering subsidies and taxes), but the private perspective. Lease prices usually represent at-site values, since the buyer typically does not have to pay the water district assessment costs the seller has incurred to maintain a water right. This practice is likely due to the fact that the water right owner (seller) will have paid the annual assessment costs before deciding to offer water for lease. Thus, water lease rates, while providing interesting evidence of short-term private demand and supply for irrigation water, may be of limited value for long-term public planning.

Market Prices for Perpetual Irrigation Water Rights. Time series data on prices for perpetual water rights are increasingly available for analysis. Like annual lease rates, prices for perpetual water rights reflect private rather than social accounting stance, but differ on other grounds. They are long-run and at-source values because buyers and sellers presumably account for all production, processing, and conveyance costs in their calculations of willingness to pay and to sell. Transactions for perpetual water rights are capitalized values, reflecting the anticipated present value of future net benefits. For estimating irrigation water values in long-run planning, prices on markets for perpetual water rights are more appropriate than lease rates. See Section 3.12 for additional discussion of water rights markets.

5.4.2 The Land Value Method for Valuing Irrigation Water

The U.S. Water Resources Council's *land value* method (1983) is based on simple comparisons of the selling prices of irrigated lands with the prices of lands that are nonirrigated but otherwise similar. It assumes that buyers and sellers in the land market are rational and fully informed, and that the observed land prices represent the amount a fully informed buyer would pay for the rights to a perpetual stream of returns from land ownership, which is the discounted present value of the stream of net rents. The price data from both alternatives (with and without irrigation) must be comparable in all other respects, such as soil quality and climate. Prices of actual market transactions are preferred, but estimates can also be obtained from self-reporting by owners or from estimates by professional real estate appraisers or sales agents (although such knowledgeable specialists may be scarce, particularly in developing countries). Land value will probably be most effective in desert areas distant from urban markets, where rights to irrigation water supplies constitute the major source of market value for irrigated crop land. Value to irrigation water rights may be inferred without a complex data collection and statistical analysis, with more or less readily available published data on real property sales combined with a simple budgeting procedure.

Imputing a value of water via land value requires at least four steps:

1. From land market transactions, determine the difference in prices for farms (per unit area, e.g. per acre or hectare) with irrigated land and those without. Several years of market observations may be necessary. The observations should be adjusted to account for inflation in land prices.
2. Estimate the amount of water (acre-feet, cubic meters) typically available each year to each unit of irrigated land. Divide the price difference obtained in step 1 by this figure to derive an estimate of the gross unit value of water.
3. Convert to an *annual* equivalent value. Insert the unit value difference, an appropriate interest or discount rate, and a planning period assumption into the present value expression and solve for the annual equivalent unit value of water. Hence, to convert the difference in land prices to an annual value of the type usually used in cost–benefit analysis (and comparable to that derived by the residual method), an interest or discount rate and a planning period must be selected and an assumption made how the (unknown) annual values of the interest rate behave over the years of the planning period. For land asset purchases, a long planning period is usually assumed. (For discussion of the assumptions and formulas, see Section 3.12.2 and particularly equation 3-19.) This procedure yields an *at-source* rather than an *at-site* measure, because buyers and sellers of land are assumed to incorporate an estimate of expected water costs in their calculation of expected future net rents to land and water. Thus the estimated value will be net of water costs and will be lower than the standard at-site value, which measures willingness to pay for water at the farm receiving point.
4. Derive the annual at-site value by adding the estimated cost of water to the at-source value.

Implementing Valuation from Land Market Data. If an annual lease equivalent is desired, should the analyst employ the market rate or a social rate of discount to convert capitalized values into annual values? Should it be a real or a nominal rate? Should a premium be added to reflect risk of the investment? The uncertainty of what interest rate to assume indicates that the answers are to some degree arbitrary. The usual approach is to try to approximate the discount rate used by market participants, say, on long-term loans for land purchases.

Rather than simply assuming a future stream of constant annual rents, market participants may assume a growth in land value due to general price inflation or to localized demand for nonagricultural land uses. In nations with a history of general price inflation and inadequate financial institutions, irrigated farm land is likely to be seen as a relatively safe store of value. Land ownership may be regarded as a social status symbol. For all of these reasons, the price of irrigated land may be larger than could be inferred from the capitalization of current net incomes at observed interest rates.

Prices on the agricultural land market in the United States do not relate to leases or net income in the simple fashion shown in the expression $V = A/r$. The real (inflation-adjusted) market price for farm land has shown wide cyclical swings, even when interest rates and net incomes are stable. Some of the best minds among agricultural economists have studied these land price fluctuations and failed to fully explain them. Clark et al. (1993), after analysis of land prices and annual incomes in both the United States and the state of Illinois, conclude that the simple asset pricing model does not adequately explain farmland price movements. Nevertheless, Falk and Lee (1998) show via a sophisticated analysis of Iowa farmland prices that, over long periods, farmland prices are mostly explained by permanent fundamental forces: changes in annual rents and interest rates. Within a shorter time frame (which may still be longer than a decade), they report that land prices tend to contain a fad element and overreact to temporary external changes. One of the most elaborate studies, by Just and Miranowski (1993), concluded that, although returns from farming are clearly important, expectations of future farmland price changes and macroeconomic phenomena (inflation and real rates of return on alternative uses of capital) also influence the market value of farmland. See Moss and Schmitz (2003) for more recent contributions to this literature.

Further, if any of the market value is attributable to potential real appreciation from nonagricultural (residential, industrial, or recreational) demands for the land, this factor should be accounted for by deducting the premium attributable to potential nonagricultural demand from the imputed irrigation gains. Because of the difficulty in estimating such a premium without formal econometric techniques, the land value method must be used with caution whenever this factor is judged to be significant.

Although formal econometric studies of agricultural land markets in developing nations are scarce, similar cyclical swings in the relationships between farm land prices and rents are likely. One example from Brazil (Brandao and de Rezende 1990) reported that the ratio between real farm land prices and real annual land rents varied as much as threefold during the period 1966–1988 (a period characterized in that country, however, by a serious episode of hyperinflation, highly variable interest rates, and, for a time, a government policy of negative real rates of interest for agricultural land purchases using government credit).

Because of its basis in actual real estate market transactions, the land value method merits further application, testing, and refinement. As a gross measure of benefit, market prices for irrigated versus nonirrigated lands can help form a preliminary judgment of the contribution of irrigation water and the likelihood of a project's economic feasibility. At the very least, if the observed differential between market prices per unit land area for irrigated lands and nonirrigated lands in a project region are considerably smaller than the public investment per acre required to provide a new irrigation water supply, estimates of project benefits must be examined carefully and skeptically. The land value approach (reflecting an at-source value) also can provide a first-order approximation of the forgone benefits of a market transfer of water.

Nevertheless, although less expensive, the land value method lacks the rigor of the standard hedonic property value method, principally because of the "omitted variables" problem. The net contribution of water is ideally estimated via statistical regression analysis, which controls for variations in significant factors other than the existence or nonexistence of irrigation. Cost and time considerations aside, a full hedonic pricing analysis, which uses formal statistical methods on observations of actual transactions and related factors to isolate the effect of water rights on farm land prices, is preferred to the simpler and less demanding land value approach.

5.4.3 The Hedonic Property Value Method Applied to Valuing Irrigation Water

Preliminaries. The formal statistical analysis of farm sales prices to isolate the net economic contribution of irrigation water is an example of the *hedonic property value* approach to water and environmental valuation. If agricultural land and real estate markets in a study area are active and competitive, then a statistical comparison of farm land values derived from samples of land sales representing various intensities of irrigation water supply per unit area of crop land can be used in a revealed preference valuing of irrigation water. Most economists are more comfortable with revealed preference— resource values derived from actual market behavior of buyers and sellers— than with *ex ante* calculations from models of assumed producer behavior.

The hedonic concept is mainly applied in the public goods context (see Chapter 4). But it is also applicable to producers' goods to the extent that market prices for producers' assets reflect the various attributes of those assets. Palmquist (1989) is credited with developing a general model for hedonic analysis of farm land markets. Land sale prices include willingness to pay for an associated bundle of rights to irrigation water as well as the value of the land itself. Data must allow the contribution of irrigation water to be statistically isolated from that of the land and other components of the sale prices, particularly proximity to urban land markets, soil quality, and presence of durable capital items (farm buildings and residences). This formulation has been exploited in surprisingly few instances for valuation of irrigation water.

To recapitulate Section 3.12, a typical approach to the topic would begin with a model such as:

Reported selling price of farm = $f(L, V, D, W)$

where

$L =$ land in farm (acres, hectares)
$V =$ value of farm buildings and residences ($)
$D =$ distance to nearest town (miles or kilometers)
$W =$ amount of water right (acre-feet or cubic meters)

The variables may also be expressed, where relevant, in per acre or hectare units. Some studies have included more detail on the quality of the land. If the data covered a period of rapid land price change, the year of the sale might be an explicit variable. It is important for the statistical validity of the method that amounts of water rights relative to land area vary significantly across the regional sample.

Previous Applications of Hedonic Property Value to Valuing Irrigation Water. Probably the earliest applications of hedonic value to irrigation water were Milliman (1959) and Hartman and Anderson (1962). These works predated the general adoption of the term "hedonic," but anticipated major developments of the hedonic property value method in the 1970s and later. Hartman and Anderson collected data from public records of sales of irrigated farms from 1954 to 1960 in a part of northeastern Colorado in which a federal water supply project had recently been completed (supplying the Northern Colorado Water Conservancy District). They gathered prices for 44 farm sales, together with the corresponding estimates of water rights, acreage of cropland, and other factors hypothesized to influence the sales value, such as the value of capital improvements and the distance to nearby towns. Linear regression analysis of the attributes on sales prices yielded a coefficient for each attribute. The coefficient on water rights holdings was interpreted to yield the incremental value that a typical perennial water right added to the price of an acre of farm land. With data on water availability per acre, an assumed interest rate, and assuming a long planning period, this coefficient provided the basis for an estimate of the value per acre-foot of water. Although the coefficient for water supply in their regression equation had the expected positive sign, it was not significantly greater than zero at conventional probability levels (e.g. 10%). Unit values of irrigation water were nevertheless calculated. The reported values were low—on the order of $3 per annual acre-foot in late 1950s price levels when a 10% discount rate was used to convert the estimated capital value to an annual value per acre-foot.

Crouter (1987) examined price and related data for 53 irrigated farm sales from the same region, but from about a decade later (1970s). Although Crouter's statistical methods were more sophisticated, the sample of transactions was not large, and she too was unable to find a statistically significant effect of irrigation water rights on farm sales price.

Torell et al. (1990) used ordinary least squares regression to statistically analyze sales of irrigated and nonirrigated lands to measure the value of *in situ* groundwater for irrigation in the High Plains region in the western United States. In the chosen study area (parts of Colorado, Kansas, Nebraska, New Mexico, and Oklahoma), essentially all water used for crop irrigation is drawn from the huge Ogallala-High Plains groundwater deposit which underlies major portions of a six-state region. These stocks of groundwater are largely nonrenewing, so the water table is declining after several decades of large-scale pumping for irrigation. The estimated value of water stocks at any specific site will depend on, among other factors, market participants' perception of the remaining water stocks and the years of economic life remaining at that site. The research of Torell et al. was notable for the detailed data set and the very large sample size. Over 7,200 observations of farm sales (of which over 1,100 were for farms that were all or in part irrigated) were obtained from federal farm lending agency records. The data, which encompassed seven years (1979–1985), permitted the analysis to control for the value of homes and buildings. For the water supply measure, the researchers separately obtained (from U.S. Geological Survey publications) physical data on groundwater stocks which differentiated irrigated parcels by the estimated amount of water underlying each parcel (based on saturated thickness and storage coefficient in the aquifer). The authors reported average values (in early 1980s price levels) over the entire region of about $3.90 per acre-foot of water in storage, with individual state estimates ranging from $1.50 to $8.35. The authors remarked that their estimates were much lower than those reached by economic studies in the region based on residual analyses using the farm budgeting technique.

A Quasi-Hedonic Approach. Faux and Perry (1999) studied the value of farm land from a sample of 225 farm sales in a desert valley in eastern Oregon during the years 1991–1995. The quantities of water rights for the individual land parcel sales were apparently not available, so rather than actually including a variable for water supply in their econometric model, Faux and Perry evaluated the effect of soil quality on farm land prices. Because water quantity is not reported for the individual sales observations and is not an independent variable in their hedonic equation, this effort cannot, strictly speaking, be labeled a hedonic property value study for irrigation water value. Hence, I label this a "quasi-hedonic" approach. From common knowledge that lighter-textured soils in the region yield higher land prices because they are better adapted to certain high-valued specialty root crops such as potatoes or onions, the authors partitioned their observations according to soil quality. The poorest soils were not irrigated and offered little productivity without water. Thus, from the results comparing prices of nonirrigated lands and prices of irrigated lands of each of the various soil qualities, they measured the effect of soil quality on land prices. They reported that the measured net returns to land differed by a factor of about five, depending on the quality of the soils. Using a discount rate of 6%, they then converted their estimate of the increment in land value attributable to soil quality to an annual value for each soil type. The water supply component of their study was introduced by assuming a uniform 2.5 acre feet per acre rate of irrigation water use over all sales in the study. These assumptions enabled them to derive a value per unit water volume (acre-foot). The estimates ranged from $9 to $44 for the lowest to the highest productivity irrigated soils, with a mode of about $18 per acre-foot. These conclusions, it appears, rest on the assumption that all of the rents are attributable to water and none to soil quality.

Why Are Hedonic Estimates of Irrigation Water Value Lower than Those Derived from Residual Methods? Torell et al. (1990) compared their hedonic valuations of irrigation water with typical valuations derived in their study region via residual (farm budgeting) methods, and found that their hedonic results were much smaller (in $ per acre-foot) than are those derived from residual methods. This divergence can be attributed to several factors.

Hedonic methods measure a different concept than standard valuation procedures. Hedonic property value of irrigation water measures an at-source (or water cost-adjusted) value rather than the at-site measure conventionally derived by residual methods. That is, the stream of net rents being priced on irrigated land markets will reflect expected revenues net of the expected costs of production (the latter including the expected costs of water to the land in question). To further derive an at-site estimate of water-related rents, estimated costs of obtaining water would have to be *added* to the corresponding at-source value. This is a point that apparently has not been recognized in the hedonic property value literature applied to valuing irrigation water.

To illustrate the significance of water costs when deriving an at-site value from hedonically-derived at-source values, we can refer again to the Torell et al. (1990) study of the Ogalalla High Plains aquifer described above. That study found annual at-source values averaging about $4 per acre-foot and ranging from about $2 to about $8 per acre-foot. Statewide average data on irrigation water costs from the 1998 Farm and Ranch Irrigation Survey (U.S. Bureau of the Census) can be added to the at-source values to provide some indication of corresponding at-site values. Table 20 of the Farm and Ranch Survey reports costs of water per acre-foot in the High Plains states ranging from $7 (Colorado) to $28 (Oklahoma) for an average of about $18 per acre-foot. These estimates are composites of groundwater costs and surface water costs, some of the which benefit from federal subsidies to capital costs and energy costs and others reflect century-old assets whose initial investments have long ago been amortized. Adding the average at-site value of $4 per acre-foot to the average water cost of $18 yields an estimated average at-site value of about $22 per-acre foot. It is noteworthy that the costs of water in this case are much larger than the at-site rents estimated by Torell et al.

Comparisons between residual and hedonic estimates must be made in equivalent contexts. Many residual estimates of irrigation water value are Marshallian short-run in concept, so they ignore some fixed costs and are appropriately much larger than the long-run estimates derived by hedonic methods under otherwise similar production conditions.

Even when the intent of a residual analysis is to derive a long-run value, if it ignores some inputs (perhaps by following some official procedural manual) the results may nevertheless overstate the "correct" value. Applied residual analysis may inadequately account for opportunity costs of owned resources, such as equity capital, management, and entrepreneurial skills. In the writer's view, because of such omissions, residual estimates in the literature tend to be biased on the high side.

More generally, the values that participants in the land market assume regarding future product prices, production costs, and interest rates are not observable, so the effects of these considerations are not readily resolved. Studies using the residual approach may use different prices for inputs and outputs or different crop yields than those implicit in the land market transactions. In particular, the interest rates used to discount a projected stream of net incomes in land market transactions may differ from that assumed in applications of the residual method.

Model specifications and data sets adopted in some hedonic property value studies applied to irrigation water yield estimates which on closer inspection tend to be on the low side. Both of the northern Colorado studies (Hartman and Anderson 1962; Crouter 1987) studied limited data sets, so larger numbers of sales observations might have yielded more statistically satisfactory results.

However, another explanation for these relatively low hedonic estimates might be the choice to exclude nonirrigated land sales in either data set, in which case hedonic property value estimates of the value of irrigation would be low. Irrigation water supplies per acre are not uniformly distributed across farms, but are clustered around the economic optimum supply. When all observations represent sale prices of irrigated lands (and none of nonirrigated lands), the range of water supplies across observations are likely to be limited and the observations all drawn from comparatively high levels of water input. Relatively little change in output per unit water input would be expected among the observed sales. In technical production economic terms, the observations are all for farm sales whose water supplies were clustered near the point on the production function where the output is at a maximum and value marginal product is approaching zero. Hence, the corresponding differences in capitalized value of irrigated lands across the sample can also be expected to be limited.

Consider now only the model formulation used by Torell et al. (1990). Even though these researchers sampled many sales of nonirrigated and partially irrigated lands, the lower than expected value of *in situ* water in their study may be partially due to model specification. The authors report inclusion of an independent variable reflecting expected annual net income per acre for each farm, based on published farm budget estimates for the main crops in the respective states. In this writer's view, this net farm income per acre variable is not statistically independent of the land price per acre dependent variable, which itself presumably represents the capitalized value of future net incomes. Inclusion of expected net farm income per acre as an independent variable is thereby likely to lead to a downward bias on the water supply coefficient and hence yield a corresponding underestimate of the value of stored water.

Finally, consider a case where growing urban markets drive an active demand for irrigation water rights. The derived value would be more a measure of urban water demand than in agriculture. Farmers may hold water rights as a speculative investment (as their "pension fund"), rather than selling as soon as water rights prices exceed the expected value in agriculture. It is not immediately obvious how one would control for this consideration in a hedonic study of irrigated land prices.

5.4.4 A Quasi-Hedonic Example: A "National Average" Unit Irrigation Water Value for the United States

An interesting and instructive market-based estimate of a unit value (in dollars per acre-foot) for irrigation water can be obtained from reported farm land market prices, here based on statistical analysis of secondary data from counties throughout the United States. The approach is termed a *quasi-hedonic* method for two reasons. First, the data points for the variables in the statistical analysis—farm land price and various shift variables—are not from individual observations on farm sales transactions.

Instead they are from secondary sources: county-wide averages of prices and other land characteristics reported by the U.S. Bureau of the Census. Second, the water use data are national averages from outside the statistical analysis. The example also bears a resemblance to the benefit transfer method, since it involves taking research results developed for one purpose and adapting to another problem.

In and of itself, a national average unit irrigation water value has no allocative significance. But it provides an interesting empirical estimate of the net economic contribution of irrigation water. An estimated unit value of water based on actual market behavior, even indirectly through the land market, can serve as a cross-check on conventional deductive techniques, and can provide an important piece of evidence on which to base water policy discussions.

The method begins with an estimate of the amount that the presence of irrigation adds to the market price of farm land. By dividing by the average water delivered per acre, the contribution to land value per acre-foot is obtained. Finally, by inserting an interest rate into a standard capital asset value formula, an annual value per acre-foot is derived. The initial value obtained by this procedure is an at-source measure. Thus the estimate will be a value net of water costs and will be lower than the standard at-site value. An estimate of the at-site value can then be obtained from this exercise by adding the estimated annual cost of water to the at-source value derived by the procedure.

Data Sources. The basic land price data is based on a somewhat unlikely source, a rigorous and extensive econometric analysis of the climatic and economic factors affecting farmland values in the United States by Mendelsohn and Nordhaus (1996). Mendelsohn et al. (1994) developed a "Ricardian" land value econometric model for understanding and measuring the potential economic effects of global warming on United States agriculture. With advanced econometric procedures and an admirably extensive database, they studied the effects of numerous factors (over thirty variables, mainly representing determinants hypothesized to influence farm productivity and revenues) on farm real estate prices. Agricultural data, including the dependent variable—farm land prices—and values of products sold and market inputs were represented by data from over 2,900 counties drawn from the 1982 Census of Agriculture. The effect of climate was accounted for by linear and quadratic terms for precipitation and temperature in January, April, July, and October. Data were also obtained for "control" or shift variables, to account for differences in factors such as soils (including texture, salinity, slope, permeability, and water capacity), flood proneness, presence of wetlands, and altitude. The analysis controlled for nearness to markets and urban centers. They used the results in a highly innovative way to infer future economic effects from hypothetical global climate changes.

In a subsequent "Reply" to critics, Mendelsohn and Nordhaus (1996) added irrigated acreage per county to the list of explanatory variables in a re-estimation of the Ricardian model. They found that the use of irrigation water added an average of about $910 to the value of an acre of farm land in 1982. The regression coefficient for the irrigation variable is large and highly significant. The reported t-statistic was a convincing 17.4, implying, for the irrigation variable, a relatively small standard error of the regression coefficient of $52 per acre. The reported $910 per acre is equivalent to the capitalized value of rents to water net of water delivery charges. Put another way, it is the capitalized value of the water-cost adjusted rents per acre shown in equation 5-2c above.

The Mendelsohn-Nordhaus estimate of the increment to the value of farmland added by irrigation seems plausible. But the "irrigation" coefficient derived in the econometric analysis may not fully capture the contribution of irrigation to land values. It is possible that some of the impact is reflected in other coefficients, such as one of the climatic variables. Conversely, the irrigation variable may reflect inputs other than water.

The estimated value of the capitalized incremental income from irrigation (rounded to $900) will be combined with data from the U.S. Geological Survey's periodic reports of water use and an appropriate discount rate to derive an estimate of the national average value per acre-foot of irrigation water used by farms.

What Measure of "Water Use" to Employ? To develop a measure of the unit value of water, a metric to represent quantity of water use is needed. Several measures are conventionally employed to measure the volume of irrigation water use, depending on the purpose of the measurement. These are withdrawal, delivery, and consumption. For measures of national average water use, refer to the U.S. Geological Survey's *The Use of Water in the United States in 1980* (Solley et al. 1983). This document reports acres irrigated, water withdrawal, conveyance losses, and consumption for the major water-using sectors, including irrigation, for 1980. This report is issued every five years, so it provides water use data for the closest year available to Mendelsohn and Nordhaus' 1982 sample. Although it would be preferable to have the water use and land value measures from the same year, acres irrigated and water use per acre probably do not vary greatly from year to year.

Although each water use measure has its place in water economics, I begin with delivery (the amount withdrawn net of conveyance losses) as the most suitable measure of water use for this data set. This choice is consistent with water supply and cost conditions most likely to be reflected in market prices for irrigated lands, because costs of having water delivered to the farm headgate will be incorporated into the market participants' expected net returns calculations.

Derivation. Solley et al. (1983, Table 5) report about 170 million acre-feet of water withdrawn to irrigate 58 million acres of crop land. Adjusting for

Table 5-1. A Quasi-Hedonic Estimate of National Average *At-Source* Values of Irrigation Water ($ per acre-foot) under Alternative Incremental Land Price and Interest Rate Assumptions

	Assumed Increment to Land Value Provided by Irrigation ($/Acre)		
Assumed Interest Rate (%)	*$720*	*$900*	*$1080*
5	14	18	22
7	20	25	30
9	26	33	39

Note: Assuming 2.5 acre-feet of water delivered per acre. Results rounded to nearest dollar.

estimated delivery losses of 26 million acre-feet (about 19%) yields a total of 144 million acre-feet delivered to farms. This implies about 2.5 acre-feet per acre as the nationwide average delivery of water per acre for irrigated lands in 1980. Combined with the Mendelsohn-Nordhaus estimate of the incremental value of irrigation (rounded to $900), these figures ($900/2.5) imply a value (capitalized stream of future net income) of an acre-foot of water delivered in perpetuity of about $360.

The next step is to insert the land value increment per acre-foot (as the capitalized value V) and an interest rate into the simplified capital value expression equation 3-20: ($V = A/r$) and solve for A. For a base interest rate, I assume that farm land markets discounted annual net income at a rate of about 7% in the early 1980s.

Table 5-1 presents the results of these calculations, with an assessment of the sensitivity of the results to alternative land price increments and interest rates. For the basic land price increment of $900 per acre, 2.5 acre feet of water per acre and r at 7%, the annualized at-source value would be $360 × 0.07 or about $25 per acre-foot ($0.02 per cubic meter) in 1982$.

Sensitivity to Alternative Parameter Assumptions. It is instructive to calculate the sensitivity of the above results to alternative values of the interest rate or the increment to land price added by irrigation (shown in Table 5-1). The derived value of water is directly related to the assumed interest rate: the higher (lower) the interest rate, the higher (lower) the inferred value of water. At $900 per acre, a 5% interest rate would imply an annual value of irrigation water of around $18 per acre-foot. At a 9% rate of interest, the annual value would be about $33 per acre-foot.

Similarly, a higher (lower) value of the increment to land price added by irrigation would lead to higher (lower) inferred value of irrigation water. For example, a 20% increase in the assumed increment to land prices added by irrigation would lead to a corresponding increase in the derived value of irrigation water. Using the base 7% interest rate, the implied at-source value of irrigation water from a land price increment of $1080 per acre would be about $30 per acre-foot, and $20 per acre-foot for an increment of $720 per acre.

Table 5-2. A Quasi-Hedonic Estimate of National Average *At-Site* Values of Irrigation ($/acre-foot) under Alternative Assumptions for Incremental Land Price and Estimated Cost of Water Supply)

Producer's Cost of Water ($/acre-foot)	Assumed Increment to Land Value Provided by Irrigation ($/acre)		
	$720	$900	$1080
$9	29	34	39
$12	32	37	42
$15	35	40	45

Note: Assuming 2.5 acre-feet delivered per acre; interest rate = 7%. (Results rounded to nearest dollar.)

Water is increasingly scarce in the semi-arid and arid regions of the western United States. The estimated values of water would be expected to be higher there. However, the more arid regions also use more water per acre, so a more localized value per acre-foot imputed by this method might not greatly differ.

Converting from At-Source to At-Site Values. The standard measure of the value of irrigation water is the willingness to pay for water at the farm receiving point (the at-site value). To derive this measure from the quasi-hedonic estimates (which are at-source values) shown in Table 5-1, one needs to add an estimate of the cost of water to farms. Table 5-2 illustrates this step and the sensitivity of the results to alternative increments in land value due to irrigation or the cost to farmers of acquiring water. The most likely national average cost of delivered water per acre-foot would be about $12 per acre-foot (which, based on the U.S. Census 1998 *Farm and Ranch Irrigation Survey*, Table 20 (US Department of Commerce 1998), was approximately the national average cost of irrigation water in 1994, adjusted for inflation to 1982). The sensitivity analysis employs alternative irrigation water costs of $9 and $15 per acre-foot. The resulting estimates center on $37 per acre-foot and range from $29 to $45. Note that these are costs faced by private irrigators; they incorporate federal or other subsidies and do not include indirect or external costs.

Concluding Thoughts. The capitalization formula used above reflects only the simplest possible assumptions about expectations on future land prices. A formula reflecting a more dynamic land market, reflecting systematic future real land price changes, might be warranted.

The farm land market data used in the Mendelsohn-Nordhaus study represents what would be termed a private value, reflecting the prices of crops, water, and other inputs experienced or expected by farm buyers and sellers. However, much of the irrigation water supply in the United States is subsidized by the federal government. Water users supplied by federal projects pay only a fraction of actual costs of capturing, storing, and delivering water to farms. Moreover, some crops produced under irrigation are subsidized by federal farm income support programs (e.g. cotton, rice). Subsidies to credit and pumping energy may further influence the market value of irrigated land. Hence the actual capitalized net income accounted for in farm land market prices is higher than it would be under a social accounting stance which reflected the full social cost of providing water and the social prices of agricultural crops. Although the social value of irrigation water would clearly be less than measured above, it is not obvious how one would adjust the basic national data to reflect these considerations.

The 1982 estimate might be adjusted to more recent price levels, say, year 2000. The most appropriate deflator appears to be the U.S. Department of Agriculture's "Index of Prices Received by Farmers: All Crops" (U.S. Department of Agriculture 2002). Since 1982 the value of that Index has fluctuated above and below its 1982 value, but in 2000 it was not much different from 1982. With no clear evidence of a trend in prices received for crops, no adjustment is necessary. In fact, farm land prices in 1982 were not particularly representative of longer-term trends. The year selected for the analysis represents land prices that were just a year or so past the peak real price of farm land in the United States over a long cycle which had begun in the 1950s (Moss and Schmitz 2003). During this period, real (inflation-adjusted) farm land prices almost tripled, peaked in 1981, and then fell by almost 40% by 1987. Adjusted for inflation by the Gross Domestic Product Implicit Price Deflator, by the late 1990s national average farm land prices had regained only about half of the loss registered between 1981 and 1987). Thus, this 1982 estimate of the contribution of irrigation to farm land prices is likely to be larger than would have been derived with data from some "average" year of that period or from a recent year.

Finally, one cannot realistically point to any single measure as *the* value of irrigation water. Each of the factors hypothesized in this simple model to influence irrigation water value—measure of water quantity, interest rate, whether the measure is at-site or at-source, and the nonwater components of irrigation—can have a considerable impact on the derived estimates. The exact parameter values one should assume in making the final estimate are not clear. Nevertheless, the most plausible assumptions ($900 per acre increment in market value from irrigation; 7% interest rate; 2.5 acre-feet of water per acre) lead to an at-source value of $25 per acre-foot. Further, adjusting by the estimated cost of water to farmers of $12 per acre-foot yields a national average at-site value of $37 per acre-foot.

5.4.5 Concluding Assessment of the Hedonic Property Value and Related Methods Applied to Irrigation Water

Most economists are more comfortable with resource values derived from actual market behavior of buyers and sellers, than with results using assumed behavior and data. If agricultural land and real estate markets in a potential irrigated farming study area are active and competitive, then statistical or less formal comparisons of farm land values derived from samples of land sales representing various intensities of irrigation water supply per unit area of crop land can provide useful and relatively convincing revealed preference approaches to valuing irrigation water.

Challenges confront the analyst implementing the hedonic approach to valuing irrigation water. One has to locate a natural experiment where both nonirrigated and irrigated lands of relatively similar climate and market conditions are bought and sold on a competitive market. Even then, there will be the usual time and resource costs of obtaining satisfactory data of farm sales prices, water rights, and the associated attributes of the land. In a pure hedonic study, for each transaction some estimate of the amount of irrigation water available per unit land must be available, and the observations on water supply must vary widely enough for a satisfactory statistical estimate. It is preferable to have sales of nonirrigated lands in the data set as well. Measures of the various shift variables, such as proximity to urban centers and measures of capital improvements (farm buildings and even residences), usually need to be incorporated in the data set. Since the sales price data are usually obtained from public records, additional study of the conditions applicable to each sales observation, perhaps with survey techniques, is necessary to measure these shift variables. To derive an at-site measure of net rents, an estimate of the costs of obtaining water is needed. Advanced proficiency with data manipulation and econometric techniques is usually required to derive reliable results. Because use of the method faces significant demands for data and econometric skills, the full hedonic approach is likely to have a relatively limited potential for estimating the value of irrigation water except in research contexts. These considerations together likely explain the limited number of studies in the literature.

The hedonic property value method measures past experience at a given location and under given economic and institutional conditions, which may not be applicable to other places and conditions. The hedonic property value method will likely be most useful in serving as a benchmark against which other irrigation water valuation methods can be evaluated. No study has yet, to my knowledge, performed both a hedonic property value and a residual valuation of irrigation water value for identical conditions. Studies of this sort should be encouraged, and would help resolve questions about both methods.

5.5 Other Inductive Methods Using Primary and Secondary Data for Valuing Irrigation Water

Applications of inductive techniques for estimating benefits of irrigation water supply are less common in the literature than deductive techniques.

Inductive techniques typically require expensive and time-consuming surveys of water use, practices, and crop yields, unless they are based on secondary data collected for purposes other than resource valuation.

5.5.1 Econometric Valuation of Irrigation Water from Primary Data

Farm survey data has been analyzed to estimate the value marginal productivity of irrigation water, particularly in developing countries. Econometric (regression) techniques can be applied to data collected by a survey specifically designed for this analysis or, less often, from general-purpose government surveys of farmers such as agricultural censuses.

Hussain and Young (1985) fitted a Cobb-Douglas function to farm survey data collected in a region in Pakistan. Because of the country's generally arid climate, agricultural crop production is largely carried out with the aid of irrigation. Investment in water-saving technologies (canal and ditch lining) and augmented groundwater supplies was the policy under study.

The conditions of water supply available to farmers differs widely across Pakistan. Some farms have nonperennial water supplies and irrigate only in summer, others can irrigate with surface water throughout the year, and still others can supplement surface water with groundwater or by informal exchanges with neighbors with excess surface or groundwater supply. This variation permits a valid statistical inference of the influence of irrigation on the value of production. Data collection was funded by the World Bank and the Government of Pakistan in an ambitious project called the "Water and Power Development Authority-World Bank Extended Farm Management Survey." About 2,000 farmers were personally interviewed in the three provinces with extensive irrigated agriculture (Sind, Punjab and North West Frontier) regarding the 1976–1977 crop year. About 400 watercourses (local ditches that are the final stage of the delivery system) were selected randomly for study. Every eighth farmer was selected for interview from each watercourse by proportionate sampling. The survey obtained detailed information on use of land, irrigation water, labor and cash inputs (such as seed, pesticides, and fertilizer), and on the yield and value of crop production. Because of the difficulty of measuring actual irrigation application, water use was measured by the number of irrigations. Conventional wisdom assumed an average of three acre inches per acre per irrigation.

The model was fit to several functional forms, including Cobb-Douglas, transcendental, and Generalized Cobb-Douglas. The standard Cobb-Douglas form (in which all variables are expressed in natural logarithms of their observed values) provided the best fit to the data. (For both empirical and computational reasons, the Cobb-Douglas formulation has been among the most frequently used for fitting agricultural production data. It provides a good, and often the best, statistical fit among functional forms. Because it is linear in logarithms, it is relatively easy to fit with ordinary least squares (OLS) methods. Results are convenient to derive and interpret, since the coefficients are the production elasticities (Heady and Dillon 1969.) The estimated production function represents a composite of crops rather than one single crop. Conventional t-tests on the coefficients and the Coefficient of Determination (R^2) = 0.62 show a relatively good fit to the data. The coefficient for the irrigation variable was positive, large, and significantly different from zero at the 99% level of probability. Solving the estimated equation at the mean number of irrigations showed that an additional application of irrigation water per year yields a marginal value amounting to several time the cost of the most likely alternative water supply, in this case pumping groundwater. This result illustrates the strong economic incentives for Punjab farmers to invest private funds in groundwater supplies during the study period.

Several studies have taken the less common approach of estimating water productivity via a cost function approach. A study by M.R. Moore et al. (2000) is based on interviews at over 500 irrigated crop farms in the Pacific Northwest. The authors measured the decreases in producers' surplus (forgone benefits) from possible pumping cost increases linked to the federal government's recovery program for endangered salmon in the Columbia-Snake River Basin. Individual observations on farms, taken from federal surveys of irrigated farms in the region, together with secondary data on prices, electricity costs, and other variables, constitute the data base. Because the data contained observations of farms which did not produce all of the typical crops in the region, an advanced econometric technique, the censored regression (tobit) model is appropriate for estimating the cost function.

5.5.2 Econometric Studies with Aggregate Regional Secondary Data

Most economic studies of irrigation using secondary data from multiple farms do not yield direct measures of the per unit value of irrigation water. But they can throw light on the relative impact of public expenditures on irrigation development. Ruttan's (1965) analysis of county-level time series data used regression techniques to estimate regional production functions with a dependent variable of total value of farm output and independent variables of irrigated land, nonirrigated land, labor, operating expenses and quantity of capital (livestock and machinery). (Note that the variable representing irrigation is area of irrigated land, not volume of water.) Ruttan then derived marginal value products of irrigated land from his estimated function. He concluded that the marginal value product of irrigation approximated the marginal private (subsidized) cost (as predicted by economic theory), but was much lower than the full social cost of providing the water via federal programs.

A spate of econometric studies in the United States in the late 1960s and early 1970s used secondary data to study the role of water resource development in regional economic growth These studies concluded that water resource development in general and irrigation projects in particular showed little positive impact on regional economic growth. Fullerton et al. (1975) studied the effect of federal irrigation development in the western United States, applying econometric techniques to county-level government statistical series. They reported little statistically measurable impact on regional income and employment. Similarly, Cicchetti et al. (1975) examined effects on regional economic growth in the southwestern states of U.S. Bureau of Reclamation investments in water resource projects and other public expenditures using data from 1950, 1960, and 1970 for 21 multi-county subregions in Arizona, Colorado, New Mexico, Utah, and Colorado. The subregions were chosen on the basis of having within their boundaries Bureau of Reclamation water projects in operation since at least the late 1930s. They performed two types of tests. The dependent variables in each test were regional per capita income and value of regional farm production. The independent variables in the first test were Bureau of Reclamation capital stock measures and employment. Independent variables in the second test included several classes of federal water project expenditure (irrigation, hydropower, flood control, recreation) and several types of state and local government expenditures. In the first test, pooled time series and cross-section data were fitted with regression techniques to a Cobb-Douglas specification. The second test involved fitting linear models of the *changes* in regional per capita income and value of farm production. The second test analyzed both a pooled times series-cross section for the whole period, and decade-to-decade changes. Positive and statistically significant effects on regional income growth of federal investments in hydropower, recreation, and flood control and of state and local expenditures on education, roads, health, and police services were reported. However, the variables representing federal investments or expenditures on irrigation did not emerge as major influences on either income or farm output. Irrigation capital was found to have a small influence on the value of farm production in the Cobb-Douglas model. No statistically significant influences on either regional income or the value of regional farm output were found in any of the statistical tests performed.

C.V. Moore et al. (1982) performed an *ex post* evaluation of 18 U.S. Bureau of Reclamation irrigation projects using land value comparisons. They reported that only 6 of the 18 projects showed an increase in land value greater than the present value of the subsidy implicit in the cost recovery rules. The authors drew the implication that the *ex post* social benefit–cost ratios were less than 1.0 for the remaining 12 projects.

M.R. Moore (1999) studied a federal Reclamation project in the Sacramento Valley in northern California to measure what he termed farmers' "ability to pay" for irrigation water. (What the author terms ability to pay is apparently the marginal revenue product, which is a suitable measure of private long-run at-site economic willingness to pay for irrigation.) With econometric techniques, he fitted a multi-output revenue function to 10 years of revenue and water input data from 19 irrigation districts that varied in water supply per acre, cropping mixes, and productivity. Moore reported values between $44 and $65 per acre-foot for 1989 from the various districts. The approach can be labeled as yielding an at-site measure. However, the method may include charges properly assigned to nonwater owned inputs—such as management and equity capital—as part of the ability to pay for water, and thus overstate its value and farmers' willingness to pay.

The International Food Policy Research Institute (IFPRI) recently studied policies designed to enhance rural economic growth and reduce poverty in developing countries. Each study used state or provincial time series data for India and China. Fan et al. (1999) used 1970–1993 state data on expenditures in India in a cross-section time-series econometric study. They found that irrigation development distantly trailed road building, agricultural research and development, and education in its impact on poverty reduction, although irrigation investments showed a somewhat more favorable impact on productivity. Evenson et al. (1999) assessed the effects of public investment in research, extension, and irrigation together with private investment in agricultural research on the growth in total factor productivity in India. Data were from nearly all districts from 13 states in India from 1956 to 1987. The marginal internal rate of return to investments in irrigation was found to be about 5% in each of several model specifications. This modest rate of return is probably considerably lower that the expected social opportunity cost of capital in that nation. In contrast, public expenditures on agricultural research and extension were reported to yield marginal internal rates of return of 58% and 45%, respectively. Fan et al. (2002) analyzed the roles of specific public investments—agricultural research and development; irrigation; rural education; and infrastructure such as roads, electricity, and telecommunications—in fostering growth and reducing poverty. A simultaneous equation model was fitted to provincial-level data for 1970–1997. For the nation as a whole and for each of three economic zones, the authors reported high returns to investment in education, agricultural research and development, and rural infrastructure, but "[i]nvestments in irrigation had only modest impact on agricultural production, and even less impact on poverty reduction, even after trickle-down benefits were allowed." The overall inference, summarized in Fan and Hazell 2001, is that rates of economic return to investments in irrigated agriculture have been low in recent decades, particularly when compared to the return on alternatives for improving the livelihoods of the rural poor, such as agricultural research, education, or rural road construction. These results imply a negative net present value of irrigation investments when benefits and costs are discounted at real interest rates appropriate to developing countries (10%

or greater). Fan and Hazell further conclude that irrigation project investments remove only one-tenth as many people from poverty per unit of monetary investment as investment in agricultural research. This evidence suggests that public food production policies emphasizing agricultural research and extension programs would be more productive uses of scarce capital and more effective in reducing poverty than further investments in irrigation water projects.

The estimated low economic value of irrigation water is, moreover, consistent with less formal observations on the outcomes of past public irrigation water policies. The economic benefits realized from irrigation development by the Bureau of Reclamation and the Bureau of Indian Affairs (both part of the U.S. Department of Interior) in the last four decades in the southwestern United States have proven disappointing. The Central Arizona Project and the Navajo Irrigation Project brought economic problems instead of prosperity, in spite of enormous subsidies in both cases (Wilson 1997; Young and Mann 1993). Holland and Moore (2003) report that considering the availability of groundwater, the Central Arizona Project was built many decades too soon. The federal government has long found it difficult to obtain a higher rate of cost recovery from farmers on even highly subsidized water supplies (Franklin and Hageman 1984). Perhaps the reluctance of farmers to repay irrigation project costs has more of an economic basis than previously thought.

5.6 Deductive Techniques for Valuing Irrigation Water: The Residual Method and Variations

The residual method and its variations are the most frequently used approaches to applied shadow pricing of irrigation water. They are deductive techniques of nonmarket valuation, deriving shadow prices from models of individual economic decisions made by firms and households. Sections 3.4 and 3.5 were devoted to the derivation of the basic long-run residual model. The relevant formulas for both the at-site and at-source measures are shown earlier in this chapter (equations 5-2a and 5-2b).

A residual method for valuing irrigation water is a special case of the well-known process of performing farm budget or *cost and return* (CAR) analysis. Ahearn and Vasavada (1992) and AAEA Task Force (1998) provide comprehensive reviews of the conceptual and measurement issues of calculating costs and returns in agricultural production in the United States. They assume a private accounting stance. Brown (1979) provides an earlier, less detailed exposition geared to public accounting stance contexts in developing countries. Their extensive discussions of measuring quantity and pricing of inputs and outputs in farm cost and return budgeting (many not yet resolved) illustrate the complexity of what might seem to a nonspecialist a simple set of problems. Analysis from a social accounting stance poses even more difficulties.

5.6.1 General Considerations Arising in Residual Valuation of Irrigation Water

Valuing irrigation water appears to be a relatively straightforward task from the accounting perspective, but inaccuracies or biases in the estimation can arise at two levels: individual crops and aggregation to a representative farm. The conceptual framework for an individual crop consists of the specification of the physical production function and the pricing of inputs and products. The physical production function specifies the quantities of all necessary inputs and the associated outputs. Pricing of both inputs and outputs involves judgments as to whether market or shadow prices should be used for each input and output, and, if shadow prices are necessary, how they are to be derived. Aggregation to the farm level involves the choice of cropping pattern: which crops to grow and what proportion of the land is allocated to each.

As emphasized in Chapter 3, biases can be introduced by several types of errors or omissions. The residual method is extremely sensitive to small variations in assumptions about the nature of the production function as well as input or output prices, so it is most suitable where the residual claimant (in this case, water) contributes a significant fraction of the value of output. In particular, omitting the cost of any input that should be represented in the production function means the contribution of that omitted input will be attributed to the residual claimant, thereby overstating the economic benefit of water.

Section 3.9 criticizes some official planning procedures (e.g. Bergman and Boussard 1976; Gittinger 1982; and pre-1980s U.S. Bureau of Reclamation planning practices) for recommending that certain costs of labor or capital can be ignored in deriving residual irrigation values. These recommended methods are inconsistent with the welfare economics-based theoretical models of residual net income reviewed earlier. Ignoring the opportunity costs of certain owned inputs may be appropriate in some short-term contexts, but in long-run planning from a public or social accounting stance—the case most often encountered in public irrigation policy analysis—the model developed above (equation 5-2a) is applicable. *To omit the cost of scarce labor and capital inputs is in effect to treat them not as costs but as benefits to society.* The calculated social welfare measure (the residual claimant) is correspondingly increased (i.e. overestimated), which favors public water project investments over alternative private (and public) uses of scarce labor and capital funds.

A crucial question is how to forecast price and yield changes over the life of the plan. For example, irrigation planning often involves long (fifty years or more) time horizons. Analysts often include a forecast of improved productivity over the life of the plan. Errors may be introduced by overestimating technical progress, or by underestimating the corresponding increased levels of nonwater inputs (fertilizer, pesticides, human capital) necessary to achieve the predicted level of output.

Historically crop prices have tended to decline with technological improvement. Improved yields imply adverse effects on product prices. Yet the author has reviewed irrigation project plans prepared for the U.S. Government in which yields were forecast to increase at a constant percentage annually, but input costs and commodity prices were assumed to remain constant over the life of an investment. Such a practice increases estimated economic benefits and boosts the chances of economically justifying an investment, but is unlikely to accurately forecast future prices and net returns (Young 1978).

Accurately predicting price and productivity changes over long planning horizons is challenging if not virtually impossible. A reasonable solution is to use current prices and production technologies. This assumes that the positive effects of technology on productivity will be offset by the negative effects of falling prices.

5.6.2 Pricing Inputs and Outputs in a Residual Irrigation Analysis

Biases may arise from improper pricing of inputs or outputs. An overpessimistic price for a commodity results in a residual that is too low, although the opposite error of overoptimism is more frequently encountered. Over- or under-pricing inputs induce corresponding but opposite effects on the estimated value of the residual.

Pricing Inputs from the Private Accounting Stance. In the private accounting stance, inputs and outputs should be priced in residual evaluations according to expected prices for the good or service. For those inputs and products whose prices are relatively stable and not influenced by public policy, the currently observed price will suffice. If current observations are not available, previous prices with an adjustment for expected inflation may be appropriate. If prices have fluctuated, a multi-year (such as five to seven years) average can be calculated.

Pricing from a Public Accounting Stance. Projecting input prices for social project analysis creates some special problems, particularly with labor, capital, and taxes. In residual analysis, shadow pricing of inputs for agricultural projects has uncritically inclined to low or absent charges, with net benefits correspondingly overestimated. The consequent openhanded spirit for funding irrigation projects is a substantial source of the failure noted earlier of irrigation plans to live up to expectations.

Where labor markets are not unduly distorted by government intervention, the going market wage (including fringe benefits) will reflect social opportunity costs and be appropriate for economic evaluation. These labor market conditions likely hold in developed country economies.

However, in developing countries it is often recommended that labor costs (wage rates) be adjusted for market imperfections. Early models of imperfect labor markets emphasized that the shadow wage rate should equal the forgone marginal productivity of workers. In the presence of unemployment, the forgone marginal productivity of previously unemployed labor was taken to be zero, and the shadow wage rate was accordingly set to be zero.

Jenkins and Harberger (1995) rightly believe that the forgone productivity approach understates the correct shadow wage rate. Even in times of unemployment some jobs remain unfilled, suggesting that the prevailing wage cannot entice workers into the job market. Work yields disutility relative to leisure, and the "unemployed" often have productive alternatives in the informal economy. The supply price of labor required to induce people to work on the project in question is the measure of the shadow wage. Hence the shadow wage rate should approach or equal the market wage. Shadow wage rates should, moreover, be set to reflect differing skill levels of the employee classes, and are also expected to vary between different times and locations. (See Dinwiddy and Teal 1996, Chapters 8 and 9 for an alternative view.)

Human inputs to irrigated crop production consist of more than just unskilled and skilled field labor hired on regular labor markets or family members whose efforts can be priced at going wage rates. Particularly in specialty fruit and vegetable crop production, noncontractual or owned human inputs including management and creativity must be accounted for. The difficulty is that these noncontractual resources are typically rewarded after the fact as part of the returns to the enterprise, and their wages are not readily ascertained

Pricing capital is another major concern in social cost–benefit analysis. In some common water valuation problems, flows of services are realized over time, and a rate of interest appears in the corresponding valuation model. In addition to the rate at which benefits and costs are discounted (the social discount rate) in a cost–benefit analysis, an interest rate must be specified in residual analysis.

Observed market interest rates vary widely, depending on such considerations as the duration and risk of the debt instrument and expected inflation, so choosing an interest rate for valuing water may be challenging. The economic theory of intertemporal choice indicates how to aggregate single-period values over time. The standard economic theory concludes that utility-maximizing individuals under competitive conditions will borrow or lend so that they equate the market rate of interest with their marginal rates of time preference between present and future consumption. Producers borrow when the anticipated rate of return on investments exceeds the interest rate, while capital owners lend if the interest rate exceeds their time preference. The market interest rate reveals preferences for the tradeoff between present and future consumption and production opportunities and thus represents a "price" of capital to employ in economic evaluation. However, in the presence of taxes, inflation, or other capital market imperfections, the observed market rate will be inappropriate for public policy analysis, and some adjustment is called for. The subject of the social rate of discount is beyond the scope of this analysis. (See Boardman et al. 2001, Chapter 10 for a recent survey of the debate.) For what it is worth, my own view is that for medium-term (30–50 years) water planning decisions in developed economies, the real social discount rate should be from 6% to 8%, based on both the public and private opportunity cost of capital and the perceived risk of the investments.

S oly h,yh)

Taxes are another point of contention in residual analysis of irrigation investments and policies. As with the treatment of labor and capital (addressed in Section 3.9), I offer a view somewhat at variance from World Bank prescriptions on taxes. Gittinger (1982, *317*) argues that for social analyses, taxes are merely transfer payments, not payments for resources used in production. So, he concludes, taxes are not deducted as a cost when deriving the incremental net benefit stream. One may agree that at the national level, certain taxes (e.g. income taxes) can be regarded as transfer payments and not considered in the residual analysis. However, at regional or local levels, sales and *ad valorem* real estate taxes may be regarded as payments for the business's share of local public goods such as road networks, health and public safety, and the like. They can be regarded as part of the cost of doing business. Thus, I believe that these types of taxes should be incorporated even in a social cost–benefit analysis.

On the output side, the analyst must establish which crops are likely to be produced under both the "with" and "without" irrigation conditions and the area predicted to be devoted to each. The recent history of cropping patterns in the region should be a guide. (There is a tendency to assume a generous area of high-valued crops, resulting in an upward bias on net rents; see Section 5.6.3.) Another issue is the basic level of yields relative to assumed input levels. The level of all inputs, including irrigation water, must correspond to appropriate local production practices in order to correctly identify the incremental contribution of irrigation water to production.

Professional farm management practice sometimes assumes that the production technology follows "best management practices." Best management practices may in application reflect above average yields. If corresponding above average input levels are not assumed, then estimated rents will be higher than warranted.

Issues in Specifying the Physical Production Function. The production functions (the amount of inputs and the associated yields) for irrigated crops can be conveniently divided among nondurable capital inputs, durable capital inputs, land, labor, and general overhead and management (including taxes, insurance).

In agricultural production, the main expendable (nondurable) inputs are seed, fertilizer, pesticides, and energy (fuel and electricity). The main concern for water valuation is to assure that all inputs expected to be used are included and in the correct quantity. The use of a Table of Operations and Inputs as described in Section 5.6.5 provides an explicit accounting of input factors, which, when reviewed and approved by experienced technical specialists or derived from a random sample survey of farmers, ensures completeness and accuracy.

Durable capital inputs, such as tractors (and their associated planting, tillage, and other equipment), harvesters, and buildings, present more difficulties than nondurables. According to convention, the unit budgets represent one year's operations; so annual depreciation and opportunity interest on the one year's portion of the life of a durable item of equipment must be quantified and costed out. (See Burt 1992 for a review of the major theories of depreciation and opportunity interest rates appropriate to farm management budgeting.) Depreciation and opportunity interest rates should be in real not nominal terms.

A potential pitfall associated with costing durable equipment is using only the equipment item's expected life, rather than the project planning period as the time period over which the item is depreciated. One of the rules of cost–benefit and other forms of discounted cash flow analysis calls for a comparable time period for all durable investment items. For example, the economic life of a durable production input—say, a sprinkler system that will last 15 years—is less than the project life or planning period that may be 50 years or more. If the average annual depreciation is represented for the 15 years rather than the 50 years, the cost will be understated. The present value of the cost of periodic replacements of the durable items throughout the planning period should be added onto the cost of the initial item before depreciation is calculated.

Perennial tree and vine crops (as well as certain long-lived forage and pasture crops such as alfalfa) present an issue of accounting for the initial investment in establishing the orchard or crop. If detailed year-by-year budgets are not performed, some way of amortizing the fixed cost of initiating the investment must be provided in the annual cost and return budgets. The usual approach is to charge an "establishment cost" which, similar to the treatment of machinery and other durables, represents a conversion of the initial investment in establishing the orchard or crop into an average annual cost over the expected life of the investment.

Owned Inputs. A particular challenge in the residual approach is pricing nonwater owned or noncontractual inputs. These inputs include equity capital, land, management, and entrepreneurship (see Section 3.7).

Data Collection. Careful and detailed farm surveys are the preferred method of determining the historical "without" trends in farm size, cropping options, production technologies, input mixes, and crop yields. (See Casley and Lury 1987; Salant and Dillman 1994; or Rea and Parker 1997 for discussions of survey research procedures.) However, when time and study resources preclude a survey, secondary data from government, university, and extension service reports may have to suffice. Brief "mini-surveys" of farmers to verify the accuracy of secondary data may provide a suitable compromise between complete reliance on secondary data and the time and cost demands of a careful survey. For the "with" cases, forecasts of all the above variables for the relevant planning period must be made.

Short-Run or Long-Run Models? The omission-of-variables problem often occurs when a Marshallian short-run modeling framework is used to represent a long-run planning situation. In short-run analysis, such as measuring forgone returns in the context of temporary shortages, it is appropriate to treat certain production inputs as fixed and to omit charges for those fixed inputs in calculating the residual value as a measure of forgone benefits. Water project analysts trained in private farm budgeting methods in traditional academic programs in agricultural economics may incorrectly apply these techniques to irrigation benefit estimation in long-run contexts. For example, a typical farm management planning exercise is to determine the annual mix of crops that will maximize returns to owned farm resources, such as land, water, labor, and management. This is usually a short-run planning problem, but if applied to measuring benefits to an investment in water supply or forgone benefits of transferring irrigation water to alternative uses, it would impute the values of *all* owned resources to water. Although short-run models have their place, the Marshallian long run is appropriate in most water development and allocation policy and planning, and all factor inputs should be treated as variable and costs assigned to them.

Cropping Patterns. On the lands of any existing or proposed irrigation project, numerous crop alternatives are possible. The planning process must aim to predict with reasonable accuracy what crops are to be grown "with" and "without" irrigation. The proportion of acreage devoted to each crop must be specified. These proportions are usually based on historic patterns derived from official agricultural statistics.

5.6.3 Returns to Water from High-Valued Crops

Application of the residual method to the production of so-called *high-valued* crops (also often called *specialty* crops) presents further complexities in valuing irrigation water. Specialty crops are those that yield a relatively high gross annual income per unit land area (per acre or hectare) and employ a correspondingly high level of productive inputs. High-valued crops are of particular interest in valuing irrigation water because, in addition to yielding a high gross return per unit land, they tend to generate a large return over variable costs (i.e. a high return to owned inputs). In some frequently used versions of the residual method, they yield especially generous unit returns to irrigation water. Yet the equimarginal principle suggests that when water is a fixed input, returns to water should be more or less the same for all crops on a given farm or resource region. Where water is a variable input, it should be allocated so that the value marginal product equals the incremental cost of water. A large difference in values of water for different crops is unexpected.

Several explanations of the anomaly come to mind:

- The contractual costs are understated for the specialty crop, so that the residual is overstated.
- Price or yield is overestimated on the specialty crop.
- The data are accurate, but reflect a temporary disequilibrium in the market, which will be corrected over time as more supply is called forth by the high residual rents.
- The true opportunity cost of noncontractual inputs (equity capital and management) are not fully accounted for.

In any case, the results call into question the use of the residual approach to value irrigation water use on specialty crops.

For the most part, the impressive values often imputed to irrigation of specialty crops reflect inappropriate accounting for owned inputs. Only a limited part of the high returns to the owned inputs of the specialty crop firm, it is argued, are actual rents or returns to water, and isolating the contribution of water in this case via the residual approach is not a simple and straightforward process.

What Are High-Valued Crops? High-valued is a relative term, and there is no precise criterion to distinguish high-valued crops. Most are perishable fresh vegetable, vine, and tree fruit products that deteriorate quickly if not harvested and sent to market in a timely way, and are especially susceptible to weather, pest, and disease damage. Accordingly, production of such crops is subject to higher risk of low yield and quality. These crops do not often benefit from national agricultural policy intervention and so are especially subject to wide market price fluctuations. On the cost side, production of high-valued crops generally entails large inputs of labor and materials such as fertilizers and pesticides. Orchards and vineyards require a large initial investment and a long period of maturation before a significant amount of production can be harvested and a recovery of capital investments can begin. High-valued crops also call for a higher degree of supervisory talents than staple field crops. The farm firm entering into the production of high-valued crops must assemble a set of specialized, relatively scarce resources: ample capital funds backed by a willingness to assume high levels of risk, perhaps for a long gestation period, together with specialized production, management, and marketing abilities.

Official manuals of procedure for water planning do not agree on an approach to high-valued crops, or even whether there is a special issue. Neither OECD (1985) nor the World Bank (Gittinger 1982) raise it as a problem (although neither of them addresses cost and return budgeting at the level of detail undertaken here). The U.S. Water Resources Council's *Principles and Guidelines* (1983, Section 2.3.2) defines 10 *basic* crops (seven grains— rice, wheat, corn, sorghum, barley, oats, soybeans—plus hay, pasture, and cotton). It assumes that the production of basic crops is limited primarily by the availability of suitable land and that any public irrigation project would not materially affect national prices of basic commodities. In contrast, production of all other crops—more or less those I am calling high-valued crops—are said to be limited by market demand, risk aversion, and supply factors other than the availability of suitable land. Further, from a national point of view, nonbasic crop acreage added by new irrigation projects would (except in special cases) merely displace similar crops on already producing lands (irrigated or otherwise) elsewhere. Although some exemptions are allowed, the immediate conclusion is that there is no reason for subsidized government water supply programs to augment specialty crop production, and no net national benefit would accrue to expanded production of such crops. Although the document's language is not entirely clear, the implication is that net income from any nonbasic crops would not normally be considered in calculating national economic benefits from irrigation.

Measurement Issues in High-Valued Crop Production. Measurement of benefits of irrigation of high-valued crops may be called for in studies of proposals for reallocating water among sectors. Programming models developed to represent regional agricultural water demands should not exclude an important class of products.

In using a residual approach to measure the value of irrigation water on a high-valued crop, the primary challenge is how to charge for owned inputs other than water. Once estimated opportunity costs of owned managerial and capital inputs plus costs of purchased inputs are deducted from expected revenues, is it then correct in irrigation water valuation on high-value crops to assign all remaining returns to the water residual? Even when charges for owned inputs are included, the calculation of net returns to high-valued crops in public irrigation water planning activities frequently show a relatively large return to irrigation water. Does this finding represent a uniquely high actual return to irrigation water, or is it a continued overstatement? There are reasons to believe that most of such estimates of high returns to water in specialty crop production are, from a long-term public perspective, an overstatement.

From a theoretical point of view, two principles of resource allocation suggest that irrigation of high-valued crop does not yield high returns to water. In the allocation of limited input supplies, from the equimarginal principle, it follows that in equilibrium, returns to an input at the margin should be equal among all alternative uses. If water applied to specialty crops yields higher returns than other crops, an optimizing producer will reallocate limited water supplies from the lower return uses to higher return uses, and thus increase total net returns. This adjustment will continue until marginal returns are equated among alternative opportunities. Similarly, where water is freely available at a given incremental cost, the self-interested producer will use water up to the point where the value marginal product is equal to the marginal input cost. Thus, assuming similar incremental costs of water throughout the region, the value marginal product of water should be more or less the same for all adapted irrigated crops. These theoretical perspectives lead one to expect that the marginal returns to water used to irrigate high-valued specialty crops should not differ markedly from those yielded by standard field crops on the same farm or even in the same region.

In fact, if water were highly valuable for producing specialty crops, we would expect more water and associated lands to be allocated to their production. But high-valued crop production represents only a modest part of total irrigated crop production. In the irrigated areas in the southwestern United States, irrigation water largely goes to serve the basic crops, particularly grains, cotton, rice, and sugar, that are assisted by the government's farm price and income support programs.

The economic theory of capital asset markets suggests that high returns to specialized fixed inputs such as irrigated lands and associated water rights should mean correspondingly high prices for the package of rights to land and water suitable to producing such crops. High returns to lands and water rights suitable for high-valued crop production would be reflected in annual or seasonal rents. Moreover, these high returns or rents would be capitalized into prices for land and associated water rights. But only where lands especially suited for high-valued crop production are limited in supply do the land and water markets reflect that scarcity. Also, as shown earlier in this chapter, those few studies applying hedonic property value methods to irrigation water report low values of irrigation water.

However, it can theoretically be expected that high-valued crops may yield a *somewhat* higher public, long-run return to water than standard field and forage crops as a reflection of differential and locational rents. For example, irrigated wheat produced in an arid area such as central Arizona would likely yield no particular locational or productivity advantage over rain-watered wheat produced in the grain belt. However, irrigated vegetables on the same land could benefit from productivity advantages due to climate, particularly the ability to produce crops throughout the year, and perhaps earn locational rents as well. (See Reynolds and Johnston 2003 for supporting data from Florida and California.) These differential and locational rents to irrigated vegetables are legitimately counted as public welfare gains from the introduction of water. Annual lease rates and land sale prices do show a premium relative to lands that may not be as adaptable to high-valued crop production. (The hedonic property value study in eastern Oregon by Faux and Perry 1999, for example, showed that land sales prices varied widely according to soil quality and adaptability to specialty crop production.) Thus formal analysis and informal observation indicate that the most productive soils and those relatively free of salinity—thus more productive for specialty crop production—exhibit higher lease or sale prices. However, these limited premiums on lease rates and prices for land suitable for high-valued crop production are not sufficient to justify the typical project planners' estimates of high returns to water in specialty crops.

These considerations lead to an alternative hypothesis: Water may seldom be the scarce resource for high-valued crop production. The scarce resources are likely to be the special skills required for producing the crops, combined with ownership of capital willing to incur the high risks to gain the significant potential returns.

Therefore, even after accounting for locational and differential rents, those high net returns to high-valued crop production are likely to include some unaccounted-for rents to owned inputs other than water. Some of these composite rents should be attributed to human input (management, technical skills, creativity) and to risk capital, and they should not all be assigned to irrigation water. They are not so much a signal of the scarcity of specialty products and the water resources necessary to produce them as a sign of the scarcity of the technical, managerial, and entrepreneurial skills required to produce specialty crops. In order to avoid overestimation, as discussed in the previous section, imputations to risk-bearing and management are needed.

How Much Area to Allocate to High-Valued Crops? If a large area of high-valued crops is projected in the plan, as is often observed in irrigation development proposals, this can greatly influence the results of an economic feasibility test, as well as how water is valued in these uses. Proposals for enhanced irrigation may assume a much larger proportion of resources devoted to specialty crop production than historically has been observed. For example, Wilson's (1997) *ex post* evaluation of the U.S. Bureau of Reclamation's Central Arizona Project noted that the original planners three decades earlier had forecast not only very high returns to high-valued crop production, but many times more area devoted to vegetable crop production than had ever been observed in the project service area and much more than was subsequently observed once the project was completed. These forecasts of large areas yielding high returns played a significant role in the original finding of economic feasibility. Wilson described a project whose outcome was economically much less favorable than was forecast at the planning stage.

In most countries, only a small proportion of lands are devoted to high-valued crop production. In California—renowned as the fruit and vegetable basket of the United States—citrus and deciduous fruit, grape, and vegetable production, while relatively large, still account for less than 40% of total agricultural acreage and probably a smaller proportion of water use in the state (U.S. Department of Agriculture 2003). As argued by the U.S. Water Resources Council (1983), any specialty crop production which occurs on a new irrigation project is likely to merely displace production elsewhere in the nation. Accordingly, in few countries is there reason to assume shortages of fruits and vegetables that government investments are needed to alleviate.

Valuation of benefits to irrigation by residual methods should therefore be supplemented by methods based on observations on land markets (see Section 5.4). These can be relatively simple lease or sales markets studies or, preferably, more sophisticated hedonic property value studies. The land market approach has the advantage that a renter of irrigated land will not be willing to pay any more than the rents from land and water (or, for a buyer, the capitalized future stream of such rents). Such renters or buyers cannot be expected to pay for risk capital and management skills that cannot be transferred with the land and water rights. Thus, those who rent or buy land for purposes of crop production can be better relied upon to estimate the correct rents to irrigation water than analysts without a stake in the outcome of their studies.

Concluding Remarks on High-Valued Crops. The large returns to water estimated for high-valued crops largely represent inadequate accounting for returns to owned inputs other than water. A significant portion of these high returns are best understood as economic rents to specialized owned inputs other than water. Hence, the residual approach to valuing irrigation water for specialty crops is correspondingly subject to error. In cases where there are large returns to owned inputs, and the returns are likely to be dominated by payments to scarce managerial talent and to capital willing to take risks, crediting these returns to the water resource will overstate the returns to the water residual. Therefore, the residual method is best suited to valuing water in simple production processes, but less adaptable to high-valued crops or industrial processes. Residual estimates of irrigation water value should be treated with considerable caution, more so in complex production processes.

Although it is not suggested that specialty crops always be eliminated from calculating irrigation benefits, the Water Resources Council's recommendation of eliminating such crops altogether is attractive. It must be demonstrated that no displacement of other producers in the country is likely. It may be that the new development has a location advantage—in terms of transportation costs or productivity—in which cases, the reduced costs of production and marketing would be a real welfare gain. To avoid erroneously attributing labor efforts to the residual water resource, a contribution of owner/operator managerial efforts to crop production should be recognized and priced at rates higher than the going wage for field labor. In view of the difficulty of establishing prices and quantities for management, the opportunity cost approach of assigning a percentage (8% to 10% of gross sales) as a charge for management for specialty crops is an appropriate compromise. An opportunity rate of return on equity capital should be set high enough to adequately reflect the actual production and marketing risks involved in specialty crop production. The amount of land area projected to be devoted to high-valued crop production in plans for new irrigation projects should not exceed the proportion in the "without project" area.

5.6.4 Should Net Returns to Livestock Production Be Credited to Water?

A related question is whether to include returns from livestock and poultry operations in the computation of irrigation benefits. Farms with irrigated crops also frequently produce livestock, relying in part on forages and feeds produced on the farming operation. These are often, in effect, sold through farm livestock and poultry feeding operations rather than directly sent to the open market. Consequently, irrigation project planners often choose to incorporate livestock activities into their estimates of irrigation water value.

Livestock should *not* be included in the budgeting of irrigation water values. A project providing an increment to irrigation water supply directly augments only feed and forage production, not livestock production. In principle, by importing feed into the project region, livestock could be grown in the absence of the project. The livestock enterprise can best be regarded as a form of secondary processing for the feeds and forages, rather than a primary enterprise directly impacted by the irrigation water supply. Introducing another intermediate good enterprise into the analysis opens the way for additional errors in imputing benefits to incremental water supplies.

Like cultivation of specialty crops, livestock production is typically more demanding of managerial and entrepreneurial skills and of capital, and often faces more production and marketing risks than regular field crop production. It is difficult to accurately measure and price owned managerial, entrepreneurial, and capital inputs. Moreover, in competitive market conditions, the income differential from livestock sales (meat, milk, or fiber) should reflect the costs of inputs plus the opportunity costs of management and risk-taking needed to attract resources into livestock production. A correct accounting for those costs would yield a return identical to the value of water in producing forage crops.

The farm land market does not include livestock returns as a return to land and water when a farm is sold. Livestock are separable assets and are sold separately when a farm is sold. *A private purchaser of farm land and associated irrigation water rights would not be willing to pay for the capitalized returns from livestock enterprises; neither should evaluation of a public policy for augmenting or reducing agricultural water supply count livestock returns as direct benefits of water supply augmentation.*

In irrigation planning exercises, it is simpler and more accurate to directly price the incremental forage than to impute a price through the livestock enterprises. Markets for feeds and forages can often be analyzed to avoid the potential problems. Feed grains and forages produced under irrigation and intended for livestock production can be valued at the cost of acquisition. If these products are scarce in the project region, the market price will reflect the cost of importing from feed and grain surplus localities. Fresh forages used for livestock grazing may seem difficult to price; however, rental markets for grazing by the week or month can often be identified, making it possible to use the rental rate to price the increased forage outputs. Forages are bulky commodities and their market prices depend on transportation costs. Forage prices are likely to be sensitive to local supplies, so the conventional simplifying assumption of constant output prices may be inappropriate in cases where forages are an expected significant output of an irrigation supply or rehabilitation project.

5.6.5 The With-Without Test in the Residual and Change in Net Rent Methods

A residual analysis for valuation of irrigation water requires the assembly of farm budgets for the "with" and "without" cases. Farm budget analysis draws on agricultural production expertise, economics, and accounting to infer returns to proposed alternatives (AAEA Task Force 1998). A partial budget analyzes changes which have a short-run effect on the total farm organization of resources and focuses on variable cost and incremental returns. A "complete" budget may consider major changes in farm assets and is appropriate for proposals which affect resource organization and income in the long run. Water planning activities nearly always require the complete budget approach.

The Representative Farm Model. A "representative farm model," sometimes called a "pattern farm" (Gittinger 1982, *287–288*), can portray a farm scenario or aggregate a regional total. Because it is impractical to evaluate each individual farm, simplification to one or more representative farm models is common practice. The representative farm model lists a farm's principal resources, which can include the land (including soils of varying productivity), labor supply, climate, financial status, machinery and equipment inventory, and buildings. Researchers often model several representative farms, depending on the amount of resources or their main production emphasis (field crops, perishable crops, livestock). Overall evaluation may then include separate analyses of small, medium, and large field crop farms; specialty crop farms; resource productivity (such as that due to variations in soil quality or microclimate); managerial capability; or financial strength.

A farm model also lists the production options available to the producer, including the range of feasible crop and livestock enterprises and the technological options for production. The model should be based on realistic assumptions about productivity of resources, markets available to dispose of products, and managerial capability.

The Unit Table of Operations and Inputs. The starting point for detailed and explicit farm budget analysis is called a Unit Table of Operations and Inputs, or simply a Schedule of Operations. A technical unit is usually a land unit (acre, hectare or fraction thereof) or an animal unit (one head of livestock); the table represents the physical and economic opportunities for producing a technical unit of a farm enterprise. For the purpose of analyzing irrigation decisions, a land measure is the appropriate unit. The table also provides a common format for displaying the necessary assumptions regarding the production of an agricultural enterprise.

A Unit Table of Operations and Inputs for each crop makes explicit each step required for crop production, its timing, its resource requirements, and the resulting outputs. Table 5-3, patterned after those found in farm planning textbooks (e.g. Hedges 1963), provides an example. The assumptions correspond to an inventory of machinery and equipment (appropriate to the size and financial status of the representative farm) which a farmer can call upon to produce the crop in question.

To ensure realism, operations and input tables such as Table 5-3 are best developed in a collaborative process with plant and soil scientists, agricultural engineers, and especially local agricultural extension specialists. These tables reflect developed country technology and pricing. For developing country conditions, adjustments would be needed.

The next step is to assemble a Unit Crop Budget to calculate and display the net returns over variable costs per unit land for each crop option.

The Total Farm Budget. Table 5-4 illustrates the Total Farm Budget, which combines the information in the Unit Crop Budgets to determine Farm Income Net of Variable Costs, and then, by deducting fixed or overhead costs, Net Return to the residual claimant(s).

The Total Farm Budget includes the "with" and "without" conditions. After the "Value Incremental Net Rent" is calculated (Line F), the ultimate object of the analysis—estimated net benefit per unit water—is imputed in Line H.

Table 5-3. Representative Format for Unit Table of Operations and Inputs (One Hectare for One Crop)

Crop			Projected Yield per Hectare		
	Machinery		*Per Hectare Inputs*		
	Power Source	*Equipment*	*Machine*	*Labor*	
Operation	*(size & type)*	*(size & type)*	*Hours*	*Hours*	*Materials*
Seedbed preparation					
Step 1					
Step 2					
Step 3					
Step 4					
Plant					(seed)
Fertilize					(fertilizer)
Pesticide					(chemicals)
Cultivate					
Irrigate					(water, cubic meters)
Harvest					(bags, ties)
Haul					(miles)
Store					(months)

Table 5-4. Representative Total Farm Budget Format for With and Without Analysis of Irrigation Developments

	Part I - Return Over Variable Cost by Crop			
	"Without" Development Situation		*"With" Development Situation*	
Item	*Crop A $*	*Crop B $*	*Crop C $*	*Crop D $*
A. Revenues per Hectare				
1. Projected Yield/Hectare				
2. Projected Price/Unit				
3. Projected Revenue/Hectare				
B. Variable Costs per Hectare				
1. Land Preparation				
2. Plant				
3. Fertilizer and Pesticide				
4. Other Pre-Harvest Operations				
5. Irrigation				
6. Harvest				
7. Hauling and Storage				
8. Management Charge				
9. Operating Interest				
10. Total Variable Costs				

continued on next page

Table 5-4. Representative Total Farm Budget Format for With and Without Analysis of Irrigation Developments *(continued)*

	Part I - Return Over Variable Cost by Crop			
	"Without" Development Situation		*"With" Development Situation*	
Item	*Crop A $*	*Crop B $*	*Crop C $*	*Crop D $*
C. Total Return Over Variable Cost: "Without" and "With" Development				
1. Return Over Variable Cost/ Hectare				
2. Hectares				
3. Total Crop Return Over Variable Cost				
4. Total Farm Return Over Variable Cost				

Part II - Net Return to Farm Operations		
Item	*"Without" Development Situation $*	*"With" Development Situation $*
D. Annual Overhead and Annualized Capital Costs (Total Farm)		
1. Land Development		
2. Machinery and Equipment		
3. Buildings		
4. Transport		
5. Irrigation Water Supply		
6. Irrigation Water Distribution		
7. General Overhead(Taxes, Insurance, Office)		
8. Total Farm Capital and Overhead Costs (Sum of 1-7)		
E. Net Farm Income (C3-D8)		

Part III - Change in Net Income Calculation $
F. Change in Net Income ("With" minus "Without")
G. Cubic Meters of Water Delivered
H. Net Benefit per Unit Water Delivered ($/Cubic Meter)
I. Cubic Meters of Water Depleted
J. Net Benefit per Unit of Water Depleted ($/Cubic Meter)

5.6.6 Mathematical Programming Models for Irrigation Water Valuation

An automated form of the Change in Net Rent method can be represented by mathematical programming models. Mathematical programming has been adapted to irrigation water valuation over the past several decades, driven by refinement of the method and more powerful computers. Mathematical programming allows much more realistic modeling of irrigation decisions than simple budgeting. But it demands more analytic training and resources than most agency planning teams possess. Nevertheless, with the expansion of personal computers and the increasing skills and training of evaluation staffs, the technique will be adapted to more real world planning. See Chapter 3 for an overview of the basic characteristics of mathematical programming models. See Williams 1999 for a general discussion of building mathematical programming models to represent the resource allocation decisions of an optimizing firm. Rae 1994 and Hazell and Norton 1986 discuss mathematical programming models applied to farm decisions and aggregated agricultural policy issues.

The basic Change in Net Rent approach requires the analyst to make a number of *a priori* judgments or assumptions about crop species and acreage allotted to each; the crops' responses to alternative amounts and timing of water; and irrigation water distribution technology. A more realistic model of farmer behavior would make these considerations endogenous or internal to the model. Analysts who wished to introduce farmers' choices regarding crop mix, water application rates, and production technologies as decision variables in their models were quick to take advantage of mathematical optimization techniques, such as linear or quadratic programming. Anderson (1968), while retaining the fixed crop acreage assumption of the whole-farm budget approach, utilized computer simulation to represent multi-stage crop response to alternative amounts and timing of water application in a model of an irrigation delivery system.

Numerous applications of linear programming to irrigation planning followed, only a few of which can be mentioned here. Early models (e.g. Burt 1964) provided only for omission of marginal crops in response to increased price or scarcity. Young and Bredehoeft (1972) modeled sequential or multi-stage decision processes and crop response to varying water application rates, and found that the water application portion of the Anderson (1968) model could be more easily and accurately represented by a linear program. Bernardo et al. (1987) included representations of seasonal crop response to water (based on highly detailed agronomic simulations) and irrigation application technology. (See Section 5.3.)

A programming model of a representative farm situation is usually specified to maximize net return to the residual claimant (the water resource) subject to constraints on water and other resources. Solving for each of a number of increments of water supply derives the net return from the incremental change in the objective function (Burt 1964; Bowen and Young 1986; Bernardo et al. 1987; Chaudhry and Young 1989). The objective function value for each solution provides an estimate of the value of water. The multi-crop marginal benefit function can then be determined.

Modeling on a microcomputer provides an opportunity to increase the detail in representing the farmer decision maker, incorporating a wide range of technological production options, input levels, and crop choices as endogenous to the model solution, although the programming approach demands more analytic resources. More specialized hardware and software and a higher level of training are needed to formulate and solve programming models, and the additional detail calls for specification of more cropping and irrigation activities. To ensure accuracy, more attention must be paid to basic assumptions and procedures.

Mathematical programming models have been used extensively to assess economic impacts of proposed water policies. Bowen and Young (1986) studied the allocative and distributive effects of alternative irrigation water charging policies in Egypt. Michelsen and Young (1993) formulated a short-run programming model to measure forgone benefits when dry-year options might be sold to urban water supply agencies to provide adequate water supplies in case of periodic drought. Booker (1995) estimated forgone benefits of a severe, sustained drought in the Colorado River Basin. Adams and Cho (1998) studied tradeoffs between water use for agriculture and for enhancing habitat for endangered fish species in the Klamath Basin, Oregon with short-run models of below normal and drought scenarios.

An alternative is to derive a demand function by solving the model for a range of water prices and recording the corresponding optimal water use rates. Scheierling et al. (2004c) reviewed the literature on irrigation water demand, finding a mean price elasticity of about –0.5 and a range of from near zero to about minus two. Meta-analysis results suggest that estimates may be higher if they are calculated at a higher irrigation water price, if a long-run time-frame of analysis is used, if low-valued crops are prominent in the analysis, and if switching to more efficient irrigation technologies is included as an adjustment option.

Most examples of mathematical programming to study irrigation demand and benefits have been partial equilibrium, deterministic, and static. Howitt et al. (1980) modeled irrigation decisions with quadratic programming to allow crop prices to vary with regional output of irrigated crops. Optimization models of intersectoral regional water allocation by Vaux and Howitt (1984) and Booker and Young (1994) incorporate demand functions for irrigation water and other demand sectors to solve for optimal prices of water in a regional or basin-wide context. Taylor and Young (1995) developed a discrete stochastic sequential programming

(DSSP) model of sequential uncertain multi-crop production processes reflecting uncertain water supplies characteristic of irrigated agriculture in southeastern Colorado. They show that benefits increase with increasing reliability of water supplies. Dinar and Letey (1996) modeled water allocation in five of California's most important agricultural producing areas with a programming model that allowed for changes in cropping patterns, irrigation intensity, and, in particular, irrigation technology to study the effects on net income of alternative means of meeting reduced water supplies required by federal requirements for increased supplies for environmental needs.

Most programming-based irrigation water demand analyses have focused on demand for water *deliveries* to the farm. Scheierling et al. (2004a, b) extended these approaches by developing derived demands for *consumptive use*. They found that pricing and subsidy policies designed to encourage adoption of water-saving technologies so as to reduce water deliveries may have little impact on region-wide consumptive use of water.

Advances on the conventional static mathematical programming models include Dudley (1988), who used dynamic programming to represent the sequential choice problem faced by Australian irrigators faced with limited water supplies. Knapp (1992) reviewed dynamic optimization with extensions to water quality and drainage. Dynamic programming provides a rigorous representation of the problem of sequential water use decisions in the face of uncertain water supplies. However, it sacrifices some realism because its heavy computational demands limit the analysis to one crop at a time.

Computable general equilibrium (CGE) models (see Section 3.9.1) are a promising approach to modeling water allocation issues. Berck et al. (1991) appears to be the first application of CGE modeling to estimate forgone irrigation benefits. The model was designed to study the effects of hypothetically removing increments of up to 50% of the base irrigation water supply from a four-county region in the southern San Joaquin Valley in California. This application used an IMPLAN data base and calculated both value added and proprietors' income forgone from removal of water. The proprietors' income measure allowed for opportunity costs of land (incorporating three soil productivity classes) and labor (although only one quality of labor was represented). The proprietors' income measure thus overcomes many of my objections (Section 3.9.1) to using value added as a measure of economic value in a producers' good context. Goodman's (2000) comparison between market transfers and additional water storage in southeastern Colorado is another example of CGE modeling of irrigation water allocation. Still another example is Watts et al. (2001), who used the CGE approach to analyze tradeoffs among irrigation and other offstream and instream uses in the context of policies for protecting endangered fish species in the Colorado River.

5.7 The Alternative Cost Method Applied to Valuing Irrigation Water

When estimates of a direct demand schedule prove difficult, the alternative cost method may provide a solution (see Section 3.11). Willingness to pay is limited by the amount required to implement the least-cost alternative method of delivering the same goods or services. The alternative can be any feasible way to accomplish the identical purpose. If the cost of the alternative is less than the estimated direct benefits, the cost of the alternative should be used as the measure of benefit.

The alternative cost method has not received much attention in valuing irrigation water, but where hydrologically, technically, and institutionally feasible, the full costs of extracting groundwater might be used as an alternative to surface water supply. However, only if groundwater is plentiful and readily renewed via natural processes will this be a straightforward exercise in calculating costs of groundwater extraction; if groundwater stocks are limited and nonrenewing, several indirect costs might need to be added to conventional groundwater extraction costs. These could include:

- external (uncompensated third-party) costs, including pumping cost increases due to water table decline from over-rapid extraction;
- subsidence leading to structural damage on the surface or intrusion of poor quality water; and
- the user cost (the forgone future benefits of present use) of exploiting a depleting resource base.

Complete and accurate estimates of the present value of external costs and user costs from pumping are likely to be relatively difficult for project planners.

The relevance of alternative cost approaches is illustrated in discussions of the economic feasibility of the U.S. Bureau of Reclamation's massive Central Arizona Project, which brings water from the Colorado River to the Phoenix and Tucson areas of central Arizona. Early in the planning stages, W.E. Martin emphasized that the cost of groundwater pumping would remain less than even the subsidized cost of the project supply, implying that the project's actual benefits would be much lower than determined by the residual approach (see, for example, Bush and Martin 1986). Subsequent to the completion of the project, the farmer beneficiaries in fact adopted a privately rational approach and, rather than purchasing the federal project water, continued to use the less expensive groundwater. Additional federal support was necessary to finance the revenue shortfall (Wilson 1997). Holland and Moore (2003) incorporate the alternative cost of groundwater in a sophisticated evaluation of water management policies in Central Arizona, confirming Martin's earlier assessment.

5.8 Measuring Benefits of Improved Quality of Irrigation Water

5.8.1 Dissolved Mineral Salts and Crop Irrigation

Dissolved mineral salts (usually called salinity) are the major water pollutants affecting the productivity of irrigated crops (Young and Horner 1986). Mineral salts, dissolved through natural processes as water passes over soils and rocks, are found to greater or lesser degrees in all surface and groundwaters. When water is utilized for irrigation, part of the applied water evaporates through plants and soil surfaces but the minerals remain, becoming concentrated in irrigated soils. Many of the world's irrigated regions draw water from river basins where normal runoff from ancient marine sediments pick up dissolved salts. In arid and semi-arid regions, natural rainfall is typically inadequate to leach out accumulated salts from soil root zones.

A buildup of salinity in soils reduces crop yields. A high total concentration of salts can affect crops through osmosis, or a specific ion may be toxic. Eventually it may become unprofitable to produce crops. Irrigated areas, unless carefully managed, risk becoming waterlogged and building up salt concentrations that will eventually make the soil infertile. This process is thought to have brought about the demise of a number of ancient irrigation-based societies. Salinization by irrigation threatens a large part of the world, and significant technical, political, and economic challenges must be overcome to preserve irrigated agriculture in the long term (Hillel 2000).

Dissolved salts of economic significance are mainly the chlorides, sulfates, nitrates, and bicarbonates of sodium, calcium, potassium, and magnesium. Although the effects of the particular ions on crop productivity vary, sodium and chlorides are typically the most damaging, particularly to fruit, citrus, and vegetable crops. However, because of the variety of potential ions and the difficulty of isolating their individual effects, the usual approach is to lump all salinity into a macro measure termed total dissolved solids (TDS). Generally speaking, the least sensitive crops are also the least valuable, so areas irrigated with highly saline waters tend to emphasize low-valued crops. Selenium, a trace element often found in runoff from ancient marine shales, is another element concentrated by irrigation processes. The recognition of serious effects of small concentrations of selenium on wildlife and fish initiated a large and expensive program for abatement in the 1980s. See Dinar and Zilberman 1991.

Increases in soil salinity and the consequent damage to irrigated crops are caused by not only decisions of individual farmers, but also the actions of other irrigators upstream. To avoid damage to their own crops, farmers apply water in excess of crop evapotranspiration needs (the excess is called the leaching fraction) to dilute the salts and drive them below the plants' root zone in their own fields. These concentrated mineralized waters are transmitted to downstream users (agricultural and otherwise), reducing productivity of water and land. Salinity damages to water users downstream of irrigated regions are textbook examples of external diseconomies. Besides excess salinity, the water remaining in the root zone may be contaminated with nutrients, pesticides, and herbicides. When flushed into the hydrologic system, these contaminants may also affect the downstream water users and ecosystems. Damage from dissolved minerals is aggravated in hydrologic basins where no natural drainage to an ocean is possible. Minerals may accumulate enough to terminate irrigation. These *irrigation-induced water quality problems* call for economic appraisal of proposed public interventions to reduce the damage.

Farmers can mitigate the effect of salinity on net income. Salt resistance varies widely among crops; high-valued fresh vegetable and fruit crops are typically the most susceptible and grain and forage crops the most resistant. The most frequent adjustment is to shift to more salt resistant, but usually less profitable crops. If water supplies are adequate, larger or more frequent irrigations can leach out salts from the root zone. High-efficiency irrigation methods (sprinklers, drip irrigation) can offset water shortages to the same effect. Dinar et al. (1992) used a statistical procedure—the maximum likelihood tobit method—to analyze farm survey data to study farmer adoption of irrigation technologies in the San Joaquin Valley. Economic research on salinity damages has thus addressed both the optimal individual on-farm response to salinity in irrigation water and the benefits of mitigating external costs or damages due to upstream irrigation practices.

5.8.2 Deductive Methods for Measuring Salinity Damages to Irrigated Crops

Deductive methods for measuring salinity impacts are based on production functions that reflect changes in crop yields. This relationship has been studied extensively by soil and crop scientists. Dan Yaron was a pioneer in controlled field experiments; see Yaron and Bresler (1970) for a basic model and an application to chloride ion effects on citrus production in Israel. This and other papers by Yaron on salinity and irrigation are collected in Dinar and Zilberman 2002. Production functions developed via computer simulation have since become a basic form of modeling salinity impacts on crop growth (Letey and Dinar 1986; Cardon and Letey 1992). Because salinity affects the soil root zone, a physical model of how salinity concentration in the intake water is translated into salinity concentrations in soil moisture is combined with a biological model of the effects on plant growth and productivity.

Economic benefits of salinity abatement can be estimated by the Change in Net Rent method. The increase in crop yields from reduced water and soil salinity will increase production or reduce costs, and consequently increase net income. Kan and Knapp 2002 is a recent example of economic modeling of effects of salinity on crop production and income.

Each of the farmer responses to changed salinity can be incorporated into either cost-and-return budgets or mathematical programming representations designed to estimate the Change in Net Rent due to a change in salinity of irrigation water. The mathematical programming model can reflect the range of potential irrigator responses to salinity—changing to crops with greater salinity tolerance; changing the frequency, timing, or amount of irrigation water applied; and changing water application technologies.

Most of the initial studies of salinity damages have focused on the areas served from the Colorado River Basin and the San Joaquin Valley. Although government agencies reported early efforts, the study of effects of Colorado River salinity on California's Imperial Valley by C.V. Moore et al. (1974) was probably the first regional study of salinity damage in the peer-reviewed literature. Most subsequent efforts at measuring benefits of salinity reduction have adopted the mathematical programming approach. A common strategy has been to formulate several farm decision models reflecting yields and operating costs representative of differing levels of salinity. The effect of salinity on productivity and costs for individual crops is based on findings by agronomic researchers. Solution of the several models provides estimates of net farm income at alternative salinity levels, which differ according to their selection of crops and irrigation technologies. Comparing the alternative solutions provides increments (or decrements) of net income from different water salinity levels. Gardner and Young (1988) also studied the Imperial Valley, measuring the effects on regional net farm income from various hypothesized salinity levels. They found the model results to be quite sensitive to which soils the salt-sensitive vegetable crops would be grown on in the event of rising salinity. Booker and Young (1994) and Booker (1995) used linear programming models to derive salinity damage functions for incorporation into nonlinear optimization models of water allocation among instream and offstream water uses in the Colorado River Basin. Lee and Howitt (1996) also studied the Colorado River Basin with nonlinear optimization models to find optimal salinity control policies. They modeled irrigated agriculture with Cobb-Douglas production functions in land, capital, and water quality, estimated by a unique two-step procedure that Howitt (1995) calls "positive mathematical programming;" this calibrates programming models to observed farmer production behavior. Lee and Howitt's final step, in effect a benefit transfer, augmented the second-step models to incorporate the effects of salinity on crop productivity, based on results derived by Letey and Dinar (1986).

5.8.3 Econometric Techniques for Measuring Salinity Damages to Irrigated Crops

Aside from controlled field experiments, econometric estimates of economic losses from salinity or benefits of salinity abatement have been infrequent. However, economic surveys of farmer production practices and crop yields can be valuable though under-used resources for estimating the value of irrigation water and the effects of salinity.

In an econometric study of a region in Pakistan, Hussain and Young (1987) fitted a Cobb-Douglas function to farm survey data to measure the adverse impacts of salinity on irrigated crop production. Over 40 million acres (about 16 million hectares) are irrigated in the Indus Basin in Pakistan, the largest contiguous irrigated area in the world. These lands are increasingly damaged by salinity, some originally in the soil and some concentrated by irrigation with salt-laden ground and surface water. Individual farmers can do little to control salinity; their efforts would likely be subverted by their neighbors' and upstream producers' failure to adopt similar discipline. Reduced salinity is a public good, and dealing with salinity becomes a matter of public concern. In a country with a rising ratio of population to arable land, salinity has been an intractable public agricultural policy problem for decades.

Methods. The authors analyzed an unusual, if not unique, pair of coordinated farm surveys conducted for the World Bank and the government of Pakistan in 1976 to measure damage from salinity in soils and water. The procedure derived damage estimates under actual production conditions. The general approach was to collect field data to statistically fit a function in which soils and water salinity measures are arguments in a production relation, controlling for levels of other major inputs (fertilizer, labor, number of irrigations).

The two surveys sampled over 550 randomly selected farmers on watercourses: the channels or ditches at the end of a canal system that finally deliver water to individual farmers. Three farmers on each watercourse—one from each third of its length—were randomly chosen to be interviewed. (Both water supply and soil salinity vary widely but systematically from head- to tail-end of individual watercourses. Fields nearest the canal enjoy more and better water; hence the sample along each watercourse.)

One survey was a conventional farm economic survey. Every selected farmer was interviewed by trained interviewers concerning production inputs (such as land, labor, seed, and chemicals) and corresponding crop production and revenue of each crop grown during the previous crop year. The portion of the survey reported here covered three winter crops (local wheat, improved wheat, and mustard) on the 140 observations taken in Punjab Province, Pakistan's most important agricultural region.

The parallel survey, conducted by crop and soil specialists on the same farms in the same year, gathered samples of minerals in soil and irrigation water. Electroconductivity (a general measure of salinity), magnesium–calcium ratios, and sodium absorption ratios in the soil were measured from samples taken at each of five different soil layers (down to 72 inches) on each farm; high values of these measures are known to reduce crop productivity. The electroconductivity of irrigation water was also measured. All economic variables (input and output data) were converted to per acre terms. To prepare for statistical analysis, the two data sets were merged on a computer.

Regression analysis of the data with the objective of estimating a marginal damage function for salinity in soils was performed in three steps. The first used stepwise multiple regression, to relate yield for each crop to input levels and all the soil and water chemistry variables. Four functional forms were tested. The standard Cobb-Douglas or exponential form best fit the data and is the most convenient analytically—the regression coefficients are the production elasticities. (See Heady and Dillon 1969). The remaining discussion reports only the Cobb-Douglas results.

The initial statistical analysis detected a high degree of multicollinearity among the soil chemical measures, both with soil depth and across the varying measures. Correlation coefficients among electroconductivity variables for the five soil layers were quite high: as much as 0.87 for one of the crops. Similar high correlations were found among the soil layer observations for both magnesium–calcium and sodium absorption ratios. When correlations among two independent variables are high, there is little knowledge gained by including both in the regression analysis, and common practice is to omit or replace one of the variables. Therefore, for each of the soil chemistry measures, the five variables representing the five soil layers were replaced by their respective means and the stepwise regressions again performed. This second stage analysis still found high correlations between the mean electroconductivity and each of the other two soil chemistry measures. Because the electroconductivity variable was selected first in the stepwise procedure, it alone was used to represent soil salinity in the third stage of the analysis, and the other two measures were deleted from the last regression runs.

Results. The final models, as measured by the Coefficient of Determination (R^2), fit the data reasonably well. The effects of soil and water salinity, the variables of most interest here, yield interesting results. The coefficient on the soil salinity has the expected negative sign, and the coefficients on this variable are all significantly less than zero at the 90% probability level. A 1% change in soil electroconductivity changed yield (with the opposite sign) of both local wheat and mustard by about 5%. Moreover, improved wheat is even more sensitive to salinity, showing about a 12% negative response to a 1% increase in electroconductivity. However, the coefficients on irrigation water salinity are not significantly different from zero at conventional probability levels for any of the crops.

The final step in the overall analysis is to derive the marginal value products of the independent input variables and marginal value of damage from salinity. Conventionally, this is done by taking the derivative of the function with respect to each variable and evaluating the derivative at the mean of the individual independent variables. Comparing the marginal value products with opportunity costs of the inputs indicates the degree to which a change in the independent variable could improve economic efficiency. In general, irrigation water supplies are short relative to land and increased water supplies could add greatly to value of production. Marginal soil salinity damages per unit electroconductivity are found to be Rupees (Rs) –18 for local wheat, Rs –63 for improved wheat, and Rs –14 for mustard. (At the time of the survey, the exchange rate was about Rs 9.9 = 1US$.)

Discussion. This type of analysis provides a useful portrayal of water quality damages to irrigated crops under actual production conditions. Research resources did not permit a complete analysis of both summer and winter crop data. For a full policy analysis of the benefits of salinity control, the summer crop damages would need to be computed as well. The combined survey approach required a relatively large amount of resources for data collection and specialized skills of soil scientists, as well as economists proficient in survey research and econometrics. A recurring tension between the research methodologies of economists and soil and crop scientists is evident in studies of this sort. Soil and crop scientists are, for the most part, highly skeptical of employing survey techniques instead of controlled experiments for measuring production relationships. Economists tend to be more comfortable with studying actual behavior of economic agents, and rely on larger sample sizes and statistical techniques designed to handle errors in observations. For a country as dependent on irrigation and as affected by salinity as Pakistan, the knowledge gained from this research based on actual field conditions would likely be well worth the effort and resources.

Because of the long-term significance of salinity for irrigated crop production throughout the world, further extension and refinement of both deductive and inductive approaches for measuring benefits of reducing salinity will be a fruitful endeavor.

5.9 Concluding Remarks on Valuation of Irrigation Water

Valuation of increments and decrements of irrigation water supply is one of the most significant issues in water economics. Throughout the world, irrigation of agricultural crops accounts for a large portion of water withdrawals and by far the largest amount of water consumptively used. Although water for irrigation can be quite valuable, the marginal uses of irrigation water (particularly where soils, water quality, climate, and market conditions limit crop productivity and value) are typically less economically' valuable than alternative offstream and instream commodity purposes: for industry, power generation, and residential uses. Increasingly, public environmental uses are also found to be more economically valuable than marginal uses of irrigation water.

Section 5.1 observed that in a review of previous estimates of irrigation water values a few anomalies are found, among them a systematic inconsistency between econometrically-based *ex post* valuations analyzing observed land and water market behavior and valuations based on deductive models of hypothetical farmer decisions. Behavior-based valuations consistently show lower (in dollars per unit volume) valuations than those grounded on the more common deductive models relying on models of hypothetical producer actions.

This is partly because these approaches tend to measure different things. The land value and the more complex hedonic property value methods estimate at-source values that are, other things equal, lower than at-site measures. Behavior-based methods are most appropriate for estimating at-source, *ex post* values for long-run private contexts although they can be adjusted to yield at-site values. Because they measure past behavior at a specific place and for a specific period, these methods are more useful for validating conceptual models and cross-checking deductive studies than for evaluating proposed investments or allocation decisions. The methods based on observed market behavior also have the advantage, weighty to most economists, of being based on actual rather than hypothetical farmer decisionmaking. The residual methods are, however, widely adaptable for *ex post* or *ex ante*, long-run or short-run, public or private planning.

Nonetheless, deductive techniques as conventionally applied to evaluating proposed irrigation water resource investment and allocation policies appear to yield overestimates of willingness to pay for water. Deductive techniques are liable to omission of variables (particularly opportunity costs of owned inputs) and overly optimistic price and productivity assumptions. Especially for high-valued crops, inadequate accounting for rents to owned managerial inputs and equity capital may lead to an overstatement of the net returns to water. When an inappropriate conceptual framework is adopted, as when value-added or related measures from regional economic models are adduced as measures of willingness to pay, deductive techniques are subject to serious overestimation. More generally, where owned inputs other than water are also specialized, so that their "prices" are determined as rents once the results of previous decisions can be observed, the results of residual analysis are subject to an unavoidable indeterminacy.

The measured "value" depends on the decision or policy context in which the estimate is developed. Analysts must distinguish between private and public accounting stances, short-run and long-run decisions, at-source and at-site values, per period and capitalized values. Proper accounting for the contributions of specialized owned inputs is vital in applying residual techniques. It is hoped that this more fully developed framework can bring more realism to applied irrigation water valuation.

6

Valuing Water Used by Industry

Industrial water use refers broadly to water used as an input in the production of goods and services in other than agricultural activities. *Commercial* water users include restaurants, hotels, retail and wholesale trades, and offices. These uses are conventionally those in which water use is primarily for human consumption and sanitation on the business premises, and are mostly purchased from municipal supply agencies. Thus, I have chosen to include commercial uses with municipal uses in Chapter 7.

The many types of industries, even more types of water-using production processes, and corresponding variation in demand structures all make economic benefit assessment a challenge. It is often difficult to obtain the data necessary to estimate demand equations or develop models of production; the extensive academic and government research in crop production is not mirrored in manufacturing industries. In the field of water valuation, the class of industrial uses is among the least studied and the techniques for benefit measurement are probably the least developed.

The use of water in industrial processes is a producers' good as introduced in Chapter 3. The producers' demand for water is a derived demand, influenced in part by the demand and prices for the goods and services produced by the use of water. Industrial water demand is also determined by the technology available for production and input prices. (See Hanemann 1998 for a more detailed discussion.) This chapter discusses valuation of industrial water in offstream uses with inductive and deductive techniques. Inductive methods are further subdivided into direct demand analysis (fitting the relationship between water withdrawals and prices or costs) and production function analysis (deriving the value marginal product via statistical fitting of a production function). The remainder of the chapter takes up instream industrial use in hydroelectric power and inland navigation.

6.1 Industrial Water Use

Water typically represents a small portion of the manufacturing firm's total cost of production. Manufacturing businesses tend to have access to low-cost water directly from surface or groundwater sources or from public utilities. In resource allocation decisions, costs of capital, labor, energy, and other raw materials tend to overshadow the costs of water even where large amounts of water are used. This fact is critical for water valuation by either inductive or deductive techniques, since it will be difficult to isolate the role of a minor input such as water in the firms' overall costs and revenues.

Water use can be considered as either a variable input or a fixed input. Whether a nonagricultural industry supplies its own water or purchases it from a water utility, in most industrial uses the firm is free to choose the optimal level of water use, so the assumption that water is a variable input would seem to fit. In probably the only formal test of this point, Dupont and Renzetti (2001), using data from surveys of manufacturing water use in Canada, have confirmed that intake water is appropriately modeled as a variable input. It is assumed here that water can be regarded as a variable input in industrial processes, available in whatever supply is needed, but at a cost that depends on the amount taken. Thus, the industrial firm is hypothesized to choose the amount of water to withdraw by equating value marginal product (VMP) with the Marginal Input Cost. The valuation of industrial water will proceed from the theory of input demand and accordingly will most often be implemented by estimating the VMP function. An exception to the generality that water is a variable input in industrial situations may be found in hydroelectric power generation, where water supply is limited by characteristics of the site. As in agriculture, the economic rent model is most applicable to water valuation in that case.

The VMP (demand) function will usually cover a wider range of water prices than found in competing (e.g. agricultural) production uses. In most industries, water contributes a small portion to the value of output, and the choke point (the price at which the amount demanded falls to zero) on a demand curve for industrial water is typically much higher than it is for agriculture. A working approximation may be that industries can pay, if not "whatever it takes," quite large amounts compared to agriculture to acquire water for production purposes. Price is not irrelevant, however. Firms with relatively high water demands—pulp and paper, steel, and chemical producers that need generous amounts of water—tend to locate their plants where water is cheap and plentiful; they are seldom found in water-short regions.

Short-run models, in the Marshallian sense, represent situations in which the plant and equipment are assumed to be invariant. Fixed costs are appropriately treated as sunk, and ignored for the calculations. In long-run situations, plant and equipment can also become variable, and in residual models their costs are deducted from revenues when deriving measures of value. Thus, short-run models will yield higher values than long-run models. I am unaware of any *ex ante* estimation of short-run values for industrial water use. However, Wade et al. (1991) report that during the California drought of 1988–1992 members of a sample of the California manufacturing sector were willing to spend relatively large amounts (over $1,300 per acre-foot—equivalent to more than $1 per cubic meter) to avoid shortages, implying a very low absolute short-run price elasticity.

If, as is often the case, the goal of the valuation exercise is to derive an estimate of at-source water value for comparison with values in alternative uses, steps beyond industrial water demand equations will be necessary. Studies of the economic demands for water by industries almost always focus on demand at the factory or enterprise level, i.e. the at-site value. The commodity is sometimes treated and delivered to the site of use. However, much of the water used by industry is self-supplied, drawn directly from ground or surface water sources and, if necessary, treated for use in the production process. Part of the water withdrawn may be recycled and used again. Moreover, some types of industrial uses can function with water of lesser quality. For example, brackish water is often used for cooling water in thermoelectric power plants. Hence, some further adjustments, which will differ according to the type and quality of the water supply, are required to extract an estimate of at-source water value.

Industries use water for an enormous range of production processes, which we can classify as offstream (withdrawal) or instream (nonwithdrawal) water uses. The most common offstream application of water in developed countries is cooling industrial processes, particularly for thermoelectric power plants. Waste disposal, sanitation, and, in the beverage and food industries, inclusion in the firm's products are other typical offstream industrial uses. In the United States, thermo-electric power plants accounted for 33% of withdrawals but only 3.7% of consumptive use in 1995 (Solley et al. 1998). Manufacturing and processing industries—chemical production, petroleum refining, pulp and paper production, food processing, and mining—constituted the remaining portion of industrial uses. Cleanup, sanitation, and fire protection accounted for most of the balance of industrial water uses. Over all, the domestic/commercial category represented 11% of withdrawals and 7% of consumption, while industry took 8% and 5% respectively.

Instream uses involve primarily hydroelectric power generation. However, water-borne transportation of freight and to a lesser extent passengers is also a common (usually public) enterprise. Instream industrial uses are typically linked with public capital investments to supply intermediate goods. Water-related capital investments include dams and reservoirs, which in turn serve investments in power plants or elements of inland waterways. Instream industrial water uses typically require large supplies of water, but they are not highly consumptive. Water must be held ready to float ships or barges or generate electricity, but little of that water—other than that evaporated from reservoir surfaces—is actually consumed or lost to the atmosphere. Nevertheless, release of water for power generation or navigation may imply forgone benefits in alternative uses, as exemplified in the United States by increasing conflicts among recreational users, hydropower plants, and water transportation enterprises, especially during droughts. Policy decisions on allocation of water among these competing uses need to be informed by estimates of economic benefits or forgone values in each alternative.

A useful early survey of issues in industrial water demand analysis is presented in a collection of papers edited by Kindler and Russell (1984); see chapters by Stone and Whittington; and Russell. Their main topic is the effects of price and other factors on water use. Gibbons 1986 and Renzetti 2002a both touch briefly on industrial water demands. Renzetti 2002b is another collection of early papers on the economics of industrial water use, some of which deal with demand and valuation issues. But our main concern—deriving at-source values (for raw water) in industrial use—has been largely ignored.

6.2 Inductive Techniques for Valuing Water in Offstream Industrial Uses

Inductive estimates of industrial water values offer the same advantages and disadvantages as inductive studies of other user classes (see Section 3.12). Professional judgment—what functional form to use; what ancillary data to include; production function versus cost function—can influence the reported results. No one study can be decisive in determining price-elasticity and willingness to pay.

6.2.1 Estimation of Industrial Demands and Values

The statistical or econometric approach makes inferences from actual observations of quantities consumed and costs of water, together with data on other explanatory variables. An abstract demand function asserts a hypothetical connection between water delivered (the variable to be explained) and factors influencing the dependent variable. Parameters of demand equations in this approach are inferred statistically, usually with multiple regression techniques. (Numerous textbooks present the theoretical and applied statistical aspects of the issue, e.g. Mittelhammer et al. 2000).

Economic theory suggests that in addition to the price of water, the prices of other factor inputs, the type of technology or production process, the product mix, and output level are significant variables in explaining the quantity of water withdrawn for industrial use. This generalization can be expressed in a model of an optimizing producer's demand for water input:

$$Q_w = Q_w(P_w, P_i, P_a; X; S) \tag{6-1}$$

where Q_w is the amount of water received by the producers in a specified time period; P_w the price of water; P_i a vector of prices of other productive inputs (capital, labor and materials); X the quantity of product to be produced, and S represents a vector of other factors such as technology and climate. (See Hanemann 1998 or Spulber and Sabbaghi 1998 for more complete development of these input demand models.)

Data to estimate the function can come from repeated observations at different times on the same enterprise (time series data) or simultaneous observation of many enterprises during the same period (cross-sectional data). Data can be primary (collected directly from the producing firms) or secondary (obtained from already-published data such as government reports or records).

To obtain enough observations to develop reliable industrial water demand functions is expensive and time-consuming. Not many research agencies are willing to do so. Many firms resist spending the time and effort to provide academic researchers with the necessary statistics. Thus, some data sets are small samples and others are collected only when a government agency compels reporting of water use.

The number of observable cases where water is volumetrically priced is limited. Instead of purchasing water from public supply agencies, many industries use their own groundwater or surface water; the cost may not be readily separable from general firm expenditures for utilities or materials. Statistical estimation of an industrial water demand function requires observations reflecting a range of real water costs. But time series data for one industry rarely exhibit much variation in real water rates, so demand equation estimates based on cross-sectional data are more common in the literature. Because of all these obstacles, studies based on large samples of industrial water use and costs collected specifically for water demand studies are unusual.

The demand model must define the "price of water" variable for the statistical analysis. Average cost is often easier to obtain, but when water is purchased within a block rate pricing system, such a definition may imply a cost which is endogenous (price depends on the quantity used). Economic theory implies that profit-maximizing firms equate marginal value with marginal price. If marginal price is not used, the model could be mis-specified and the resulting coefficients biased (Billings and Agthe 1980). If the price variable P_w' is an average price obtained by dividing the total payments for water TP_w by the quantity taken Q_w,

$$P_w' = TP_w / Q_w$$

the price variable is not independent of the dependent variable Q_w. Consequently the estimated coefficient on P_w and the coefficient of determination R^2 will both be biased upward, as will the price elasticity derived from the estimated model.

Because of the above obstacles, the literature reports only a few econometric studies of industrial water demand. Studies of industrial water demand up through the early 1980s used single-equation representations of the model in equation 6-1. Turnovsky (1969) used an ordinary least squares (OLS) approach to analyze data from 19 towns in Massachusetts for the period 1962–1965. Estimates of price elasticity ranged from about –0.5 to about –0.8. Rees (1969) obtained a very detailed set of data from a large sample of manufacturing firms in southeast England. She reported elastic responses to price in a number of industries, ranging from about –1.0 to as high as –6.7. Both these researchers used average revenue for the price variable, which probably led to an overstatement of responsiveness to price. For a small sample of New Jersey chemical plants, De Rooy (1974) estimated separate demand equations for cooling, process, steam, and sanitation intake water. A weighted average of the cost of water intake and the estimated cost of recirculation was employed as the water price variable. He reported price elasticities of –0.35 for process water, –0.9 for cooling water and –0.6 for steam generation. Stone and Whittington (1984) studied a small sample of paper manufacturers in the Netherlands. Babin et al. (1982) switched to a cost function approach; they fitted state-level observations on major water-using American manufacturing industries to a translog cost function model. In both these studies, demand was usually found to be price-inelastic, but elasticity calculations in the various industries ranged widely: (in absolute values) from near zero to almost one. Schneider and Whitlach (1991) also report a price-inelastic demand for industrial water in Columbus, Ohio.

Referring to this earlier literature, Renzetti (1992) noted:

> All of these studies use the average cost of water acquisition to represent the price of water. This is significant for three reasons. First, it introduces a simultaneity bias into the estimation because the quantity of water appears on both sides of the regression equation...Second, because most firms face water prices in the form of declining block rates, representing price by the average cost of acquisition may imply

that the demand equation is not identified. In this case, the analyst cannot determine whether a negative coefficient on the price variable represents the negative slope of the demand equation or of the utility's water price schedule. Finally, it may lead the demand equation to be mis-specified, since economic theory predicts that firms respond to marginal, not average prices in their decisionmaking.

To avoid the problem of simultaneity bias, Renzetti (1992) approaches industrial demand via a cost function. His study is based on about 2,000 individual Canadian firms in a 1985 cross-sectional water-use survey. The sample encompasses almost 95% of Canadian manufacturing water use. The data includes expenditures, costs, and quantities of water intake, partitioned into seven industrial sectors. Following a suggestion in the residential water demand literature, Renzetti creates an instrumental variable to represent the price of water. In addition to the large sample, he goes beyond earlier approaches by modeling industrial water demand as reflecting four components: intake, treatment prior to use, recirculation, and discharge. The cost function is represented by a translog functional form. Lacking data on marginal prices, he encounters difficulties in specifying the price variable. Renzetti finds that industrial water demand in Canada is price inelastic. The average price elasticity for intake water in Canadian industries is –0.38, while individual industry elasticity estimates range from –0.15 to –0.59. Renzetti also confirms that recirculation of water is a substitute for both water intake and water discharge, and concludes from this that economic incentives such as effluent fees are likely to encourage both reduced water intake and increased recirculation. From another sample of Canadian manufacturing firms, Dupont and Renzetti (2001) report a price elasticity of intake water demand of –0.77, a somewhat more elastic response than found previously. Reynaud (2003) has studied industrial water demand from a sample of 51 firms located in southwest France. Also using a cost function approach, he reports a relatively inelastic demand at –0.29.

These empirical findings of price-inelastic industrial water demand under conditions of metered supply contrast with anecdotal evidence of elastic demands in many developing countries. Where water has been unmetered or a volumetric price set very low, introduction of meters or a relatively small price increase is said to have a major rationing effect, implying a more price-elastic industrial demand. There are very few attempts at measuring industrial water demand in developing countries. However, I. Hussain et al. (2002) studied industrial water use in Sri Lanka, based on a national time series data set comprising monthly consumption for 1994–1998, a period during which the real price of water was raised significantly. Testing both linear and log-log functional forms, they reported –1.3 as the price elasticity of demand for industrial water withdrawals.

6.2.2 An Example from a Developing Country

Wang and Lall (2001), using survey data from China, found some support for the hypothesis of elastic demands for industrial water withdrawals in developing countries. They made use of plant-level data collected by the State Environmental Protection Administration to analyze pollution control policy. The agency survey recorded outputs and inputs for the year 1993 from over 2000 medium and larger factories that discharged significant wastes into water bodies. Wang and Lall subjected a portion of the data set to an econometric value productivity analysis.

Because the data had been collected for other purposes, some adjustments were necessary to prepare the data for the productivity analysis. Total value of output was measured in 1993 yuan. Flows of capital input such as depreciation and interest were not available, so year-end capital stocks were used to represent capital. The labor input was measured by year-end number of workers. The raw materials variable was represented by the pollution discharges to waters, on the premise that they were highly correlated with raw materials inputs (but ignoring the fact that some of the raw material intake would also leave as final products, solid wastes, or releases to the atmosphere). For lack of data, energy use was ignored in the empirical analysis. Finally, water was represented by annual water intake measured in cubic meters.

For the main analysis, additional explanatory variables were incorporated as binary (dummy) variables. These included: regional location, size of enterprise, and private versus public ownership. Further, 16 additional binary variables were included, each representing one of 16 producing sectors: food and beverages, textiles, chemicals, petroleum refining, power generation, etc. As their preferred specification from which they calculated marginal value productivities and price elasticities, the authors chose the translog form. This allows a great range of substitution patterns, and it is quadratic in the logarithms (meaning that the function incorporates cross-products and squared terms). The estimated coefficients on the variables related to water were highly sensitive to model specification.

From the estimated production function, the authors derive a value marginal product of water intake, which, since water is measured as physical intake quantity, I interpret as an at-site measure. The estimated sectoral values extend widely, from a low of 0.05 yuan per cubic meter in the power generation sector to a high of 26.8 yuan per cubic meter in the transportation equipment sector. The overall average for the sample was reported as 2.45 yuan per cubic meter. Large variations were reported between regions; as expected, the water-short North reported an average marginal value much larger than that found in the South. Wang and Lall also report estimates of price elasticity of water demand ranging from –1.20 for leather goods to –0.57 for power generation. The overall sample average was reported as –1.03 or approximately unitary elasticity, an estimate that is somewhat larger (absolute value) than others in the literature (e.g. Renzetti 1992).

The study illustrates the complications in obtaining data and estimating marginal value productivities for water as an input to industrial production. Here the authors obtained data collected for a different purpose from a nonrandom sample of firms drawn from a list of plants identified as major industrial polluters.

Ideally, the researcher would choose a random sample of all sizes and types of profit-maximizing industries. One would also prefer to use direct measures of raw materials inputs and energy. In spite of these limitations, the large number of observations and the detailed reporting of major inputs and output make this data set attractive for econometric production function analysis. Future work of this sort needs to emphasize improved data collection procedures.

6.2.3 Concluding Thoughts

The small role of water in the typical industrial cost structure makes it difficult to obtain statistically reliable estimates of value marginal product. Analysts performing a regression analysis to estimate the marginal value or demand for industrial water use are typically content to demonstrate that the coefficient representing price is significantly different from zero, calculate the price elasticity of demand, and confirm that the effect of price on quantity used is negative in sign.

For policy analysis, the most commonly desired value of industrial water is that for at-source water. The at-source value of water is the appropriate measure for evaluating intersectoral water allocation options, where the value of raw water for industries is to be compared on the same terms with, for example, the value of raw water for agriculture, households, or the environment. However, the most common data on industrial water value measure willingness to pay for water from public water supply agencies—an at-site value embodying costs of capture, storage, treatment, and delivery. Hence, some adaptation of the at-site demand functions estimated in most empirical industrial water demand studies will be required. A form of the benefit transfer method is one way to make such a conversion (see Section 6.3.4).

6.3 Deductive Techniques for Valuing Water in Offstream Industrial Uses

Several deductive approaches employing constructed models have been applied to valuing industrial water uses. As with irrigation water, residual approaches can be applied. Some analysts have adopted mathematical programming, a similar but more flexible and realistic approach. Cost function models, benefit transfer, and alternative cost formulations may also be applicable.

6.3.1 Basic Residual Approaches to Industrial Water Valuation

The residual method as applied to industrial water valuation is typically based on engineering design studies for the industry or plant; these identify feasible water-using unit processes, alternative designs and inputs and their operating conditions, and associated costs. This information is incorporated into a budget designed to ascertain the costs and returns associated with alternative technologies and water use amounts. The simplest form would budget out discrete alternatives with partial budget formulations. Spreadsheet software on personal computers has made this convenient.

Residual methods of valuing water use in industry must account for opportunity costs of all nonwater inputs. This technique is subject to a number of pitfalls. As with crop irrigation (see Chapter 5), in order to assign a residual to water, prices or opportunity costs musts be assigned to elements of the income statement that are, in normal business accounting practice, actually residual returns themselves.

Water, while essential to many industrial processes, typically reflects only a very small portion of total input costs and the corresponding value of incremental output. As with inductive techniques, the residual is highly sensitive to all assumptions made about the production process, particularly the price assigned to any noncontractual inputs in the industrial process. The smaller the marginal product of an input relative to the total output, the higher the likelihood of an inaccurate estimate of the residual. For example, a typical industrial corporation is capitalized through a financial contribution from its owners as well as from borrowings from banks and bondholders. These returns tend to vary with the perceived risk of the enterprise. Also, Schumpeterian rents (from entrepreneurship and innovation), may account for a significant part of profits. Within a range of plausible assumptions about the opportunity cost of owned or borrowed financial capital and about the contribution of human inputs such as management and entrepreneurship, the estimated residual value of water might vary widely, even from a negative to a large positive value. Estimates derived by the residual method in industrial contexts should be accepted with caution.

6.3.2 Limitations of Value Added from Input-Output Models

The value-added method based on regional input-output models was prominently applied to the industrial sector several times in the early development of nonmarket benefit estimate procedures in the field of water resources.

Section 3.9.1 critiqued value-added as a measure of willingness to pay. The true return to water in long-run decision contexts is only a part of the net rents accruing to natural resources, and a much smaller fraction of the total value-added. Of course, the relative amounts of purchased goods and services compared to value added will vary from firm to firm and from industry to industry. When inexperienced analysts mistakenly assume that the term value-added (regularly used in regional economic models) represents the appropriate economic welfare concept, such as value marginal product or value incremental net rent, they impute not only the marginal value of water but the productivity of the other primary resources, such as profits, interest, depreciation, wages, and salaries. The uncritical use of value-added as a measure of marginal value product has yielded large, erroneous estimates of marginal industrial water values.

6.3.3 Mathematical Programming Models

Mathematical programming models can be formulated to select the combination of processes which maximize firm profits or minimize costs. (See Williams 1999 for a general discussion of applying mathematical programming to economic models of production.) As with programming models of agricultural water use, the definition of objective function is key. A long-run formulation—with the objective function defined to measure net return after all costs—is usually appropriate for water development planning exercises. The demand function is approximated by solving the model for a number of alternative water prices and recording the amount of water required at each price. Solutions are often repeated under alternative assumptions about product prices, resource constraints, rate of return, and depreciation of capital and water use technology, to determine sensitivity to alternative model specification and to learn more about the nature of response patterns. As in agricultural applications of mathematical models, the Value Incremental Net Product for an increment of water supply is imputed to the value of industrial water. The objective function needs to be carefully specified so as not to attribute to water the productivity of other resources such as labor or financial capital.

An improved optimization model of an industry can also be formulated to incorporate alternative water-use technologies, and then solved for varying constraints on water. Alternative cost (see Section 3.1.1), which imputes a value via cost-saving between technologies, may in effect be incorporated into a mathematical programming model. The production activities in the model represent a number of technical opportunities of varying cost and water use efficiency, and solution of the model yields dual values which automatically impute cost saving to alternative water use levels.

In the 1970s, Clifford Russell developed probably the first application of mathematical programming to industrial water demands. See Russell (1984) for a review of the procedure and citations of the earlier literature. Stone and Whittington (1984) employed a cost-function approach to study industrial water demand for a hypothetical steam-powered electric power plant for the Vistula River region in Poland. Because of the complex relationships among withdrawal, consumption, and discharge of water, and the availability of a number of alternative water use technologies, they formulated a mixed-integer mathematical programming model with cost-minimization as the objective function. The model comprised approximately 350 rows and 1400 columns. (With present-day computing capacity, the impediment to implementing such a model is not computational capacity but the resources to define the relevant technical relationships and gather the necessary data.) Manipulation of the model yielded demand functions for water intake in the form of predictions of water withdrawals, consumptive use, and discharges for a range of hypothesized water costs. A number of possibilities for substitutions of alternative water use technologies at varying cost added to the realism of the model. Specifically, the costs and water use for each of eight alternative cooling system configurations and their associated water withdrawals were incorporated in the model. Cost-minimizing solutions for each of a range of alternative water supply constraints traced out the demand function. Price elasticities of demand were also derived. Solutions to this model would be quite sensitive to assumptions about the cost of alternative technologies, the opportunity cost of capital, and other owned inputs. Although the engineering structure of the model is described in considerable detail, the economic assumptions regarding costs are quite general. For example, annual depreciation charges are simplified to 4% of capital investments, implying a 25-year straight-line depreciation with zero salvage value. The real opportunity cost of capital is assumed to be 8%. It would be of interest to know how labor or other costs of human input were priced. In spite of these reservations, this is a promising avenue for deriving *ex ante* demands for industrial use of water.

6.3.4 Benefit Transfer for Industrial Water Valuation

In contrast to at-site values, at-source values of industrial water are usually needed for evaluating intersectoral water reallocation proposals. Data on which to base at-source values for industrial firms are ordinarily not directly observable, so an alternative method is required. A deductive approximation via benefit transfer is a quick and easy approach by which values or demand functions estimated for one or more sites or circumstance are employed to assign benefits or value to other sites or circumstances.

In the case of water resources planning, benefit transfer methods have been applied mostly in environmental and outdoor recreational contexts (see Section 4.9), but the broad approach is applicable for valuation of off-stream water uses as well.

The method described here for deriving an at-source value from data on water delivered to households and industries was first proposed and implemented by James and Lee (1971, *314–315*). It can be shown that some plausible assumptions inserted into such a formula can yield a useful approximation of incremental gross economic benefits. The first step is to find a gross benefit, measured as the integral of the demand curve for water for the change of water quantity being valued. (The demand function is taken from previous studies of different sites, so this is a case of benefit transfer.) Four parameters or empirical measures are needed for the gross benefit or value estimate. The first two consist of a *price-quantity point*—an observed consumption quantity taken during a specified period and the price then in effect. The third measure is a hypothetical change in quantity that is to be valued, and the fourth is an estimate of the price elasticity of demand. The integral of the demand curve for a pre-specified range of water quantity can be derived to find the measure of gross benefit. To then determine an at-source value of industrial water for purposes of intersectoral allocation, it is necessary to adjust the benefit estimate to reflect the derived demand for at-source water in a watercourse. Studies of demand for industrial water measure the willingness to pay not only for water itself, but for the services involved in capturing, transporting, treating, storing, and delivering water. Therefore costs of these services must be deducted from the estimated willingness to pay for water supply. This second step defines the at-source value as the *imputed producer surplus per unit of raw water.* The detailed formulas and a case example applied to residential uses are presented in Section 7.4.

6.4 Valuing Water in Instream Industrial Uses: Hydropower

Hydroelectric power plants and waterborne transportation are the primary industrial instream water uses. Electric power plants are often operated by public sector agencies rather than private firms. But the valuation process is more akin to that for private intermediate goods than for other instream uses.

6.4.1 Preliminaries

Hydropower is more flexible and in some ways more environmentally friendly than thermal-powered electricity generation. Hydropower plants last longer and cost less to operate and maintain, but more to build. Hydropower does not produce the air pollution of fossil-fueled plants.

However, hydropower reservoirs slow down streams and change water temperatures. They may inundate important scenic, historic, and recreational sites, although they may create new flat-water recreational opportunities. Because of the ease with which hydropower plants can increase and decrease output, hydropower is often most attractive when used for supplying power at peak daily demand periods. However, because electricity demands tend to rise in winter from heating and lighting needs, demands for water releases for hydropower generation often conflict with irrigation and, to a lesser extent, residential demands for water, both of which tend to rise in summer. Water released in winter for hydropower may be unusable for summer irrigation unless downstream storage can capture it. Economic analysis can clarify the tradeoffs between these competing uses.

6.4.2 Characterizing the Production of Hydroelectric Power

Energy production from hydropower depends on three factors: the amount of water that flows through the turbines, the distance that the water drops (the *effective head*), and the power plant efficiency. For a specific hydropower installation, energy production (Qe) for a given period t (hours, days, months, years) in kilowatt-hours (kWh) is computed as:

$$Qet = H_t * V_t * Ef_t * C \qquad\qquad (6\text{-}2)$$

subject to the following definitions and constraints:

$$H_t = Ep_t - Es \qquad\qquad (6\text{-}3)$$

$$H_t \geq Hm \qquad\qquad (6\text{-}4)$$

$$Qet_t \leq Mg \qquad\qquad (6\text{-}5)$$

$$V_t \leq Mq \qquad\qquad (6\text{-}6)$$

where:

$\quad H_t$ = average head in feet during period t;
$\quad V_t$ = water flow volume (in acre-feet) per unit time;
$\quad Ef$ = generator efficiency (typically assumed to be about 0.80 or 0.85);
$\quad C$ = 1.0253 (a constant to convert from acre-feet into kWh);
$\quad Ep$ = average pond (reservoir) elevation in feet during period;
$\quad Es$ = tailwater elevation in feet during period;
Hm = minimum head for intake;
Mg = maximum generator capacity in kWh per unit time; and
Mq = maximum turbine capacity in Q per unit time.

Put in words, equation 6-2 asserts that the production of electricity (in kWh) is the volume of water times the constant reflecting the theoretical kilowatt hours generated per unit volume per unit head times the generator efficiency, all multiplied by the effective distance the water falls. The constraints require that estimated production be limited to maximum turbine and generator capacity.

Estimating the value of water in hydropower generation begins with determining the gross value of electricity output by assigning an alternative cost price to units of output. Care must be taken to distinguish between base load generation and the more valuable peak load output.

6.4.3 Issues in Hydropower Evaluation

Most economic evaluation of hydropower is intended to assess the overall economic feasibility of a proposed investment in hydropower production capacity, in which case a specific value of water for hydropower is not at issue. For, say, an intersectoral allocation study, however, isolating the marginal value of water from the total value requires additional steps. Because the electricity is produced from a combination of resources (capital investment; operating, maintenance, and repair costs; water) the marginal contribution of water can be derived from an additional deductive process employing the residual technique.

The first step is to value the electricity produced from a specific plant. Because electricity is typically sold into a power grid relying on a number of sources (hydro plus thermal), it is seldom convenient or even possible to derive the demand for the hydro portion of a region's or a country's electrical supply. Because electricity prices are often set by government policy, which seldom reflects the marginal cost of new supply, observed electricity rates may be inappropriate for economic evaluation. Therefore, in the first step, the value (shadow price) of electricity is usually calculated via the alternative cost method, based on an estimate of the cost of the next likely increment of electrical power. The second step is to calculate, via the residual method, the portion of the total value of the electricity output attributable to the water used for generation.

An analyst may elect to estimate short-run and long-run values. Marshallian short-run value or rent is derived by deducting only operation, maintenance, and repair (OM&R) from total value of output. Long-run values are developed by further deducting capital investment costs (annualized equivalent costs of outlays for dam, reservoir, and generating plant allocated to the power function). For a given site and electricity market, long-run values are therefore less than short-run. Another pair of values represent peaking and baseload generation. Peaking power electricity is typically much more valuable than baseload generation because of the cost of bringing less efficient and more expensive alternative thermal capacity briefly on line. Thus, water for peaking is more valuable than for base load generation. The alternative cost valuation of peaking power is particularly difficult because of the site-specific characteristics of alternative peaking capacity and the ambiguities of allocating fixed costs between peaking and baseload operations.

The accounting price of electricity is determined by the alternative cost method. The OECD (1998) report "Projected Costs for Generating Electricity: Update 1998" offers procedures and data for estimating generating costs. Dowlatabadi and Toman (1991) discuss the cost differences between alternative technologies and mention environmental costs, which in certain cases should be added to capital and operating costs. Adding environmental damages as a cost of the alternative will, of course, properly credit hydropower with that cost saving. For symmetry, environmental costs of the dam and reservoir should be included in the cost of the hydropower facility.

Experience over the last two or three decades with the costs of electricity generation shows that predicting the alternative generating costs over a long planning period introduces an unavoidable degree of uncertainty. Technological improvement has increased the efficiency of power from thermal energy plants (a trend one hopes will continue, although the forecasts for cost-saving from nuclear power several decades ago proved very optimistic). The real, social costs of energy inputs (such coal or natural gas) into electricity generation have varied widely with fluctuations of investment in production capacity and perceived relative scarcities. Public policies designed to reduce air pollution can be expected to increase electricity costs, although technological advances in the electricity industry seem to partially offset these effects.

The analyst who undertakes to estimate the alternative cost of electricity generation "from scratch" faces a major task. This effort may be avoided if the planning department of the relevant public or private power provider can be tapped for estimates of the cost of the next increment of power to the service area.

A limited number of studies of hydropower values, mainly assessing tradeoffs with competing water uses, are found outside of the gray literature. Houston and Whittlesey (1986) and Hamilton et al. (1989) studied the tradeoffs between irrigation and hydropower in the Snake-Columbia River Basins, finding that additional diversions for irrigation would cost more in forgone energy than would be gained. Booker and Young (1994) and Booker (1995) developed hydropower benefit functions for incorporation into nonlinear optimization models of water allocation among instream and offstream water uses in the Colorado River Basin. Harpman (1999) studied the short-run forgone benefits of changing water release regimes to improve downstream environmental conditions. He extended previous approaches by developing an hourly constrained optimization model of power operations on the Glen Canyon Dam. Harpman simulated the operation of the dam under historical operating rules and under modified rules based on Endangered Species Act considerations that reflected new restrictions on flows. The changes reduced the peak power generation from the dam and correspondingly increased the base load generation. With a cost based on alternative methods, Harpman found that the new operating rules would reduce the value of hydropower from the dam by over $6 million per year.

6.4.4 Example: Deriving the Value of Water in Hydropower Generation

This example from the Colorado River Basin is an adaptation of a model formulated by Albery (1968) for computing the value of water.

The Model. Albery derives the maximum willingness to pay for water given the competition of the cheapest alternative source of electricity. According to alternative cost, the willingness to pay equals the saving from using the hydropower option. This saving can be interpreted as the economic rents to the water resource. (Although they don't extend their discussion to deriving a unit value of water, Zuker and Jenkins 1984 provide a useful discussion of the conceptual and empirical issues in derivation of hydropower rents.) Albery's model can be adapted to derive both long-run and short-run estimates.

Let:

$G =$ capital cost ($) per installed kilowatt (kW) capacity of generating facilities, site work, and dams;

$T =$ capital cost ($) per installed kW capacity of transmission facilities (including transmission lines and substations);

$K =$ capital cost ($) per installed kW capacity of total project $(G + T)$;

$\alpha K =$ annualized charges on capital investment, where α is the capital recovery factor for the assumed planning period and interest rate; (αK may be considered equivalent to annual interest and depreciation on investment);

$\beta K =$ annual costs of operation and maintenance (for simplicity, β is assumed to be a constant percentage of capital cost);

$e =$ overall hydraulic, mechanical, and electrical efficiency;

$f =$ annual capacity utilization factor (ratio of average load on the plant to installed generating capacity);

$h =$ effective mean head in feet (pond elevation minus tailwater elevation);

$q =$ flow in cubic feet per second (cfs) at maximum output (all equipment assumed operating at normal full load capacity);

$x =$ value ($) of one cfs of water for one year;

$z =$ value ($) of one acre-foot of water; and

$y_f=$ accounting price of electricity (cents per kWh) at load factor f (alternative cost of generation plus transmission).

Albery's definitions and formulas (given in English units) are derived as follows:

The available maximum output of the hydro plant in horsepower (hp) is:

Installed capacity (hp) $= 0.1135eqh,$

where 0.1135 is the weight of one cubic foot of water (62.5 lbs) divided by 550 (foot-pounds/sec/hp). Converting hp to kW,

Installed capacity (kW) $= 0.0848eqh$

Then:

Total capital cost ($) $= 0.0848eqh(K)$

and

Total annual cost ($) *excluding* the value of water
$= 0.0848eqh(K)(\alpha + \beta)$ (6-7)

Total annual cost ($) *including* the value of water
$= 0.0848eqh(K)(\alpha + \beta) + xqf$ (6-8)

Electricity generated (kWh/year) $= 0.0848eqhf$ (8760)   (6-9)

or 8760 hours in one year.

Dividing (6-8) by (6-9) yields costs of generating hydropower in $/kWh:

$$= \frac{[0.0848eh\ (K)(\alpha + \beta)] + xf}{0.0848ehf\ (8760)} \quad\quad (6\text{-}10)$$

Deriving the Value of Water. The next step is to estimate the net rents to water by subtracting the cost of the hydro option from the cost of the more expensive thermal option:

Setting (6-10) equal to the value (alternative cost) of delivered electricity:

$$\frac{[0.0848eh\ (K)(\alpha + \beta)] + xf}{0.0848ehf\ (8760)} = \frac{y_f}{100} \quad\quad (6\text{-}11)$$

Equation 6-11 is a general expression which for a given hydropower site (or series of sites on a river) can be solved for x (the value of water in dollars of one cubic foot per second for one year), assuming particular values for capital cost $[(K)(\alpha + \beta)]$, efficiency (e), head (h), capacity utilization factor (f), and the value (alternative cost) of the electricity (y_f).

An Illustration. Assume $\alpha + \beta = 0.075$, and $e = 0.85$, and solve to find a general expression for the value of water (in cfs for one year):

$$x = 0.63hy_f - 0.0054hK/f \qquad (6\text{-}12)$$

Equation 6-12 gives a value of water that is an explicit function of head, value of energy delivered, capital and operating costs, and annual capacity utilization factor.

Finally, the value in cfs for one year (a flow, denoted x) can be converted into a volume z (value per acre-foot) using the constant 721.1 to represent the number of acre feet equivalent to one cfs flowing for one year.

$$z = \frac{x}{721.1} \qquad (6\text{-}13)$$

A Short-Run Estimate. An estimate of the Marshallian short-run value of water for hydropower is often needed, because the capital cost of long-lived hydro plants is frequently treated as "sunk" and ignored in water allocation decisions. The short-run value can be derived from equation 6-11 by simply setting K equal to zero and solving with the appropriate other parameters:

$$x = 0.63hy_f \qquad (6\text{-}14)$$

A Sample Calculation. Assume the following for the model parameters and variables, roughly representative of multiple sites on the Colorado River Basin:

> $K =$ \$235 per installed kilowatt capacity;
> $h =$ 450 feet of total head;
> $e =$ 0.85;
> $\alpha =$ 6%;
> $\beta =$ 1.5%;
> $f =$ 0.50; and
> $y_f =$ \$0.039/kWh (i.e. alternative cost is 3.9 mills per kWh).

Under these assumptions, the long-run value of water in generating electricity would be about \$5 per acre-foot.

The estimated short-run value—ignoring the annualized capital costs of installing a hydropower generating plant—would be significantly higher, about \$20 per acre-foot. For intermediate-term reallocations among sectors, the short-run value would be appropriate (the storage reservoir and generating facilities presumably wouldn't change).

A Final Remark. Electric power generation (whether by hydro or thermal technologies) is characterized by long-lived, capital-intensive investments. Cost estimates are sensitive to whether historical or replacement costs are used, by what interest rate (especially whether private or social) is adopted, and by the assumptions about efficiency of the generating processes. As noted by Zuker and Jenkins (1984, Table 4-2), estimates of hydropower rent can vary widely, even for same site, depending on the assumptions made. As always, sensitivity analysis on key assumptions is advised.

6.5 Valuing Water in Instream Industrial Uses: Waterborne Transportation

Inland water transport, used mainly for certain bulk commodities, has one major advantage: low operating cost, largely due to the low motive force required to overcome fluid friction. Disadvantages include high capital investment requirements, indirect routes, slow travel (which makes it inappropriate for perishable or time-sensitive cargo), periodic closure (as in winter or extreme water flow conditions), impossibility of door-to-door service, and the need for extensive dock facilities. Waterborne transportation requires a nearly constant supply of water when the channel is operational. This leads to conflict with alternative uses along a river system. For example, releases of water from storage so as to maintain channel depth often conflict with needs to save the stored water for use at another time by hydropower or irrigation facilities.

Water-based transportation economics extends beyond inland waterways. Because this book centers on valuing water in competitive situations, and because of lack of resources and experience, this section is limited to a brief comment on valuation of inland waterway transportation.

6.5.1 Measuring Gross Benefits of Investments in Inland Waterways

Although a number of conceptual analyses and empirical studies of the economics of waterborne transportation (often classed as *navigational* uses of water) were conducted several decades ago in the United States, interest among economists has declined. The basic method of appraisal of navigation projects is an alternative cost method, calculating the expected cost saving (both capital and operating costs) over alternative transportation methods such as rail or trucking. Eckstein (1958) provided an early critique of the techniques of economic appraisal of navigation by public agencies. Howe et al. (1969) developed techniques for evaluating both public and private waterborne transportation decisions.

The cost of the alternative service can be posted rail rates or an estimate of the social marginal costs of the alternative transportation service. The latter is usually more appropriate, but a more challenging undertaking. Marginal rail costs will usually be less than rail rates, due to the large fixed costs. The volume of traffic that will use water transportation facilities, or the increment in volume due to some investment in improved facilities may be troublesome to compute. The U.S. Water Resources Council's *Principles and Guidelines* (1983) contains a brief summary of standard U.S. Government evaluation procedures. The typical economic appraisal of navigation expenditures assigns a zero opportunity cost to water itself. Although this assumption may be appropriate in some cases (should no actual opportunity costs to alternative water uses exist), it is not a generally valid supposition.

6.5.2 Skeptical Views of Navigation Feasibility Studies

Beginning with Eckstein's (1958) early critique, independent analysts have been skeptical of the findings of economic feasibility of many public navigation projects. In their view, studies have been prone to use too low an interest rate, too high a cost saving estimate, too high an incremental barge traffic projection, an inappropriate mix of materials to be transported, and inadequate consideration of environmental costs.

Huszar (1998) provides a recent example of such skepticism in a critique of the official feasibility study for a navigation proposal called the Paraguay-Paraná Waterway. Prompted in part by the formation of the Southern Cone Common Market, the waterway would improve transportation within and between Uruguay, Argentina, Paraguay, Bolivia, and Brazil. The system was intended to improve year-round navigation on the Paraná River system and its major tributary, the Paraguay River, by large ships and barge trains from the harbor at Nueva Palmira, Uruguay to Cáceres, Brazil, a distance of over 3400 km. The route would pass through the Pantanal National Park in Brazil, one of the world's largest wetlands. The plan contemplated construction and dredging costs of over US$1 billion, and operating and maintenance costs of over $US3 billion over the next 25 years. The expected benefits of the project would be reduced risk of interruptions in service due to seasonal low river flows, reduced transportation costs due to larger barge trains, and time saving because of continuous navigation. An intergovernmental coordinating committee directed major economic, engineering, and environmental feasibility studies by consortiums of consulting firms in 1996. For its base case, the feasibility study reported an internal rate of return of 55%.

Huszar criticized the study's general approach to the cost–benefit analysis and specific measures of direct and forgone economic benefits, the latter aspect being of interest here. In its estimate of the cost of transporting regional products via alternative transportation methods, the feasibility study assumed that nearly all regional production and all petroleum imports would be transported via the waterway. However, Huszar argued that these shipping volumes would be unlikely to materialize given the imminent completion of a railroad in the project area, the existence of competing waterways to the north in Brazil, and planned highway improvements. Huszar also challenged the feasibility study's projections of growth in shipments to and from the region, citing other studies of expected regional growth. Finally, he pointed out that the study underplayed what could be significant forgone environmental benefits to fisheries and to the Pantanal region. His general conclusion was that the project would actually bring negative net economic returns.

6.5.3 Finding an At-Source Value of Water for Navigation

An at-source valuation of water applies steps similar to those for hydropower to a specific reach of river with specific navigational structures (such as locks, reservoirs, and docks). The operating costs and, if long-run, the capital costs of the navigational structures are subtracted from the estimated gross benefits, yielding an estimate of the economic rents to water. The inferred economic rents from the economic appraisal of the navigation structures are imputed to the water resource.

Both short-run and long-run rents may be calculated. In a long-run context, the residual rents to water will not be positive for an investment that is itself not cost-effective. Once the investment is in place, and costs are sunk, a positive short-run value may be derived, even if the original investment was not economically feasible. However, most water allocation decisions nowadays will not involve either building or abandoning structures to provide navigational services, so the need will mainly be for short-run water values. Then some estimate of water use to supply the system of structures is inserted to derive a value per unit volume of water.

Young and Gray (1972) estimated long-run values for a number of river basins in the United States. They began with historical public investment and operating costs. To calculate annual rents to impute to water, they adopted a social opportunity cost of capital theory (which holds that because of interventions in the capital markets, the social discount rate should be higher than the real federal borrowing rate). Thus, they annualized investment costs with a higher social discount rate than had been used in the initial appraisals. They found positive rent to water for only four systems: the Mississippi, Ohio, and Black Warrior Rivers, and the Illinois Waterway. Negative long-run rents were found for several others, including the Missouri, Columbia, Arkansas, and Tennessee.

Gibbons (1986) skeptically summarizes some short-run water value estimates from a U.S. Army Corps of Engineers study. That report found substantial (greater than $200 per acre-foot) short-run average water values for the Ohio River and the Illinois Waterway, but much smaller values ($6 or less per acre-foot) for the Mississippi, Columbia, and Missouri Rivers.

These studies attempted to find an average value over the representative year for water used in navigation projects. In fact, many allocation decisions will be seasonal. For example, during springtime high flow periods, the incremental values of water for navigation will be negligible, perhaps even negative, whereas when water is short and in demand from other sectors (hydropower, irrigation) a considerable economic incentive will emerge to accommodate the large fixed public and private investments in transportation facilities. Very short-run values will be needed for use in decisions regarding tradeoffs among these competing uses in such situations.

As with hydropower rents, the assumptions regarding cost of capital and length of investment life are pivotal in assessing navigation investments, and sensitivity analysis will be appropriate.

Calculating the social economic benefits of investments and water allocation policies related to inland waterborne transportation has attracted little interest lately among academic economists, at least in the United States. The further step of finding the rents per unit volume attributable to water for intersectoral water allocation has seen even fewer efforts. Nevertheless, in view of increasing conflicts between water released for waterborne transportation purposes and for competing purposes such as hydropower, recreation, and floodwater management, more effort seems warranted.

6.6 Concluding Remarks on Valuation of Industrial Water

Most of the economic research on industrial water demand has focused on offstream uses in manufacturing facilities: cooling, process water, and incorporation into products. Additional important benefits classed as industrial are derived from a few instream uses, such as hydroelectric power generation and inland waterborne transportation. Among manufacturing facilities, the level of withdrawal ranges from very small (perhaps only for little more than employee sanitation) to relatively large (cooling thermal electric power plants or producing chemical products). Even among the larger offstream users, the evidence suggests that the contribution of water to the value of industrial production is minor next to other inputs such as capital equipment, labor, management and other raw materials.

Perhaps because of its complexity, the topic of industrial water demand and valuation has attracted relatively little interest. Most of the limited number of efforts have used econometric techniques with annual (mostly secondary) data on production and input use from surveys of manufacturing enterprises to estimate the effects of water cost on withdrawals. These studies have found the demand for water withdrawn for industrial purposes to be generally price-inelastic, although it is likely that model specifications adopted for most of the early studies (using average price rather than marginal price) resulted in an overstatement of the elasticities. The varied sources of water (both purchased and self-supplied) complicate specifying a variable to represent marginal price or cost of water. Recent research has developed complex methods to solve the problem of price specification. These econometric studies generate long-run *ex post* at-site values of water intake. Short-run estimates of *ex ante* or at-source willingness to pay are not easily derived from these econometric studies.

Residual methods, which in general are flexible and adapted to forecasting the effects of proposed policy initiatives, are deemed even less useful in industrial water valuation, primarily because of the difficulties in accurately estimating the opportunity costs of capital, management, entrepreneurship, and other owned inputs. Except perhaps in the instream cases—hydropower and waterborne transportation—plausible variations in the opportunity costs of owned inputs would overwhelm the minor contribution of water to the total value of output. In particular, the use of unadjusted value-added measures from regional input-output models should be avoided. Mathematical programming methods based on cost function rather than residual rent models may hold promise, but have been infrequently attempted. Applied economic valuation of industrial water use still deserves further exploitation by resource and environmental economists.

CHAPTER
7

Valuing Water in Municipal Uses

Among the variety of municipal uses of water, residential (also called household or domestic) use dominates, with commercial and public also parts of the mix. Like the producers' good uses, municipal water use is also a private good; one person's use conflicts with the potential benefits derived by others. Residential water use includes indoor uses for sanitation, drinking, and cooking, and outdoor uses for lawns, gardens, and occasional washing of cars and driveways. In arid areas, outside uses may account for a major portion of demand, so climatic factors are important in the demand model. Residential use is appropriately classified as a final consumption good, in contrast with the intermediate or producers' goods (agricultural, industrial) uses of water discussed in the previous two chapters. Commercial water uses, mainly nonmanufacturing business enterprises including restaurants, hotels, retail and wholesale trades, and offices, have received limited separate treatment from economists, but are also briefly mentioned in this chapter. The commercial category does not fit conveniently into our classification system, because although commercial water use is technically a producers' good, the category represents uses in which water is primarily for human consumption and sanitation on the premises. Government (or public) water uses include government agencies, schools, and other public services, including irrigation and care of public parks and recreational facilities. Because government uses are so varied and water sales to government entities are not often volumetrically priced, this class of use is seldom subjected to economic demand analysis. This class of demand is not separately discussed here.

Most analysts have had to rely on consumption and price data from water supply agencies, whose customers encompass residential, government, and commercial uses. Because it was often difficult to obtain data

246

isolating other municipal customers from residential uses, most early investigations of municipal water demand focused on total municipal consumption. The resulting empirical estimates of water demands reflect behavior of a wider range of users than purely household demands. With the increased use of meters to measure deliveries to individual customers and with improved municipal record-keeping, water demand studies can now usually distinguish at least among residential and commercial categories. Most such studies are based on average water use by user class, but some analysts have turned to surveys of individual household water users.

7.1 Demand and Value of Water in Residential Uses: Overview

Most residential water is captured, treated, stored, and delivered to the consumer. In developed countries and increasingly in cities throughout the world, the water is filtered and treated for impurities, disinfected (and perhaps further modified, such as by fluorinating), and delivered to residences under pressure and on demand. In contrast, in developing country villages, towns, and those parts of cities not supplied by more advanced systems, water may be made available only at neighborhood taps or pumps, or delivered in containers by roving water sellers. Throughout the world, particularly in rural areas, many households supply themselves with water of widely varying quality from surface or groundwater sources. The reliability of supply, which ranges from near certainty in urban systems in developed countries to high uncertainty elsewhere, is an important component of willingness to pay for domestic water.

The economic value most often desired for residential water investment and allocation appraisals is at-source value. This is the derived demand for raw or untreated water in a stream or other body, a measure comparable to derived demands from other sectors such as agriculture, industry, or the environment. In contrast, the most readily observable value is at-site value, the willingness to pay at the point of use—in this case, the household. The characteristics of the product purchased by users differs greatly in time, place, and form from those of raw water in watercourses. Accordingly, the analyst needs to begin with a demand relation for the treated, delivered product, and develop from that a derived value for raw water. In what follows, the issues of estimating at-site demand relationships are discussed first, followed by methods of estimating the value of raw water.

Empirical residential water demand studies typically postulate that the quantity of water demanded per connection varies with the "appropriate" measure of price of domestic water, prices of related goods, income of domestic water consumers, climate, and municipal water conservation policies. The demand function (the relationship between quantity taken and price) is represented graphically by the demand curve, or abstractly as:

$$Q_w = Q_w (P_w, P_a, Y, Z) \tag{7-1}$$

where Q_w refers to the individual's level of water use in a specified time period; P_w refers to the price of water; P_a denotes the price of an alternative water source; Y is the consumer's income; and Z is a vector representing other factors such as climate, nonprice water conservation policies, and consumer preferences. Where observations are from beyond a single period, an average price index representing prices of all other goods and services may be also used as a deflator. Consumers are hypothesized to adjust water consumption behavior and, in the long-run, to modify water-using appliances in response to changes in residential water price. Residential water consumption thus varies inversely to price changes. (See Hanemann 1998; Howe 1998; and Arbues et al. 2003 for more detailed discussion and applications to residential water demand.)

Price elasticity indicates the magnitude of the effect of a change in price on the amount demanded by consumers. The demand for residential water is expected to be price-inelastic (that is, a given change in price will lead to a less-than-proportional change in quantity used): the anticipated absolute value of the price elasticity is less than 1.0. This expectation is generally confirmed by empirical studies. One reason is that expenditures for household water represent a small portion of consumer outlays. Another is that there are no close substitutes for water in most of the uses found in a household.

A demand that is price-inelastic does not mean that there is *no* response to price (although some noneconomists continue to believe household water use is independent of price). The demand elasticity estimate usually refers to a specific point on the demand function. Except in the special case of a constant-elasticity demand function, the elasticity will vary. Elasticity estimates are conventionally reported for the mean of the price and quantity observations from which the demand function was derived.

The majority of the residential water demand literature has used inductive (mainly econometric) techniques to analyze mostly secondary data on residential water use to measure an at-site value. This emphasis likely derives from the fact that information on at-site demands and elasticities is the most useful for informing pricing and supply policies for municipal water suppliers. A few studies have employed hedonic pricing, expressed preference valuation, or deductive methods. The benefit transfer method can derive at-source values of residential water demand from estimates of at-site demand.

7.2 Econometric Methods for Measuring At-Site Residential Water Demand

Where the appropriate data are available, economic analysts usually apply econometric methods to modeling residential water user response to price. These use formal statistical techniques to infer willingness to pay from observations on quantities consumed, together with the corresponding data on prices and such shift variables as income and climate (see equation 7-1). Residential water demand is very site-specific, varying with a range of natural and socioeconomic factors. The parameters of the demand equations are inferred via multiple regression techniques, with a final goal of deriving estimates of the price and income elasticity of at-site demand.

7.2.1 Previous Studies

Econometric modeling of residential water demand began with relatively simple single-equation models using aggregate data from a cross section of suppliers. Because the rate structures of residential water suppliers often change in tandem with changes in the general price level, time series data from a single supplier are not often able to provide a sufficient range of variation in real water price to measure an effect of price. Observations on individual household water use (disaggregated data) are more costly and difficult to obtain, and less frequently used. More recent studies, recognizing some of the complexities of the subject, adopt multi-equation approaches using advanced statistical models to studying residential water demand. Hanemann (1998) reviews the theory and application of residential water demand analysis and identifies more than 50 articles and reports from the pre-1992 literature in the United States on the subject. Renzetti (2002a, Chapter 3) provides an authoritative summary of the literature, with a commentary on methodological issues.

Howe and Linaweaver (1967) first applied modern econometric techniques to residential water demand, with methods and findings that still stand up well. They analyzed data from United States suppliers differentiated by region according to indoor and outdoor uses. Average values from each supplier composed the data base. Water price was represented by the combined value of the marginal water and sewage price blocks in which the average consumption was observed. Quantity was the average water use per account per day. They found that indoor demand was quite price-inelastic (about –0.2) while the price elasticity of outdoor demand ranged from –0.4 to –1.6, the higher value presumably reflecting the availability of substitute water supplies (rainfall) in the humid regions. Howe (1982) later restudied the data with newer techniques. Martin and Thomas (1986) combine a range of price-quantity points from the U.S. with observations on very high-priced situations in Kuwait and Australia. They note that these diverse data points trace out an approximately constant unitary elasticity demand curve, although few other studies report results in this range.

Schneider and Whitlach (1991) produced one of the most comprehensive municipal water demand studies in the literature. They analyzed a very large data set (some thirty years of individual accounts from a number of communities supplied by the water system of Columbus, Ohio), and derived short-term and long-term demand functions for each of five sectors (residential, commercial, industrial, government, and schools) as well as for the total of all metered demand accounts. Renzetti (2002a) remarks, however, that the authors' methods may not account for the decreasing block rate employed by the water utilities in the sample during the study period, implying that the demand functions may not have been measured. From a sample of Texas counties, Griffin and Chang (1991) reported results consistent with Howe and Linaweaver's earlier finding that water demand differs between winter and summer. Their study showed somewhat more inelastic demand in winter (about –0.3) than in summer (about –0.4). Lyman (1992), using individual household data, compared peak with off-peak demands from a small Idaho city, finding a quite elastic response to peak prices, while long-run off-peak demand was inelastic with respect to price.

Several recent articles exemplify the challenges of estimating residential water demand equations and the approaches analysts have developed to deal with them. Hewitt and Hanemann (1995) implemented an integrated discrete-continuous choice demand model to test statistical methodologies. They reassessed a portion of a data set developed by Nieswiadomy and Molina (1991) representing five years of individual household observations for Denton, Texas. Their hypothesis was that demand measurement should consider the block rate specification. They found seasonal residential demand elasticities in the neighborhood of –1.5. Since this estimate falls well outside the range of any previously reported, a replication of the method with other data sets was in order. One was soon performed by Pint (1999), who further tested the role of model specification with sophisticated quantitative methods. She studied individual household responses to water price increases in an urban central California district during the interval 1982–1992. Part of that period corresponded to a serious drought, and pricing was adopted as a primary policy response; real water prices increased by 450% during the study period. The data were bi-monthly observations from 599 households. Large amounts of computer time (hundreds of hours on a mainframe processor) were required to solve the models. Fixed-effects models were not successful in modeling water demands with these data. The most plausible findings were derived with maximum likelihood methods of the sort employed by Hewitt and Hanemann (1995). Pint's findings of summer elasticities of –0.20 to –0.47 were more within the conventional range of estimates than those reported by Hewittt and Hanemann. although, contrary to typical results, Pint reported winter demand to be more responsive to price than summer demand.

Various nonprice conservation policies, such as public information campaigns, low-flow toilet rebate programs, and water rationing policies can obscure the relationship between price and demand. Renwick and Green (2000) analyzed cross-section monthly time-series data for eight large water agencies in California for the period 1989–1996 to isolate the effects of nonprice conservation policies and water price. They report that both price and demand-side management policies reduce residential use of water. Gaudin et al. (2001), noting that price elasticity is likely to decrease with increasing price, test functional forms that reflect that consideration. The data set was five years (1981–1985) of monthly observation from 221 Texas communities, originally compiled by Griffin and Chang (1991). Alternative functional forms were tested using an average price specification. The authors conclude that the parsimonious Stone-Geary functional form yields estimated demand functions that are comparable to results from more demanding flexible forms. The Stone-Geary specification also permits an estimation of the portion of the demand function that may be nonresponsive to price.

7.2.2 Specific Issues in Econometric Measurement of Residential Water Demand

Type and Number of Observations. Sufficient observations on prices and water use for developing reliable water demand functions have been difficult to obtain, mainly because of the limited number of cases where water is volumetrically priced (although the proportion of water suppliers using meters has increased greatly in recent years, especially in developed countries). If reasonably accurate data from metered deliveries are not available, average delivery per connection may be used as an approximation, but system leaks and other unaccounted-for losses will introduce an unknown degree of inaccuracy. Leakage may be substantial, sometimes near 50% in developing countries (Howe 1971a; Young et al. 1996; Saleth and Dinar 1997). Illicit connections contribute to the total of unaccounted-for losses. However, part of the estimated "losses" may be simply due to worn, inaccurate meters.

Because there is little variation in the price charged to customers of a given supplier, usually a cross-section (simultaneous observation of behaviors during the same period) of utilities must be sampled. Less frequently, data to estimate the function can come from repeated observations over time on the same utility (time series data), or a combination of cross-section and time series observations. Use of either type requires a wide enough actual variation in the real price variable to yield statistically reliable results.

Some have argued that observations on individual household behavior are preferable. But Espey et al. (1997) found that although about 20% of the studies used in their meta-analysis were based on individual household observations, there were no statistically significant differences in price elasticity estimates between the two types of data.

The Simultaneity Problem. Because price varies systematically with quantity in a block rate pricing system, ordinary least squares (OLS) estimates would be biased. Hence, some form of simultaneous equation estimating system may be needed to avoid the bias.

Specifying the Price Variable: Marginal versus Average Price. Average price is computed as the total revenue divided by the quantity of water, while the marginal price is cost to the household of the marginal increment as provided in the rate schedule. Unlike a competitive market, the water supply schedule for a household is established by the monopoly water supplier, which typically sets rates more or less reflecting costs of service. Rate schedules include combinations of a fixed fee with a flat rate, increasing or decreasing block rates, and nonmetered rates (fixed fee only). The estimation of residential water demand is complicated by an administered rate schedule; if a block rate structure is employed, price is endogenous, varying with the amount of water consumed.

Foster and Beattie (1981), among others, propose that because water represents a small portion of expenditures, consumers do not find it in their interest to become informed on the details of the rate schedule. Thus marginal price is less relevant than average price because average price is the price actually perceived by consumers. The average revenue position seems to be supported by goodness of fit statistics in econometric studies of residential water demand.

However, for fully knowledgeable consumers, most analysts agree that the residential water demand function would be correctly specified with the marginal price obtained from the respective rate schedule. Moreover, as Billings and Agthe (1980) have observed, when average price is used, an upward bias is introduced in the measures of both price elasticity and goodness of fit. They adopt a solution proposed by Nordin (1976), that employs a two-variable representation of water price. One variable is the marginal price operative at the quantity purchased by the household. The second variable, the "difference" variable designed to reflect the income effects of changes in inframarginal rates, is the difference between the household's actual utility bill and what would have been paid if all units of water had been taken at the marginal price. However, Billings and Agthe found the estimated coefficient on the difference variable to be much larger than theory would suggest (although of the correct sign). Other researchers have failed to find the expected sign or a statistically significant coefficient for the difference variable. This may simply mean that it is small compared to total household income. Early in the debate, Howe

(1982, *716*) commented that the interpretation of the difference variable and the justification for the magnitude of its estimated coefficient "remain something of a mystery."

Griffin and Martin (1981) observed that OLS methods produce a biased estimate when the price paid by the household varies with consumption, as it does with a block rate pricing structure. Jones and Morris (1984), using instrumental price estimates to address this problem, found that this method produced results that were not basically different from OLS approaches, and concluded that average price procedures would be appropriate where data limitations preclude more precise demand specification.

Analysts continue to debate over water consumers' knowledge and decision mechanisms, and the proper econometric specification of the demand function. Only after the perceived price has been correctly specified can the effect of conservation and other demand parameters be tested. Nieswiadomy (1992) used cross-sectional data on aggregate demand in 450 cities in the United States to test whether consumers respond to average or marginal prices, and concluded that they responded to average price (see Renzetti 2002a, Chapter 4 for more detail). Taylor et al. (2004) point out that the better goodness of fit for the average price formulation is more a statistical artifact than an empirical confirmation of consumer behavior. Letting R denote the utility's sales revenue, the average revenue is R/Q_w. Therefore, the demand function (omitting shifter variables) is actually $Q_w = f(R/Q_w)$, and the variable Q_w appears in both sides of the expression. The variables are not independent; the estimated coefficient on average revenue is biased upward towards unity, and the price elasticity of demand will also have an upward bias. Taylor et al. estimated residential water demand using marginal and average price for a sample of Colorado utilities. When rate schedules included fixed fees, specification of average price biased estimates of price elasticity toward unity and inflated goodness of fit measures. Biased estimates resulted from an embedded identity in average revenue created by the fixed fees. When fixed fees were purged from the data, levels of significance fell sharply for average price, but not for the marginal price specification. Price elasticity from the marginal price model was –0.3. Interestingly, conservation programs had no significant effect on the preferred marginal price specifications. The meta-analysis of residential price elasticity studies by Espey et al. (1997) found that studies using average price as the measure of price showed a significantly larger elasticity than did those employing marginal price, consistent with the point of Taylor et al. (2004) that average revenue specification leads to a biased estimate.

Additional Considerations in Specifying the Residential Water Demand Function. In addition to accurate measures of the price and quantity variables, data must be found for the important ancillary or shifter variables in the residential demand model. These additional variables include consumer income and, in data sets for large regions, climatic factors. Nonprice water conservation policies and incentives may be additional considerations.

Available data on these shifter variables may not coincide with the jurisdiction for which the price and quantity data are obtained, introducing possible inaccuracies. Measures of household income, if available, are usually developed from periodic national censuses of political subdivisions, which may not correspond to the water supply agency's service area or the date of the water consumption data set. In developing countries, an underground economy may also distort income estimates. Similarly, climatic instrument stations may not adequately reflect average conditions in a water service region. Analysts who attempt to control for qualitative variables such as water conservation programs face the problem of deciding what actually constitutes a conservation program.

7.2.3 A Meta-Analysis of Studies of the Price Elasticity of Residential Demand for Water

Considerable variation is found among the estimates of the price elasticity of demand for residential water. Espey et al. (1997) undertook a meta-analysis of 24 studies in the United States, each of which provided one or more estimates of price elasticity, for a total of 124 data points. Among the studies, the estimated price elasticities ranged from −0.02 to −3.33, while −0.51 was the mean of all observations. The meta-analysis tested the hypothesis that the variation in these estimates arise from one of four broad types of sources:

- variation caused by differences in model specification, including the significant variables incorporated into the model as well as functional form (linear or nonlinear);
- variation arising from variables included in the models, such as income, rainfall, temperature, and household size, as well as data characteristics such as whether data are cross-sectional, time-series, or pooled, and whether the price variable is marginal or average price;
- environmental setting (winter or summer) and geographic location (arid or humid regions); and
- the estimation technique, e.g. OLS or other more complex multi-equation techniques.

A total of 25 binary variables were incorporated into the regression model.

Espey et al. analyzed the data using three model specifications: semilog, linear, and Box-Cox, with the latter showing significantly more explanatory power. Elasticity estimates did *not* vary significantly whether the study used individual household observations or aggregate data, time-series or cross-section data, linear or log linear models, OLS or more complex estimation techniques. On the other hand, elasticity estimates were significantly *higher* if they employed an average rather than a marginal specification of the price variable, if they were based on increasing block rate schedules, if they were from long-run models, if they included commercial uses in the data base, or if they represented summer demand. Estimates were found to be *less* elastic than average demand if they represented winter demand.

These results will be useful to researchers in designing future studies. They will also be a valuable basis for exercises in benefit transfer (to estimate benefits in situations not previously studied). Espy et al. decline to draw further inferences from the study. Readers may come up with their own judgments, but these results suggest that the price elasticity of demand for residential water in the United States in the long run, accounting for the average cost bias and excluding commercial users, will likely fall between –0.3 and –0.6: an inelastic demand, but not unresponsive to price. Dalhuisen et al. (2003) extended the Espey et al. 1997 analysis, adding more recent studies and using an alternative econometric technique. However, some of their results raise questions. For example, their finding that using average revenue as the price measure reduces the absolute value of the elasticity estimate conflicts with Taylor et al. 2004 (see Section 7.2.2).

7.3 Other Methods for Estimating At-Site Residential Water Demand

Expressed preference (contingent valuation and choice modeling), hedonic property value analysis, and an engineering-technical (deductive) approach have all been applied to municipal water use.

7.3.1 Other Inductive Methods

The contingent valuation method (CVM) was developed for valuing goods or services that cannot be valued either directly or indirectly from market observations. (The method was introduced in Section 4.6; applications to environmental goods are shown in Chapter 8.) CVM has occasionally been attempted for residential demands in industrialized nations. Thomas and Syme (1988) applied the technique to valuing residential water use in the Perth metropolitan area of Australia. An example of application of CVM to domestic water demand in a developing country situation is provided in Section 7.6.2.

Gordon et al. (2001) summarize an interesting choice modeling (see Section 4.7) approach to assessing alternative proposals for investment in additional domestic water supply capacity. They examined domestic water users' valuation of five options for meeting future water needs of the water utility supplying the Canberra, Australia region. As of 1996, with a population of some 340,000 growing about 2% per year, the utility could foresee that within a decade their two water supply dams and reservoirs would be insufficient to meet demands for municipal water. The utility could employ additional structural or engineering options, with some expected environmental costs, or focus on demand management or recycling. Gordon et al. addressed the general question: given the tradeoffs, which option would the public prefer? The analysis generated willingness to pay estimates for each option relative to a basic limited response to potential shortages, and a willingness to pay estimate for preventing a reduction in household water supply.

A revealed preference approach, the *hedonic property value* method (see Section 3.12.3), can measure the willingness to pay for the water supply attribute when housing prices can be shown to be affected by the availability of improved water supplies. In developed countries, where the natural experiment of varying residential water supply is an unusual occurrence, the hedonic approach will seldom apply, but this method may find use in developing countries. See the North and Griffin (1993) hedonic study of housing markets in the Philippines in Section 7.6.1.

Colby et al. (1993) employed a hedonic property value technique to study the water rights market in a sparsely populated region of western New Mexico. Sellers were mainly agricultural users and buyers were mostly municipalities or industries. Water rights prices were found to be significantly influenced by water right priority dates, size of transaction, geographic area within which the right could be transferred, and buyer characteristics. (Farmers were able to sell water rights to towns and industries at higher prices than they received from other farmers.)

7.3.2 An Engineering-Technical Approach

Residential water demand has been studied with an *engineering-technical* (deductive) approach in one case of which the writer is aware. Howe (1971a) described the water use and the operating and capital costs of alternative technologies for indoor household water use (including toilets, showers, and washing machines). Assuming cost-minimizing consumers, he calculated the water price at which the consumer would find it desirable to adopt each technology, and thus traced out a price–quantity relationship for a representative household. He also analyzed sensitivity to alternative household discount (interest) rates. Although this study provides important understanding of tradeoffs for inside household uses, I know of no other replication of this approach.

7.4 Finding an At-Source Value of Residential Water from an At-Site Demand Function

Since derived household demand regarding at-source water is not directly observable or valued in properly functioning markets, some method of converting at-site values to at-source values is needed.

7.4.1 A Procedure for Deriving an At-Source Value for Residential Water

At-source and at-site values reflect very different economic products. Significant resources are involved in the capture, storage, treatment, and delivery of raw water to the customer. Conveyance losses must also be accounted for. One reasonably practical approach consists of imputing the consumer surplus from at-site domestic water demand to derive the measure of the at-source value.

Young and Gray (1972) have adapted a standard formula for the integral of a constant elasticity demand function (James and Lee 1971, *314–315*) to estimate an at-source value of residential water. A demand function is obtained by assuming a functional form and inferring an empirical demand function from an observed price-quantity point on that function. In this approach, gross economic value of some assumed change in water availability is found by integrating under the inferred demand function for the assumed quantity change. Then, subtracting for costs of supply, consumer surplus is isolated. Finally, an at-source water value is derived by adjusting for delivery losses.

The example shown here assumes a constant-elasticity demand function for simplicity and because it is plausible given other empirical results on residential water demand. The application requires only four data items:

- a price-quantity point—an observed price in effect during a specified period;
- the corresponding water deliveries observed during that same period;
- a hypothetical change in quantity that is to be valued; and
- the assumed price elasticity of demand.

The quantity terms can reflect either an aggregate or a per household estimate of water use. The procedure infers a second point on an empirical demand function from an initial point (the price-quantity observation), assuming the constant-elasticity form of the demand function. The procedure can be extended to find any point on the demand function, given an initial starting point and a demand elasticity (Gibbons 1986).

Finding the Gross Value of an Increment of Delivered Water. For the constant-elasticity form, the area under the demand curve between two specified quantities can be derived by solving an equation reflecting the quantities at two points and the price appropriate to the initial one of those points (Figure 7-1). Assuming that the price elasticity of demand (denoted ε) is known and is constant over the relevant range (and is not equal to 1.0), and that the relevant initial price P_1 and quantity Q_1 can be specified, then the area under the demand curve (the desired measure of value, denoted V) for a change in quantity from Q_1 to Q_2 is given by:

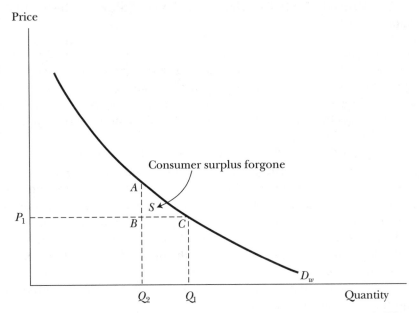

Figure 7-1. Consumer Surplus Forgone from Reduction in Domestic Water Supply

$$V = \left(\frac{P_1 \times Q_1^{\frac{1}{\varepsilon}}}{1 - \frac{1}{\varepsilon}} \right) \left(Q_2^{1-\frac{1}{\varepsilon}} - Q_1^{1-\frac{1}{\varepsilon}} \right) \tag{7-2}$$

This expression represents the entire area under the demand curve for the specified quantity change, and, as such, represents the value of an increment of treated water delivered to the final user. The expression $1/\varepsilon$ (the inverse of the price elasticity of demand) in equation 7-2 is commonly called the "price flexibility of demand." It reflects the proportional change in value to users from a given change in quantity consumed, the relationship of interest in many water valuation contexts.

Any empirically and theoretically reasonable functional form of the demand function can be assumed, but forms other than the constant-elasticity expression would of course require different formulas. For example, Griffin (1990) compares the results from employing Cobb-Douglas and translog functional forms, finding that the results are sensitive to the functional form chosen. He further notes that the translog form is more empirically realistic—in that price sensitivity falls as price rises—but solving the equation is more complex.

Imputing a Value of Raw Water. Studies of demand for tap water measure the willingness to pay not only for water itself but also for the services involved in capturing, transporting, treating, and storing water. Therefore the costs of these services must be deducted from the estimated willingness to pay for tap water before the estimates can be properly compared with demand for instream uses or for raw water abstracted for irrigation or industry. When residential water can be assumed to be priced to fully recover the costs of supplying it (i.e. full-cost pricing and no producer surplus), the average revenue can be subtracted from the total willingness to pay to derive the net consumer surplus imputable to raw water.

Therefore, the next step is to adjust the consumer demand function to reflect the derived demand for raw water in a watercourse. Let the expression $(P_1 \times Q_1)$—price times quantity—represent the amount paid for the water. (Employing the users' cost of water in this fashion requires the assumption that the water utility prices at average cost, an assumption that is usually tenable.) To obtain an estimate of the consumer surplus (S) associated with the change (reduction) in quantity from Q_1 to Q_2, the consumer's cost of the increment of water $[(P_1)(Q_1 - Q_2)]$ are subtracted from V (the total benefit or value):

$$S = V - [(P_1)(Q_1 - Q_2)] \tag{7-3}$$

For intersectoral water allocation it is often convenient to express the raw water value in volumetric units. So, dividing the increment in consumer surplus by the assumed change in the volume of water yields an estimate of the net benefit per unit volume of water associated with the quantity change.

Adjustment for Water Delivery Losses. Losses due to leakage, pilferage, and meter error are inevitable, but must be taken into account in an allocation formula. Multiplying the derived value per unit times the percentage available for use by customers, equivalent to 1.00 minus percentage lost, yields the final estimated value of raw water to the utility's customers. This net benefit is the value of raw water, which is sought to compare with other raw water values.

Gibbons (1986) and Saleth and Dinar (1997) show extensions and further applications. Griffin (1990) extends this type of analysis to the long-period case, incorporating an assumption for population growth and calculating the net present value per acre-foot over the project life.

7.4.2 Example: Application of a Benefit Transfer Method to Finding an At-Source Residential Water Value

The above procedure can be employed directly by using the price elasticity developed in a specific municipal water demand study (as in Saleth and Dinar 1997), or by a benefit transfer method using a price elasticity estimate derived from other research. A short-run drought water allocation issue emerged some years ago in the Philippines (Young et al. 1996). This case is an application of benefit transfer because the elasticity estimates are drawn from previous research, rather than being taken from an original study of the case at hand.

Background. Manila is the core of a sprawling, rapidly growing megacity of over 8 million people as of 1996. The Metropolitan Waterworks and Sewerage System (MWSS) was the main supplier of water to the Manila region. MWSS relied on the Angat River—which originates in a separate hydrologic basin north and east of Manila, and discharges into the sea north of the metropolitan area—for 90% of its raw water supplies. The Angat Reservoir stores water for both the municipality and an irrigation system that serves some 28,000 hectares in the lower Angat basin. MWSS transports its water entitlement from the reservoir to the coastal plain for treatment and delivery to their customers. Local surface and groundwater provided the balance of MWSS's supplies.

At the time of the study, MWSS supply capacity was unable even in times of normal water supply to provide an around-the-clock water supply to all customers. A drought in 1995 highlighted the fact that MWSS was inadequately prepared to deal with drought, particularly in the short-term before a new transbasin project was scheduled to come online. One alternative source of water was transferring (temporarily or permanently) a portion of the irrigation water rights to Angat Reservoir waters. Philippine water law provides for water rights on a priority system (first in time—first in right). Water rights are tradable, and can be permanently transferred by purchase. Higher priority irrigation water can be temporarily transferred to a lower priority municipal water supply agency in an emergency, under the supervision of the National Water Resources Board (NWRB), subject to compensation to the irrigation water users for forgoing their water. Among other goals, the study aimed to determine the economic value of a short-run drought emergency transfer of some irrigation water rights to the MWSS customers (for the purpose of determining whether those benefits exceeded the forgone benefits in the irrigated area).

From MWSS data for 1994, the paying customers were divided into three groups. The first included the small domestic accounts which numbered about half a million or 70% of all accounts, but represented only 30% of the volume of sales. They averaged about 250 cubic meters (m^3) of water use per year, and paid an average rate of P5.75 per m^3 (P = Philippine Peso, approximately US$0.04 in 1996). This average rate comprised a base charge, to which was added a 10% environmental improvement fee, and a currency adjustment factor of about P1.25 per m^3. Because the average customer in this group took the above quantity (250 m^3) at the marginal price of P5.75, these figures are used as the initial price-quantity (P_1, Q_1) points. The other two groups consisted of larger domestic users and large users who were primarily commercial and industrial accounts. For brevity, the results for those groups and for the aggregate are not shown here.

Next, an estimate of the price elasticity of demand (ε) was needed. For the benefit transfer, estimates of long-run price elasticity for domestic water uses reported in the existing literature were considered. The available estimates ranged from –0.3 to –0.7. (Studies that use an average rather than a marginal price to represent the price variable in the demand equation generally overstate the true elasticity. The meta-analysis by Espey et al. 1997 reported an average estimate of about –0.3 for the United States when adjusted for this factor.) Given the larger proportion of income devoted to expenditures on water in this developing country, one would expect a somewhat more elastic demand. Conversely, for a drought response, a short-run, less price-elastic demand was thought to be appropriate. For the analysis, two cases of price elasticity of demand were tested: –0.15 and –0.30. These were judged be roughly half the probable long-run elasticity levels.

The final assumptions related to the magnitude of a potential drought-induced reduction in water supply and the leakage losses. Two shortage scenarios were assumed: one that the monthly supply during a short-term dry season drought would be reduced by 20% from that taken by customers at existing tariff rates, and a second scenario with a 10% shortage. Estimates of the percentage of nonrevenue water that was leakage (as opposed to pilferage, meter error, and public uses) vary widely. It was assumed that leakage represents 77% of nonrevenue water and 45% of total production. (By adjusting only for the leakage component of nonrevenue water, the study credited a value to the portion of nonrevenue water attributable to nonpaying water users, whether it was legal use from standpipes, under-recording by meters, or illegal use from unauthorized connections.) Solving equation 7-2 for the integral under the various scenarios yielded estimates of the total benefits per cubic meter lost to drought for MWSS customers.

Table 7-1 shows a portion of the estimates of the value of raw water for municipal uses. The figures represent the imputed economic value of raw water at Angat Reservoir after adjustment for leakages, and are designed to be commensurate with value estimates for irrigation diversions at the same location. The estimated economic values vary significantly with the assumed parameters. For example, the value imputed to Angat water for small domestic users is P3.4 per cubic meter for the case of lower assumed price elasticity and larger assumed shortage. This estimate falls all the way to P0.5 per cubic meter for the inverse assumptions.

These estimates should be regarded as rough approximations. For example, they do not recognize the possible public health benefits (although public health benefits may not be much reduced by a temporary

Table 7-1. Estimated Economic Values of Raw Water at Angat Reservoir, Philippines, for Municipal Uses

	Elasticity Assumptions	*Results*
Scenario 1: Shortage 20%	–0.15	P3.4/m³
	–0.30	P1.3/m³
Scenario 2: Shortage 10%	–0.15	P1.2/m³
	–0.30	P0.5/m³

Note: Average of small domestic accounts only.

drought shortage). Further, the static model and the assumption that all needs for water could be met on demand fail to reflect the reality of MWSS's sporadic delivery system. Clearly, there would be value to reliable supply, but there was little way to measure that value without a more intensive study effort.

7.5 Measuring Benefits of Residential Water Supply Reliability

In addition to the quantity of residential water, customers value the reliability with which water is available. The reliability dimension is not captured in the conventional water demand function, which assumes full reliability. Because increased reliability comes at increased costs, estimates of the household benefits from increased reliability are of interest. Hour-to-hour or day-to-day reliability of residential water supplies may have measurable value to customers. Some municipal water supply systems in developing countries, for example, cannot reliably deliver water on demand throughout the full 24-hour day, every day of the week, even to customers with piped connections (Nickum and Easter 1994). Households in such situations show a willingness to pay for water supply reliability in several ways:

- investing in home storage tanks;
- illegally installing suction pumps to pull water from the distribution system, which reduces pressure for others and greatly increases the risk of contamination of the main system; and
- investing in shallow domestic wells.

Altaf et al. (1993) measured willingness to pay for improved reliability from a sample of Pakistani households with private connections that typically supplied water only a few hours per day. Responses to a contingent valuation question, "What is the most your household would be willing to pay to ensure water was available from your private connection 24 hours per day, every day of the week, with good pressure?", indicated that they would be willing to pay more than double the existing tariff for improved reliability.

Reliable water supply throughout the range of climatic fluctuations, particularly during droughts, is also of value. Clear evidence is found in water markets in the western United States. Property rights in water are typically assigned according to prior appropriation (first in time—first in right), such that the most reliable supply belongs to those with the earliest priority of right. Market prices in those instances vary significantly by priority, with the highest price being paid for the earliest priority rights (Colby et al. 1993).

There is not a large empirical literature on the value of domestic water supply reliability during droughts, although interest has increased in recent years. Some studies employed the contingent valuation method (CVM). In the gray literature, Carson and Mitchell (1987) reported a CVM survey of California voters regarding their annual willingness to pay for water supply reliability, finding that median annual household willingness to pay to avoid shortages ranged from $83 for a mild shortage up to $258 for the most severe case.

Howe and Smith (1994) studied the value of reliability in three small cities in Colorado using a relatively sophisticated form of CVM. Respondents to a mail survey were asked both willingness to pay (WTP) and willingness to accept compensation (WTA) questions. For the two cities with unreliable water supplies, a conservative estimate of aggregate WTP was insufficient to cover the costs of improved reliability. For the third city, whose water supply was highly reliable, the cost saving from reduced reliability was found to be more than sufficient to cover aggregate WTA through reduced water bills.

Griffin and Mjelde (2000) recently extended the Howe-Smith approach to modeling water supply reliability issues, incorporating the potential for analyzing a range of potential shortage events. They sampled over 4800 households in seven Texas cities by mail. Two issues were analyzed: WTP to avoid a current shortfall, and WTP/WTA to modify future reliability. In an innovative touch, each questionnaire included information from the household's past water bills. However, almost 70% of the responses to the current shortfall question were what the authors termed "protest" bids, which might be due to the unusual form of the contingent value question. It asked what respondents would be willing to pay to be exempted from a hypothetical program restricting outdoor water use, not what they were willing to pay for an increased supply. Respondents may have thought it inappropriate to permit some to buy their way out of a temporary shortfall. The results also indicated that consumer valuations of current shortfalls were not consistent with their valuations of future shortfalls. These findings provide further evidence of the general point that it is not easy to communicate probabilistic information to respondents in studies employing CVM. In the limited developing country literature, Hoehn and Krieger (2000) considered WTP for improved reliability in their study of residential water demand in Cairo, Egypt.

7.6 Valuing Residential Water in Developing Countries

Much of the earth's population—particularly in rural portions of developing nations—has no access to piped potable water in their homes. Improved access will yield health benefits and reduced water carrying effort, particularly for women. Tradition has assumed that for low income villagers, only provision of the most basic services—hand pumps or public taps—would be justified. Although governments and donor agencies make considerable investment in potable water supplies in rural areas of developing countries each year, lasting success of these programs has been elusive. Most village water systems improved by outside donor agencies are inadequately maintained and used incorrectly; many are abandoned soon after installation. Better understanding of preferences and behavior regarding water supply of rural households will contribute to more economical and effective programs. Traditional demand models used where water is metered are inapplicable for assessing village water demands, and improved methods must be developed.

7.6.1 Research on Residential Water Demands in Developing Countries

Residential water demand in developing countries that lack meters has not been much studied with the standard econometric analyses used in the United States and elsewhere in the developed world. Saleth and Dinar (1997), as part of a larger study on municipal water supply policy in Hyderabad, India, performed a sophisticated econometric investigation of domestic water demand for that city. A study of urban water use in Sri Lanka by I. Hussain et al. (2002) used a national time-series data set tracking monthly consumption for 1994–1998, when the real price of water in that country was rising significantly. Testing both linear and log–log functional forms, they reported a residential demand elasticity of –0.18, which is somewhat lower than typical findings, even in developed countries.

When housing prices are affected by the availability of improved water supplies, *hedonic property value*, a revealed preference method, can measure the willingness to pay for the water supply attribute. North and Griffin (1993) studied a housing market in the Philippines, using data from 1978 to estimate the rent premium attributable to an improved water supply. A measure of imputed monthly rent (the estimated monthly rental value of homes owned by their occupants) was regressed on variables representing the attributes of the house, including size, location, number of rooms, nature of construction, and type and distance of the water source from each house. A statistically significant measure of the value of access to piped water supply was obtained, although the implied valuation was small relative to the cost of supply.

In the many smaller developing country municipalities where water supplies are not metered, researchers have adopted expressed preference methods. From the late 1980s, a concerted effort has been mounted under sponsorship of international agencies to formulate improved methods. Whittington and Swarna (1994) summarize research into economic benefits of potable water supply projects in developing countries. They discuss and illustrate the use of cost saving, contingent valuation, and hedonic property value methods. (See Whittington and Choe 1992; World Bank Water Demand Team 1993.) A household can benefit in two ways from installation of an improved water supply:

- saving in resources used to obtain water under the old system, from not having to purchase water from vendors, fetch water from a distant source, or boil water;
- the consumer surplus from the increased water purchased at a lower total cost.

However, this overlooks the problem of choosing a water source. In the "without" scenario, households may obtain water from open wells, public taps on a limited distribution system, or water vendors; cost, quality, proximity, and reliability may vary. Whittington and Swarna argue that a discrete-continuous decision process must be incorporated to successfully model village water demand (see also Mu et al. 1990).

Whittington (1988) provides a practical, useful handbook for the design and conduct of household surveys of willingness to pay in developing countries. He addresses questionnaire design and implementation of the survey, including sampling, translation of the questionnaire, and recruitment and training of enumerators. An appendix provides examples of questionnaires used in Haiti, Nigeria, and Tanzania. Whittington (2002) is concerned that too CVM surveys in developing counties are poorly designed and poorly executed. (See Casley and Lury 1987 for additional discussion of the problems of data collection in developing countries.)

In addition to evaluating demand for potable water in developing countries, nonmarket valuation methods have also been employed to estimate willingness to pay for sanitation services. Whittington et al. (1992) studied the demand for improved sanitation services in Ghana. McClelland et al. (1994) studied the value of both water and sanitation services in a small town in Uganda. Their study is summarized in Section 7.6.2 as an example of nonmarket valuation techniques for evaluating demand for water in developing country small city context. In contrast to the focus on village water supply of most developing country applications, Hoehn and Krieger (2000) investigated residential water supply and sanitation issues in Cairo, one of the largest cities in the world. For a cost–benefit analysis of water supply issues using contingent referendum valuation, the authors developed a textbook analysis of four aspects of residential water supply: willingness to pay for water connection, improved reliability of existing water service, wastewater connections, and network maintenance to eliminate sewer overflows. McConnell and Rosado (2000) used defensive behavior methods to study how the costs of boiling or filtering tap water or purchasing bottled water affected willingness to pay for relatively risk-free drinking water in a city in Brazil.

7.6.2 Example: A Contingent Valuation Study in Uganda

McClelland et al. (1994) report an interesting study of demand for water and sanitation services in Lugazi, Uganda, a town of about 20,000 about 40 kilometers east of the capital, Kampala. There was no piped water in the study area, and most residents obtained their water from natural springs or rainwater collection systems. About 25% of the households (40% in dry season) purchased water from vendors who filled jerricans (20-liter containers) at the springs and transported them (usually by bicycle) to customers.

The study represented an initial step in a new approach to water supply and sanitation planning in Uganda, in which the sector investment was to be demand-driven, meaning that households would be provided the services for which they are willing to pay. Beneficiaries were allowed to choose a level of service and informed of the cost. The study was done in 1994 with a "rapid appraisal" approach, completing data collection in just a few weeks using a limited form of random sampling. In addition to willingness to pay for household water, the study covered supply side activities (such as water vendors) and sanitation needs. Only the contingent valuation study of household demand for water is summarized here.

Data Collection. The water demand survey team, consisting of expatriate economists and local staff, interviewed 384 people from approximately 8% of the town's households. The enumerators, who helped finalize the questionnaire and choose locally appropriate wording, were all college-educated. Nearly all of the enumerators had experience in survey research, and all could converse in the language most common among town residents. The research began with training the interviewers and designing the questionnaire. Pretests of the questionnaire were conducted for several days and revisions made daily before a final version was adopted. Enumerators were directed to interview the head of household (or spouse) in every fifth house along the main road and every third house in selected clusters in the town. In addition to questions about willingness to pay for improved water services, the questionnaire also asked about respondents' existing water situation and the socioeconomic and demographic characteristics of the household. Questionnaires were collected and reviewed twice daily; where needed for correction or clarification, the respondent was contacted again. The population was interested in the issue; a 99% response rate was reported.

Table 7-2. Percent of Lugazi Respondents Who Indicated That They Would Use the Proposed Public Taps at Different Prices per Jerrican

First Price per Jerrican	Buy from New Public Taps	Continue to Use Existing Sources	Don't Know
25 Shillings	89%	10%	1%
50 Shillings	78%	19%	3%
100 Shillings	49%	51%	0%

The questionnaire in a contingent valuation survey must include sufficient detail in the description of the proposal for interviewees to realistically evaluate their willingness to pay for the service or product. The policy proposed was a system of public water taps to be installed in neighborhoods throughout the town. After an introductory statement setting the stage for the CVM questions, respondents were shown pictures and diagrams of how the public tap system might appear. They were assured that the water supply would be reliable and of good quality. Public water taps would be within 200 meters of every home and would be open daily from 7 a.m. to 7 p.m.

Two different payment options were assessed: a pay-by-the-jerrican system, and a system of fixed monthly fees that would provide unrestricted access to the public taps for those who had paid.

For the pay-by-the-jerrican questions, the sample was divided into three sub-samples of approximately equal size, each facing a different price of water per jerrican—25, 50, or 100 shillings (US$1 = approximately 950 shillings in 1993). The going price for a jerrican of water from a water vendor was 100 shillings. Similarly, for the question related to a monthly payment for unlimited access to a public tap, three sub-samples were asked if they would accept or reject monthly charges of either 1000, 4000, or 7000 shillings.

Response to First Contingent Valuation Question. "Suppose that the price of water per jerrican at the public tap was _____ shillings. Would your household decide to buy most of your water from the public taps or would you decide to continue using vendors and/or springs?" The results are shown in Table 7-2.

Response to Second Contingent Valuation Question. "Suppose there was a system of public taps in your neighborhood and that everyone who paid a fixed monthly fee could obtain as much water as they wanted from the public tap. If the monthly fee was _____ shillings, would you use the public taps or would your household continue using existing sources?" Table 7-3 shows the results.

Statistical Analysis. To analyze the responses about paying a monthly fee for unlimited access to public taps, the data were subjected to a multivariate regression statistical analysis employing a probit model. The dependent variable was the probability that the respondent would decide to use

Table 7-3. Percent of Lugazi Respondents Indicating That They Would Use the Proposed Public Taps at Different Fixed Monthly Fees

First Price-Fixed Monthly Fee	Buy from New Public Taps	Buy from Existing Sources	Don't Know
1000 Shillings/mo.	91%	9%	0%
4000 Shillings/mo.	63%	34%	3%
7000 Shillings/mo.	24%	69%	7%

public taps. The independent variables, mainly derived for the socioeconomic and demographic questions in the survey, included the monthly price, an estimate of household wealth (as a proxy for income), education level, whether or not the household already purchased water from vendors, number of children in the household, the gender of the respondent, and whether or not the household owned or rented their residence.

Discussion. The results of the pay-by-the-jerrican analysis showed a robust demand for the proposed public taps at each price offered. A substantial proportion of the population would support the public taps, even at the highest price. Respondents who would pay the highest amount indicated that vendors were not entirely reliable and, in addition to improved reliability, they expected the taps to provide better quality water.

Table 7-3 shows that respondents to the fixed monthly fee questions were similarly interested in public taps, but were quite responsive to the various price alternatives. The probit analysis found that the potential use of public taps was negatively related to monthly price and strongly significant. The probability of preferring taps was also positively associated with wealth and with prior use of vendors. Level of education, gender, and number of children in the household were not statistically significant influences on willingness to pay for public taps.

Clearly, a careful application of nonmarket valuation techniques, survey research procedures, and statistical methods can, even in a relatively short time, generate useful information on the value of water and sanitation services in developing countries.

7.7 Valuing Water in Commercial Uses

Commercial water use has received little attention in the municipal water demand literature. Lynne et al. (1979) analyzed commercial water demand in Miami, Florida via a mail survey. They organized responses by sectors, finding a wide range of elasticities across sectors. Elastic responses were found, curiously, in department stores, and inelastic demands in hotels and motels. Williams and Suh (1986) analyzed municipality-level data for publicly supplied commercial establishments in the United States. They tested several price specifications (including both average and marginal price) and reported elasticities ranging from –0.14 to –0.36, depending on the price specification. Commercial water demand was much less price-elastic than industrial water demands in the same data set. Schneider and Whitlach (1991) examined commercial water use as part of a study of water demand in the Columbus, Ohio, metropolitan area with a pooled cross-section time-series data set over an 18-year period. Short-term elasticities in the commercial sector were reported as –0.2 while –0.9 was found for the long-term case. Renzetti (2002a, *47*) suggests that the declining block rate structures in effect during the study period may have accounted for part of the reported negative effect of price on water use. Malla and Gopalakrishnan (1999) studied industrial (in this case, food processing) and, separately, nonfood industrial and commercial water demand for the City and County of Honolulu, Hawaii. They reported price elasticities in the food industry of from –0.3 to –0.4, depending on whether Ordinary Least Squares or Generalized Least Squares was the statistical technique employed. The water demand in the nonfood industries and commercial establishments was found to be nonresponsive to price, with elasticities in the neighborhood of –0.1 or less. Finally, the meta-analysis on residential water demand performed by Espey et al. (1997) found that when commercial accounts were included in the observations on municipal water use, the reported elasticity was somewhat higher.

When I. Hussain et al. (2002) studied demand for water in Sri Lanka (see Section 7.6.1), they found a statistically significant effect of price on the demand for water in the industrial sector, but for commercial use the coefficient on the price variable was not significantly different from zero.

7.8 Concluding Remarks

Economists have devoted considerable effort to studying residential water use in the past three decades, mostly in North America. They have employed increasingly complicated econometric methods to study demand facing municipal water supply utilities. The empirical observations that are the basis for the econometric studies are most often average annual deliveries per household from cross-section samples of several municipalities, although a significant fraction of researchers have analyzed individual households. Time-series data from a specific municipality or combined time-series and cross-sectional data from multiple communities are also represented. These studies of at-site values find that demand for residential water depends primarily on the price of water (including the rate structure), consumer income, and climate. Demand is price-inelastic, with most estimates falling in the range from –0.2 to –0.6. Results are sensitive to model specification, particularly whether average or marginal price is the measure. In order to deal with the measurement issues that occur with increasing block rates, more complex, expensive, and statistically challenging methods have been applied.

For developing countries, residential water and sanitation demand studies are increasingly useful for designing and evaluating proposals for improved water supply, quality, and management policies (such as cost recovery and tariff-setting). However, conventional econometric studies are more difficult in this setting, and other nonmarket methods (mainly expressed preference) have been employed. This literature is not extensive. Because at-source values for residential water use are not observable in both developed and developing economies, a benefit transfer approach is suggested as a workable alternative for estimating at-source values.

Valuation of Selected Water-Related Public Goods

This chapter discusses methods of valuing noncommodity water uses: water-based recreation, water quality improvement, and the reduction of flood risks. Unlike offstream private good benefits, these exhibit benefits of a public or collective good nature, in that once they are provided, consumers cannot readily be excluded from using them.

The principal means of measuring public goods benefits—expressed preference (contingent valuation and choice modeling) and revealed preference (travel cost and hedonic property value)—were discussed in Chapter 4. These methods are the most developed in the environmental economics literature (Freeman 2003; Champ et al. 2003; Bateman et al. 2002; Bateman and Willis 1999; Herriges and Kling 1999). For water quality improvement or flood risk reduction, another technique—*damages avoided*—is sometimes used; willingness to pay for these public goods is the value of damages avoided by the public project or program.

8.1 Valuing Instream Flows and Reservoir Levels for Outdoor Recreation

8.1.1 Overview

An increasingly significant economic benefit from water is its value for recreation, aesthetics, and fish and wildlife habitat (see Section 1.1.2). Water quality is a significant component of recreational and aesthetic enjoyment of water in its natural surroundings, so measuring benefits of water quality improvement activities is also an important issue.

The economic value of water-based recreation is traditionally measured in terms of what are called "visitor days": the value placed by one recreationist on visiting a site for all or part of one day (Loomis and Walsh 1997, Chapter 3). However, for measuring recreational gains or forgone benefits in the course of evaluating investments in increments of water supply or of intersectoral reallocation proposals, estimates of derived at-source demands for water are more appropriate. This section focuses less on the overall measurement of benefits of water-based recreation and more on estimating the marginal value of changes in water supply.

8.1.2 Alternative Methods for Valuing Water Levels

Levels in streams and lakes can directly affect the quality of boating experiences, success at sport fishing, scenic beauty, and suitability for swimming and wading; they have long-term effects on the viability of fish and wildlife habitat (Loomis 1998). As demand for instream flows increasingly competes with offstream values, economists have sought to develop techniques for estimating the marginal economic contribution of instream flows.

The most frequently used techniques are expressed preference methods, such as the contingent valuation method (CVM) and choice modeling (CM). But revealed preference methods, including travel cost and hedonic property value, have also been adopted.

In CVM studies, respondents are asked to directly value increments or decrements of flow or reservoir level. Daubert and Young (1981) reported one of the earliest CVM studies of instream flow values, based on a personal interview survey of 120 recreationists on the Cache la Poudre River in northeastern Colorado. The respondents were divided approximately equally among three groups: whitewater rafting and kayaking, fishing, and streamside activities (picnicking and camping). Photographs of varying levels of instream flows, combined with descriptions of the implications for recreation, were used to elicit marginal values of increments or decrements of flows for each class of water-based recreational activities, from which benefit functions relating flows to value were derived. Recreationists involved in whitewater boating exhibited a willingness to pay directly correlated with water flows throughout the range of flows offered in the questionnaire. (Due to low flows when the photographs were taken, whitewater enthusiasts apparently did not reach a point of decreasing marginal willingness to pay for increased flow.) Closer to expectations, the functions reflecting the value of both fishing and picnicking displayed a maximum willingness to pay (WTP), beyond which it declined, presumably because decreased utility or increased risk of high water reduced the value. The authors compared their estimates to use of the water for crop irrigation, and showed that during some seasons water released for recreation was more valuable than for irrigation. Ward (1987) and Duffield et al. (1992)

are other applications of CVM to valuation of instream flows. These studies indicate that instream flow values at certain times and places may exceed those for offstream use in agriculture, and suggest that a shift in incentives might lead to reallocation and improvements in net economic benefits. (See Loomis 1998 for a general review.)

Garrod and Willis (1999, Chapter 10) report on their choice modeling study of water flow and quality values in south west England, a region favored with over 4,000 miles of rivers. Here reduced flows may be caused by abstractions by urban water supply companies, hydroelectric power generation, and reservoirs. Inadequate flows shorten the angling season and impede the reproduction of salmon and trout. Shortage of dilution water can reduce the quality of water as well. Respondents were presented with choice cards that stated hypothetical annual costs per household of meeting environmental quality targets for beach cleanliness, water quality, and river flows. Rather than using some direct measure of volume per unit time, the policy options for reducing or remedying low river flows used "miles of river without acceptable flow levels" as the measure of impact. Hence, although suitable for the authors' purposes, the results cannot be readily converted to a monetary measure of WTP for water volume such as that used in studies in the western United States. Cards reflecting 64 alternative policy combinations were prepared. Each respondent was asked to choose options on four randomly chosen cards. The statistical analysis of responses from self-identified users of rivers in the region yielded, among other results, an estimate of marginal WTP of £0.08 annually per respondent for a one-mile reduction in length of unacceptably low flow rivers. Nonuser respondents showed a positive but not statistically significant WTP for a reduction in low-flow river miles. Regional population estimates were used to aggregate these results, first to a total value for each river basin and then to a present value of benefits to be compared with capital costs of the proposed improvements.

In a benefit transfer study of the impact of a potential severe, sustained drought on the Colorado river in the southwestern United States, Booker and Colby (1995) assembled data on the demand for water-based outdoor recreation. They distinguished between reservoir and free-flowing river uses. The former represents primarily fishing and water skiing, while the latter includes fishing and whitewater rafting. From the literature survey, they developed equations that reflected WTP for volumes of water. These equations, combined with similar equations for other water uses in agriculture, industry, and homes, were subsequently used in the river basin model to solve for the effects of drought on net economic benefits of offstream and instream economic activities.

Mahan et al. (2000) measured the value of proximity to wetlands in the area of Portland, Oregon, from a sample of over 14,000 residential transactions. Each 1,000 feet closer to a wetland increased a home's value by about

$400 after controlling for factors like attributes of the residence. Colby and Wishart (2002) analyzed over 7,000 transactions in Tucson, Arizona, to assess the value of proximity to a riparian corridor along an intermittent desert stream. They reported that homes and vacant lots located 1.5 miles from the riparian corridor sold for about $10,000 less than similar properties situated 0.1 mile away. See Section 4.3.2 for a hedonic value study of lake levels by Lansford and Jones (1995).

8.1.3   Example: Using the Travel Cost Method to Value Stored Water During Drought

The U.S. Army Corps of Engineers (USACE), among its other duties, is responsible for most major flood damage alleviation programs in the United States. It controls numerous reservoirs whose original or primary purpose was floodwater retention. Many of these generate considerable economic value as public sites for water-based recreation. Demands by recreationists for amply filled reservoirs are increasingly competitive with floodwater management, releases for instream flows for navigation and recreation, crop irrigation, and other uses. Thus, recreational values of water are useful in assessing tradeoffs in reservoir management.

Ward et al. (1996) developed travel cost estimates of the marginal value of water for reservoir-based recreation at several Corps of Engineers reservoirs in its Sacramento District in central California. On-site visitor use data were collected from visitors to ten USACE reservoirs during 1983–1985 at the beginning of what became the 1985–1991 California drought. Most of the reservoirs and their substitutes experienced wide water level fluctuations due to limited inflows and competing demands for agricultural water and other uses. Reservoir draw-downs typically reduce recreational visits because of reduced surface area, diminished aesthetics, expanded mud flats, reduced water for fish habitat, and because facilities such as docks and boat ramps may become inoperative. These fluctuations facilitated the estimation of a travel cost model with enough variation in water level to isolate effects based on travel cost and visitor demographic effects. The water level changes during the drought were significant enough to permit derivation of marginal water values over a wide range of reservoir sizes and lake levels. Since response to reservoir status was expected to vary significantly by user class, demands from day-users and overnight campers were studied separately.

Model Specification. The dependent variable was total reported visitation from county i to site j during year t. Independent variables included four classes that, according to economic theory, affect recreation visitation: price (cost of travel), demographic factors, site characteristics (reservoir water status), and nature of substitutes. The recreationist samples included 462 campers and 264 day visitors. A number of sources were drawn upon to develop the database of independent variables for explaining visitation, including the Natural Resource Management System inventory of site facilities developed by the Corps of Engineers; state fish and game agency records of fish stocking; U.S. Census sources; and data on substitute non-Corps reservoirs. The following model was hypothesized:

$$V_{ijt} = f(P_{ijt}, OWN\_RP_j, OWN\_PF_{jt}, CHR_{jkt}, DEM_{iLt}, DEM_{iLt},$$
$$SUB\_RP_s, SUB\_PF_{ijt}) \qquad\qquad (8\text{-}1)$$

where:

$V_{ijt} =$ total visits from county i to site j in year t;

$P_{ij} =$ price (travel cost) from county i to site j in year t (round trip miles times travel cost per mile plus entry fee). Travel cost includes an opportunity cost of time valued at one-third the county average hourly wage by zone of origin;

$OWN\_RP_j =$ recreation pool in surface acres at the "own" site j;

$OWN\_PF_{jt} =$ average percentage full of OWN_RP_j, weighted by the distribution of monthly visitation over year t;

$CHR_{jkt} =$ characteristic variable k of site j in year t;

$DEM_{iLt} =$ demographic variable L of county i in time t;

$SUB\_RP_{ij} =$ water-based recreational substitute index for county i and site j, where SUB_RP_s is the recreation pool surface in acres at substitute reservoirs, reflecting the round trip miles from county i to substitute site s; and

$SUB\_PF_{ijt} =$ substitute index of percentage full for county i and site j in time t.

In addition, two hydrologic variables were used to assign volumes and surface acres to various levels of a reservoir's OWN_PF_{jt}, permitting the translation of values per surface area into values per acre-foot of water. They are:

$SA_{jt} =$ average monthly surface acres at site j in year t;

$VOL_{jt} =$ computed acre-feet of water volume corresponding to SA_{jt}.

Indices:

$i =$ county of visitor origin;

$j =$ Corps reservoir of visitor destination;

$k =$ one of eight reservoir characteristic variables;

$L =$ one of four visitor demographic variables;

$s =$ one of 145 substitute reservoir destinations in the market area;

$t =$ one of three years of visitor sampling (1983–1985).

Econometric Results. After tests of model specification, a log-linear form was chosen for both the camping and day-use models. The estimated coefficients all have the expected signs. The coefficients for travel cost are highly significant and negative. The coefficients for percentage of full surface area are strongly positive, implying that visitation falls as any reservoir level, and associated surface area, drops. The larger coefficient on the day-use model indicates that with reduced water levels, day-use visitation declines faster than camping visitation. Variability of monthly lake levels was also negative and highly significant, indicating a disutility for uncertainty in lake levels and surface areas among recreationists. Coefficients on variables representing percentage full at substitute reservoir sites were also negative, as anticipated, and statistically significant.

Derivation of Water Value. Equation 8-1 reflects the demographic, site characteristics, travel cost, and substitute variables that affect visitation. Consumer surplus is obtained by finding (from a table of definite integrals) an integral of the econometric equation. The integral is determined for each reservoir for each county for each year up to a travel cost at the outer limit of the assumed market area (175 miles for campers and 125 miles for day users).

The incremental value of water is derived by further manipulation of the consumer surplus expression. The annual economic value of an additional acre-foot of water held at a reservoir in county j at site i in year t is obtained by differentiating the consumer surplus expression with respect to water volume to derive a "water valuation" equation, which is solved for each reservoir under alternative water level assumptions.

The researchers found that annual recreational values per incremental acre-foot of water ranged from $6 at Pine Flat Reservoir to more than $600 at Success Lake for the range of the lake levels observed in the sample Corps reservoirs. During droughts or in times when demands for competing water uses are high, economically efficient basin management will draw down reservoirs that have the lowest marginal values for recreation. The authors note that draw-downs in large, isolated reservoirs with steep banks produce relatively small losses in regional recreation benefits. Conversely, drawing down reservoirs with high recreational values per acre-foot could impose unnecessarily large economic losses on the region's visitors; these reservoirs typically have few substitutes, are located near population centers, or have shallow slopes at the waterline. This analysis helps water managers identify trade-offs between recreation benefits and the benefits of competing users.

8.2 Valuation of Water Quality Improvements

The effects of pollution on human health and quality of life and on wildlife habitat are significant political issues in most nations. Governments that fail to recognize that the environment is a scarce resource and permit it to be a free good will fail to achieve an economically efficient allocation of environmental resources and bring on an unhealthy and unpleasant environment. When there are no costs or constraints for using scarce environmental services as a sink for residuals, producers and consumers have no incentive to control their discharges to the environment (Bergstrom et al. 2001).

8.2.1 Preliminary Concepts

Environmental economists have devoted considerable effort to the problem of managing water pollution. In the modern world, environmental pollution is an inevitable and pervasive consequence of the production and consumption activities of humankind. Raw materials are extracted from the environment and processed into consumer goods by the production sector. Some wastes (residuals) from the production process are returned to the environment. The household sector returns byproducts of consumption to the environment. The *materials balance principle* asserts that over the long term the mass of residuals discharged to the environment by consumers and producers will equal the mass of materials originally extracted from the environment to make production and consumption goods. In consequence, the environment is a scarce resource, as important for its capacity as an assimilator of residuals as it is as a source of materials.

An implication of the materials balance principle is that residuals discharges must be balanced among the various environmental outlets. Residuals must end up somewhere, as mass or energy. Thus, discharges into watercourses must be managed in conjunction with waste disposal to the atmosphere and discarding to landfills. Reducing the amount of wastes discharged into water will not solve the overall problem if the wastes are merely sent elsewhere into the environment.

Water pollution originates from either *point sources* or *nonpoint sources*. Point source pollution is emitted from a single pipe or ditch through which the pollutant is transported to a water body. Regulation and monitoring of compliance with regulations can focus on the point of discharge. Nonpoint sources are those for which there exists no single source of pollutant discharge. They are most often associated with human uses of land such as farming, forestry, and construction. Soil particles eroded from farm or forest lands and washed into lakes or streams are a primary example. Fertilizers and pesticides can be carried off the soil surface or percolate into groundwater deposits. However, much nonpoint-source pollution originates from natural processes, e.g. organic matter from forests or dissolved mineral solids (salinity) from both surface and underground contact with sedimentary rock formations.

A basic issue of water quality management is the level of water quality that should be targeted by public policy: the point that economists call the economically optimal level of water quality. The other fundamental issue is the package of policy instruments that should be adopted to achieve the desired standard for point and nonpoint-source pollution.

A paradox faces policy makers in dealing with water quality. On the one hand, in their role as producers or householders, people prefer to be entitled to discharge wastes at will. Dumping rather than treating wastes transfers costs to others distant in time and space. Thus dischargers must be induced to take steps contrary to their perceived self-interest. On the other hand, the public as consumers of the environment desires near zero pollution. This would be enormously expensive or even impossible unless important industries are closed down. Recognizing the need for tradeoffs in this as in other instances of resource scarcity, economists have proposed a model based on economic efficiency. The economic value of reducing discharges (or improving ambient water quality) is an essential element of this model.

Figure 8-1 illustrates the standard economic model of optimum pollution control. Consider a damaging pollutant or residual being discharged to a river. Assume that the adverse effects of this pollutant are known, and that monetary values can be placed on these effects. The damaging discharges can be reduced by treatment or process changes at a known cost. The decision variable of interest is residuals concentration, shown on the horizontal axis. Treatment cost (T) rises (moving from right to left) as the residual concentration falls. The willingness to pay of beneficiaries is assumed to be measured by the damages avoided by the treatment. Damages avoided (D) falls (also moving from right to left) as residual concentration is reduced. For initial units of improvement, the cost of initial increments of improved water quality are likely to be fairly small, while the water user's (receptor's) willingness to pay (damages avoided) will likely be fairly high. The total cost of disposing of residuals in the water is the sum of damages and treatment costs (given by the curve $T + D$). The point R_1 defines the optimum level of pollution control, at the minimum of total cost. This is the point at which economic analysis suggests should be the target or optimal level of environmental quality. Neither emitter or receptor will be entirely pleased with this compromise position, the receptor preferring treatment to the threshold of damages (at R_0) while the emitter prefers not to incur costs of treatment, (staying at R_2).

Note that this model is subject to the criticisms of applied utilitarianism noted in Chapter 2. The cost–benefit analysis model places damage costs to receptors on an equal footing with the costs of treatment by polluters. On its face, the model implies that cost should be borne by the least-cost avoider, whether that entity is the source of or the victim of the pollutant. Within the range where the incremental damages to receptors are less than the incremental costs of treatment (to the left of R_1), the model does not require the polluter to meet a higher standard. Advocates (e.g. Bucha-

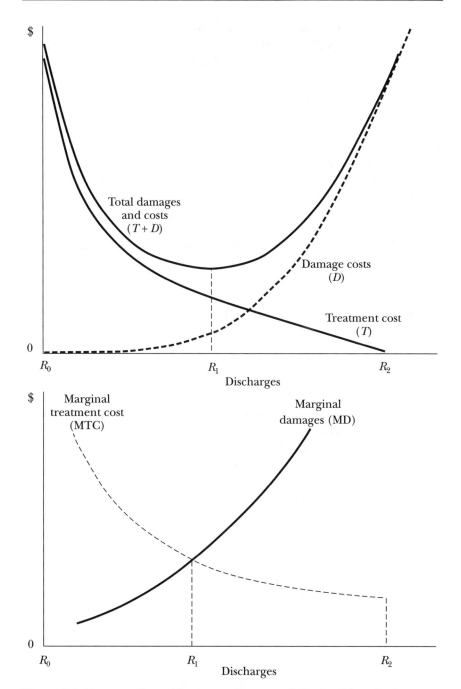

Figure 8-1. Damage Costs, Treatment Costs, and Optimal Level of Pollution Control

nan 1977) of a *Pareto safety* rule (no uncompensated third-party damage) and environmental philosophers arguing for a criterion of *avoid doing harm* (Goodin 1992) contend that public pollution control policy should strive to minimize all damages to third parties.

Estimating the economic benefits of water quality improvement is among the most frequently encountered but most difficult tasks of water valuation. Benefits may be received by both users and nonusers. Users can be offstream producers, offstream consumers, and public good beneficiaries. User benefits accrue to recreational water users, to municipal and industrial users, and sometimes to agriculture. Freeman 2002 provides a recent overview and assessment of the benefits of environmental regulations in the United States, including water quality improvement.

Nonuse benefits—particularly in the form of avoiding toxic waste damages to environmental flora and fauna—have come into prominence in the last decade or so. (Recall from Chapter 4 that nonuse values are benefits received from knowing that a good exists, even though the individual may never directly experience it.) Interest in nonuse values was boosted by the Exxon *Valdez* accident in 1989. A number of cases involving nonuse (or passive use) values related to water have attracted the attention of resource economists. See Bishop et al. (1997) and Carson et al. (1999) for conceptual and measurement issues.

Expressed preference methods are the most appropriate here. Loomis et al. (1991) surveyed households in California to determine willingness to pay to protect and expand wetlands and to reduce contamination of wildlife habitat. They reported that California households would pay $254 per annum in additional taxes for an increase in wetland acreage with an associated 40% increase in bird population. Cummings et al. (1994) report a willingness to pay for preservation of endangered fish species of $3.42 per household in a sample taken from a southwestern United States city. Loomis et al. (2000) used a dichotomous choice CVM approach to value a proposed restoration of the South Platte River in the semi-arid plains of eastern Colorado. At stake were dilution of wastewater, natural purification of water, erosion control, fish and wildlife habitat, and recreation. About 100 respondents reported an average willingness to have their water bills increased by $252 annually to implement the plan.

Kopp (1992) advocates the concept of nonuse value, while Cummings and Harrison (1995) provide a challenge. Despite its increasing acceptance, applying nonuse environmental value to policy assessment continues to be controversial.

In general, economic benefits of water quality improvements are measured by changes in consumer and producer surpluses (Freeman 2003; Ribaudo and Shortle 2001). The compensating surplus—the reduction in income that would maintain utility at the same level as before the water quality improvement—is the preferred concept. Benefits are, as usual, defined as WTP for an environmental improvement. In practical terms, WTP is often measured in terms of *damages avoided* from a water quality enhancement program. The economic benefit to water users is conceptualized as the WTP to avoid potential damages from water pollutants. On the producer side, damages include increased costs of production and decreased output. For consumers, damages mean the potential expenses for defending against water pollution and the reduced utility associated with water use, such as the taste of drinking water or biological or chemical sources of water-borne diseases.

Degradable effluents are organic materials decomposed by stream biota into their inorganic constituents. Their potential for environmental damage depends on the concentration of the pollutant, which in turn depends on the distance and time from the point of discharge, temperature, rates of flow, and the quality of the receiving waters. Sophisticated biophysical models are needed to accurately forecast the effects of changes in discharges on downstream pollutant concentrations.

8.2.2 Recreational Benefits of Water Quality Improvement

Early studies of the effects of water pollution in the humid eastern United States concluded that the costs of water quality improvement for municipal and industrial users would greatly exceed the benefits, meaning that the primary damages are in the form of reduced value of recreational services. Attempts to estimate damages to industrial water users have found minimal effects. For many industrial processes, such as cooling of electric power plants, change in water quality within the normally experienced ranges has little impact. The quality requirements for other processes such as food processing or electronics manufacturing are so high that some degree of treatment is necessary anyway. Treatment costs for many industries are not particularly sensitive to water quality.

Several studies have examined the recreational benefits of water quality improvement. If sites vary according to water quality, it may be possible to infer the incremental value of the improved quality from a travel cost analysis. An early effort was reported by Feenberg and Mills (1980), who formulated a logit model of site visitation in the Boston area. Smith and Desvousges (1986) developed estimates of the value of improved water quality from a sample of U.S. Army Corps of Engineers reservoirs. In addition to contingent valuation and simple travel cost models, Smith and Desvousges developed a generalized travel cost model to infer the value placed on water quality improvements by recreationists. The model yielded results that were implausibly large, illustrating the problems of extrapolating beyond the range of site characteristics from which the model was estimated. Carson (1991) attempted to measure the value of varying degrees of improvement in water quality (boatable, fishable, and swimmable) at the national level. Estimated annual benefits of achieving nationwide swimmable quality waters in the United States were in the $20 billion range, which the authors concluded was probably not enough to offset the cost.

Choice modeling (CM) has also found application to valuing recreational aspects of water quality. In a complex and sophisticated study, and perhaps the earliest application of CM to the case of water management, Adamowicz et al. (1994) measured recreationists' valuation of water availability and quality in Alberta Province in western Canada. The authors conducted a parallel revealed preference (travel cost) study of recreation in the same region. The CM study attempted to explain the choice of recreational sites as conditioned by attributes like water quality, distance to be traveled, catch rates, and opportunities for boating, swimming, or fishing. The data were collected via a telephone survey of recreationists, who were also asked to provide data on actual recreational activities on which a travel cost study could be based. Both the CM and the travel cost studies showed that distance to be traveled, water quality, catch rates, and the availability of boating, swimming, or fishing influenced the valuation of the sites. The authors' final step was to combine the CM and the travel cost data for a joint model. The survey had been designed with this in mind, so that a random utility formulation could be employed in the statistical estimation. Their conclusion was that the combined approach improved the statistical estimates. Measures of WTP for marginal improvement in water quality as well as for other desired attributes could be derived from the joint model.

D'Arge and Shogren (1989) used the hedonic property value method to measure the value of water quality for recreational home owners on a pair of neighboring lakes in Iowa which exhibited contrasting water qualities due to different depths, summer temperatures, and nutrient inflows, particularly from neighboring agricultural activities. The authors employed hedonic pricing, a survey of local real estate agents, and a contingent valuation survey of site dwellers' willingness to pay for improved water quality. They regressed observed house prices near both lakes against various attributes of the sample, including area under roof, date of construction, quality of construction, size of lot, and proximity to a lake. A dummy (binary) variable for the site with higher quality water provided a measure of the willingness to pay for improved water quality. Sales prices for recreational homes on the lake with better quality water were higher, controlling for other factors, than prices of homes on the other lake. This application of the hedonic pricing method serves to confirm that consumers do in fact exhibit a positive willingness to pay for environmental improvement. The approach requires unique data sets, which are unlikely to be available to use for deriving specific benefit estimates for planning water policy initiatives.

8.2.3 Example: Application of the Hedonic Property Value Approach to Valuing Demand for Protection Against Water Quality Degradation

Boyle et al. (1998) used the hedonic property value method to measure demand for protecting freshwater lakes in Maine from nutrient loading, algae growth, and the associated reduction in water clarity.

Eutrophication (algae blooms brought on by excess nutrient content) reduces the clarity of lake water. It is the result of nonpoint pollution from land use practices in the watershed (agricultural production, forestry harvest, and residential housing development), and frequently also from natural sources. It decreases the aesthetic appeal and reduces recreational values, which can translate into reduced prices of lakefront properties. Measures of the value of improved clarity can help in determining the level of public funding to allocate toward nonpoint pollution regulation.

Boyle et al. implemented a two-stage hedonic property value study to estimate lakefront property owners' demand for improved water clarity on Maine lakes. The first stage used data on lakefront property transactions to estimate a hedonic price equation which explained lakefront home prices in terms of the characteristics of the house, associated land, frontage of the lake, and water clarity. The second stage combined the first stage findings with a mail survey of the property purchasers to derive a demand function for water clarity.

Stage 1: Factors Explaining Lakefront Property Prices. The authors formulated a hedonic pricing model which depicted property price (PP) as dependent on a vector of property attributes; characteristics of the structure on the property; characteristics of property location; and an environmental variable reflecting both the total surface area of the lake (SA) and water clarity (WATERC). Property price was hypothesized to increase with water clarity, but at a decreasing rate, so the water clarity variable was expressed in natural logarithms. Because of collinearity between lake area and clarity, for the environmental variable the authors employed a multiplicative term ($SA \cdot \ln WATERC$). The property location variable was expressed as distance to the nearest city. Some dummy variables were incorporated for lakes with unusual features not captured by other variables in the model, such as proximity to larger towns or susceptibility to flooding.

In symbols, the model is expressed as:

$$PP = \Sigma_j \, \beta_j A_j + \beta_{wc}(SA \cdot \ln WATERC) \tag{8-2}$$

where PP = property sales price, A_j is a vector of property characteristics hypothesized to affect the selling price and the β's are coefficients to be estimated.

Stage 1: Data. Selling prices and property attributes were assembled for lakefront property sales on 36 lakes in Maine, grouped into 7 market areas to facilitate estimation of the implicit prices used in the second stage. The 862 observations in the data set were limited to transactions regarding single-family homes with lake frontage or unimproved parcels of less than 20 acres with lake frontage during the years 1990–1995.

Water clarity can be measured by a flat, circular device called a "secchi disk" that is black and white on alternating quadrants. The disk is lowered into the water on a metered line, and the depth (in meters) at which the disk disappears is a measure of clarity. The Maine Department of Environmental Protection and volunteers have recorded numerous secchi disk readings each summer on Maine lakes. The water clarity measures used for this analysis were measured by the minimum secchi disk readings reported by the Department during the summer of the year the property was sold.

Property sales price (PP) was inferred from public tax records. Public tax assessment records provided the data on characteristics of structures and land. The characteristics of structures—intended to distinguish between rustic cabins and year-round residences—were square feet of living area, presence of a full bath, and central heating. Feet of frontage on the lake was the land characteristic included in the model.

Stage 1: Analysis and Results. Equation 8-2 was fitted with the data described above for each of the seven market areas. The water quality variable was positive for six of the seven market area equations, and significantly greater than zero at the 1% level of significance for four of the areas. For the most part, the key variables were of expected sign and significantly different from zero at the 10% level of significance or better. Coefficients of determination (R^2) ranged from 0.50 to 0.68.

Stage 2: Demand for Water Clarity. The partial derivative of the estimated hedonic price function with respect to an attribute yields the marginal implicit price of that attribute. Marginal implicit prices vary across the multiple markets, which permits the identification of the demand curve for that attribute. The estimates of marginal implicit price for each property in the sample, together with the quantities of water quality purchased, are used to estimate the demand for water clarity. The second stage demand is represented as:

$$Q^i_{wc} = f(P^i_{wc}; P^i_k; Z_i) \qquad (8\text{-}3)$$

where Q^i_{wc} is the quantity of water clarity purchased, P^i_{wc} is the price of water clarity, P^i_k is a price vector of substitutes or complements to water clarity, and Z_i is a vector of demographic characteristics and other factors hypothesized to influence demand for water clarity. Two variables are included in P^i_k: the implicit price of living area and the implicit price of feet of lake frontage, both also obtained in Stage 1. The variables in $\mathbf{Z}$,

WTP for Water Clarity

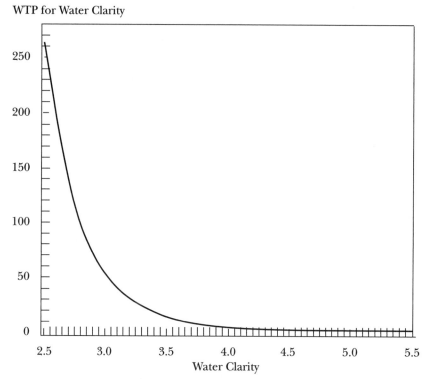

Figure 8-2. Hedonic Estimate of Demand for Water Clarity on Maine Lakes

Source: from Boyle et al. 1999.

obtained from a mail survey of property purchasers in the seven market areas, included:

- the income of the purchasing family;
- a binary (dummy) variable equal to 1 if the purchaser had visited the lake before purchasing the property;
- another dummy variable, 1 if the purchaser had friends or relatives who also owned property at the lake;
- a dummy variable for expectations of improvement in clarity; and
- a dummy variable for expectations of deterioration in clarity.

Figure 8-2 shows the resulting demand curve for water clarity. Conforming to *a priori* economic reasoning, the marginal value of water clarity is seen to be quite high at low levels of clarity, but decreases rapidly as satisfactory clarity levels are reached.

A large sample of transactions and an ample number of lakes (providing a wide range of observations on water clarity) yielded useful value estimates. The analysis benefitted from research resources large enough to collect data on price and other attributes of the transactions as well as to survey the attributes of purchasers. Competence in economic modeling, data collection methods, and statistical techniques were needed to bring the project to a successful conclusion.

8.2.4 Water Quality Benefits via a Benefit Transfer Method

Morgan and Owens (2001) undertook to estimate the economic benefits of water quality legislation for the Chesapeake Bay region for the period 1972–1996. The Chesapeake Bay is the largest estuary on the Atlantic coast of the United States, and receives water from portions of six states. The legislation in question was the federal Clean Water Act of 1972 (and subsequent amendments and associated regulations). Although these were not the only pollutants, the study focused on nitrogen and phosphorous loadings from both point and nonpoint sources, plus atmospheric deposits of nitrogen. These nutrients encourage algae growth, which in turn adversely affects aquatic life and human recreational and health values. Implementation of the laws and regulations took the form of control programs to regulate fertilizer applications on farmlands and management of animal wastes (nonpoint sources), and upgrading wastewater treatment facilities (point sources). Six categories of benefits were taken to be relevant for valuing water quality improvements in the Bay: recreation (boating, fishing, swimming), commercial fishing, health, nonuse values, property values, and regional economic impacts. Two previously published water quality benefit studies of portions of the Chesapeake Bay region were the basis for the extrapolations in this benefit transfer exercise. The researchers adjusted for general price level changes and drew on secondary data on population growth and economic change to extrapolate to a larger area, a wider range of recreation benefits, and a higher degree of nutrient removal. The authors report a range of annual benefits of $360 million to $1,800 million in 1996 dollars. Even so, they were unable to address the effects of toxic chemical reduction, nonuse benefits, commercial fisheries, and the impacts of the policies on the populations of tributary waterways. With estimated treatment costs of around $900 million, the authors cautiously concluded that net benefits were likely to be positive, but acknowledged a wide range of uncertainty.

8.2.5 The Benefits of Water Used for Waste Dilution: An Alternative Cost Approach

Polluted waters can be improved by diluting them with a source of higher quality. Release of dilution water can yield economic benefits by reducing damage to subsequent water users or by decreasing the costs of treating effluents. The provision of dilution water incurs corresponding costs. These can be the cost of constructing storage for release as dilution water or, more likely, the forgone benefits of alternative instream uses of water for hydropower or recreation or withdrawal for irrigation, municipal, or industrial purposes.

Interest in the potential economic benefits of waste dilution arose in the late 1960s in the United States as a possible response to environmental degradation, a concern that led to the passage of environmental quality legislation. Because of the difficulties of directly estimating damage functions, a form of the alternative cost approach was developed. Enhanced waste treatment before discharge was the alternative abatement technology chosen in those early studies. The conclusions were that dilution was a very low-valued method of pollution damage reduction. That is, waste treatment was found to be less expensive than constructing water storage primarily for waste dilution. These findings probably account for the limited interest in this subject in recent years. Gray and Young (1974) adapted the alternative cost method to forecast the value of dilution water for several major river basins in the United States, focusing on diluting biochemical oxygen demand (BOD) loadings (although the model would work for other pollutants).

8.2.6 Integrated Management of Water Supplies and Water Quality

Water supply and water quality have typically been considered independently, but it is increasingly clear that integrating the quantity and quality aspects of water management is essential. Spulber and Sabbaghi (1998) have developed an elaborate formal economic framework which integrates the two considerations by means of quality-graded demand and supply functions for water. A discrete set of water supply and demand functions is envisaged, each representing a defined water quality. This important extension from the traditional approach—simply ignoring water quality—permits simultaneous representation of both the quantity and quality dimensions in analysis of intersectoral allocation issues. While the model is theoretically quite attractive, the authors have attempted no empirical implementation, and it remains to be seen if this will be a fruitful approach in practical policy analyses.

Booker and Young (1994) developed an empirical optimization model combining hydrologic and economic relationships for the Colorado River Basin (see also Booker 1995). The main water quality problem is dissolved mineral solids (salinity), which arises naturally in runoff from the sedimentary rock formations in the watershed, and secondarily from irrigation drainage. Salinity damage functions by subregion and type of use (urban and agricultural) quantify the economic effects of quality degradations. The hydrologic model routes water and salinity downriver, and the economic optimization model balances water quantity (including hydropower) and quality considerations. See also Lee and Howitt (1996) for an alternative approach to basin-wide modeling of salinity impacts in the context of basin-wide water management.

8.2.7   A Special Municipal Water Quality Issue: Reductions in Salinity

In arid and semiarid regions, such as the southwestern United States, rivers often naturally display high levels of salinity (see Section 5.8.1). Residential water users may suffer adverse effects from elevated salinity levels. Salinity in domestic tap water may result in corrosion and scale damage to appliances, fixtures, and pipes, reducing their useful life. It may also impose additional work cleaning mineral deposits from fixtures, and increased expenditures for bottled water, home water treatment, soaps, and detergents. Many people dislike the taste imparted by excessive mineral content, although at the levels of salinity most often encountered, mineral salts are an inconvenience, not a threat to health. In an early study, McGuckin and Young (1981) formulated an optimization model to test the economic feasibility of desalinating in the lower Arkansas River Basin in eastern Colorado. This river picks up salts from sedimentary rocks formed from ancient seabeds; these are then concentrated by evapotranspiration from irrigation. Water users in the Arkansas River Basin experience some of the highest dissolved solids readings in the United States, as high as 3600 mg/liter in the eastern prairies. The authors used benefit transfer (based on previous estimates of per household damages from dissolved solids in southern California) to quantify benefits of reduced salinity.

The U.S. Government has expended considerable effort and funds toward reducing salinity in the Southwest, especially in the Colorado River, which flows through several states into Mexico and the Gulf of California. A number of studies have undertaken to estimate the economic benefits of this type of program. In spite of the widespread opinion that water quality improvement is generally a good thing, the assessments by Gardner and Young (1985, 1988) of the methods used to economically justify the Colorado River Salinity Program suggest that skepticism of the methodology behind these programs is warranted. Moreover, in spite of claims by the Colorado River Salinity Program that salinity causes many hundreds of millions of dollars of annual damages, the issue raises relatively little public concern.

Economic benefits to residential water users from salinity reduction can take the form of either increased life span of water-using household appliances or reduced defensive expenditures (such as purchasing bottled water). Because individual households cannot purchase water of varying quality, directly estimating the demand function for water quality improvement is not possible. Most studies of salinity damages have focused on the value of increased service lives of water-using household appliances. Benefits are measured as willingness to pay up to the economic value of the damages to avoid experiencing such damages.

Studies of salinity damages to household appliances adopt a four-stage approach to estimating benefits of salinity abatement:

1. Obtain data on the service lives of water-using appliances over a range of salinity levels, usually from households and local plumbers and appliance repair people.
2. Estimate statistically the relation between tap water salinity and life of water-using appliances.
3. Estimate the cost of ownership of affected appliances for alternative salinity levels over the life of a home.
4. Calculate the damages avoided (the reduction in appliance ownership cost) for a specific reduction in salinity.

Ragan et al. (2000) studied the segment of the Arkansas River in southeastern Colorado. Salinity here ranges from 100 mg/liter in the high mountains to 3600 mg/liter in towns in the eastern prairies, thus providing a natural experiment on the effects of salinity on households. Using mailed questionnaires, the authors surveyed both households and businesses thought to know the effects of salinity. Previous studies had measured appliance life only with reference to the age at failure. Those studies had relied on estimates from plumbing contractors of the life of appliances. For improved accuracy of estimated appliance service lives, this study obtained data on both ages of in-service appliances and ages at failure of appliances that had previously failed. A statistical technique new to this field was adapted to model the effect of salinity on appliance lives: the *accelerated testing method.* The Weibull distribution provided the best statistical fit to the data. Dishwashers, water heaters, garbage disposers, water softeners, and evaporative coolers showed statistically significant reductions in service life with increasing salinity.

Analysis of the plumber appliance repair survey estimated a much larger influence of salinity on service life. However, because these respondents were few in number, their estimates varied widely, and they could not provide data on in-service appliances, the authors concluded that the household survey results were more representative of actual salinity damages.

In comparison to the economic study by which the Colorado River Salinity Control Program has been economically justified (Lohman et al. 1988), Ragan et al. found no statistically significant effects for some appliances (including automobile radiators, which were a significant source of estimated damages in the study used to support the federal salinity control program), and for appliances common to both studies their estimates of salinity damages were only one-third or less. These differences likely originate from two sources. One is the improvement in research methodology, such as inclusion of in-service appliances in the database, more advanced statistical methods, and a wider range of salinity in the observations. The other source may be a change in the underlying demand parameters, particularly from reduced damage due to technological improvements in appliances over time. Manufacturers appear to be making appliances with materials that are less affected by salinity in the range found in most of the affected municipalities.

Although these findings are from another river basin, the dissolved solids composition is reasonably similar to that of the Colorado River. These results further call into question the net economic benefits yielded by the U.S. Department of Interior's large investment in salinity management on the Colorado River and suggest the need for re-evaluating that program.

8.2.8 Measuring Benefits of Reducing Waterborne Health Risks

Two approaches have been applied to measuring damages from outbreaks of waterborne diseases and from chemical pollutants: the defensive behavior and the damage cost models (see Section 4.4).

Harrington et al. (1991) studied an outbreak of waterborne giardiasis that affected several thousand people in Luzerne County, Pennsylvania in 1983–1984 (giardiasis is a particular form of diarrhea carried by a one-celled water-borne microscopic parasite). Harrington et al. studied both the damage costs of the illness and defensive (averting) behaviors to avoid the adverse effects. They hypothesized that willingness to pay to avoid acute illness is equivalent to the cost of treatment and any lost earnings. The second category, defensive or averting behavior, represents the costs of actions people take to reduce their exposure to environmental contaminants. Harrington et al. estimated costs of boiling water and of obtaining uncontaminated water as their estimate of defensive costs. See Lee and Moffitt 1993 for further theoretical development of defensive costs, Abdalla et al. 1992 for application to chemical contamination of groundwater, and McConnell and Rosado 2000 for defensive behavior-based valuation of improved drinking water quality in a city in Brazil. CVM has also been applied to these topics. Bergstrom et al. (2001) present a collection of empirical studies of the benefits of improving groundwater quality using a rigorous option price conceptual framework and expressed preference methods. See Dickie (2003) for a complete and rigorous review of defensive behavior and damage cost measures of the costs of illness.

8.3 Measuring Benefits of Flood Risk Reduction

Floods inflict property damage, economic disruption, injury, disease, and death throughout the world. In the United States, floods have caused an estimated average damages of $2 billion per year over the past 30 years;

damages from the Mississippi Valley floods of 1993 exceeded $12 billion. Even so, annual flood damages have a minor impact on the national economy. Flood damages are more severe in undeveloped countries. An extreme example is Bangladesh, where much of the population lives on a floodplain. Monsoon rains combined with runoff from the Himalayas frequently bring serious inundation, with heavy fatalities and property damage.

To reduce losses from flooding and to make the best use of valuable floodplain lands, governments throughout the world expend resources for structures to change flow regimes and adopt nonstructural policies to influence behavior of floodplain occupants. Public floodplain management programs produce benefits in the form of reduced risk of loss from floods. (Some writers misleadingly refer to flood risk reduction programs as "flood prevention" or "flood protection." Floodplain management can reduce risks, but does not completely prevent damages from floods.)

Structural programs for flood risk reduction generally reduce risks of flood damage by changing the timing and rates of flow of floodwaters. For example, a dam and flood storage reservoir can capture the peak of high flood flows and slowly, safely release them later. Embankments or levees can be built to contain most high flows.

Since damaging floods rarely recur at a given site, individual homeowners and businesspeople usually know little of the risks of locating on floodplains. Unregulated private floodplain use tends to locate on flood plains to take advantage of apparent amenity, locational, and construction cost advantages. Nonstructural methods often involve reducing incentives to choose dangerous locations. Other nonstructural programs may work to change land use and runoff in upper watersheds or may consist of warning systems to alert floodplain residents of impending danger. Publicly mandated flood insurance and its premium costs linked to risks is designed to confront the potential home or business owner with the expected cost of their siting decisions and hence discourage uninformed decisions to build on flood-prone sites. Public land use regulations are another approach to changing private behavior regarding location on floodplains.

8.3.1 Prefatory Remarks on Flood Risk Reduction Benefits

Economic evaluation of floodplain management policies was given impetus in the United States by the Flood Control Act of 1936, which directed that flood control projects should be undertaken "if the benefits to whomsoever they may accrue are in excess of the estimated costs, and if the lives and social security of people are otherwise adversely affected." Subsequently, by legislative and administrative action, federal water agencies adopted the key phrase *benefits to whomsoever they may accrue are in excess of the estimated costs* as a guideline. This phrase is generally regarded as the modern impetus for establishing a primary role for economic analysis in public investment planning and for formalizing the techniques of cost–benefit analysis. Consequently, the economic approach to flood risk reduction follows general cost–benefit analysis principles, measuring the tradeoffs associated with purchasing additional risk reduction. Measuring benefits of flood hazard alleviation includes a probabilistic element in the evaluation of benefits, reflecting the uncertainty of flood events. As in the pollution control model, benefits of flood damage mitigation are typically measured as willingness to pay to avoid damages.

Flood risk reduction programs exhibit benefits that tend to be of a public or collective good nature, meaning that once these benefits are provided, potential public good users cannot be readily excluded from enjoyment of its benefits. Thus the nonmarket valuation techniques developed for environmental public goods—stated preference and revealed preference—are applicable, but these have been attempted mainly in academic settings. A deductive method called property damages avoided (PDA) is relied upon most often for valuation of flood risk reduction benefits in actual planning circumstance. PDA calculates the expected property damages avoided by the project or policy in a with-policy versus without-policy comparison. The general methods for estimating the economic benefits of flood risk reduction are similar to those used in other contexts, but imperfect knowledge of flood probabilities and likely damages from flood events and the potential for intangible consequences, including the risk of death, make their application difficult and contentious. Compared to the literature on environmental quality benefits, for example, that on measuring flood risk reduction benefits is sketchy.

8.3.2 An Overview of the Optimal Response to Flood Hazards

Estimation of flood hazard reduction benefits assumes rational, fully informed flood plain occupants willing to pay up to the present discounted *expected* (probability-weighted) value of their losses to avoid them (Herfindahl and Kneese 1974, *257*). Structures are built and nonstructural policies are adopted to influence behavior of floodplain occupants. Flood hazard adjustments are subject to diminishing marginal expected returns because they protect mainly against the more frequent events. The incremental expected losses typically decline rapidly with initial levels of expenditure, but level off as additional damage reduction is more difficult to attain. Mitigation costs tend to rise at an increasing rate with increased degrees of mitigation. Costs of protection tend also to be nonlinear. In the case of structural adjustments to floods (such as dams and reservoirs) the volume (and hence costs) is a power of the height, so additional protection is obtained at disproportionate expense.

The evaluation of structural flood alleviation projects is site specific, depending on hydrologic conditions and the nature and density of present and prospective human activity on the floodplain. Unlike most of the values discussed previously, benefits of flood hazard reduction are estimated in probabilistic terms. The expected annual damages represent the monetary value of physical and other losses that can be expected in any given year based on probability and magnitude of flood losses. Probabilities of inundation in the PDA method are based on statistical analysis of historical flows rather than on the subjective perceptions of potential or actual floodplain residents.

8.3.3 Basic Steps in Measuring Flood Alleviation Benefits

The approach developed by the U.S. Army Corps of Engineers is sketched here. See the U.S. Water Resources Council's (1983) *Principles and Guidelines* for a summary of accepted procedures. More detail is found in USACE 1988. (The Flood Hazard Research Institute at Middlesex Polytechnic University [Parker et al. 1987; Penning-Rowsell et al. 1992, Chapter 5] presents an approach keyed to the United Kingdom; an updated, combined edition is anticipated.)

The following basic steps compose a simplified process of benefit estimation:

1. Identify *existing* (without-project) conditions:
   - delineate potential affected floodplain area;
   - determine floodplain characteristics (structures, infrastructure, etc);
   - determine expected flood damages for existing floodplain conditions.

2. Identify *future* without-project conditions:
   - forecast future activities, structures, and land uses in the affected floodplain area;
   - estimate expected future (without-project) flood damages for each year of planned project life.

3. Identify future with-project conditions:
   - forecast future with-project activities, structures, and land uses in the affected floodplain area;
   - estimate future (*with-project*) flood damages over project life.

4. Compute estimated benefits (expected flood damages *with* versus *without* project).

8.3.4 Estimating Flood Alleviation Benefits in Urban Settings

The greatest benefit of flood alleviation is reduced damage from incursion of floodwater into structures. Physical damage includes damage to residences, buildings, and their contents, including loss of furniture, equipment, and, in the case of commercial and manufacturing entities, raw materials. It also includes damage to infrastructure such as streets, highways, and utilities. Nonphysical damage is disruption of normal activities that cannot be recaptured:

- income losses (lost wages or profits);
- emergency costs, such as evacuation, flood-fighting, cleanup costs, and added expense of public safety (police, fire, and military patrol); and
- the cost of temporary relocation due to forced evacuation, short-term moving of people, food, and transportation.

Expected annual damages are usually estimated by a team of hydrologic and hydraulic (H and H) engineers together with economists. Three basic relationships are the foundation of the process of estimating flood damage alleviation benefits; these three are used to derive a fourth relationship. (See Figure 8-3.) These relationships are each estimated for the "with" and "without" project scenario. Two of the four basic relationships are derived by the H and H team. The first, represented in the lower left quadrant of Figure 8-3 is the *discharge-frequency* (or *discharge-probability*) function, which describes the probabilities of occurrence of various discharges (cubic meters or cubic feet per second) above flood stage. A low discharge has a higher frequency than a high discharge. Thus, the curve relating frequency to discharge (with discharge on the horizontal axis and frequency on the vertical axis) slopes downward to the right.

The second relationship relates discharge to elevation of water surface above flood stage, the *stage-discharge* (or *rating*) curve. Elevation (stage) increases with discharge, usually at a decreasing rate. The stage-discharge curve is shown in the upper left quadrant of Figure 8-3.

The third relationship is developed mainly by economists. The *stage-damage function* expresses how much monetary damages are expected at any flood stage. As depicted in the upper right quadrant of Figure 8-3, as flood elevation rises, damages are expected to increase (at an increasing rate).

The fourth relationship, the *damage-frequency* function, is shown in the lower right quadrant of Figure 8-3. It is derived by combining the other three. The stage-damage and stage-discharge functions are first combined to estimate the direct recurring damages as a function of discharge. Then this relationship is combined with discharge-frequency to yield a relationship which expresses damages as a function of frequency of occurrence. Low damages occur with higher frequency than high damages. The area under this last curve (the integral of the probability function) is the mathematical expectation of damage.

Next, to estimate benefits of a proposed flood alleviation intervention (which may be structural or nonstructural), the above process is repeated for expected hydrologic and damage conditions with the project in place

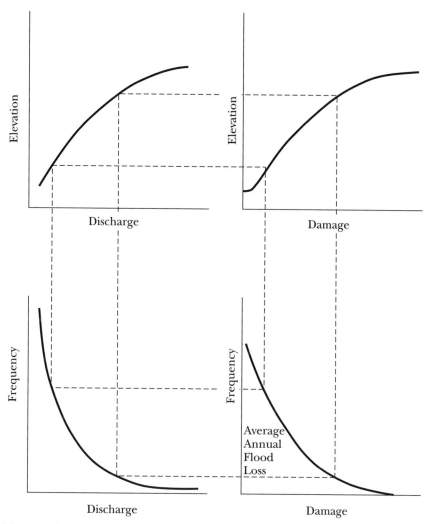

Figure 8-3. Conceptualizing the Computation of Annual Economic Damages from Floods

(see Figure 8-4). Suppose that the proposal is for increased reservoir storage. Hydrologists estimate the influence of an increase in storage on flood flows with the probability of various peak discharges. To derive the with-project probability damage function, this effect is tracked through the other relationships. The with-project damage-frequency relationship will presumably shift so that the damages are lower at any given probability of occurrence.

Deriving the estimate of benefit is the final step. The integral (area under) the new curve is determined as before. Then the difference between the two integrals (as shown in Figure 8-4) is the measure of the

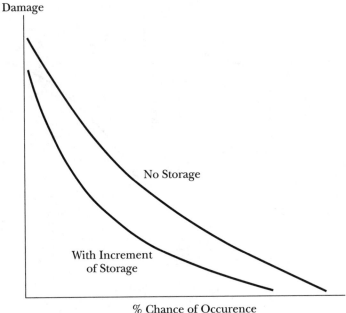

Figure 8-4. Computation of Floods Risk Reduction Benefits

benefit: the expected value of damage reduction linked to the proposed increment of storage. The floodplain resident's WTP is this expected value of damages avoided from the proposed project.

The incremental value of potential increases in storage capacity is determined by a series of calculations as shown above, changing the flood stage assumptions incrementally to reflect the change in storage. These calculations will facilitate tracing out a curve mapping the expected value of benefits to the increments of storage. This relationship would be expected to exhibit diminishing marginal returns, increasing at a decreasing rate.

The economist on the feasibility study team is designated to estimate the monetary value of damages for both the with- and without-project situations. This assignment can be broken down into seven steps:

1. *Prepare an inventory of the existing floodplain.*
   Survey floodplain properties as the basis for estimating potential damages from flood events. Record the number and types of structures in the floodplain, their susceptibility to damage, and the estimated value of the structures and their contents; in particular, note their elevation. Classify structures as residential, industrial, or commercial. Because a complete enumeration is expensive and time-consuming, a statistical sampling procedure is usually employed, but on-the-spot inspections of larger commercial and industrial properties are usually required.

2. *Establish depth-damage relationships.*

   Many factors influence the extent of flood damages, and no single quantitative relationship is available to predict in monetary terms the effects of floods on structures. A survey of a sample of businesses and homeowners to determine damages incurred in a recent flood can be extrapolated for floods above and below the reference flood. Because of the time and expense involved, it is more common to develop stage-damage data for a given floodplain by using generalized data embedded in a computer program, although the result is probably less accurate.

3. *Calculate damage-frequency relationships.*

   The probability of given level of flood damage is obtained from joint solution of the stage-discharge, discharge-frequency, and stage-damage relationships. Damage-frequency relationships are often organized by damage category and river reach. Within reach, they may be expressed according to land use groupings: residential, commercial, industrial, utilities, transportation, and public uses.

4. *Determine expected annual damages.*

   The expected annual damage is defined as the expected value of flood loss in any given year. It is calculated by finding the integral under the damage-frequency function. Computer programs are available to perform these calculations.

5. *Estimate flood damages in the without-project scenario.*

   To complete the estimate of flood damages for the without-project scenario, future physical and socioeconomic conditions in the affected area must be estimated. Establish an economic and demographic data base. Forecast future growth in the population and the regional economy for several points in time. 10-year intervals up to 50 years are typical. The U.S. Army Corps of Engineers bases its projections on those developed by the Office of Business Economics, U.S. Department of Commerce. Derive changes in land use in the project area. Within each land use category, predict the number and elevation of physical units, their future values, and their susceptibility to floods.

6. *Estimate flood damages for the with-project scenario.*

   This process is similar to step 5, but based on a different set of assumptions.

7. *Calculate benefits.*

   Find the differences in expected damages between the with-project and without-project scenarios. Estimate the effect of the project on the probability of various peak discharges; presumably the intervention will reduce the probability of higher discharges. This effect is traced through the other hydrologic relationships to the damage-frequency relationship. Once again, the integral under the damage frequency relationship is derived. The difference between the two integrals is then the measure of the expected value of the benefit from the project.

This procedure can absorb considerable time and resources, as well as calling for specialized analytic and quantitative skills. However, computer software to calculate standardized damage estimates can reduce the effort.

8.3.5 Estimating Agricultural Damages Avoided

Flood risk reduction benefits in rural and agricultural settings are estimated using a similar methodology to measure the damages avoided to agricultural crop production.

Estimating Crop Damages Avoided. In evaluating flood risk reduction programs, crop production must be estimated and valued for both the with- and without-project scenarios. The U.S. Army Corps of Engineers *Procedures Manual: Agricultural Flood Damages* (1987) breaks the process down into three steps:

1. For the area affected by the project plan, identify current land use and cropping patterns. Then forecast land use for both the with-project and without-project scenarios over the relevant planning horizon. For simplicity and convenience, divide the project area into subareas called damage reaches, each of which is represented by average conditions for the with- and without-project scenarios. The subareas should be reasonably homogeneous in soil capability, and existing and expected cropping patterns. Data-reporting boundaries (such as county or district subdivisions) may influence the choice of damage reaches, as may the location of stream gauges and major watershed subdivisions (tributary boundaries). The analyses for the subareas are then aggregated to the total project area.

2. Once the damage reaches are decided upon, forecast land use and cropping patterns (the area devoted to the various crops produced in the study area) for the with- and without-project scenarios. A land use study ascertains the amount of land devoted to various farm uses such as crops, pastures, and forests, according to elevation. Protection from inundation may permit farmers to switch from low-valued enterprises such as livestock pasture to higher-valued crops, a process called intensification. But use caution to avoid injudiciously projecting changes to higher-valued crops and thereby inflating forecasts of expected benefits of flood risk reduction proposals.

3. Determine the benefits of the reduced risk of flooding on a crop-by-crop basis. In the simpler case, there is no change in cropping pattern between the with-project and the without-project scenarios. *Damage reduction benefits* accrue from increased yields or reduced production costs. They are calculated as the change in net income between the with-

plan and without-plan scenarios. If cropping patterns do change in the with-project scenario, *intensification benefits* result, as the new crops will likely yield higher gross and net income than the crops grown in the without-project case.

Estimation of damage reduction and intensification benefits will call for a detailed understanding of agricultural production, because the damages avoided will depend on when in the annual production cycle the inundation occurs and how deep the flood is. The budgeting procedure thus considers production costs and yield impacts at various stages of the crop cycle. The damage estimate can be based on a relationship called a *crop-loss function*, which expresses the percentage loss in net income for each day of the year. From this relationship, the maximum potential loss for any given date can be found. The loss would be zero from the year's beginning until planting, then increase to a maximum toward normal harvest date, then fall back to zero after the end of harvest season. If the flood occurs early in the production season, replanting may be possible. Such events impose lower yields and greater costs than a flood-free season. A flood so late that replanting is impossible will cause far greater losses.

Estimating Non-Crop Agricultural Damages Avoided. Damages other than to agricultural crops include impacts on "other agricultural properties" including homes, farm buildings, fences, and farm equipment. Flooding of access roads may affect lands that are not themselves flooded. Livestock production may suffer increased cost of feeds when pastures are flooded, heightened susceptibility to diseases, or even drowning. "Off-site sediment reduction" refers to the cost of removing flood-deposited sediment from roads, bridges, or drainage systems in rural areas (see USACE 1987, Chapter VIII).

8.3.6 Other Research on Flood Alleviation Benefits

Beyond governmental evaluations, the literature contains few studies of flood damage alleviation benefits (see Section 8.3.3). Shabman (1994) provides probably the first comparison of alternative techniques for measuring flood risk reduction benefits for the same locality. Estimates using PDA, land price analysis, and contingent valuation methods were each computed for a floodplain in Roanoke, Virginia. Benefit estimates varied significantly across techniques; in particular, the CVM approach yielded willingness to pay estimates which did not systematically increase with an increasing probability of inundation. This may be another instance of the difficulty that contingent valuation researchers face in communicating potential risks to lay respondents.

Land Value and Hedonic Property Value Methods. A number of hedonic property value studies have been published on the effect of location relative to a floodplain on housing values. Other studies have investigated the effect of actual flood events on housing values. The theoretical underpinning of hedonic methods suggest that this approach is of limited value in estimating potential damages avoided for assessments of flood risk reduction proposals. The method assumes that buyers and sellers recognize the actual physical differences in the level of characteristics to be valued. Although market values for riparian property may be to some degree influenced by a history of inundation, it seems unlikely that the real property market can accurately reflect risk, particularly those events embodying a small probability of large damages that are the most significant for public policy.

Several recent hedonic investigations into floodplain property values in the United States have shown that housing prices are negatively linked to the cost of mandatory federal flood insurance. Harrison et al. (2001) analyzed almost 30,000 residential property transactions over an 18-year period in the county surrounding Gainesville, Florida. They found that after controlling for attributes of residence location, size, and age, homes within the 100-year flood zone sold for significantly less than equivalent homes outside the floodplain. Part of this difference was attributed to direct perception of the flood risk itself and part to the present (discounted) value of future flood insurance premiums. Schultz and Fridgen (2001) employed the hedonic property value method to study the effect of floodplain location on housing values in Fargo, North Dakota and Moorhead, Minnesota, using data from over 4000 sales in 1995–1998. Location on the 100-year floodplain lowered house prices by about $10,000, or about 10%, after controlling for structural, neighborhood, and environmental variables. Schultz and Frigden further conclude that the measured reduction in house prices closely reflects the present value of the stream of mandatory flood insurance premiums discounted over 20 years at the average historical mortgage rate of 7.6%. This seems to indicate that the real estate market accurately reflects the present value of costs of flood insurance, but further implies that home purchasers do not contemplate any significant additional financial risks to living on the 100-year floodplain. A second model, isolating those home sales that occurred following a severe 1997 flood, did show a slight decrease in prices of houses on the 100-year floodplain. Shultz and Frigden also found that location on the 500-year floodplain had a positive and statistically significant net effect on house values. The authors observe that unlike occupants of the 100-year floodplain, home sellers on the 500-year floodplain are not required to disclose that fact to potential buyers or to carry flood insurance.

These findings imply that house price differentials across floodplains mainly reflect the cost of mandatory federal insurance (and thus, incidentally, behave in conformance with the neoclassical model). But hedonic methods provide little further information on market participants' perception of expected flood damages beyond that already embedded in the flood insurance premiums. Under United States conditions of mandatory flood insurance, hedonic property value studies seem to hold limited prospect for estimating benefits of public flood risk reduction.

8.3.7 Concluding Remarks on Measuring Flood Risk Reduction Benefits

The property damage avoided method, which reflects the present value of real (inflation-free) expected property damages avoided by the project or policy, has been the principal means of estimating urban flood risk reduction benefits. Shabman (1994) and other writers criticize the PDA method for ignoring nonproperty effects such as individual and community disruption, medical expenses, productivity losses, and preflood anxiety. James (1994) further argues that the conventional approach is incomplete in the case of Bangladesh and other localities where inundation of homes and farms is a frequent fact of life. In his view, a focus on property damages ignores the point that the primary benefits of flood damage reduction policies in such countries are "the intangible values of better lives for people..."

Other valuation issues arise in assigning values to the potential loss of life and to psychological effects of flood events. Although deaths from floods are a major risk for few of the world's population, the topic of valuing risks to life cannot be ignored in economic evaluations of flood risk reduction. The issue is controversial, because many criticize the implication that life can be valued as if it were a commodity. Risk analysts acknowledge that society is unwilling to place a monetary value on saving an individual from certain death. However, society does value safety, or conversely, *reductions in risks* to life. This point is exemplified in public decisions which trade off public safety (from such risks as pollution, hazardous wastes, highway or airline transportation, and floods) against limited budget allocations. Although increased government spending might further reduce risks, given the limitations of budgets and the presence of alternative uses for scarce public funds, no feasible policies can be expected to reduce the risk of loss of life to zero. A number of nonmarket approaches can be used to infer the value society places on reducing risks to life and health (e.g. Viscusi 2001). Economic valuation of flood risk reduction would be rewarded by more attention from the natural resource economics research community.

CHAPTER
9

Conclusions

The analysis presented in this book demonstrates several key points. First, rather than valuing water *per se,* resource and environmental economists performing nonmarket valuations actually develop monetary measures of individuals' preferences for consequences of policy proposals or events. Such consequences might be improved water supply or reliability for off-stream water users. Others include water's role as public goods, such as environmental or habitat preservation. Likewise, economists develop monetary measures of the gains in well-being that result from policies that reduce water degradation or those that address excessive or inadequate water supply. Using money as the measuring rod for valuing inputs and outputs enables economists to compare benefits with money costs of investments or with forgone values in alternative uses.

Valuation results therefore depend on which specific water services are being valued, as well as where and why the valuation exercise is being conducted. Values tend to differ according to which commodity or environmental use is being valued. Valuations are also affected by characteristics of the study region: climatic factors and water quality cause variance in results on the supply side, as do population, income, and the structure of the regional economy on the demand side. Finally, the results of a valuation effort vary according to the policy context within which the valuation takes place. Estimated values vary, other factors equal, according to whether an at-site or an at-source value is desired, whether a private or a social value is needed, whether a long-run or a short-run estimate is intended, and whether the value is expressed as a per-period (usually annual) or capitalized asset value.

Valuation methods can be divided into two broad categories. Inductive methods use statistical techniques to infer economic values from data on observed human behavior. Deductive approaches derive estimated willingness to pay from constructed models that hypothesize human motivations together with measured or predicted conditions of production or consumption. Deductive models have advantages of simplicity, flexibility, and the ability to analyze hypothesized future policy options. They can, in principle, incorporate alternative assumptions about prices, interest rates, and production technology, permitting tests of the sensitivity of assumptions to unknown future conditions. Many analysts, however, prefer to determine economic benefits using inductive techniques, which are based on observations of economic behavior in actual situations. In some cases, inductive models can be used to analyze previous policies and natural experiments. Then again, inductive models have limits too: evaluating hypothesized policies may involve assumptions that lie outside the range of available historical observations.

As we have seen, an analyst's judgment remains important in determining results at a number of points in the process. First, judgment takes place when the model is formulated. For both deductive and inductive methods, significant choices must be made concerning which variables will be included and what functional form of production and demand relationships will be assumed. In deductive models, empirical parameters such as interest rates, production functions, and price levels are also critical. For inductive methods, the characteristics of the data set—for example, the number of observations, or whether the sample approximates randomness—are important factors in determining how useful the results will be. Refinement of techniques needs to continue, particularly in the sector of the producers' good, to resolve the apparent divergence between estimates derived by inductive and deductive methods.

Estimating the economic values and benefits of water-related policies is seldom an easy task. Analysis of demand-side issues in water policy decisions requires a level of resources, specialized skills, and training equal to that of our colleagues in the engineering and hydrologic disciplines who study supply-side issues. Effective measurement of water values calls for expertise in application of all the tools of the applied economist's trade: data collection, optimization modeling, statistical analysis, research reporting, and many more. Our task is to exercise the necessary skill and spend the time and resources required to make use of these tools. In doing so, we can derive conceptually consistent and empirically valid measures of the value of water and continue to enhance our contribution to economically efficient water resource management.

References

Abdalla, C.W., B.A. Roach, and D.J. Epp. 1992. Valuing Environmental Quality Changes Using Averting Expenditures: An Application to Groundwater Contamination. *Land Economics* 68(2): 163–169.

Adamowicz, W.L., J.J. Louviere, and M. Williams. 1994. Combining Revealed and Stated Preference Methods for Valuing Environmental Amenities. *Journal of Environmental Economics and Management* 26(2): 271–292.

Adams, R.M., and S.H. Cho. 1998. Agriculture and Endangered Species: An Analysis of Tradeoffs in the Klamath Basin, Oregon. *Water Resources Research* 34(10): 2741–2749.

Ahearn, Mary C., and U. Vasavada (eds.). 1992. *Costs and Returns for Agricultural Commodities: Advances in Concepts and Measurement.* Boulder, CO: Westview Press.

Albery, A.C. 1968. Forecasting Demand for Instream Uses. In *Forecasting the Demands for Water,* edited by W.R.D. Sewell and Blair T. Bower. Ottawa, Canada: Department of Engineering, Mines, and Resources.

Altaf, M.A., D. Whittington, and V.K. Smith. 1993. Rethinking Rural Water Supply Policy in the Punjab, Pakistan. *Water Resources Research* 29(7): 1943–1954.

American Agricultural Economics Association (AAEA) Task Force on Commodity Costs and Returns. 1998. *Commodity Costs and Returns Estimation Handbook.* Ames, IA: Iowa State University Press.

Anderson, Elizabeth. 1993. *Value in Ethics and Economics.* Cambridge, MA: Harvard University Press.

Anderson, R.L. 1961. The Irrigation Water Rental Market: A Case Study. *Agricultural Economics Research* 8: 54–58

———. 1968. A Simulation Program to Establish Optimum Crop Patterns on Irrigated Farms Based on Pre-Season Estimates of Water Supply. *American Journal of Agricultural Economics* 50: 1586–1590.

Anderson, Terry L., and D.R. Leal. 1990. *Free Market Environmentalism.* Boulder, CO: Westview Press.

Arbues, F.M., A. Garcia-Valinas, and R. Martinez-Espineira. 2003. Estimation of Residential Water Demand: A State-of-the-Art Review. *Journal of Socio-Economics* 32: 81–102.

Arrow, Kenneth J., J.R. Solow, P.R. Portney, E.E. Leamer, R. Radner and H. Schuman. 1993. Report of the NOAA Panel on Contingent Valuation. *Federal Register* 58: 4601–4614.

Ayer, H.W., J. Prentzel, and P. Hoyt. 1983. *Crop-Water Production Functions and Economic Implications for Washington.* Staff Report AGES 830314. Washington, DC: U.S. Department of Agriculture.

Babin, F., C. Willis, and P. Allen. 1982. Estimation of Substitution Possibilities between Water and Other Production Inputs. *American Journal of Agricultural Economics* 64(1): 148–151.

Barry, Peter J., John A. Hopkin, and C.B. Baker. 1995. *Financial Management in Agriculture,* 5th ed. Danville, IL: Interstate Press.

Bartik, T. 1988. Evaluating the Benefits of Non-Marginal Reductions in Pollution Using Information on Defensive Expenditures. *Journal of Environmental Economics and Management* 15(1): 111–127.

Bash, P.K., and R.A. Young. 1993. *The Role of the South Platte Tributary Aquifer in Northeastern Colorado Irrigated Agriculture: Results of a Survey.* Completion Report No. 173. Fort Collins, CO: Colorado Water Resources Research Institute.

Bateman, Ian J., and Kenneth J. Willis (eds.). 1999. *Valuing Environmental Preferences: Theory and Practice of the Contingent Valuation Method in the US, EU, and Developing Countries.* Oxford: Oxford University Press.

Bateman, Ian J., Richard T. Carson, and W. Michael Hanemann. 2002. *Economic Valuation With Stated Preference Techniques: A Manual.* Northampton, MA: Edward Elgar Publishing.

Baumol, William J. 1993. *Entrepreneurship, Management and the Structure of Payoffs.* Cambridge, MA: MIT Press.

Becker, Gary. 1993. Nobel Lecture: The Economic Way of Looking at Behavior. *Journal of Political Economy* 101(3): 385–409.

Bell, Clive, Peter Hazell, and Roger Slade. 1982. *Project Evaluation in Regional Perspective: A Study of an Irrigation Project in Northwest Malaysia.* Baltimore, MD: Johns Hopkins University Press for the World Bank.

Bennett, J., and V. Adamowicz. 2001. Some Fundamentals of Environmental Choice Modeling. In *The Choice Modeling Approach to Environmental Valuation,* edited by Jeff Bennett and Russell Blamey. Northamption, MA: Edward Elgar Publishing.

Bennett, Jeff, and Russell Blamey (eds.). 2001. *The Choice Modeling Approach to Environmental Valuation.* Northamption, MA: Edward Elgar Publishing.

Berck, P., S. Robinson, and G. Goldman. 1991. The Use of Computable General Equilibrium Models to Assess Water Policies. In *The Economics and Management of Water and Drainage in Agriculture,* edited by A. Dinar and D. Zilberman. Boston, MA: Kluwer Academic Publishers.

Berck, P., J. Geoghegen, and S. Stohs. 2000. A Strong Test of the von Liebig Hypothesis. *American Journal of Agricultural Economics* 82(4): 948–595.

Bergman, H., and J.-M. Boussard. 1976. *Guide to Economic Evaluation of Irrigation Projects (Revised Version).* Paris: OECD.

Bergstrom, J.C., and P. De Civita. 1999. Status of Benefits Transfer in the United States and Canada: A Review. *Canadian Journal of Agricultural Economics* 47: 79–87.

Bergstrom, John C., Kevin C. Boyle, and Gregory L. Poe (eds.). 2001. *The Economic Value of Water Quality.* Northampton, MA: Edward Elgar Publishing.

Bernardo. D.J., N.K. Whittlesey, K.E. Saxton, and D.L. Bassett. 1987. An Irrigation Model for Managing Limited Water Supplies. *Western Journal of Agricultural Economics* 12(1): 164–173.

Billings, R.B., and D. Agthe. 1980. Price Elasticities for Water: A Case Study of Increasing Block Rates. *Land Economics* 56(1): 73–84.

Bishop, R.C., and T.A. Heberlein. 1979. Measuring Values of Extra-Market Goods: Are Indirect Measures Biased? *American Journal of Agricultural Economics* 61(5): 926–930.

Bishop, R.C., Patricia A. Champ, and Thomas C. Brown. 1997. Measuring Non-Use Values: Theory and Application. In *Determining the Value of Non-Marketed Goods,* edited by Raymond J. Kopp, W.W. Pommerehne, and N. Schwartz. Boston, MA: Kluwer Academic Publishers.

Blaug, Mark. 1997. *Economic Theory in Retrospect.* 5th ed. Cambridge: Cambridge University Press.

Boardman, Anthony E., David H. Greenberg, Aidan R. Vining, and David. L. Weimer. 2001. *Cost–Benefit Analysis: Concepts and Practice.* 2nd ed. Upper Saddle River, NJ: Prentice-Hall, Inc.

Bockstael, N.E., I. Strand, and W.M. Hanemann. 1987. Time and the Recreational Demand Model. *American Journal of Agricultural Economics.* 69(2): 293–302.

Bockstael, N.E., and K.A. McConnell. 1999. The Behavioral Basis of Non-Market Valuation. In *Valuing Recreation and the Environment: Revealed Preference Methods in Theory and Practice,* edited by Joseph A. Herriges and Catherine L. Herriges. Northampton, MA: Edward Elgar Publishing.

Boggess W., R. Lacewell, and D. Zilberman. 1993. Economics of Water Use in Agriculture. In *Agricultural and Environmental Resource Economics,* edited by G. A. Carlson, D. Zilberman, and J. A. Miranowski. New York: Oxford University Press, 319–372.

Booker, J.F. 1995. Hydrologic and Economic Impacts of Drought under Alternative Policy Responses. *Water Resources Bulletin* 31(5): 889–906.

Booker, J.F., and R.A. Young. 1994. Modeling Intrastate and Interstate Markets for Colorado River Water Resources. *Journal of Environmental Economics and Management* 26(1): 66–87.

Booker, J.F., and B.G. Colby. 1995. Competing Water Uses in the Southwest: Valuing Drought Damages. *Water Resources Bulletin* 31(5): 877–888.

Bouhia, Hynd. 2001. *Water in the Macro Economy: Integrating Economics and Engineering into an Analytical Model.* Burlington, VT: Ashgate.

Boulding, K.E. 1980. The Implications of Improved Water Policy. In *Western Water Resources: Coming Problems and Policy Alternatives,* edited by Marvin Duncan. Boulder, CO: Westview Press.

Bowen, R.L., and R.A. Young. 1986. Appraising Alternatives for Allocating and Cost Recovery for Irrigation Water in Egypt. *Agricultural Economics* 1(1): 35–52.

Boyle, K.J. 2003. Contingent Valuation in Practice. In *A Primer on Nonmarket Valuation,* edited by Patricia A. Champ, Kevin J. Boyle, and Thomas C. Brown. Dordrecht: Kluwer Academic Publishers.

Boyle, K.J., S.R. Lawson, and H.J. Michael. 1998. *Lakefront Property Owners' Economic Demand for Water Clarity in Maine Lakes.* Miscellaneous Report 410. Orono, ME: Maine Agricultural Experiment Station.

Brandao, A.S.P., and G.C. de Rezende. 1990. The Behavior of Land Prices and Land Rents in Brazil. In *Agriculture and Governments in an Interdependent World,* edited by Allen Maunder and Alberto Valdez. Aldershot, UK: Dartmouth Publishing.

Brent, Robert J., 1998. *Cost–Benefit Analysis for Developing Countries.* Northampton, MA: Edward Elgar Publishing.

Bromley, Daniel W. 1991. *Environment and Economy: Property Rights and Public Policy.* Cambridge, MA: B. Blackwell.

Bronfenbrenner, Martin. 1971. *Income Distribution Theory.* Chicago: Aldine-Atherton.

Brown, M.L. 1979. *Farm Budgets: From Farm Income Analysis to Agricultural Project Analysis.* Baltimore, MD: Johns Hopkins University Press.

Brown, T.C., P. Champ, R. Bishop, and D. McCollum. 1996. Which Response Format Reveals the Truth About Donations to a Public Good? *Land Economics* 72: 152–166.

Buchanan, James M. 1977. *Freedom in Constitutional Contract.* College Station, TX: Texas A&M University Press.

Bunch, J. 2004. Thirsty Aurora Inks $5.5 Million Water Pact. *Denver Post.* March 9, B1.

Burt, O.R. 1964. Economics of Conjunctive Use of Ground and Surface Water. *Hilgardia* 36(2): 1–111.

———. 1992. Allocation of Capital Costs in Enterprise Budgets. In *Costs and Returns for Agricultural Commodities: Advances in Concepts and Measurement,* edited by M.C. Ahearn and U. Vasavada. Boulder, CO: Westview Press, 259–272.

Burt, O.R., and D. Brewer. 1971. Estimation of Net Social Benefits from Outdoor Recreation. *Econometrica* 39: 813–827.

Bush, D.B., and W.E. Martin. 1986. *Potential Costs and Benefits to Arizona Agriculture of the Central Arizona Project.* Technical Bulletin 254. Tucson, AZ: University of Arizona Agricultural Experiment Station.

Cardon, G.E., and J. Letey. 1992. Soil-Based Irrigation and Salinity Management Model: II. Water and Solute Movement Calculations. *Soil Science Society of America Journal* 56: 1887–1892.

Carson, R.T. 1991. Constructed Markets. In *Measuring the Demand for Environmental Quality,* edited by J.B. Braden and C.D. Kolstad. Amsterdam: Elsevier Science Publishers.

Carson, R.T. 1997. Contingent Valuation Surveys and Tests of Insensitivity to Scope. In *Determining the Value of Non-Marketed Goods: Economic, Psychological and Policy Relevant Aspects of Contingent Valuation Methods,* edited by Raymond J. Kopp, W. W. Pommerehne, and Norbert Schwartz. Boston, MA: Kluwer Academic Publishers.

Carson, R.T., and R.C. Mitchell. 1987. Economic Value of Reliable Water Supplies for Residential Water Users in the State Water Project Service Area. Contract

Report for Metropolitan Water District of Southern California. Los Angeles, CA: Metropolitan Water District of Southern California.

Carson, R.T., N. Flores, K. Martin, and J.Wright. 1996. Contingent Valuation and Revealed Preference Methodologies: Comparing the Estimates for Quasi-Public Goods. *Land Economics* 72: 80–99.

Carson, R.T., N.E. Flores, and R.C. Mitchell. 1999. The Theory and Measurement of Passive-Use Value. In *Valuing Environmental Preferences,* edited by Ian J. Bateman and Kenneth G. Willis. Oxford: Oxford University Press.

Casley, D.J., and D.A. Lury. 1987. *Data Collection in Developing Countries.* 2nd ed. Oxford: Oxford University Press.

Champ, Patricia A., Kevin J. Boyle, and Thomas C. Brown (eds.). 2003. *A Primer on Nonmarket Valuation.* Dordrecht: Kluwer Academic Publishers.

Chaudhry, M.A. and R.A. Young. 1989. Valuing Irrigation Water in Punjab Province, Pakistan: A Linear Programming Approach. *Water Resources Bulletin* 25(5): 1055–1061.

Cicchetti, C., V.K. Smith, and J. Carson. 1975. Economic Analysis of Water Resource Investments and Regional Economic Growth. *Water Resources Research* 11: 1–6.

Ciriacy-Wantrup, S.V. 1947. Capital Returns from Soil Conservation Practices. *Journal of Farm Economics* 29: 1181–1196.

Clark, J.S., M. Fulton, and J.T. Scott, Jr. 1993. The Inconsistency of Land Values, Land Rents and Capitalization Formulas. *American Journal of Agricultural Economics* 75: 147–155.

Colby, B.C., K. Crandall, and D. Bush. 1993. Water Rights Transactions: Market Values and Price Dispersion. *Water Resources Research* 29(6): 1565–1572.

Colby, B.C., and S. Wishart, 2002. *Riparian Areas Generate Property Value Premium for Landowners.* Tucson: University of Arizona.

Crouter, J. 1987. Hedonic Estimation Applied to a Water Rights Market. *Land Economics* 63(3): 259–269.

Cummings, R.G., D.S. Brookshire, and W.D. Schulze. 1986. *Valuing Environmental Goods: A State of the Arts Assessment of the Contingent Valuation Method.* Totawa, NJ: Rowman and Allanheld Publishers.

Cummings, R.G., P.T. Ganderton, and T. McGuckin. 1994. Substitution Effects in Contingent Valuation Estimates. *American Journal of Agricultural Economics* 76(2): 205–214.

Cummings, R.G., and G.W. Harrison. 1995. The Measurement and Decomposition of Non-Use Values: A Critical Review. *Environmental and Resource Economics* 5(3): 225–248.

Cummings, R.G., S. Elliot, and G.W. Harrison. 1997. Are Hypothetical Referenda Incentive-Compatible? *Journal of Political Economy* 105(3): 609–21.

Cummings, R.G., and L.O. Taylor. 1999. Unbiased Value Estimates for Environmental Goods: A Cheap Talk Design for the Contingent Valuation Method. *American Economic Review* 89(3): 649–65.

Cummings, R.G., and L.O. Taylor. 2001. Experimental Economics in Natural Resource and Environmental Management. In *The International Yearbook of Environmental and Resource Economics 2001/2002,* edited by Henk Folmer and Tom Tietenberg. Northampton, MA: Edward Elgar Publishing, 123–149.

Dalhuisen, J.M., R. Florax, H. de Groot, and P. Nijkamp. 2003. Price and Income Elasticities of Residential Water Demand: A Meta-Analysis. *Land Economics* 79(2): 292–308.

d'Arge, R., and J. Shogren. 1989. Nonmarket Asset Prices: A Comparison of Three Valuation Approaches. In *Valuation Methods and Policy-Making in Environmental Economics*, edited by H. Folmer and E. van Ierland. Amsterdam: Elsevier.

Daubert, J.T., and R.A. Young. 1981. Recreational Demand for Maintaining Instream Flows: A Contingent Valuation Approach. *American Journal of Agricultural Economics* 63(4): 666–676.

Davis, R.K. 1963. Recreation Planning as an Economic Problem. *Natural Resources Journal* 3: 239–49.

De Rooy, J. 1974. The Price Responsiveness of Industrial Demand for Water. *Water Resources Research* 10(3): 403–406.

Diamond, P.A., and J.A. Hausman. 1994. Contingent Valuation: Is Some Number Better than No Number? *Journal of Economics Perspectives* 8(4): 45–64.

Dickie, M. 2003. Defensive Behavior and Damage Cost Methods. In *A Primer on Nonmarket Valuation*, edited by Patricia A. Champ, K.J. Boyle, and T.C. Brown. Dordrecht: Kluwer Academic Publishers.

Dinar, A., M.B. Campbell, and D. Zilberman. 1992. Adoption of Improved Irrigation and Drainage Reduction Technologies under Limiting Environmental Conditions. *Environmental and Resource Economics* 2(2): 3373–3398.

Dinar, A., and J. Letey. 1996. *Modeling Economic Management and Policy Issues of Water in Irrigated Agriculture.* Westport, CT: Praeger.

Dinar, A., and D. Zilberman (eds.). 1991. *The Economics and Management of Water and Drainage in Agriculture.* Boston, MA: Kluwer Academic Publishers.

Dinar, A., and David Zilberman (eds.). 2002. *Economics of Water Resources: The Contributions of Dan Yaron.* Norwell, MA: Kluwer Academic Publishers.

Dinwiddy, C., and F. Teal. 1996. *Principles of Cost–Benefit Analysis in Developing Countries.* Cambridge: Cambridge University Press.

Dowlatabadi, H., and M. A. Toman. 1991. *Technology Options for Electricity Generation: Economic and Environmental Factors.* Washington, DC: Resources for the Future.

Dudley, N.J. 1988. A Single Decision-Maker Approach to Irrigation Reservoir and Farm-Management Decision-Making. *Water Resources Research* 24(3): 633–640.

Duffield, J.W., C.J. Nehrer, and T.C. Brown. 1992. Recreation Benefits from Instream Flow: Application to Montana's Big Hole and Bitterroot Rivers. *Water Resources Research* 28(9): 2169–2181.

Dupont, D.P., and S. Renzetti. 2001. Water's Role in Manufacturing. *Environmental and Resource Economics* 18(4): 411–432.

Easter, K.W., and R. Hearne. 1995. Water Markets and Decentralized Water Resources Management: International Problems and Opportunities. *Water Resources Bulletin* 31(1): 9–20.

Easter, K. William, Mark W. Rosegrant, and Ariel Dinar (eds.). 1998. *Markets for Water: Potential and Performance.* Boston, MA: Kluwer Academic Publishers.

Easterly, William R. 2001. *The Elusive Quest for Growth: Economists' Adventures and Misadventures in the Tropics.* Cambridge, MA: MIT Press.

Eatwell, J., M. Milgate, and P. Newman (eds.). 1987. *The New Palgrave: A Dictionary of Economics.* 4 vols. New York, NY: Stockton Press.

Eckstein, O. 1958. *Water Resource Development: The Economics of Project Evaluation.* Cambridge, MA: Harvard University Press.

Edwards-Jones, G., B. Davies, and S. Hussain. 2000. *Ecological Economics: An Introduction.* Oxford: Blackwell Science, Ltd.

Espey, M., J. Espey, and W. D. Shaw. 1997. Price Elasticity of Residential Demand for Water: A Meta-Analysis. *Water Resources Research* 33(6): 1369–1374.

Evenson, R.E., C. Pray, and M.W. Rosegrant. 1999. *Agricultural Research and Productivity Growth in India.* Research Report 109. Washington, DC: International Food Policy Research Institute.

Falk, B., and B.-S. Lee. 1998. Fads versus Fundamentals in Farmland Prices. *American Journal of Agricultural Economics* 80(4): 696–707.

Fan, S., P. Hazell, and S. Thorat. 1999. *Linkages Between Government Spending, Growth and Poverty in Rural India.* Research Report 110. Washington, DC: International Food Policy Research Institute.

Fan, S., and P. Hazell. 2001. Returns to Public Investments in the Less-Favored Areas of India and China. *American Journal of Agricultural Economics* 83(5): 1217–1222.

Fan, S., L. Zhang, and X. Zhang. 2002. *Growth, Inequality and Poverty in Rural China: The Role of Public Investments.* Research Report 125. Washington, DC: International Food Policy Research Institute.

Faux, J., and G.M. Perry. 1999. Estimating Irrigation Water Value Using Hedonic Price Analysis: A Case Study of Malheur County, Oregon. *Land Economics* 75(3): 440–452.

Federal Inter-Agency River Basin Committee. 1950. *Proposed Practices for Economic Analysis of River Basin Projects* (the "Green Book"). Washington, DC: US Government Printing Office.

Feenberg, D., and E.S. Mills. 1980. *Measuring the Benefits of Water Pollution Abatement.* New York, NY: Academic Press.

Florax, J.G.M., P. Nijkamp, and K.J. Willis (eds.). 2002. *Comparative Environmental Economic Assessment.* Northampton, MA: Edward Elgar Publishing.

Foster, H.W., and B. Beattie. 1981. On the Specification of Price in Studies of Consumer Demand under Block Price Scheduling. *Land Economics* 57(4): 624–629.

Franklin, D.R., and R.K. Hageman.1984. Cost Sharing with Irrigated Agriculture: Promise versus Performance. *Water Resources Research* 20(8): 1047–51.

Freeman, A.M., III. 1966. Adjusted Benefit–Cost Ratios for Six Recent Reclamation Projects. *Journal of Farm Economics* 48(4): 1202–1212.

———. 2002. Environmental Policy Since Earth Day I: What Have We Gained? *Journal of Economics Perspectives* 16(1): 125–146.

———. 2003. *The Measurement of Environmental and Resource Values: Theory and Methods.* 2nd ed. Washington, DC: Resources for the Future.

Friedman, Milton. 1976. *Price Theory.* Chicago, IL: Aldine Publishing Company.

Fuguitt, Diana, and S.J. Wilcox. 1999. *Cost–Benefit Analysis for Public Sector Decision-Makers.* Westport, CT: Quorum Publishers.

Fullerton, H., W.C. Lewis, and J.E. Keith. 1975. *Regional Development: An Econometric Study of the Role of Water Development in Effectuating Population and Income Changes.* Report PRRBE.O89.1. Logan, UT: Water Research Laboratory, Utah State University.

Gabre-Mahdin, E.Z., C.B. Barrett, and P. Dorosh. 2003. Technological Change and Price Effects in Agriculture. MTID Discussion Paper 62. Washington, DC: International Food Policy Research Institute.

Gardner, R.L., and T.A Miller. 1983. Price Behavior in the Water Market in Northeastern Colorado. *Water Resources Bulletin* 19(4): 557–562.

Gardner, R.L., and R.A. Young. 1985. An Economic Evaluation of the Colorado River Salinity Control Program. *Western Journal of Agricultural Economics* 10(1): 1–12.

Gardner, R.L., and R.A. Young. 1988. Assessing Strategies for Control of Irrigation-Induced Salinity in the Colorado River Basin. *American Journal of Agricultural Economics* 70(1): 37–49.

Garrod, Guy, and Kenneth G. Willis. 1999. *Economic Valuation of the Environment: Methods and Case Studies.* Northampton, MA: Edward Elgar Publishing.

Gaudin, S., R.C. Griffin, and R.C. Sickles. 2001. Demand Specification for Municipal Water Management: Evaluation of the Stone-Geary Form. *Land Economics* 77(3): 399–422.

Gibbons, D.C. 1986. *The Economic Value of Water.* Washington, DC: Resources for the Future.

Gittinger, J. Price. 1982. *Economic Analysis of Agricultural Projects.* Baltimore, MD: Johns Hopkins University Press.

Gleick, Peter H. 1998. *The World's Water: The Biennial Report on Freshwater Resources.* Washington, DC: Island Press.

Goodin, R.E. 1992. Ethical Principles for Environmental Protection. In *The Moral Dimensions of Public Policy Choice: Beyond the Market Paradigm,* edited by J.M. Gillroy and M. Wade. Pittsburgh, PA: University of Pittsburgh Press.

Goodman, D.J. 2000. More Reservoirs or Transfers: A Computable General Equilibrium Analysis of Projected Water Shortages in the Arkansas River Basin. *Journal of Agricultural and Resource Economics* 25(2): 698–713.

Gordon, J., R. Chapman, and R. Blamey. 2001. Assessing the Options for the Canberra Water Supply: an Application of Choice Modeling. In *The Choice Modeling Approach to Environmental Valuation,* edited by Jeff Bennett and Russell Blamey. Northampton, MA: Edward Elgar Publishing.

Gray, S. L., and R. A. Young. 1974. The Economic Value of Water for Waste Dilution: Forecasts to 1980. *Journal of the Water Pollution Control Federation* 46(7): 1653–1663.

Griffin, A.H., and W.E. Martin. 1981. Price Elasticities of Water: A Case of Increasing Block Rates: Comment. *Land Economics* 57(2): 266–275.

Griffin, R.C. 1990. Valuing Urban Water Acquisitions. *Water Resources Bulletin* 26(2): 219–225.

Griffin. R.C., and C. Chang. 1991. Seasonality in Community Water Demand. *Western Journal of Agricultural Economics* 16(2): 207–217.

Griffin, R.C., and G.W. Characklis. 2002. Issues and Trends in Texas Water Marketing. *Water Resources Update* 121: 29–33.

Griffin, R.C., and J.W. Mjelde. 2000. Valuing Water Supply Reliability. *American Journal of Agricultural Economics* 82(2): 414–26.

Haab, Timothy C., and Kenneth E. McConnell. 2002. *Valuing Environmental and Natural Resources: The Econometrics of Non-Market Valuation.* Northampton, MA: Edward Elgar Publishing.

Hamilton, J.R., N.K. Whittlesey, and J. Ellis. 1991. Economic Impacts, Value Added and Benefits in Regional Project Analysis. *American Journal of Agricultural Economics* 73(2): 334–44.

Hamilton, J.R., N.K. Whittlesey, and P. Halvorson. 1989. Interruptible Water Markets in the Pacific Northwest. *American Journal of Agricultural Economics* 71(1): 63–75.

Hammack, J., and G.M. Brown, Jr. 1974. *Waterfowl and Wetlands: Toward a Bioeconomic Analysis.* Baltimore: Johns Hopkins University Press.

Hanemann, W.M. 1992. Preface: Notes on the History of Environmental Valuation in the U.S. In *Pricing the Environment: the European Experience,* edited by Stale Navrud. London: Oxford University Press.

———. 1994. Valuing the Environment through Contingent Valuation. *Journal of Economics Perspectives* 8(4): 19–43.

———. 1998. Determinants of Urban Water Use. In *Urban Water Demand Management and Planning,* edited by D.D. Baumann, J.J. Boland, and W. M. Hanemann. New York: McGraw Hill, 31–95.

———. 1999a. The Economic Theory of WTP and WTA. In *Valuing Environmental Preferences,* edited by Ian J. Bateman and Kenneth G. Willis. Oxford: Oxford University Press, 42–96.

———. 1999b. Welfare Analysis with Discrete Choice Models. In *Valuing Recreation and the Environment: Revealed Preference Methods in Theory and Practice,* edited by Joseph A. Herriges and Catherine L. Kling. Northampton, MA: Edward Elgar Publishing.

Hanemann, W.M., and B. Kanninen. 1999. The Statistical Analysis of Discrete-Response CV Data. In *Valuing Environmental Preferences: Theory and Practice of the Contingent Valuation Method in the US, EU, and Developing Countries,* edited by Ian J. Bateman and Kenneth J. Willis. Oxford: Oxford University Press, 302–441.

Harberger, A.C. 1974. *Project Evaluation: Collected Papers.* Chicago, IL: Markham.

Harpman, D.A. 1999. Assessing the Short-run Economic Cost of Environmental Constraints on Hydropower Operations at Glen Canyon Dam. *Land Economics* 75(3): 390–401.

Harrington, W., A.J. Krupnick, and W.O. Spofford, Jr. 1991. *Economics of Episodic Diseases: Benefits of Preventing a Giardiasis Outbreak.* Washington, DC: Resources for the Future.

Harrison, D.M., G.T. Smersh, and A.L. Schwartz, Jr. 2001. The Environmental Determinants of Housing Prices: The Impact of Flood Zone Status. *Journal of Real Estate Research* 21(1): 3–20.

Hartman, L.M., and R.L. Anderson. 1962. Estimating the Value of Irrigation Water from Farm Sales in Northeastern Colorado. *Journal of Farm Economics* 44(1): 207–213.

Hausman, J.A. (ed.). 1993. *Contingent Valuation: A Critical Assessment.* Amsterdam: Elsevier.

Hazell, Peter B.R., and Roger D. Norton. 1986. *Mathematical Programming for Economic Analysis in Agriculture.* New York, NY: Macmillan Publishing Co.

Heady, Earl O. 1952. *Economics of Agricultural Production and Resource Use.* New York, NY: Prentice-Hall.

Heady, Earl O., and J.L. Dillon. 1969. *Agricultural Production Functions.* Ames, IA: Iowa State University Press.

Hedges, T.R. 1963. *Farm Management Decisions.* Englewood Cliffs, NJ: Prentice-Hall.

Hellerstein, D. 1995. Welfare Estimation Using Aggregate and Individual Observation Models. *American Journal of Agricultural Economics* 77(3): 620–630.

Herfindahl, O.C., and A.V. Kneese. 1974. *Economic Theory of Natural Resources.* Columbus, OH: Merrill Publishing Co.

Herriges, Joseph A., and Catherine L. Kling (eds.). 1999. *Valuing Recreation and the Environment: Revealed Preference Methods in Theory and Practice.* Northampton, MA: Edward Elgar Publishing.

Hewitt, J.A., and W.M. Hanemann. 1995. A Discrete/Continuous Approach to Residential Water Demand under Block Rate Pricing. *Land Economics* 71(2): 173–180.

Hexem, R.W., and E.O. Heady. 1978. *Water Production Functions for Irrigated Agriculture.* Ames, IA: Iowa State University Press.

Hillel, Daniel. 2000. *Salinity Management for Sustainable Irrigation.* Washington, DC: World Bank.

Hoehn, J.P., and D.J. Krieger. 2000. An Economic Analysis of Water and Wastewater Investments in Cairo, Egypt. *Evaluation Review* 24(6): 579–608.

Holland, S.P., and M.R. Moore. 2003. Cadillac Desert Revisited: Property Rights, Public Policy and Water Resource Depletion. *Journal of Environmental Economics and Management* 46(1): 131–155.

Holmes, T.P., and W.L. Adamowicz. 2003. Attribute-Based Methods. In *A Primer on Nonmarket Valuation,* edited by Patricia A. Champ, K.J. Boyle, and T.C. Brown. Dordrecht: Kluwer Academic Publishers.

Horowitz, John K., and Kenneth McConnell. 2002. A Review of WTA/WTP Studies. *Journal of Environmental Economics and Management* 44(3): 426–447.

Houston, J.E. Jr., and N.K. Whittlesey. 1986. Modeling Agricultural Water Markets for Hydropower Production in the Pacific Northwest. *Western Journal of Agricultural Economics* 11(2): 221–231.

Howe, C.W. 1971a. The Role of Technological Change in Municipal Water Demand. In *The Impacts of Technological Changes, Public Policies and Changing Market Conditions on the Water Use Patterns in Selected Sectors of the U.S. Economy, 1979–1990,* prepared by Charles W. Howe, C.S. Russell, and R.A. Young for the U.S. National Water Commission. Report No. NWC-EES: 71-001. Washington, DC: Resources for the Future.

———. 1971b. *Benefit–Cost Analysis for Water System Planning.* Water Resources Monograph No. 2. Washington, DC: American Geophysical Union.

———. 1976. Effects of Economic Growth on Economic Development: the Conditions for Success. *Natural Resources Journal* 6: 939–956.

———. 1982. The Impact of Price on Residential Water Demand: Some New Insights. *Water Resources Research* 18(4): 713–716.

———. 1998. Forms and Functions of Water Pricing: An Overview. In *Urban Water Demand Management and Planning,* edited by D.D. Baumann, J.J. Boland, and W.M. Hanemann. New York, NY: McGraw-Hill Company, 181–189.

Howe, Charles W., J.L. Carroll, A.P. Hunter, Jr. and W.J. Leininger. 1969. *Inland Waterways Transportation: Studies in Public and Private Management and Investment Decisions.* Washington, DC: Resources for the Future.

Howe, C.W., and K.W. Easter. 1971. *Interbasin Transfer of Water: Economic Issues and Impacts.* Baltimore, MD: Johns Hopkins University Press.

Howe, C.W., and F.P. Linaweaver. 1967. The Impact of Price on Residential Water Demand. *Water Resources Research* 3(1): 13–32.

Howe, C.W., and M.G. Smith. 1994. The Value of Water Supply Reliability in Urban Water Systems. *Journal of Environmental Economics and Management* 26(1): 19–30.

Howitt, R.E. 1995. Positive Mathematical Programming. *American Journal of Agricultural Economics* 77(2): 329–342.

Howitt, R.E., W.D. Watson, and R.M. Adams. 1980. A Reevaluation of Price Elasticities for Irrigation Water. *Water Resources Research* 16: 623–28.

Hussain, I., S. Thrikawala, and R. Barker. 2002. Economic Analysis of Residential, Commercial and Industrial Uses of Water in Sri Lanka. *Water International* 27(2): 183–193.

Hussain, R.Z., and R.A. Young. 1985. Estimates of the Economic Value Productivity of Irrigation Water in Pakistan from Farm Surveys. *Water Resources Bulletin* 26(6): 1021–1027.

Hussain, R.Z., and R.A. Young. 1987. Salinity Damages to Irrigated Crops: Economic Measurements from a Farm Survey in Pakistan. In *Proceedings, 19ᵗʰ Conference, International Association of Agricultural Economists*, Malaga, Spain, July 1985, edited by Bruce Greenshields. Aldershot, UK: Dartmouth Publishing Co.

Huszar, P.C. 1998. Overestimated Benefits and Underestimated Costs: The Case of the Paraguay-Parana Navigation Study. *Impact Assessment and Project Appraisal* 16(4): 295–304.

James, L.D. 1994. Flood Action: An Opportunity for Bangladesh. *Water International* 19(2): 61-69.

James, L. Douglas, and Robert R. Lee. 1971. *Economics of Water Resources Planning.* New York, NY: McGraw-Hill.

Jenkins, G.P., and A.C. Harberger. 1995. *Manual: Cost–Benefit Analysis of Investment Decisions* (Draft). Prepared for World Bank by Harvard Institute for International Development. Cambridge, MA: Harvard Institute for International Development.

Johansson, Per-Olov. 1993. *Cost–Benefit Analysis of Environmental Change.* Cambridge: Cambridge University Press.

Jones, C.V., and J.R. Morris. 1984. Instrumental Price Estimates and Residential Water Demand. *Water Resources Research* 20(2): 197–202.

Just, R.E. 1991. Estimation of Production Systems with Emphasis on Water Productivity. In *The Economics and Management of Water and Drainage in Agriculture*, edited by A. Dinar and D. Zilberman. Boston, MA: Kluwer Academic Publishers.

Just, R.E., D.L. Hueth, and A. Schmitz. 1982. *Applied Welfare Economics and Public Policy.* Englewood Cliffs, NJ: Prentice-Hall.

Just, R.E., and J.A. Miranowski. 1993. Understanding Farmland Price Changes. *American Journal of Agricultural Economics* 75: 156–168.

Kahn, A. E. 1966. The Tyranny of Small Decisions. *Kyklos* 19(1): 23–47.

Kahneman, D., and J.L. Knetsch. 1992. Valuing Public Goods: the Purchase of Moral Satisfaction. *Journal of Environmental Economics and Management* 22(1): 57–70.

Kahneman, D., and A. Tversky. 1979. Prospect Theory: An Analysis of Decisions Under Risk. *Econometrica* 47(1): 263–291.

Kamarck, Andrew M. 1983. *Economics and the Real World.* Ann Arbor, MI: University of Michigan Press.

Kan, I., and K.C. Knapp. 2002. Microeconomics of Irrigation with Saline Water. *Journal of Agricultural and Resource Economics* 27(1): 16–39.

Keiper, Joseph S., Ernest Kurnow, Clifford D. Clark and H.H. Segal. 1961. *Theory and Measurement of Rent.* Philadelphia, PA: Chilton Co.

Kelso, M.M., W.E. Martin, and L.E. Mack 1973. *Water Supplies and Economic Growth in an Arid Environment: An Arizona Case Study.* Tucson, AZ: University of Arizona Press.

Kindler, Janusz, and Clifford S. Russell. 1984. *Modeling Water Demands.* London: Academic Press.

Knapp, K. 1992. Irrigation Management and Investment under Saline, Limited Drainage Conditions: 1. Model Formulation. *Water Resources Research* 28(12): 3085–3090.

Knight, Frank. 1921. *Risk, Uncertainty and Profit.* New York, NY: Houghton Mifflin.

Kopp, Raymond J. 1992. Why Existence Value Should Be Used in Cost-Benefit Analysis. *Journal of Policy Analysis and Management* 11(1): 123–130.

Kopp, Raymond J., W.W. Pommerehne, and N. Schwarz (eds.). 1997. *Determining the Value of Non-Marketed Goods.* Boston: Kluwer Academic Publishers.

Krutilla, J.V. 1967. Conservation Reconsidered. *American Economics Review* 57(3): 787–796.

Krutilla, J.V., and O. Eckstein. 1958. *Multiple Purpose River Development.* Baltimore, MD: Johns Hopkins University Press.

Kwak, Seung-Jun, and C.S. Russell. 1996. Exploring the Value of Drinking Water Protection in Seoul, Korea. In *The Economics of Pollution Control in the Asia Pacific,* edited by Robert Mendelsohn and Daigee Shaw. Brookfield, VT: Edward Elgar.

Lansford, N.J., Jr., and L.L. Jones. 1995. Recreational and Aesthetic Value of Water Using Hedonic Price Analysis. *Journal of Agricultural and Resource Economics* 20(2): 341–355.

Lee, D.J., and R.E. Howitt. 1996. Modeling Regional Agricultural Production and Salinity Control Alternatives for Water Quality Policy Analysis. *American Journal of Agricultural Economics* 78(1): 41–53.

Lee, L.K., and L.J. Moffitt. 1993. Defensive Technology and Welfare Analysis of Environmental Quality Change with Uncertain Consumer Health Impacts. *American Journal of Agricultural Economics* 75(2): 361–366.

Letey, J., and A. Dinar. 1986. Simulated Crop-Water Production Functions for Several Crops When Irrigated with Saline Waters. *Hilgardia* 54(1): 1–32.

List, J.A. 2003. Does Market Experience Eliminate Market Anomalies? *Quarterly Journal of Economics* 118(1): 41–71.

Lofting, E.M., and P.H. McGauhey. 1963. *Economic Value of Water: Part III: An Interindustry Analysis of the California Water Economy.* Contribution No. 67, California Water Resources Research Center. Berkeley, CA: University of California.

Lohman, L.C., J.G. Milliken, and W.S. Dorn. 1988. Estimating Economic Impacts of Salinity on the Colorado River. Report to US Bureau of Reclamation. Denver, CO: Denver Research Institute.

Long, R.W. 1988. Aggregate Marginal Returns from Western Irrigated Agriculture. *Water Resource Bulletin* 24(2): 1117-1124.

Loomis, J.B. 1992. The Evolution of a More Rigorous Approach to Benefit Transfer: Benefit Function Transfer. *Water Resources Research* 28(3): 701–705.

———. 1998. Estimating the Public's Values for Maintaining Instream Flow: Economic Techniques and Dollar Values. *Journal of the American Water Resources Association* 34(5): 1007–1014.

———. 1999. Contingent Valuation Methodology and the US Institutional Framework. In *Valuing Environmental Preferences: Theory and Practice of the Contingent Valuation Method in the US, EU, and Developing Countries,* edited by Ian J. Bateman and Kenneth J. Willis. Oxford: Oxford University Press.

Loomis, J.B., W.M. Hanemann, and B. Kanninen. 1991. Willingness to Pay to Protect Wetland and Reduce Wildlife Contamination from Agricultural Drainage. In *The Economics and Management of Water and Drainage in Agriculture,* edited by A. Dinar and D. Zilberman. Boston, MA: Kluwer Academic Publishers.

Loomis, J.B., B. Roach, F. Ward, and R. Ready. 1995. Testing the Transferability of Recreation Demand Models Across Regions: A Study of Corps of Engineers Reservoirs. *Water Resources Research* 31(3): 721–730.

Loomis, J.B., T. Brown, B. Lucero, and G. Peterson. 1997. Estimating the Validity of the Dichotomous Choice Question Format in Contingent Valuation. *Environment and Resource Economics* 10(3): 109–123.

Loomis, J.B., K. Traynor, and T. Brown. 1999. Trichotomous Choice: A Possible Solution to Dual Response Objectives in Dichotomous Choice Contingent Valuation Questions. *Journal of Agricultural and Resource Economics* 24(2): 572–583.

Loomis, John B., and Richard G. Walsh. 1997. *Recreation Economic Decisions: Comparing Benefits and Costs.* 2nd ed. State College, PA: Venture Publishing.

Loomis, J.B., Paula Kent, Liz Strange, Kurt Fausch, and Alan Covich. 2000. Measuring Total Economic Value of Restoring Ecosystem Services in an Impaired River Basin: Results from a Contingent Valuation Survey. *Ecological Economics* 33(1): 103–117.

Louviere, J.J. 2001. Choice Experiments: an Overview of Concepts and Issues. In *The Choice Modeling Approach to Environmental Valuation,* edited by Jeff Bennett and Russell Blamey. Northampton, MA: Edward Elgar Publishing.

Louviere, Jordan J., D.A. Hensher, and J. D. Swait. 2000. *Stated Choice Methods: Analysis and Applications.* New York, NY: Cambridge University Press.

Lyman, R.A. 1992. Peak and Off-Peak Residential Water Demand. *Water Resources Research* 28(9): 2159–2167.

Lynne, G., W. Luppold, and C. Kiker. 1979. Water Responsiveness of Commercial Establishments. *Water Resources Bulletin* 14(3): 719–29.

Maass, A., M. M. Hufschmidt, R. Dorfman, H.A. Thomas, S. A. Marglin, and G.M. Fair. 1962. *Design of Water Resource Systems.* Cambridge, MA: Harvard University Press.

Mahan, B., S. Polasky, and R. Adams. 2000. Valuing Urban Wetlands: A Property Price Approach. *Land Economics* 76(1): 100–113.

Makowski, Louis, and Joseph M. Ostroy. 2001. Perfect Competition and the Creativity of the Market. *Journal of Economic Literature* 39(2): 479–535.

Mäler, Karl-Göran. 1985. Welfare Economics and the Environment: Markets. In *Handbook of Natural Resource and Environmental Economics,* Vol. I, edited by A.V. Kneese and J. L. Sweeney. Amsterdam: Elsevier.

Malla, P., and C. Gopalakrishnan. 1999. The Economics of Urban Water Demand: the Case of Industrial and Commercial Use in Hawaii. *Water Resources Development* 15(3): 367–374.

Mann, R.W., E.W. Sparling, and R.A. Young. 1987. Irrigation Development and Regional Economic Growth: Evidence from Northern High Plains Groundwater Resource. *Water Resources Research* 23(9): 1711–1716.

Marshall, Alfred. 1920. *Principles of Economics: An Introductory Volume.* 8th ed. New York, NY: Macmillan.

Martin, W.E., and J.F. Thomas. 1986. Policy Relevance in Studies of Urban Water Demand. *Water Resources Research* 22: 1735–1741.

McClelland, E., J. Davis, and D. Whittington. 1994. *A Rapid Appraisal of Household Demand for Improved Water and Sanitation Services in Lugazi, Uganda.* Contract Report for Ministry of Natural Resources, Government of Uganda. Chapel Hill, NC: CVM, Inc.

McConnell, K.E., and M.A. Rosado. 2000. Valuing Discrete Improvements in Drinking Water Quality Through Revealed Preferences. *Water Resources Research* 36(6): 1575–1582.

McFadden, D. 1974. Conditional Logit Analysis of Qualitative Choice Behavior. In *Frontiers in Econometrics,* edited by P. Zarembka. New York, NY: Academic Press.

———. 2001. Economic Choices. *American Economic Review* 91(3): 351–378.

McGuckin, J.T., and R.A. Young. 1981. On the Economics of Desalination of Brackish Household Water Supplies. *Journal of Environmental Economics and Management* 8(1): 79–91.

McKean, J.R., D.M. Johnson, and R. Walsh. 1995. Valuing Time in Travel Cost Analysis: An Empirical Investigation. *Land Economics* 71(1): 96–105.

McKean, J.R., R.G. Taylor, G. Alward, and R.A. Young. 1998. Adapting Synthesized Input-Output Models for Small Natural Resource-Based Regions. *Society and Natural Resources* 11: 387–399.

McKean, Roland. 1958. *Efficiency in Government Through Systems Analysis.* New York, NY: Wiley.

McLean, D. 1993. Environmental Values and Economic Tradeoffs: Conflict and Compromise. In *Environmental Risk, Environmental Values and Political Choices,* edited by J.M. Gillroy. Boulder, CO: Westview Press.

Mendelsohn, R., W.D. Nordhaus, and D. Shaw. 1994. The Impact of Global Warming on Agriculture: A Ricardian Analysis. *American Economic Review* 84(4): 753–771.

Mendelsohn, R., and W.D. Nordhaus. 1996. The Impact of Global Warming on Agriculture: Reply. *American Economic Review* 84(5): 1312–1315.

Merrett, Stephen. 1997. *Introduction to the Economics of Water Resources.* London: UCL Press.

Michelsen, A.M. 1994. Administrative, Institutional and Structural Characteristics of a Functioning Water Market. *Water Resources Bulletin* 30(6): 1–12.

Michelsen, A.M., J.F. Booker, and P. Peterson. 2000. Expectations in Water Rights Prices. *International Journal of Water Resources Development* 16(2): 209–219.

Michelsen, A.M., and R. A. Young. 1993. Optioning Agricultural Water Rights for Urban Water Supplies During Drought. *American Journal of Agricultural Economics* 75(4): 1010–1020.

Miller, R.E., and P.D. Blair. 1985. *Input-Output Analysis: Foundations and Extensions.* Englewood Cliffs, NJ: Prentice-Hall.

Milliman, J.W. 1959. Land Values as Measures of Primary Irrigation Benefits. *Journal of Farm Economics* 41(2): 234–243.

Mills, E.S. 1993. The Misuse of Regional Models. *Cato Journal* 13(1, Spring/Summer): 29–39.

Minnesota IMPLAN Group. 2003. IMPLAN Software and Data Files. Stillwater, MN: MIG Inc.

Mitchell, R.C., and R.T. Carson. 1989. *Using Surveys to Value Public Goods: The Contingent Valuation Method.* Baltimore, MD: Johns Hopkins University Press.

Mittelhammer, R., G.C. Judge, and D. Miller. 2000. *Econometric Foundations.* New York, NY: Cambridge University Press.

Moore, C.V., J.H. Snyder, and P. Sun. 1974. Effects of Colorado River Water Quality and Supply on Irrigated Agriculture. *Water Resources Research* 10(4): 137–144.

Moore, C.V., D.L. Wilson, and T.C. Hatch. 1982. *Structure and Performance of Western Irrigated Agriculture with Special Reference to the Acreage Limitation Policy of the U.S. Department of the Interior.* Bulletin 1905, Division of Agricultural Sciences. Berkeley, CA: University of California.

Moore, M.R. 1999. Estimating Irrigators' Ability to Pay for Reclamation Water. *Land Economics* 75(4): 562–578.

Moore, M.R., N.G. Gollehon, and D. H. Negri. 1992. Alternative Forms for Production Functions of Irrigated Crops. *Journal of Agricultural Economics Research* 44(3): 16–25.

Moore, M.R., N.R. Gollehon, and D.M. Hellerstein. 2000. Estimating Producer's Surplus with the Censored Regression Model: An Application to Producers Affected by Columbia River Basin Salmon Recovery. *Journal of Agricultural and Resource Economics* 25(2): 325–346.

Moore, M.R., and A. Dinar. 1995. Water and Land as Quantity-Rationed Inputs in California Agriculture: Empirical Tests and Water Policy Implications. *Land Economics* 71(4): 445–461.

Morgan, C., and N. Owens. 2001. Benefits of Water Quality Policies: the Chesapeake Bay. *Ecological Economics* 39(2): 271–284.

Morgan, M.G., and M. Henrion. 1990. *Uncertainty: A Guide to Dealing with Uncertainty in Quantitative Risk and Policy Analysis.* Cambridge: Cambridge University Press.

Morgenstern, O. 1963. *The Accuracy of Economic Observations.* 2nd ed. Princeton, NJ: Princeton University Press.

Moss, C.B., and A. Schmitz (eds.). 2003. *Government Policy and Farmland Markets: the Maintenance of Farmer Wealth.* Ames, IA: Iowa State University Press.

Mu, X., D. Whittington, and J. Briscoe. 1990. Modeling Village Water Demand Behavior: A Discrete Choice Approach. *Water Resources Research* 26(4): 521–529.

Nickum, J.E., and K.W. Easter (eds.). 1994. *Metropolitan Water Use Conflicts in Asia and the Pacific.* Boulder, CO: Westview Press.

Nieswiadomy, M.L. 1992. Estimating Urban Residential Water Demand: Effects of Price Structure, Conservation and Education. *Water Resources Research* 28(3): 609–615.

Nieswiadomy, M.L., and D.J. Molina. 1991. A Note on Price Perception in Water Demand Models. *Land Economics* 67(3): 352–359.

Nordin, J.A. 1976. A Proposed Modification of Taylor's Demand Analysis: Comment. *Bell Journal of Economics* 7(3): 719–721.

North, J.H., and C. Griffin. 1993. Water Source as a Housing Characteristic: Hedonic Valuation and Willingness to Pay for Water. *Water Resources Research* 29(7): 1923–1929.

Nyborg, Karine. 2000. *Homo Economicus* and *Homo Politicus*: Interpretation and Aggregation of Environmental Values. *Journal of Economic Behavior and Organization* 42(3): 305–322.

O'Driscoll, Gerald. 1977. *Economics as a Coordination Problem*. Kansas City, KA: Sheed, Andrews, and McMeel.

Omezzine, A., M. Chabaane, and L. Zaibet. 1998. Analysis of Water Allocation and Returns in the Sultanate of Oman. *Water International* 23(4): 249–255.

Oosterhaven, J. 1989. The Supply-Driven Input-Output Model: A New Interpretation but Still Implausible. *Journal of Regional Science* 29: 459–465.

Organization for Economic Cooperation and Development (OECD). 1985. *Management of Water Projects: Decision-making and Investment Appraisal*. Paris: OECD Publications.

———. 1998. *Projected Costs of Generating Electricity: Update 1998*. Paris: International Energy Agency (OECD Publications).

Ostrom, E., R. Gardner, and J. Walker. 1994. *Rules, Games and Common-Pool Resources*. Ann Arbor, MI: University of Michigan Press.

Palmquist, R.B. 1989. Land as a Differentiated Factor of Production: a Hedonic Model and its Implications for Welfare Measurement. *Land Economics* 65(1): 23–28.

———. 1992. Valuing Localized Externalities. *Journal of Urban Economics* 31(1): 59–68.

Parker, D.J., C.H. Green, P.M. Thompson, and E.C. Penning-Rowsell. 1987. *Urban Flood Protection Benefits: A Project Appraisal Guide*. Aldershot, UK: Gower Technical Press.

Parsons, G.R. 2003. The Travel Cost Model. In *A Primer on Nonmarket Valuation*, edited by Patricia A. Champ, K.J. Boyle, and T.C. Brown. Dordrecht: Kluwer Academic Publishers.

Pearce, David W. 1993. *Economic Values and the Natural World*. Cambridge, MA: MIT Press.

Penning-Rowsell, E.C., C.H. Green, D.J. Parker and P.M. Thompson. 1992. *The Economics of Coastal Management: A Manual of Benefit Assessment Techniques*. London: Bellhaven.

Pint, E. 1999. Household Responses to Increased Water Rates During the California Drought. *Land Economics* 75(2): 246–66.

Portney, P.R. 1994. The Contingent Valuation Debate: Why Economists Should Care. *Journal of Economic Perspectives* 8(4): 3–17.

Provencher, B., and O. Burt. 1994. A Private Property Regime for the Commons: the Case for Groundwater. *American Journal of Agricultural Economics* 76(4): 875–895.

Provencher, B., K.A. Baerenklau, and R.C. Bishop. 2002. A Finite Mixture Logit Model of Recreation Angling with Serially Correlated Random Utility. *American Journal of Agricultural Economics* 84(4): 1066–1075.

Rae, Allan N. 1994. *Agricultural Management Economics: Activity Analysis and Decision Making.* Wallingford, UK: CAB International.

Ragan, G., C. Makela, and R.A. Young. 2000. New Evidence on the Economic Benefits of Reduced Salinity in Domestic Water Supplies. *Water Resources Research* 36(4): 1087–1095.

Randall, A. 1987. *Resource Economics.* 2nd ed. New York, NY: John Wiley.

———. 1994. A Difficulty with the Travel Cost Method. *Land Economics* 70(1): 88–96.

———. 2002. Benefit–Cost Considerations Should Be Decisive When There is Nothing More Important at Stake. In *Economics, Ethics and Environmental Policy,* edited by Daniel W. Bromley and Jouni Paavola. Oxford, UK: Blackwell Publishers.

Randall, A., B.C. Ives, and C. Eastman. 1974. Bidding Games for Evaluation of Aesthetic Environmental Improvements. *Journal of Environmental Economics And Management* 1(1): 132–149.

Randall, A., and J.R. Stoll. 1980. Consumer's Surplus in Commodity Space. *American Economic Review* 66: 587–597.

Randall, A., and J.P. Hoehn. 1996. Embedding Effects in Market Demand Systems. *Journal of Environmental Economics And Management* 30(3): 360–380.

Rea, Louis M., and Richard A. Parker. 1997. *Designing and Conducting Survey Research,* 2nd ed. San Francisco: Jossey Bass.

Rees, J.A. 1969. Industrial Demands for Water: A Study of South East England. Research Monograph No. 3, London School of Economics. In *The Economics of Industrial Water Use,* edited by Steven Renzetti. Northampton, MA: Edward Elgar Publishing.

Renwick, M.E., and R.D. Green. 2000. Do Residential Water Demand Side Management Policies Measure Up? An Analysis of Eight California Water Agencies. *Journal of Environmental Economics and Management* 40(1): 37–55.

Renzetti, S. 1992. Estimating the Structure of Industrial Water Demands: The Case of Canadian Manufacturing. *Land Economics* 68(4): 396–404.

———. 2002a. *The Economics of Water Demands.* Boston: Kluwer Academic Publishers.

———. (ed.). 2002b. *The Economics of Industrial Water Use.* Northampton, MA: Edward Elgar Publishing.

Reynaud, A. 2003. An Econometric Estimation of Industrial Water Demand in France. *Environmental and Resource Economics* 25(2): 213–232.

Reynolds, J.E., and W.E. Johnston. 2003. Micro-Markets for Farmland: the Case of Florida and California. In *Government Policy and Farmland Markets: the Maintenance of Farmer Wealth,* edited by Charles B. Moss and Andrew Schmitz. Ames, IA: Iowa State University Press.

Rhoads, S.S. 1985. *The Economist's View of the World: Governments, Markets and Public Policy.* Cambridge: Cambridge University Press.

Ribaudo, M., and J.S. Shortle. 2001. Estimating Benefits and Costs of Pollution Control Policies. In *Environmental Policies for Agricultural Pollution Control,* edited by J.S. Shortle and D.G. Abler. New York, NY: CABI Publishing.

Ricketts, Martin. 2002. *The Economics of the Business Enterprise: An Introduction to Economic Organization and the Theory of the Firm.* 3rd ed. Northampton, MA: Edward Elgar Publishing.

Rodda, J.C. 1995. Whither World Water? *Water Resources Bulletin* 31(1): 1–7.

Rogers, P. 1993. *America's Water: Federal Roles and Responsibilities.* Cambridge, MA: MIT Press.

Rosen, S. 1974. Hedonic Prices and Implicit Markets: Product Differentiation in Pure Competition. *Journal of Political Economy* 82(January–February): 34–55.

Rosenbeger, R.S., and J.B. Loomis. 2000. Using Meta-Analysis for Benefit Transfer: In-Sample Convergent Validity Tests of an Outdoor Recreation Base. *Water Resources Research* 36(4): 1097–1107.

Rosenberger, R.S., and J.B. Loomis, 2003. Benefit Transfer. In *A Primer on Nonmarket Valuation,* edited by Patricia A. Champ, K.J. Boyle, and T.C. Brown. Dordrecht: Kluwer Academic Publishers.

Rosenthal, D.H. 1987. The Necessity for Substitute Sites in Recreation Demand Analysis. *American Journal of Agricultural Economics* 69(4): 828–837.

Russell, C.S. 1984. Programming Models for Regional Water Demand Analysis. In *Modeling Water Demands,* edited by Janusz Kindler and Clifford S. Russell. London: Academic Press.

Ruttan, Vernon. 1965. *The Economic Demand for Irrigated Acreage: New Methodology and Preliminary Projections, 1954–1980.* Baltimore, MD: Johns Hopkins University Press for Resources for the Future.

Salant, P., and D.A. Dillman. 1994. *How to Conduct your Own Survey.* New York, NY: Wiley.

Saleth, R.M., and A. Dinar. 1997. *Satisfying Urban Thirst: Water Supply and Pricing Policy in Hyderabad City, India.* Technical Paper 395. Washington, DC: World Bank.

Saliba, Bonnie Colby, and D.B. Bush. 1987. *Water Markets in Theory and Practice: Market Transfers and Public Policy.* Boulder, CO: Westview Press.

Scheierling, S., G. Cardon, and R.A. Young. 1997. A Discrete-Input Production Function for Modeling the Effect of Amount and Timing of Irrigation Water Applications on Crop Yield and Evapotranspiration. *Irrigation Science* 18(1): 23–32.

Scheierling, S., R.A. Young, and G. Cardon. 2004a. Determining the Price-Responsiveness of Irrigation Water Deliveries versus Consumptive Use. *Journal of Agricultural and Resource Economics* 29(2): 328–345.

———. 2004b. Can Subsidizing Improved On-Farm Irrigation Technologies Bring About Real Water Conservation? Paper presented at Universities Council on Water Resources Annual Conference, Portland, OR, July.

Scheierling, S., J.B. Loomis, and R.A. Young. 2004c. Irrigation Water Demand: A Meta Analysis of Price Elasticities. Paper presented at the American Agricultural Economics Annual Conference, Denver, CO, August.

Schiffler, M., H. Koppen, and R. Lohmann. 1994. *Water Demand Management in an Arid Country: The Case of Jordan with Special Reference to Industry.* Report 10. Berlin: German Development Institute.

Schleifer, A. 2000. *Inefficient Markets—An Introduction to Behavioral Finance.* New York, NY: Oxford University Press.

Schneider, M.L., and E.E. Whitlach. 1991. User-Specific Water Demand Elasticities. *Journal of Water Resources Planning and Management* 17(1): 52–73.

Schultz, S.D., and P.M. Fridgen. 2001. Floodplains and Housing Values: Implications for Flood Mitigation Projects. *Journal of the American Water Resources Association* 37(3): 595–603.

Schumpeter, Joseph A. 1936. *The Theory of Economic Development.* Cambridge, MA: Harvard University Press.

Scitovsky, Tibor. 1993. The Meaning, Nature and Source of Value in Economics. In *The Origin of Values,* edited by Michael Hechter, Lynn Nadel, and Richard Michod. New York, NY: Aldine de Gruyer, 93–105.

Shabman, L. 1994. Measuring the Benefits of Flood Risk Reduction. In *Risk-Based Decision-Making in Water Resources VI,* edited by Y. Y. Haimes, D. Moser, and E.Z. Stakhiv. New York, NY: American Society of Civil Engineers, 122–135.

Shogren, Jason, C. Cho, C. Koo, and John List. 2001. Auction Mechanisms and the Measurement of WTP and WTA. *Resource and Energy Economics* 23(1): 97–109.

Smith, V.K. 1985. The Foundations of Benefit–Cost Analysis. In *Benefit Assessment: The State Of the Art,* edited by Judith D. Bentkover, J.T. Covello, and J. Munpower. Dordrecht: Reidel Publishing Co.

Smith, V. Kerry, and W. H. Desvousges. 1986. *Measuring Water Quality Benefits.* Dordrecht: Kluwer Academic Publishers.

Smith, V.K., and Y. Kaoru. 1990. Signals or Noise? Explaining Variation in Recreation Benefit Estimates. *American Journal of Agricultural Economics* 72(2): 419–33.

Smith, V.K., and L. Osborne. 1996. Do Contingent Valuation Estimates Pass a "Scope Test"? A Meta-Analysis. *Journal of Environmental Economic and Management* 31(4): 287–301.

Solley, Wayne B., E.B. Chase, and W.B. Mann. 1983. *Estimated Use of Water in the United States in 1980.* Circular 1001. Washington, DC: U.S. Geological Survey.

Solley, Wayne B., R.R. Pierce, and H.A. Perlman. 1998. *Estimated Use of Water in the United States in 1995.* Circular 1200. Washington, DC: U.S. Geological Survey.

Spulber, Nicolas, and Asghar Sabbaghi. 1998. *Economics of Water Resources: From Regulation to Privatization.* 2nd ed. Norwell, MA: Kluwer Academic Publishers.

Stone, J.C., and D. Whittington. 1984. Industrial Water Demands. In *Modeling Water Demands,* edited by J. Kindler and C.S. Russell. London: Academic Press.

Taylor, L.O. 2003. The Hedonic Method. In *A Primer on Nonmarket Valuation,* edited by Patricia A. Champ, K.J. Boyle, and T.C. Brown. Dordrecht: Kluwer Academic Publishers.

Taylor, R.G., and R.A. Young. 1995. Rural-to-Urban Water Transfers: Measuring Foregone Direct Benefits of Irrigation Water Under Uncertain Water Supplies. *Journal of Agricultural and Resource Economics* 20(2): 247–262.

Taylor, R.G., J.R. McKean, and R.A. Young. 2004. Alternate Price Specifications for Estimating Residential Water Demand with Fixed Fees. *Land Economics* 80(3): 463–475.

Teegerstrom, T., and S. Husman. 1999. *1999–2000 Arizona Field Crop Budgets: Pinal County.* Extension Bulletin AZ1121. Tucson, AZ: University of Arizona.

Thomas, J.F., and G.J. Syme. 1988. Estimating Price Elasticity of Residential Demand for Water: a Contingent Valuation Approach. *Water Resource Research* 24(11): 1847–1857.

Torell, A., J. Libbin, and M. Miller. 1990. The Market Value of Water in the Ogallala Aquifer. *Land Economics* 66(2): 163–175.

Turnovsky, S.J. 1969. The Demand for Water: Some Empirical Evidence on Consumers' Response to a Commodity in Uncertain Supply. *Water Resources Research* 5(2): 350–61.

United Nations. 1992. *The Dublin Statement on Water and Sustainable Development.* International Conference on Water and the Environment. http://www.wmo.ch/web/homs/documents/english/icwedece.html (accessed September 14, 2004).

U.S. Army Corps of Engineers. 1987. *National Economic Development Procedures Manual: Agricultural Flood Damage.* Report 87-R-10. Fort Belvoir, VA: Institute for Water Resources.

———. 1988. *National Economic Development Procedures Manual: Urban Flood Damage.* Report 88-R-2. Fort Belvoir, VA: Institute for Water Resources.

U.S. Department of Agriculture. 2002. *Agricultural Prices Annual Summary.* Washington, DC: National Agricultural Statistics Service.

———. 2003. *Agricultural Statistics Annual.* Washington, DC: Government Printing Office.

U.S. Department of Commerce. 1998. *Farm and Ranch Irrigation Survey.* Washington, DC: Bureau of the Census.

———. 2000. Note on Rates of Return for Domestic Nonfinancial Corporations: Revised Estimates for 1960–1998. S*urvey of Current Business* June: 15–17. Washington, DC: Bureau of Economic Analysis.

U.S. Water Resources Council. 1983. *Economic and Environmental Principles and Guidelines for Water and Related Land Resource Implementation Studies.* Washington, DC: Government Printing Office.

Varian, H.R. 1997. *Intermediate Microeconomics: A Modern Approach.* 4th ed. New York, NY: W.W. Norton.

Vaux, H., and R. Howitt. 1984. Managing Water Scarcity: An Evaluation of Interregional Transfers. *Water Resources Research* 20: 785–792.

Vaux, H.J., Jr., and W.O. Pruitt. 1983. Crop-Water Production Functions. *Advances in Irrigation* 2(1): 61–95.

Viscusi, W. Kip. 2001. The Value of Risks to Life and Health. In *Environmental Risk Planning and Management,* edited by Simon Gerrard, R. Kerry Turner, and Ian J. Bateman. Northampton, MA: Edward Elgar Publishing.

Wade, W.W., J.A. Hewitt, and M.T. Nussbaum. 1991. *Cost of Industrial Water Shortages.* Report to California Urban Water Agencies. San Francisco, CA: Spectrum Economics.

Walsh, R.G., D.M. Johnson, and J. R. McKean. 1992. Benefit Transfer of Outdoor Recreation Demand Studies: 1968–1988. *Water Resources Research* 28(3): 707–713.

Wang, Hua, and S. Lall. 2002. Valuing Water for Chinese Industries: A Marginal Productivity Analysis. *Applied Economics* 34(6): 759–765.

Ward, F.A. 1987. Economics of Water Allocation to Instream Uses: Evidence from a New Mexico Wild River. *Water Resources Research* 23(3): 381–392.

Ward, F.A., and D. Beal. 2000. *Valuing Nature with Travel Cost Models.* Northampton, MA: Edward Elgar Publishing.

Ward, F.A., B.A. Roach, and J. E. Henderson. 1996. The Economic Value of Water for Recreation: Evidence from the California Drought. *Water Resources Research* 32(4): 1075–81.

Watts, G., W.R. Noonan, and H. Maddux. 2001. The Endangered Species Act and Critical Habitat Designation: Economic Consequences for the Colorado River Basin. In *Protecting Endangered Species in the United States: Biological Needs, Political*

Realities, Economic Choices, edited by Jason Shogren and John Tschirhart. New York, NY: Cambridge University Press.

Whittington, D. 1988. Guidelines for Conducting Willingness to Pay Studies for Improved Water Services in Developing Countries. Arlington, VA: Water and Sanitation for Health (WASH) Project, USAID.

Whittington, D. 2002. Improving the Performance of Contingent Valuation Studies in Developing Countries. *Environmental and Resource Economics* 22(1–2): 323–367.

Whittington, D., and K. Choe. 1992. Economic Benefits Available from the Provision of Improved Potable Water Supplies. Technical Report No. 77. Arlington, VA: Water and Sanitation for Health (WASH) Project, USAID.

Whittington, D., and D. MacRae. 1986. The Issue of Standing in Cost–Benefit Analysis. *Journal of Policy Analysis and Management* 5(4): 665–682.

Whittington, D., D.T. Lauria, K. Choe, and J.A. Hughes. 1992. Household Demands for Improved Sanitation Services in Kumasi, Ghana: A Contingent Valuation Study. *Water Resources Research* 29 (6): 1539–1560.

Whittington, D., and V. Swarna. 1994. *The Economic Benefits of Potable Water Supply Projects to Households in Developing Countries.* Economic Staff Paper No. 35. Manila: Asian Development Bank.

Williams, H.P. 1999. *Model Building in Mathematical Programming,* 4th. ed. New York, NY: Wiley.

Williams, M., and B. Suh. 1986. The Demand for Urban Water by Customer Class. *Applied Economics* 18: 1275–1289.

Willig, R.D. 1976. Consumer's Surplus Without Apology. *American Economic Review* 66(4): 589–597.

Wilson, P.N. 1997. Economic Discovery in Federally Supported Irrigation Districts: A Tribute to William E. Martin and Friends. *Journal of Agricultural and Resource Economics* 22(1): 61–77.

Wollman, Nathaniel, J.W. Thomas, Roy E. Huffman and Allen V. Kneese. 1962. *The Value of Water in Alternative Uses with Special Application to Water Use in the San Juan and Rio Grande Basins of New Mexico.* Albuquerque, NM: University of New Mexico Press.

World Bank Water Demand Research Team. 1993. The Demand for Water in Rural Areas: Determinants and Policy Implications. *World Bank Research Observer* 8(1): 47–70.

World Commission on Environment and Development. 1987. *Our Common Future.* Oxford: Oxford University Press.

Yaron, D. 1967. Empirical Analysis of the Demand for Water by Israeli Agriculture. *Journal of Farm Economics* 49(2): 461–473.

Yaron, D., and E. Bresler. 1970. A Model for the Economic Evaluation of Water Quality in Irrigation. *Australian Journal of Agricultural Economics* 14(2): 53–62.

Young, R.A. 1978. Economic Analysis and Federal Irrigation Policy: A Reappraisal. *Western Journal of Agricultural Economics* 3(2): 257–68.

———. 1986. Why Are There So Few Transactions Among Water Users? *American Journal of Agricultural Economics* 68(5): 1143–1151.

———. 1996. *Measuring Economic Benefits of Water Investments and Policies.* Technical Report No. 338. Washington, DC: World Bank.

Young, R.A., and J.D. Bredehoeft. 1972. Digital Computer Simulation for Solving Problems of Conjunctive Groundwater and Surface Water Systems. *Water Resources Research* 8(3): 533–56.

Young, R.A., and S.L. Gray. 1985. Input-Output Models, Economic Surplus and the Evaluation of State or Regional Water Plans. *Water Resources Research* 21(12): 1819–1823.

Young, R.A., and S.L. Gray (with R.B. Held and R.S. Mack). 1972. *Economic Value of Water: Concepts and Empirical Estimates.* Report to the U.S. National Water Commission. Publication PB 210 356. Springfield, VA: National Technical Information Service.

Young, R.A., and J.L. Horner. 1986. The Mineral Water Quality Problem and Irrigated Agriculture. In *Agriculture and the Environment,* edited by T. Phipps and P. Crosson. Washington, DC: Resources for the Future.

Young, R.A., and R. Mann. 1993. Cheap Water: A Cost-Effective Tool for Rural Development in Indian Country? In *Indian Water in the New West,* edited by T.R. McGuire, W.B. Lord, and M.G. Wallace. Tucson, AZ: University of Arizona Press.

Young, R.A., N. Whittlesey, and W.E. Martin. 1988. Aggregate Marginal Returns from Western Irrigated Agriculture: Discussion. *Water Resource Bulletin* 24(6): 1337–1339.

Young, R.A., D. Cablayan, B.Z. Haman, and R. Maloles. 1996. *Water Management and Allocation Options: Angat River System.* Report to Asian Development Bank and National Water Resources Board, Republic of the Philippines. TA No: 2417-PHI. Manila.

Zuker, R.C., and G.P. Jenkins. 1984. *Blue Gold: Hydro-Electric Rent in Canada.* Ottawa: Economic Council of Canada. (Excerpted in *The Economics of Industrial Water Use,* edited by Steven Renzetti. Northampton, MA: Edward Elgar Publishing, 2002.)

Glossary

Accounting price The value used in social or public economic analysis when the market price is unknown or judged not to be an appropriate measure of economic value; also called *shadow price.*

Accounting stance The perspective from which benefits and costs are accounted for in an economic evaluation; can be private and social (or public), measured by market prices or social prices respectively. See *standing.*

Aggregation The summing of individual observations or responses into a total. Because the preferences or resource endowments of individuals or firms may vary asymmetrically across a population, and data is derived from a sample rather than a complete enumeration, aggregation from a sample may require more complex operations than just multiplying the reported average by the number in the population.

Aquifer A geologic formation whose pores and voids may contain water which can be removed economically and used as a water supply.

Associated costs In U.S. Bureau of Reclamation terminology, a farmer's costs of resources—other than water—required to produce a crop. *At-site* economic value or benefit equals expected revenue minus associated costs.

At-site value The value of water calculated as at the site of use (farm, home, factory). By convention (but not by necessity) this is the value used in investment evaluations, to be compared with costs of supply. See *at-source value.*

At-source value The value of water calculated as at the source (stream, reservoir, aquifer). A derived demand less than at-site value by any costs of capture, transport, and treatment for use. Appropriate for use in comparing intersectoral allocations. See *at-site value.*

Averting behavior See *defensive behavior.*

Benefit, economic A monetary measure of preference, satisfaction, or welfare improvement from some change in quantity or quality of a good or service; the maximum amount that person would be *willing to pay* to obtain the improvement.

Benefit transfer The procedure by which values or *demand functions* estimated for a site or circumstance are employed to assign benefits or value to another site or circumstance.

Capitalized value The present discounted value of a stream of *per-period values* of indefinite length; the value of an asset (a property right to a stream of *per-period values*).

Cheap talk In contingent valuation studies, a reminder to respondents that they are valuing a hypothetical program, to make them less likely to unintentionally overstate their willingness to pay. See *hypothetical bias*.

Choice modeling (CM) An expressed preference method that infers *willingness to pay* in absence of markets by directly asking a sample of respondents to make choices among alternative proposed policies; assumes preferences are based on several attributes of product or situation, and values proposals by assessing tradeoffs among attributes.

Computable General Equilibrium (CGE) model Empirical model of a region, political entity, or subdivision designed to determine domestic prices, supplies, and incomes jointly via a system of nonlinear simultaneous equations.

Conjoint analysis Early survey-based form of evaluating consumer preferences; evolved into what is now more commonly called *choice modeling*.

Constructed model Model of hypothetical individual economic behavior that incorporates assumptions about motivation (profit or utility maximization), technological options, and prices; usually refers to deductive models of producer behavior.

Consumer surplus The excess in money value that an individual would pay for a good over and above the total expenditures that would be made at a given price for the good. Changes in consumer surplus associated with changes in quantity or quality of *consumers' goods* are the primary basis for measuring economic benefits of consumers goods.

Consumers' good A good or service used or consumed directly by the consumer (contrasted with *producers' goods*). Water used in households or enjoyed in the natural environment is classified as a consumers' good.

Consumption In the context of measuring water use, water *withdrawn* from a source and made unsuitable for further use in the same basin; also called *consumptive use*. Consumption mainly occurs via evaporation and transpiration, but may also be due to contamination, drainage to a saline sink, or incorporation into products.

Consumptive use See *consumption*.

Contingent Valuation Method (CVM) An *expressed preference method* which asks individuals the value (in monetary terms) of specified changes in quantities or qualities of environmental goods and services; especially useful where nonuse values are important.

Contractual inputs In analyzing producer goods, those productive inputs purchased by a firm at known prices, including materials purchased from other firms, hired labor, and other inputs whose costs are known. See *owned inputs*.

Conveyance loss Water that is lost in transit from a pipe canal or conduit by leakage or evaporation. May percolate to ground water source and be available for further use.

Costs The value of goods or services sacrificed or used up in the allocation decision; measured by the opportunity costs (forgone benefits in the best alternative use) of the resources used.

Cost–benefit analysis For public policy decisions, systematic cataloging of benefits and costs (valued in monetary units) and determining net benefits (benefits minus costs) of the proposal relative to the status quo.

Cost function method For producers' goods, a method of measuring benefits or damages avoided which is based on shifts in the industry cost or supply functions. The welfare change is the change in areas between the supply functions, and measures welfare changes via the changes in price to consumers. Alternative to *value marginal product* or *residual rent* methods.

Damage-frequency relationship In evaluating flood risk reduction projects, the relationship between flood losses and flood probability; also called loss-probability relationship.

Deductive reasoning Reasoning from general principles and assumptions to specific conclusions using logical or mathematical rules. Conclusions are only as valid as the initial assumptions. See *inductive reasoning*.

Deductive valuation techniques Valuation models (including residual, alternative cost, and benefit transfer methods) which primarily use *deductive reasoning*.

Defensive behavior Actions people take (e.g. buying bottled water to avoid the effects of degraded tap water quality) to mitigate or avoid an external cost (e.g. chemical or biological water pollution). Reductions in the costs of averting behavior may be a partial measure of the benefits of policies from reducing the externality. Also called *averting behavior*.

Delivery The amount of water provided to the point of use. *Withdrawal* minus *conveyance loss* equals delivery to the point of use. *Withdrawal* minus *return flow* (or releases) equals *consumption*.

Demand function or schedule Indicates the quantities of a good or service that individuals purchase at various prices. A single person has an individual demand schedule; all individuals in the market contribute to the market demand function.

Depth-damage relationship In evaluating flood risk reduction projects, the relationship between flood depth and economic damages to structures.

Discount rate The interest rate used to determine the present worth of a future value or cost. See *social rate of discount*.

Discrete choice question A type of contingent valuation question that asks for a "yes" or "no" answer to a willingness to pay question; also called *dichotomous choice* question.

Econometric methods The combination of economic theory and mathematical statistics to inductively infer general economic relationships from observations on consumer or producer behavior, from experimental data, or from responses to questionnaires.

Economic analysis Term used in World Bank project evaluation literature to refer to evaluation of the social (contrasted with private) profitability of alternative investments or programs. In the project evaluation literature, "social" and "economic" may be used interchangeably. However, some writers limit "economic profitability" to economic efficiency or net national income gains, while social profitability is used to refer to analysis which incorporates social considerations other than economic efficiency, such as income distribution. In economic analysis, benefits and costs are valued in terms of real willingness to pay or opportunity costs. Subsidies, certain taxes, and other income transfer policies are not counted in economic analysis. See *financial analysis*.

Embedding effect In the contingent valuation method (CVM), the finding that a particular good is ascribed a lower value when the WTP for it is inferred from the WTP for a more all-encompassing good or set of goods compared to when the particular good is valued by itself.

Endowment effect The hypothesis that a good's value increases once it is in an individual's possession.

Equimarginal principle The proposition that a net benefit or criterion function is maximized when the net marginal benefits per unit of water used are equal in all use sectors. To test for the existence or absence of equi-marginality in water economics, benefits in each sector must be measured in commensurate (willingness to pay) terms.

Existence value See *nonuse value*.

Expressed preference methods The class of methods, including contingent valuation and choice modeling, which determine by questionnaire how much a respondent would be willing to pay for a change in quantity or quality of an environmental good; useful where no complementary or substitute private goods are available from which to derive a behavior-based willingness to pay.

Extrinsic value Value that arises because a thing or act is instrumental in attaining things of *intrinsic value*; also called *instrumental value*. Economic values are extrinsic.

Financial analysis In World Bank project evaluation terminology, evaluation from the perspective of the private individual or firm affected by a project (which can be producers, consumers, or both). The purpose of financial analysis is to ascertain the appeal of the project to its intended beneficiaries. Profitability is calculated in terms of actual prices received or paid, and therefore reflects any income transfer programs (taxes or subsidies). See *economic analysis*.

Forgone benefit The value sacrificed when one resource use option is chosen over another. See *opportunity cost*.

General equilibrium analysis The mode of economic analysis in which supplies and demands in all sectors of the national (or regional) economy are represented and the prices and quantities in these sectors emerge in solution to the model; more realistic, but more difficult to implement, than *partial equilibrium analysis*. Impractical until recent development of *computable general equilibrium* (CGE) techniques.

Hedonic property value method A *revealed preference* method of isolating the value of one attribute of a complicated multi-attribute good or service (usually farm land or residences) by statistically separating the contributions of the various attributes using data from market transactions on a selected good or service.

Hypothetical bias In contingent valuation studies, the potential for bias in responses due to the fact that the respondent doesn't actually have to pay for the good or service being valued. See *cheap talk*.

Inductive reasoning Reasoning from specific empirical observations to broader generalizations, usually employing statistical techniques. The accuracy of inductive techniques depends on several factors, including the representativeness of the observations used, the appropriateness of the assumed statistical distribution, and the functional form on which the inference is based. See *deductive reasoning.*

Inductive valuation techniques A broad class of nonmarket valuation techniques, including *expressed preferences* and *revealed preferences*, which use *inductive reasoning* (usually statistical methods) to infer *willingness to pay* from empirical observations of behavior, including market transactions or responses to questionnaires. See *deductive valuation techniques.*

Input-output model A static economic model of production, ordinarily used to portray a geographic region or political subdivision for purposes of understanding the structure of the regional economy, and for making *short-run* predictions of the effects of exogenous changes in final demands on such economic variables as output, employment, and income; also called *interindustry model.*

Instrumental value See *extrinsic value.*

Interindustry model *See input-output model.*

Intermediate goods See *producers' goods.*

Intrinsic value Value assigned to things, actions, or outcomes for their own sake, independent of means of providing or attaining other items or situations of value for humans. See *extrinsic value.*

Lease rate Payment made for temporary formal and informal market exchanges of goods or assets; often called *rental rate.*

Long run In A. Marshall's simplified analytic price theory, the situation in which plant and equipment capacity is assumed to be variable, rather than fixed as it is in the *short run.* Short run and long run are distinguished not by the actual time in days, weeks, or months but by the degree to which economic actors can adapt to changing conditions.

Meta-analysis The statistical analysis of the results of previously reported research studies; used in environmental economics primarily for the purpose of improving research methods by determining the effects of differing research techniques or model specifications on measures of user demands for environmental attributes; also used to distill general empirical conclusions regarding environmental demands.

Model A structure that has been built to exhibit features and characteristics of some other object. In economics, usually refers to mathematical relationships (e.g. supply, demand, or production functions) that correspond to some real-world relationships (firms, households, markets).

Nominal price Price expressed in current money terms as of a specific date, unadjusted for inflation; even for the same amount of goods or services, may vary over time due to effects of general price inflation. See *real price.*

Noncontractual inputs See *owned inputs.*

Nonexcludable goods Good or service from which it is impossible or difficult to exclude potential users for nonpayment.

Nonmarket valuation The study of economic behavior (especially consumption, demand, production, and supply relationships) for the purpose of assigning economic values in contexts where market prices are absent or distorted. See *accounting price.*

Nonrival goods Good or service enjoyment of which by one person does not reduce the possible enjoyment by others. See *rival goods.* Nonexcludable, nonrival goods, such as water quality, are called *public goods.*

Nonuse values Benefits received from a *public good* by knowing that it exists, even though the individual may never directly experience the good. People are *willing to pay* for environmental services they will never use or experience. Sometimes called *passive use* or *existence values.* See *total economic value* and *use value.*

Opportunity cost The monetary value or forgone value of a good or service in its next best alternative use; the maximum amount it could receive elsewhere for use as a production input or for final consumption.

Owned inputs Those productive inputs owned by a firm, including the firm's equity capital, some human inputs (management and entrpreneurial creativity), and some natural resources (e.g. land). Costs of owned (or *noncontractual*) inputs are important in residual evaluation of producers' uses of water. Because their prices are uncertain—determined by the outcome of prior management and investment decisions, rather than being priced on markets—any method of pricing owned inputs creates uncertainty in residual valuation of producer uses of water. See *contractual inputs.*

Partial equilibrium analysis Analysis which focuses on a single product or market, examining the effect of simple changes in assumptions on price and output; less realistic, but more easily implemented, than *general equilibrium analysis.*

Passive-use value See *nonuse* value

Per-period value Value referring to willingness to pay for a quantity of water for particular time period (usually a year). See *capitalized value.*

Planning context Refers to whether the plans are considering the (Marshallian) *long run* or *short run.*

Planning period The length of time (in years) over which individuals, firms, or government agencies plan economic choices; also called *planning horizon.*

Primary data Original data collected for a specific research purpose. See *secondary data.*

Private goods Goods and services one person's consumption or use of which reduces the amount available to other consumers and from which nonpayers can be excluded. See *public goods.*

Producers' good A product or service used to make other goods or services (as contrasted with *consumers' goods*). Water is often a producer good, as when it is used in an industrial or agricultural process to produce goods for eventual final consumption. Also called *intermediate goods.*

Producers' surplus The returns to a producer in excess of variable costs; also payments for fixed inputs. See *quasi-rent.*

Product exhaustion theorem A microeconomic theorem important in the *residual method* of valuing *producers' goods*; also called the adding-up theorem.

Property damage avoided (PDA) The estimated present value of real (inflation-free) expected property damages avoided by a project or policy; the principal technique for estimating urban flood risk reduction benefits. Criticized for ignoring nonproperty effects such as individual and community disruption, medical expenses, productivity losses, and preflood anxiety.

Public goods Goods or services for which enjoyment by one person does not reduce the enjoyment of other persons. Potential public good users cannot be readily excluded from enjoyment of its benefits. (The definition of public goods does not mean that they are publicly owned). See *nonrival* and *nonexcludable*.

Quasi-hedonic method Sometimes used for irrigation water valuation. Value inferences based on comparisons of differences between the selling prices of irrigated lands and the prices of lands that are not irrigated, but in which the methods employed do not meet the criteria for a full *hedonic property value method*.

Quasi-public goods Environmental goods which, like public goods, can be enjoyed by one individual without affecting enjoyment by others, but only at low levels of use; above some threshold, congestion reduces the enjoyment of all users.

Quasi-rents Returns to assets regarded as fixed in the short run; usually understood to be total payments to fixed factors plus excess profits. See *rent, economic*.

Quasi-rents, composite A now little-used concept proposed by A. Marshall, referring to the special cases where a combination of resources yields a return exceeding that of the opportunity costs of the inputs; particularly relevant to valuing water in irrigation and hydropower uses.

Random Utility Theory Hypothesis that an individual's utility function may be deterministic, but may contain elements not observable by the researcher. In such instances, utility can be more realistically modeled to consist of an observable component plus a random component, and a random utility model (RUM) may apply. Discrete-choice random utility models, which portray the dependent variable as a yes/no choice (yes = 1, no = zero), are frequently used by environmental economists to model revealed preference and expressed preference choices. Logit or probit statistical models are often used to implement random utility theory.

Real price Price series adjusted for general price inflation, usually referring to a specific base year. See *nominal price*.

Regression analysis A statistical technique used to measure the relationship between a "dependent variable" (for example, annual visits to a recreational site) and "independent variables" (such as socioeconomic characteristics and cost of travel) expected to influence its behavior.

Release The portion of water *delivered* that is released or discharged to surface or ground water after use. Delivery minus release usually equals *consumption*.

Rent, economic Nonobservable income imputed to an input in limited supply; represents payment made to an input over and above the amount needed to attract any of that input to be supplied to its present employment. Rents originally were attributed only to land, but modern usage recognizes that rents may accrue to any resource in scarce supply.

Rent, market See *lease rate*.

Residual methods Class of methods used primarily for valuing nonmarketed producers' or intermediate goods; approximates the net rent or *value marginal product* of a nonpriced productive input by subtracting all other estimated costs of production from forecasted total value of output. The remaining (residual) value is assigned to the nonpriced input (water).

Return flow That portion of water *withdrawals* which returns to the hydrologic system and is further usable. Withdrawal minus return flow equals *consumption.*

Revealed preference (RP) methods Nonmarket valuation methods, including *travel cost* and *hedonic pricing,* which infer economic value from analysis of actual consumer decisions or market transactions. See *expressed preference methods.*

Risk-averse Preferring certainty to a risky outcome of the same expected value. A risk averse person would rather pay a charge greater than $100 per year than take a 1 in 2 risk of paying $200.

Risk premium For an investor, the difference between the expected returns on a risky investment and a risk-free investment. Generally, the risk premium increases with *risk aversion* and with the risk of the investment.

Rival goods Good or service enjoyment of which by one person precludes possible enjoyment by others. See *nonrival goods.*

Secondary data Published material and information not specifically gathered for the present research question. See *primary data.*

Shadow price See *accounting price.*

Short run In Marshall's simplified analytic price theory, the situation in which plant and equipment capacity is assumed to be fixed, rather than variable as it is in the *long run.* Short run and long run are distinguished not by the actual time in days, weeks, or months but by the degree to which economic actors can adapt to changing conditions.

Social rate of discount The shadow or accounting rate of interest used by public agencies to discount (calculate the present value of) future benefits and costs of public projects or policies. Determining the social rate of discount remains a controversial issue in evaluation of public water and environmental projects.

Standing The question of whose benefits and costs should count in a *cost-benefit analysis;* the region or political jurisdiction (local, regional, national, or universal) whose inhabitants' preferences are counted. See *accounting stance.*

Total economic value The sum of *use values* plus *nonuse values.*

Travel cost method (TCM) A *revealed preference* approach to valuing recreational sites that derives a demand schedule from statistical analysis of the costs of travel.

Unit-loss method A flood loss estimation method which employs standard or average loss data.

Use value Values assigned to goods and services which are actually used or experienced. See *nonuse value.*

Value-added The difference between the value of a firm's output and the value of inputs purchased from other firms; the value contributed by the firm's production process; often used in regional economics. Labor, land, and capital are treated as owned or internal, rather than externally purchased inputs. Sometimes used incorrectly as a measure of value marginal productivity or net rents of an increment of water in production.

Value marginal product The value of the additional quantity of product due to the use of an additional unit of a particular input. Important concept for valuing water in production because it is a measure of a producer's willingness to pay for an additional unit of input.

Willingness to accept (WTA) A monetary measure of the minimum amount an individual would accept rather than experiencing a lesser amount or quality of a good or service.

Willingness to pay (WTP) A monetary measure of the value an individual would pay for a specified change in quantity or quality of a good or service.

With-without principle The principle that benefits and costs should be measured as those strictly attributable to the project or policy under consideration (contrasted to measuring changes *before versus after* the policy initiative, which likely would include effects of other factors).

Withdrawal The amount of water diverted from a surface source or removed from a groundwater source for human use. Withdrawal minus *conveyance loss* equals *delivery* to the *point of use*. See *consumption*.

Approximate Conversion Factors: Water Volumes and Flows

Volumes

liter	= 1000 cubic centimeters
	= 0.2642 US gallons
gallon (US)	= 3.785 liters
	= 0.1337 ft^3
cubic meter	= the volume of water to cover one square meter one meter deep
	= 1,000 liters = 1 kiloliter
	= 35.31 cubic feet
	= 8.107 × 10^{-4} acre-feet
	= 264.2 US gallons
1,000 cubic meters	= 1 × 10^6 liter
	= 0.8107 acre-feet
1,000,000 cubic meters	= 1 × 10^9 liter
	= 810.7 acre feet
1 cubic kilometer	= 1 × 10^9 m^3
	= 1 × 10^{12} liter
	= 8.107 × 10^5 acre-feet
cubic foot	= 28.323 liters
	= 7.481 gallons
	= 0.02832 m^3
acre-foot	= the volume of water required to cover one acre (43,560 square feet) one foot deep
	= 43,560 ft^3
	= 325,851 US gallons
	= 1,233.48 cubic meters

Flow Rates

cubic meters per second	= 35.31 cubic feet per second
	= 1000 liter per sec
cubic feet per second	= 448.8 gallons per minute
	= 1.983 acre feet per day
	= 0.0283 cubic meters per second

Index

About the Author

Robert A. Young joined the faculty at Colorado State University in 1970, where he is currently professor emeritus of Agricultural and Resource Economics. He has worked as a water policy consultant for the World Bank, the U.S. Agency for International Development, the Asian Development Bank, and the United Nations.

Young's primary research interests are in applied economics and cost-benefit analysis as related to water resources. Much of his research has focused on developing and applying models for estimating the economic welfare effects of changes in water supply and quality, particularly in the case of offstream water uses, in agriculture, municipalities and industry. His policy-related research has emphasized collaboration with specialists from other disciplines, such as hydrologists, engineers, environmentalists, and attorneys.

Young's research has received awards from the American Agricultural Economics Association and the Western Agricultural Economics Association, where he served as president from 1979–1980. He received the American Water Resources Association's Iben Award for Promoting Understanding and Communication Among Disciplines Involving Water Resources (1992) and was awarded the Warren A. Hall Medal for Distinguished Contributions to Water Resources by the Universities' Council on Water Resources (2004).